SAN DIEGO

ERICKA CHICKOWSKI

Contents

Discover San Diego

San Diego is less a place and more a state of mind. Something about the constant sunshine, the sandy beaches, and the friendly people makes for a laid-back atmosphere that is as inescapable as a wave's pull to shore.

Located in the southwestern corner of the United States, the sprawling city is part of an even more expansive county of the same name. Topping out at 4,255 square miles, San Diego County is a rambling maze of geographical diversity. The sun rises over the vast Anza-Borrego Desert, the largest state park in the contiguous United States. It traces over the peaks and valleys of the San Marcos and Laguna Mountain Ranges and sets on the 70 miles of shoreline stretching up the San Diego coast.

The region is certainly one of many personalities. It is at once a sleepy navy enclave and a bustling nightspot. It is a sanctuary for the arts and a surfing mecca. Locals wear flip-flops to the opera, but won't hesitate to spend a mint to get their hair done flawlessly. Rather than creating a cognitive dissonance, these contrasts only serve to accentuate the area's colorful uniqueness.

The region's claim to fame is its temperate weather, and nothing makes it stand out so well as the bodies of water that sparkle under all of that sunshine. At every turn, there are enough bays and beaches to give even the biggest water enthusiast their fill with places to sail, fish, swim, and paddle. But no recreational activity is quite as definitively San Diego as surfing. To say San Diegans like to surf would be shortchanging the impact that the sport has on the region. Surfing isn't just a sport in San Diego, it is a way of life, permeating the culture all the way into the vernacular. You're as likely to hear a buttoned-down boardroom exec use the word "dude" as a tow-headed beachgoer in board shorts.

But don't let the easygoing nature of the residents fool you. The always-casual atmosphere belies the region's deep intellectual, philosophical, and religious roots, roots that reach as far back as the 16th century.

If there is one lesson to learn from the locals, it is that San Diego is meant to be enjoyed leisurely. The majority of the area's residents are transplants, visitors that never quite got around to leaving. So don't pack too lightly, because you might find so much to do in San Diego that you become one of them yourself.

Planning Your Trip

▶ WHERE TO GO

San Diego

Situated on a large bay protected from the Pacific, San Diego is the biggest city in the county of the same name. This geographical and cultural center is a sprawling patchwork of neighborhoods, with its downtown core creeping up to the waterfront that looks west across San Diego Bay to the tip of Coronado Island, which features one of San Diego's finest beaches, Silver Strand State Beach. On the east edge is Hillcrest and the pride of the city, Balboa Park, home to the world-famous San Diego Zoo and dozens of museums and gardens. Keep going north and you'll hit the historic first neighborhood of the city, Old Town. Even farther north is Mission Valley, home of California's first religious outpost, Mission San Diego de Alcalá.

City Beaches and Point Loma

The central core of the city of San Diego is augmented by its beach neighborhoods to the northeast. Southernmost is Point Loma, named for the peninsula that bounds the other side of San Diego Bay's inlet. Sprawling north along the ocean side of the peninsula is the warm-hued Sunset Cliffs Natural Park. Next comes the hippie town of Ocean Beach, and just over the jetties is Mission Beach, a thin strip of a neighborhood that is corralled by the ocean to the west and by the aquatic wonderland of Mission Bay Park to the east. Keep moving up the coast and you'll come across Pacific Beach, which boasts the city's hottest party scene outside of the Gaslamp district.

IF YOU HAVE...

San Diego's Balboa Park

- **THREE DAYS:** Visit Pacific Beach, the Gaslamp District, Balboa Park, and La Jolla.

- **ONE WEEK:** Add Point Loma, Coronado Island, Little Italy, and Del Mar.

- **TWO WEEKS:** Camp or stay at a resort along the North County coast.

- **THREE WEEKS:** Drive through the Laguna and Cuyamaca Mountains, visit the Palomar Observatory, and explore the vast expanses of the Anza-Borrego Desert.

La Jolla

One neighborhood up from Pacific Beach is the jewel of San Diego, La Jolla. Known for its craggy coves and sandy beaches, this is a pocket of luxury that holds the finest dining,

Mission Bay Park offers plenty of grassy areas to enjoy a picnic and watch the boats go by.

lodging, and art galleries in all of San Diego. La Jolla's varied shoreline is highlighted by the sea caves and cliffs surrounding La Jolla Cove and the traditional white sand beach of La Jolla Shores. Placed right near the cove is the posh La Jolla Village, the center of the neighborhood's culinary and shopping scene and home to the well-regarded Museum of Contemporary Art San Diego.

North County

Mostly populated along the coast and the major freeway corridors of I-5 and I-15, North County is best known for its idyllic beach towns. Southernmost is Del Mar, known as the place where the "turf meets the surf" at the Del Mar Racetrack. Next comes Encinitas, which is known for some of the best surfing breaks in all of California. Carlsbad has a

the idyllic beach town Del Mar

five-mile-long stretch of uninterrupted sand along Carlsbad State Beach. The military town of Oceanside boasts the longest fishing structure in the west, Oceanside Municipal Pier. And inland, Escondido is a cultural hub and the home of the California Center for the Arts.

Julian and Anza-Borrego

San Diego's backcountry is a rugged and ecologically diverse span of shaded riparian glades, rocky chaparral-covered mountains, and baked desert landscapes. San Diego–area mountain ranges bisect the county from north to south, starting with the Border Ranges, then moving up to the Laguna and Cuyamaca Mountains, followed hop-scotch style by the Volcan, San Ysidro, and Santa Rosa Mountain Ranges. Nestled in these peaks lies the quiet hamlet of Julian, the Sierra-like peak of Palomar Mountain, and the hidden healing waters of Warner Springs. All of the mountainous slopes drop east into the expansive Anza-Borrego Desert, home of the largest park owned by the state, Anza-Borrego Desert State Park. Explorers here are rewarded with bad-land vistas, cactus-lined trails, and palm-filled oases. Sitting on the desert's western edge is the small town of Borrego Springs.

Indian Head Mountain in Borrego Springs after a rare desert drizzle

▶ WHEN TO GO

San Diego is blessed with some of the most temperate weather in the country. The old joke is that there are two major seasons here, spring and summer.

But in reality, there is a little more nuance to the climate than that. San Diego County actually rests within numerous microclimates that can result in drastically different weather conditions from one zone to the other. Some days it can be foggy along the coast and pleasantly sunny just a few miles inland. The desert can be baking hot while it snows in the mountains.

During May and June airline tickets and hotel rates dip a little bit because during these months, along the coastal areas, ocean fog known as the marine layer rolls in thick and some days it never has the chance to completely burn off. There are a lot of nice days when the fog does go away; and this is not a problem at all in the inland areas. But it is something to be aware of if you were really counting on consistently sunny days during your trip.

July through August is the high season. The beaches are rockin', bars are open late, and the crowds are absolutely everywhere. If you don't have school vacations to worry about, try coming in September while the weather is still warm and the crowds have thinned.

In the late fall and winter the weather dips down between the low 60s and the high 50s. The locals dust off their jackets, but many cold-weather snowbirds find it heavenly. So do the surfers, who consider winter the best time to stake out local breaks. Winter usually brings the biggest swells and nicest waves.

Wildflowers blanket the desert in early spring.

Explore San Diego

▶ THE BEST OF SAN DIEGO

With so much to offer, the San Diego region can be a daunting place to visit from the vacation planner's perspective. But it is possible to condense many of the top sights, shopping trips, hiking excursions, and dining experiences down into a single week-long trip. The following itinerary offers a sample of the very best the region has to offer.

Day 1

Open your trip with a jaunt over to Coronado Island. Ditch your car in the city and take the ferry from the Embarcadero. Shop your way down Orange Avenue and stop for a bite and some people-watching at Tent City. Then mosey next door to the Coronado Historical Association to buy a ticket for a tour of Hotel del Coronado. If there's time before dinner,

you can rent a bike at Holland's Bicycles and ride up to Silver Strand State Park. Dine at Peohe's for dinner and check out the city lights reflected off San Diego Bay.

Day 2

Wake up early to hit up the city's most famous site of all, the San Diego Zoo. Be sure to get the pandas out of the way first—there's a line to get into that special enclosure. If you need to prioritize, some favorite exhibits are Monkey Trails and Forest Tales, Cat Canyon, and Gorilla Tropics. After freshening up a bit and changing into nicer threads, zip over to the Gaslamp Quarter for dinner at Trattoria La Strada or Monsoon. From there you're in a great position to find any number of clubs in which to dance the night away.

Hotel del Coronado

the view from San Diego Zoo's aerial tram

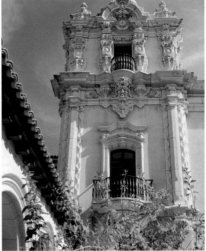
Spanish Revival architecture in Balboa Park

Day 3

Art and history abound at Balboa Park. Get a head start and arrive just before the museum doors open at 10 A.M. so that you don't miss any of the great stuff inside. Start by walking through the Timken Museum of Art, then stroll next door to the San Diego Museum of Art. Between the two of them you'll find masterpieces by El Greco, Rembrandt, and Eastman Johnson. Skip the ice cream cart and try a bento box for lunch at the Tea Pavilion at the Japanese Friendship Garden or try a full sit-down meal at El Prado. From there it is just a quick jaunt to the Museum of Photographic Arts. If you still have time before closing, check out the artifacts in the folk-art collection at the San Diego Natural History Museum. Take a break from the park by driving just a couple of minutes away to Gulf Coast Grill for dinner. Return back to Balboa for an evening performance at Old Globe Theatre.

Day 4

After the previous day's activities, you deserve a break. Sleep in as long as you like and head over to Kono's in Pacific Beach for grub. They serve breakfast all afternoon here. Now you're ready to while the time away on the beach. Grab a towel and a book and do nothing at all. Or rent a boogie board (and maybe a wetsuit) from one of the shops here to catch a few waves. When you're feeling peckish, take a break to dash across Mission Boulevard for a taste of a San Diego classic, the fish taco, at Taco Surf. Once the sun goes down unwind with the locals at Cass Street Bar and Grill for beer or Café 976 for coffee and tea.

Day 5

Trade in your bathing suit for your hiking boots with an excursion out into the county's mountains. From the city center, zip up I-15 and then take Highway 76 out to Palomar Mountain State Park. You can either hike or drive up the mountain to the famous Palomar Observatory, home of the famed Hale telescope. Once the tour is complete, you've got a choice to make: Either rough it in a tent at the nearby Doane Valley Campground and explore more local trails or trek another 40 minutes northeast via Highway 76 and 78 to Warner Springs Ranch. This resort offers a nice comfy bed, and if there's still daylight to burn, the option to cap the day's activities with a round of golf or a horseback ride under the shadows of Hotsprings Mountain. If you go to the ranch, be sure to relax in the spring-fed hot pool there, which is open past dark for a relaxing end to a busy day.

Day 6

Today you'll continue to take in the mountainous countryside by winding along more

TOP 10 FAMILY ATTRACTIONS

Planning and executing a family vacation is a lot like lion taming or snake charming. Do it right and you'll entertain and amaze. Do it wrong and you'll be hurtin'. Fortunately, San Diego affords the trip planner with a whole arsenal of tools to gain the adoration and admiration of spouse and children. Here are some of the best kid-friendly sights and destinations in the city and around the county to keep the brood content for days.

San Diego Zoo

- Delight the kids with the antics of Shamu and company at **SeaWorld.**

- Pack a lunch, plenty of sunscreen, and an umbrella to make it a day of sun and sand-castles at **Mission Beach.**

- Take a break from splashing in the ocean by pitter-pattering over the boardwalk black-top to **Belmont Park,** positioned right on the beach at South Mission.

- Check out the collection of more than 80 old steam and diesel engines, cabooses, passenger cars, and more at the **San Diego Railroad Museum** in Campo.

- Spend the day touring a real-life gold mine at **Eagle & High Peak Mines** and gorging on apple pie in the historical town of **Julian.**

- Young families can revel in the world of click-ety bricks at **Legoland** in Carlsbad. The new adjacent **Legoland waterpark** is also a great way to cool off on a hot summer's day.

- Come face-to-face with lions and tigers and bears at the world-famous **San Diego Zoo.**

- Try your hand at angling off of the West Coast's longest concrete pier, **Ocean Beach Pier.**

- In the winter, get a glimpse of a breaching grey whale aboard one of the many **whale watching tours** that depart from the Embarcadero.

- Let the kids touch as much as they want in the interactive displays at the **Reuben H. Fleet Science Center** in **Balboa Park.**

La Jolla Cove

of the region's scenic byways. You'll be heading back toward the coast, but this time it will be via Highways 78 and 79. Take 78 all the way west to the county's northernmost city, Oceanside. Spend the afternoon casting a line off of the Oceanside Pier and maybe checking out memorabilia at the California Surf Museum. In the evening you should head farther south along U.S. 101 to stay someplace close enough to allow you to spend your final day within city limits. But before you hit the road, consider a casual dinner at 101 Café. First opened in 1928, this diner is an Oceanside landmark.

Day 7

Your last day is back in the city, this time up in the La Jolla neighborhood. You'll want to start your day here with mouthwatering French toast at Brockton Villa followed by a visit to Birch Aquarium at Scripps Institution of Oceanography. This colorful home of sea life is a public interpretation of the scientific research conducted by the hometown Scripps Institution of Oceanography. Now get out there and conduct a little field research of your own! Head to La Jolla Cove and take a guided snorkel tour of the aquatic sanctuary, San Diego-La Jolla Underwater Park. You'll see bright orange garibaldi, spindly lobster, and giant sea bass in the protected waters here. End your stay with a luxurious dinner at the beachside Marine Room.

OLD CALIFORNIA CHARM

Yes, San Diegans' favorite salutation just might be "dude." Many people here do consider flip-flops with rhinestones appropriate for a formal dinner. And tattoo art is a serious medium of expression here. But coexisting with the ethos of informality is a rich tapestry of history, art, and culture. Here are some of the best historical sights in town:

GASLAMP VICTORIANS

The **Gaslamp Quarter** displays one of the finest collections of restored Victorian-era commercial buildings on the West Coast. Feast your eyes on beauties like the **Louis Bank of Commerce** and the **Yuma Building** as you walk through this historic area.

THE DEL

The grand dame of San Diego, the **Hotel del Coronado** is a stunning Victorian masterpiece whose red-hued turrets, gables, and cupolas have been drawing wealthy guests for more than 115 years.

CABRILLO NATIONAL MONUMENT

Cabrillo National Monument offers a a bird's-eye view of sheltered San Diego Bay. The highlight of the monument is the **Old Point Loma Lighthouse.** This 1850s-era building is dressed in period furniture and open for a look.

MARITIME HISTORY

Your tour of the city's waterlogged history is best facilitated by a walk down the **Embarcadero.** This is where you'll find two major floating attractions. First there's the **Maritime Museum of San Diego,** which has an impressive collection of restored vessels. Military buffs may prefer the **USS *Midway* Museum,** a retired and restored aircraft carrier. Up on deck there is a remarkable array of military aircraft to explore.

CALIFORNIAS'S FIRST MISSION

San Diego's first European settlers were the soldiers and priests of Spain. Learn about these pioneers by first strolling the grounds and visiting the small museum at **Mission San Diego de Alcalá,** California's first mission.

Mission San Diego de Alcalá, also known as the San Diego Mission Church, was founded on July 16, 1769.

PRESIDIO PARK AND OLD TOWN

Then head over to Presidio Park, the site of the city's first European settlement and fortification. Take a tour through **Junípero Serra Museum** to learn about the Native Americans who proceeded the Spaniards and the period of first settlement, as well as the shift to Mexican and American rule. Sitting at the foot of Presidio Hill is your next stop, **Old Town State Historic Park,** a recreated version of San Diego's first town square.

THE KING OF MISSIONS

Perhaps one of the best historic sights from the Mission era, however, is a 45-minute drive from the center of town. The **Mission San Luis Rey,** or the "King of the Missions," is a marvelous property full of barrel-tiled beauties and equally impressive landscaping.

SAN PASQUAL BATTLEFIELD

Another historic destination to finish off a leisurely afternoon drive in North County is in the San Pasqual Valley near Escondido. Stop off at the San Pasqual Battlefield and pick up some perspective about a Mexican-American battle that still has historians quibbling over the victor.

▶ WEEKEND GETAWAY

Sure, it can take weeks to really make a dent in the San Diego region. But not all of us have the luxury of time to take off into the countryside. Fortunately some of the very best San Diego sights are concentrated close to the city. In just a long weekend visitors can sample the sights, soak up the relaxing atmosphere, and work on an even tan to flaunt in front of envying coworkers back home.

Day 1

Start your San Diego adventure by taking a walk by the waterfront along the Embarcadero. Get a good perspective of the city by hopping aboard a San Diego Bay harbor cruise from either San Diego Harbor Excursions or Hornblower Cruises, both of which send off boats from the Embarcadero

throughout the day. Once you get back, traipse up to Little Italy to browse the shops in the Kettner Art and Design District and check out the eclectic neighborhood. Whet your whistle at San Diego's longest established bar, The Waterfront Bar and Grill, along the way. Finish everything off with a meal at one of Little Italy's trattorias, such as Mimmo's or Zagarella's.

Day 2

Today you'll spend the day in "the jewel" of San Diego, La Jolla. Start with a trip to the La Jolla branch of the Museum of Contemporary Art San Diego. Then stroll along Girard Avenue to browse the shops and art galleries. For a simple lunch with a view, pop into Goldfish Point Café overlooking La

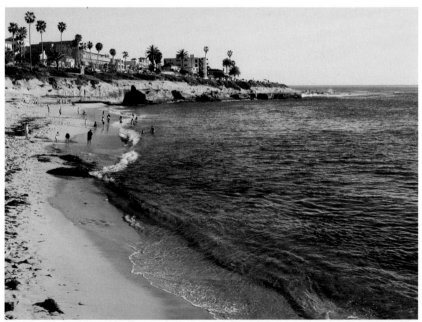

La Jolla

Jolla Cove. It is just a two-minute walk from there over to the Cave Store, where you will get a chance to descend the steep steps down to one of La Jolla's magnificent sea caves. If you still have time, sneak in a walk down to Children's Pool and check out the seals lolling on the beach. Once you're back in your car, consider driving up to Del Mar for dinner. For something more casual, try Americana right in downtown Del Mar. For a fine meal, drop into Market, near the Polo Grounds.

Day 3

This morning you'll tromp over the docks at Quivira Basin in Mission Bay Park and pick out your ride over at Seaforth Boat Rentals. Be it by motorboat, sailboat, or personal watercraft, you're going to ply the calm water of Mission Bay on your own. Bring your lunch and pack a fishing pole if you like, or maybe some water skis, and take off for a couple of hours. Once you get your feet back on solid land, drive to nearby Ocean Beach and mosey down Newport Avenue Antique Row for some relaxing window shopping until your tummy grumbles. Once you're ready, head over to Hodad's near Ocean Beach for a juicy burger and milkshake.

▶ SURF 'N' TURF

You don't have to throw away your worldly possessions, drive a VW bus, or even grow out your hair to take an authentic surf trip down the San Diego coast. Nope, all you need is a little equipment and a lot of time to take an unhurried tour of the region's best outdoor adventures both on and off the water. You don't even need a ton of money—just rely on

Windansea in La Jolla

OUT ON THE GREEN

Torrey Pines golf course

San Diego's constant sunshine and moderate climate make it a heavenly place to take a stroll along the greens and fairways of its storied golf courses, whether you're a scratch golfer or an average duffer. If you bring your clubs, consider slinging them on any one of these top-tier sets of links.

TORREY PINES

Host of the 2008 U.S. Open, Torrey Pines is one of the most iconic municipal golf courses in the nation. Set along the cliffs between La Jolla and Del Mar, you'll get your money's worth during a twilight round here. The sunsets over the ocean are amazing.

AVIARA GOLF CLUB

Home to a world-renowned golf academy and set within one of the county's nicest golf resorts, the Arnold Palmer–designed Aviara Golf Club flows along the Baitiquitos Lagoon; the grounds' water features and hazards were crafted to serve as visual extensions of the landscape.

LA COSTA

Once the long-time host of the World Golf Championship Accenture Match Play Championship, the two PGA Championship 18-hole courses at La Costa Resort offer a fine measuring stick to compare your play against some of the best. It's also set within one of San Diego's favorite resort hideaways, a getaway for the stars for decades.

SYCUAN SINGING HILLS

Tucked away in a secluded valley amid San Diego's chaparral-covered hillsides, this challenging facility has enough bunkers and water features to challenge the best of them. It's frequently voted by the locals as the best course in the county.

RIVERWALK GOLF COURSE

Conveniently located just a short chip away from downtown along the former marshes of Mission Valley, Riverwalk Golf Course will challenge you. Architect Ted Robinson Sr. brought the leisurely San Diego River into play on many of the holes here, with water hazards making an appearance on 13 of its 27 holes.

the campgrounds, hostels, motels, and cheap eats along the way. You'll have the most fun with a surfboard and a mountain bike at hand for each of the travelers in your group. Your best bet is to do these activities in fall through spring. That's when the swell comes in, the desert's cool, and the crowds are small. Because the ocean is a fickle, there's no real set itinerary for this vacation. Act like the locals and go with the flow.

Surfing

North of Oceanside, San Onofre State Park is one of the best places in the county to burn some daylight hours paddling out. Consider the longboard-friendly break at Old Man's, or make the trek up to Lower Trestles if that storied left is firing.

Farther south down to Encinitas, you can stuff yourself silly with a cheap and tasty breakfast at Pipes Café; keep your ears open at this surfer-friendly spot to hear where the waves might be best around here. Do a little reconnaissance along the coast while you digest to pick out a location for your afternoon session. The first obvious place to look is Swami's, less than five minutes away along U.S. 101. If there's no luck there, follow the highway south to Pipes and Suckouts farther south.

If the water's flat up north, backtrack north a couple of minutes to the Agua Hedionda Lagoon for some wakeboarding.

When evenings roll around, consider chillin' around a fire at one of North County's coastal campsites and making friends with some of the San Diego locals who come here to get away from the grind. Some favorite spots include San Onofre and San Elijo. If you prefer some more stimulating evening activities, a stay further south may be in order, your best bet being in Pacific Beach. Set up shop at Mission Bay Motel and hit the bars along Mission Boulevard and Garnet Avenue.

In the mornings you can stumble out of bed and head across the street to treat your hangover with a lazy breakfast at The Eggery, a perfect place to fuel up for days spent ambling up the Mission Beach Boardwalk or surfing at Tourmaline Surfing Park. Even on a calm day this combination reef and point break is worth lugging out the longboard. Plus, between here and Crystal Pier is one of the best beach scenes in the city.

Don't forget the breaks out in La Jolla, either. Windansea offers one of the nicest reef breaks within city limits, and if you head up to Torrey Pines State Reserve you'll find one of the county's very best beach breaks, Black's Beach. Here surfers coexist with a healthy contingent of nudists who use this out-of-the-way spot as a place to sunbathe in the buff.

Cycling

Clean the dust off your bike gears for an adventure through San Diego's bike paths. If

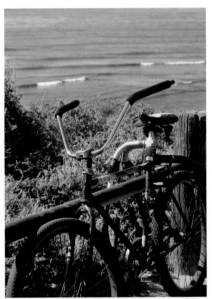

Hop on a beach cruiser to get a flavor for the coast.

ADRENALINE RUSH

hang gliding in La Jolla

With lots of year-round sunshine, San Diego has cultivated a thriving recreational sports scene. The area is home to some of the most pristine waterways, bike paths, and nature trails in the country, ideal for running, cycling, fishing, and boating.

Visitors don't have to be professional athletes or a knowledgeable locals to find the area's best activities. Participating in the following events, tours, and schools can put you right in the middle of San Diego's recreational charms without having to spend hours planning your outdoor adventure.

RUN

The **Rock and Roll Marathon** entertains its runners with bands performing along the route and a concert at the finish line.

If you like to run, but care not to race, **City Running Tours** offers a tour of San Diego sights from the unique perspective of a runner's mind.

BIKE

Adventure seekers can feel the thrill of bombing down one of La Jolla's highest hillsides on the **Mount Soledad Bike Plunge,** which ends along the beach at La Jolla shores.

Thousands of cyclists tune up their rides to join the 25-mile procession along the scenic San Diego Bay during the annual **Bike the Bay** event.

On the popular **Tour de Borrego** explore the cactus-covered vistas of the Anza-Borrego Desert during wildflower season.

SWIM

Put on a cap and dive into the water with thousands of other intrepid water lovers at one of the top roughwater swim events in the nation, **La Jolla Cove Rough Water Swim.**

TRIATHLON

San Diego is the birthplace of the modern triathlon, first held in 1974 along Mission Bay. The **Mission Bay Triathlon** is still held along the original waterway, which provides a scenic route to test your run-bike-swim mettle.

SAIL

Learn to tack and jib aboard one of **Harbor Island Yacht Club**'s instructional crafts during one of the **basic cruising weekend sailing classes,** or participate in a **live-aboard week-long learn-to-sail vacation.**

FISH

Take any one of the half-day, full-day, or multi-day deep sea fishing tours out of Point Loma's **Fisherman's Landing.**

Get up close and personal with the catch off the bow of a kayak with a tour from **La Jolla Kayak Fishing Adventures.**

FLY

Learn to hang glide or paraglide from the instructors at **Torrey Pines Gliderport,** located on a cliff overlooking the ocean in La Jolla. Or take an expert-guided tandem flight.

you are up in North County and are skunked by glassy conditions, hop on your bike for an easy spin along an abandoned stretch of Old Highway 101 that runs south of the park for a little over three miles.

Some the other more exciting land-based activities may take a bit more planning. You'll want to rise early, pack a lunch, and head east on I-8 to reach San Diego's mountains. Take Sunrise Highway, the serpentine road up through the Laguna Mountains and consider a stop along the way at Big Laguna Meadow for a scenic 10-mile mountain bike ride along the trail here. You'll have the opportunity to lengthen it if you choose to climb the hills along the spur of Noble Canyon Trail.

Hiking

If the waves aren't co-operating and you're at the city beaches, zip east along Highway 52 from La Jolla out to Mission Trails Park and hike to the top of Cowles Mountain.

Out near the desert town of Borrego Springs you can gain an appreciation of the arid ecosystem with a hike up Borrego Palm Canyon Trail to an honest to goodness oasis. Before you go, make a stop at the Anza-Borrego State Park Visitors Center and pore through its interpretive exhibits.

Bouldering and Mountain Biking

Southwest of Borrego Springs, check out the granite-speckled Culp Valley for some of the best bouldering in the county. This is also a good starting point for an epic day in the

Hike to a natural oasis in Borrego Springs.

mountain biking saddle. Nearby Grapevine Canyon presents the opportunity for an exhilarating ride for as many as 16 miles to Yaqui Well.

4x4 Adventures

The best way to get out there and actually see the desert is to hop aboard one of the retrofitted troop transport trucks operated by California Overland, which can take you to the vistas of Font's Point and many out-of-the-way slot canyons and dry lake beds.

SAN DIEGO

It seems impossible, but San Diego is at once a small little beach town and a thriving metropolis. It's an urbane center of culture and a rowdy roost for partiers. It's a surf town, it's a mountain town, a golf course, and a skate park.

The truth is, this town is hard to completely get a handle on—it's a patchwork of more than 100 neighborhoods stitched together over hundreds of square miles, a mishmash of villages, barrios, and stomping grounds. It's up to newcomers to make it what they want it to be.

The birthplace of California, San Diego is a city of great historical significance to some. It is the site of the very first of the 21 California missions founded by Spanish Franciscan priests, Mission San Diego de Alcalá. It is home to remarkable adobe haciendas of the Mexican-California period. It has one of the most impressive concentrations of restored Victorian commercial buildings on the entire West Coast. And its location on the San Diego Bay has cultivated a rich and long-running maritime and naval history.

Home of Balboa Park, San Diego is a place of great culture and learning. The park is an amazing public treasure—the second-oldest city park in the United States (just behind New York's Central Park), it's filled with beautiful and ornate Spanish Colonial Revival buildings that house the city's best museums. Collections of art, history, and science are all here, surrounded by lush and fascinating gardens and the world-famous San Diego Zoo.

Cradled between mountains and ocean, San Diego is a town of amazing recreational opportunities. The city takes its open spaces

© ERICKA CHICKOWSKI

HIGHLIGHTS

◖ **USS *Midway* Museum:** The longest-serving aircraft carrier in U.S. naval history, the *Midway* is now a floating museum. Its berthing spaces, decks, and bridge are all open for curious civilians and nostalgic vets (page 41).

◖ **Maritime Museum of San Diego:** This flotilla of historic ships celebrates San Diego's salty roots. Here visitors can duck into an

ex-Soviet sub, walk the deck of tall sailing cutters, and sit on the benches of vintage wooden yachts (page 42).

◖ **Silver Strand State Beach:** Unfolding along the southern half of Coronado Island, this stretch of dunes and beaches is a natural and recreational getaway from city madness (page 43).

◖ **Hotel del Coronado:** This renowned Victorian seaside resort, with its red cupolas and gables, is an architectural masterpiece (page 44).

◖ **Balboa Park:** The pride of San Diego, this 1,200-acre park is home to dozens of museums, stunning Spanish Colonial Revival architecture, vibrant gardens, and the world's best-known zoo (page 46).

◖ **San Diego Zoo:** Both an institution of conservation and of fun, the rambling grounds of the zoo are home to a legendary collection of animals in a natural environment (page 46).

◖ **Old Town State Historic Park:** Before San Diego became a proper port city it was a simple inland pueblo at the foot of a Spanish presidio. This park relives that history with a mix of original and reconstructed structures (page 52).

◖ **Mission San Diego de Alcalá:** This whitewashed church, a sight to behold, is living documentation of the city's ecclesiastical heritage (page 57).

◖ **Mission Trails Regional Park:** The largest urban park in the country, this mountainous open space is a sanctuary for hikers, bikers, bird-watchers, and climbers (page 58).

◖ **Chula Vista Nature Center:** This wildlife zoo situated on the Sweetwater Marsh National Wildlife Refuge offers an interesting peek into the ecological diversity of the coastal wetland (page 58).

LOOK FOR ◖ TO FIND RECOMMENDED SIGHTS, ACTIVITIES, DINING, AND LODGING.

seriously, so within city limits there are literally hundreds of parks, preserves, and trails that are meant to be hiked and biked. Anglers frequently dip their lines in lakes or in the sparkling water of San Diego Bay. Boaters ply those same waters by motor and sail. Golfers swing their way along the fairways of the city's links. And picnickers have many opportunities to just lie around and enjoy the sunshine—a pastime that is so common on the public lawns here that it is practically a city sport.

San Diego is also an easy departure point to Coronado Island, a lazy seaside getaway. A municipality all its own, Coronado is a 10-minute drive or a half-hour ferry ride across the bay from San Diego. On the north end, its idyllic tree-lined village is a place to stroll leisurely amidst shops and restaurants. And just a few minutes south is a remote seven-mile sandy strand that is perfect for a family day at the beach.

HISTORY

The San Diego River watershed was home to the oldest known people of California, the San Dieguitos. Archeological evidence shows that these Paleo-Indians were around about 12,000 years ago, probably enjoying the same mild climate that has made "Sun Diego" so famous worldwide.

The San Dieguitos' ancestors greeted Spanish explorers in 1542, when Juan Rodriguez Cabrillo landed briefly in San Diego, and again in 1602 at the landing of Sebastián Vizcaíno. It took the Spanish more than a century to return to what they called Alta California (Upper California), but they did return and San Diego was their first stop on the journey north.

When the soldiers and priests of Spain first settled San Diego, they initially chose a high perch over the San Diego River Valley to establish a military complex and a small mission to act as a center for both social and political activities. Known as Presidio Hill, this vantage point provided a defensive view of the surrounding Native American territory and acted as a symbol of dominance to the natives. Not too long after the Presidio

was established, the mission was relocated a few miles inland to be closer to running water and to distance itself from the sometimes brutal army. The hill remained an important political and military base until the Mexicans gained independence and left the Presidio to fall to pieces. During this period in the early 19th century, settlers trickled into the area, establishing a dusty pueblo at the bottom of the hill, the first real neighborhood in San Diego.

However, as San Diego transitioned from Mexican to American rule, some citizens believed that the town would never grow into a true city if it remained at the foot of Presidio Hill. The location was more than three miles away from the bay and the distance between city center and the harbor would keep the city from establishing itself as a major shipping hub of the United States.

And so the idea of New Town San Diego was born, giving rise to what would eventually become today's downtown Gaslamp Quarter.

The Gaslamp Quarter was the birthplace of modern San Diego's downtown.

© ERICKA CHICKOWSKI

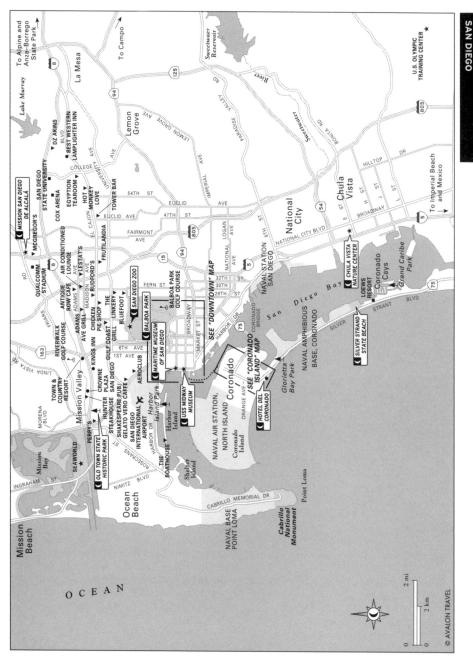

To Alpine and
Anza-Borrego
State Park

To Campo

U.S. OLYMPIC
TRAINING CENTER

Lake Murray

La Mesa

Sweetwater
Reservoir

8

125

94

Lemon Grove

RD

PARADISE VALLEY

Sweetwater River

BONITA RD

HILLTOP DR

805

To Imperial Beach
and Mexico

DZ AKINS

BEST WESTERN
LAMPLIGHTER INN

LEMON GROVE AVE

AVE

COLLEGE AVE

UNIVERSITY AVE

Chula Vista

CHULA VISTA
NATURE CENTER

5

MISSION SAN DIEGO
DE ALCALÁ

SAN DIEGO
STATE UNIVERSITY

COX ARENA

EGYPTIAN
TEAROOM

HOT ▼
MONKEY
LOVE

TOWER BAR

54TH ST

EUCLID AVE

47TH ST

FAIRMONT AVE

National
City

NATIONAL CITY BLVD

St

St

Coronado
Cays

Grand Caribe
Park

McGREGOR'S

QUALCOMM
STADIUM

RD

8

El CAJON BLVD

LESTAT'S
AIR CONDITIONED
LOUNGE

RUDFORD'S

FRUTLANDIA

EUCLID

AVE

805

94

15

FERN ST

32ND ST

30TH ST

28TH ST

NATIONAL AVE

LOGAN AVE

8TH ST

54

BROADWAY

LOEWS
RESORT

SILVER STRAND
BLVD

75

RIVERWALK
GOLF COURSE

163

ANTIQUE
ROW CAFE

ADAMS AVE

ADAMS AVE GRILL

CHICKEN
PIE SHOP

MADISON AVE

THE
LINKERY

GULF COAST
BLUEFOOT

SAN DIEGO ZOO

BALBOA PARK

BALBOA PARK
GOLF COURSE

Broadway

MARKET ST

HARBOR DR

SEE "DOWNTOWN" MAP

CORONADO
BRIDGE

75

NAVAL AMPHIBIOUS
BASE, CORONADO

San Diego Bay

SILVER STRAND
STATE BEACH

LINDA VISTA RD

TOWN &
COUNTRY
RESORT

MORENA
BLVD

Mission
Valley

KINGS INN

CROWNE
PLAZA
SAN DIEGO

HUNTER
STEAKHOUSE

SHAKESPEARE PUB/
GELATO VERO CAFFE

6TH AVE

1ST AVE

AEROCLUB

SAN DIEGO
INTERNATIONAL
AIRPORT

HARBOR DR

Harbor
Island

MARITIME MUSEUM
OF SAN DIEGO

USS MIDWAY
MUSEUM

ORANGE AVE

Coronado

NAVAL AIR STATION,
NORTH ISLAND

Coronado
Island

Glorietta
Bay Park

HOTEL DEL
CORONADO

SEE "CORONADO
ISLAND" MAP

San Diego Bay

PERRY'S

OLD TOWN STATE
HISTORIC PARK

SEAWORLD

Mission
Bay

INGRAHAM ST

NIMITZ BLVD

THE
BOATHOUSE

ROSECRANS ST

Shelter
Island

CABRILLO MEMORIAL DR

NAVAL BASE
POINT LOMA

Point Loma

Cabrillo
National
Monument

Mission
Beach

Ocean
Beach

O C E A N

2 mi

2 km

0

0

© AVALON TRAVEL

Moving an entire city is no easy task, so it isn't surprising that the transition from Old Town to New came in fits and starts. Especially considering the fact that at the time the land along the bay was completely devoid of trees or fresh water.

The first civic leader to spearhead the move was William Heath Davis, who purchased land near the bay in the 1850s with the expectation of selling lots to families and business owners. While his zeal for the plan planted a seed that would eventually germinate decades later, he was unable to sell many lots. For years the area was derisively called Davis's Folly.

Alonzo Horton was the man who actually managed to make New Town a reality. Already a successful entrepreneur when he first stepped foot in San Diego in 1867, Horton had experience marketing and developing towns out of thin air. As a young man Horton had founded a town in Wisconsin that he called Hortonville.

His westward migration brought him to the Mother Lode in San Francisco during the height of the Gold Rush, where he made a fortune selling ice to those seeking riches in the streams of the gold fields.

In the 1860s Horton heard of opportunities in San Diego and came down to check it out himself. When he arrived he found that the town had potential, but like Davis he believed that the key to building the pueblo into a proper city would be to establish the city center alongside the bay. In 1867 he bought up 960 acres next to Davis's land and began the process of promoting the area. He was tireless, sailing up to San Francisco to hawk the possibilities of San Diego and the lots on his new subdivision. He invested early earnings to build a new wharf, a hotel, and a library, and he gave away lots to congregations willing to build churches.

The only missing link was the municipal government. Stubborn Old Town residents still insisted that the future of San Diego was there, not over on crazy old Horton's waterfront property. Even though momentum was swinging in New Town's favor by 1870, Old Town still clung feverishly to the control it had over the county court system.

As long as it remained home to the county court and the county records, Old Town would stay relevant in city politics and business. And all of Old Town's staunch supporters knew it. Which is why when Horton donated building space in New Town to relocate the courthouse and records, Old Town locals fought the scheme tooth and nail.

The battle raged through legal channels until the California Supreme Court settled the matter in 1871. The court and its records were ordered to be moved from Old Town. This still didn't deter Old Town politicos. They refused to comply, going so far as to post a cannon and armed guards in front of the building that housed the court's records.

But Horton's contingent was persistent. One March night his allies, led by the county clerk, rolled in to Old Town on express wagons and forcibly removed the court's records. They loaded up the documents and left a trail of dust as they rolled back down to the waterfront, changing San Diego's future forever. From then on, it would be known as the city on the bay.

PLANNING YOUR TIME

So what *do* you want San Diego to be to you? Thinking about that before you arrive can help alleviate vacation frustration, because San Diego is a big town and no one likes to spend most of their vacation on the roads or freeways.

If it's history you want, it might make sense to stay downtown and split your time between the core downtown area and Mission Valley. While downtown you can ramble through the streets of the **Gaslamp Quarter,** which are lined with scores of restored buildings from the late 19th century. From there it is an easy walk to the waterfront to visit the **USS *Midway* Museum** or the historic ships of the **Maritime Museum of San Diego.**

In Mission Valley, the historical highlight is obvious. This is the home of the **Mission**

San Diego de Alcalá, California's first. Also adjacent to the valley is Presidio Hill, the site of the first Spanish fort and an impressive view of downtown. Sitting below the hill is Old Town State Historic Park, which provides an interesting perspective of early San Diego with its restored and original buildings from the 19th century.

Art lovers could probably spend a whole week just exploring the nooks and crannies of **Balboa Park,** so they would do well to stay in a nearby Uptown or Midcity hotel. While at the park, a stop at the Timken Museum of Art, the San Diego Museum of Art, and the Mingei International Museum are all in order. A day at the park might even be extended by staying for a production at the Old Globe Theatre, which is on the premises.

The park is also a major draw for families, who come for at least a day to check out the pandas, gorillas, and other creatures at the **San Diego Zoo.** Other kid-friendly options at Balboa include the Reuben H. Fleet Science Center, the San Diego Natural History Museum, and the San Diego Aerospace Museum.

Those looking to get away from it all without actually driving away from it all can take a ferry or drive over the Coronado Bay Bridge to Coronado Island to spend time shopping Orange Avenue or taking a walk along the beach at Silver Strand State Beach. Another active alternative is to make a trek out to the northern outposts of the city for a hike on Cowles Mountain at **Mission Trails Regional Park** or bike to the waterfalls in Los Peñasquitos Canyon Preserve.

ORIENTATION

San Diego wouldn't be a self-respecting Southern Californian city if it weren't guilty of a little urban sprawl. Geographically, this town is massive; its municipal borders bulge at a whopping 325 square miles.

Though the town is best known for its sandy beaches, the central core of San Diego is actually situated on the sheltered San Diego Bay, whose inlet from the Pacific Ocean is bounded on the north by Point Loma and on the south by Coronado Island.

Point Loma is the southernmost tip of the city's beach communities, which are in the northwestern part of the city. Because of their isolated geography and unique character, these communities have earned a chapter of their own. The rest of the city's geography is best explained region by region.

Downtown

Just east of North Harbor Drive, from the airport down to the **Coronado Bay Bridge,** are the downtown neighborhoods.

The central downtown core is south of Little Italy. This is the practical area of San Diego, where the courthouses and the county lockup are found. It is also home to the Santa Fe Depot, a major transportation hub and a beautiful building to boot. The station sits on the corner of Kettner and **Broadway,** the major east–west thoroughfare here.

Gaslamp Quarter and East Village

Just a few blocks south of downtown is the city's entertainment nerve center, the Gaslamp Quarter and San Diego's East Village. East Village tries as it might to distinguish itself from its neighbor, but most locals continue to expand their colloquial boundaries, often referring to East Village establishments as being "in the Gaslamp." Who am I to argue? I tend to do the same when describing area restaurants and bars. The neighborhood is home to Petco Park and is the heart and soul of the San Diego food and entertainment scene.

Little Italy

Just northeast of the downtown core, southwest of I-5 before it takes a little curve up toward Highway 163, you'll find Little Italy, whose major attractions lie on **India Street** and **Kettner Boulevard.** Built up by Italian and Portuguese fishermen in the early 20th century, when San Diego's waterfront catered to the town's once-mighty tuna fishing fleet,

© ERICKA CHICKOWSKI

the Gaslamp Quarter

Little Italy is now a revitalized neighborhood full of vibrant buildings, parks, and eateries.

Waterfront

San Diego's major waterfront attractions lie directly across the bay from the northern part of Coronado Island. This is where the popular **Embarcadero** area runs alongside **North Harbor Drive.** You'll find some of the city's most renowned waterside attractions here, including the famous *Midway* aircraft carrier, now retired and operating as a floating museum.

Coronado Island

The bay curves like an upside-down fish hook around the east side of Coronado Island, which runs parallel to the downtown core. Interestingly enough, Coronado is not actually an island. It's an isthmus, joined with the mainland at the border beach town of Imperial Beach.

Balboa Park and Bankers Hill

North of the I-5 S-curve is a collection of neighborhoods all tied together by San Diego's cultural and pastoral jewel, Balboa Park. Visitors will find the most amenities convenient to the park's attractions just east in Bankers Hill, which has its core north of **Laurel Avenue** and west of **5th Avenue.**

Hillcrest, North Park, and Midcity

Just north of Balboa Park lie the neighborhoods of Hillcrest, North Park, and **University Heights.** Hillcrest, the epicenter of San Diego's gay and lesbian community, is cultured, urbane, and just a little bit cheeky. Set in the canyons and mesas northeast of Balboa Park, this vibrant neighborhood is a kaleidoscopic patchwork of cozy art-house theaters, naughty leather shops, elegant cafés, vintage bookstores, and swanky night spots. Side streets are a fun maze of canyon dead ends and meandering hillside lanes sprinkled with Victorian mansions and Craftsman cottages. The main drags here are **University Avenue** and **Washington Street,** around which most of the neighborhood's best independent restaurants and boutiques are clustered. Hillcrest has long been an open-minded and welcoming community. Even though it strongly identifies with the

© ERICKA CHICKOWSKI

Hillcrest offers an eclectic smorgasboard of shopping and good eats.

gay and lesbian community, straight couples needn't worry that the proverbial record will screech to a halt when they walk arm-in-arm down the street. All are welcome and none are judged here.

Primarily a sleepy bedroom community, North Park has also made a name for itself among the restaurant- and bar-hopping set with a growing number of excellent establishments starting to gel along 30th Avenue and several other major arteries.

East of the park lies Midcity, a rather unglamorous part of town that is dominated by **San Diego State University.** Neighborhoods that surround the school include **Normal Heights, Kensington,** and **College Heights.** Though there aren't many sights to see here, these neighborhoods do have a healthy nightlife and restaurant scene due to the students and freshly graduated young'uns who live in the area.

Mission Valley and Old Town

East of I-5 along the I-8 corridor, Mission Valley runs all the way to I-15. Besides the freeways, the major roadways include **Hotel Circle North** and **Hotel Circle South,** which curiously enough have a lot of lodging options. Friars Road is another major artery, running parallel to I-8 along the valley's northern rim.

Old Town is just south of Mission Valley, on the arrow point of land bounded by **Pacific Highway** and I-8. The neighborhood sits below **Presidio Hill.**

North City

North of Mission Valley, between I-5 and eastern city limits, is North City. This expansive stretch of land includes the residential neighborhoods of **Clairemont Mesa, Kearny Mesa,** and **Mira Mesa** on the south end. These neighborhoods are directly west of the city's recreational wonderland, **Mission Trails Regional Park.**

Go north from any of these points and you'll eventually encounter the massive **Marine Corps Air Station Miramar.** Just north of the base along I-15 is the exclusive **Rancho Bernardo** community. And beyond that is where things get fun. To the east of I-15 are **Los Peñasquitos Canyon Preserve** and **Black Mountain Open Space Park.** To the west you'll find **San Pasqual-Clevenger Canyon Open Space Park.**

South Bay

Stretching from the areas south of East Village all the way down to Mexico, San Diego's South Bay area is lined with bedroom communities leading southward to the border. **Imperial**

Beach is the most southwesterly beach town in the United States, and visitors there can check out the physical barrier that runs along the beach and into the water marking the international border. **Chula Vista's** parks and wildlife refuge are a pleasant stop for families. And the border crossing at **San Ysidro** is the busiest in the world.

Sights

While there is plenty to see in most of San Diego's neighborhoods, much of the fun can be broken up by interest. On the waterfront, get a keen feeling for the city's rich naval and maritime history. In Old Town and Mission Valley, one can find much of the city's historical roots. Downtown is a grab bag of museums and architectural sights. Arts and culture organizations are concentrated in Balboa Park. And in the northern stretch of city limits, one can enjoy plenty of open space and natural beauty.

DOWNTOWN
Museum of Contemporary Art San Diego

Housed right in the heart of the 1915 Santa Fe Depot complex, the downtown branch of the Museum of Contemporary Art San Diego (MCASD, 1100 & 1001 Kettner Blvd., between Broadway and B St., 858/454-3541, www.mcasd.org, 11 A.M.–5 P.M. Thurs., Mon.–Tues., 11 A.M.–7 P.M. Fri.–Sat., $10 adults, $5 military and seniors, ages 25 and under free) offers a central location for art lovers looking to get their fix without driving out to Balboa Park or to the MCASD main branch in La Jolla. The museum features artistic touches from the renowned architect Richard Gluckman and several permanent pieces commissioned by the museum. As the second branch of the museum, MCASD Downtown shares with the La Jolla branch some 4,000 works of art and also features a rotating stock of international exhibitions.

San Diego Firehouse Museum

Also located downtown is the San Diego Firehouse Museum (1572 Columbia St., 619/232-3473, www.sandiegofirehouse-museum.com, 10 A.M.–2 P.M. Thurs.–Fri., 10 A.M.–4 P.M. Sat.–Sun., $3) in Little Italy, which gives a glimpse of San Diego's firefighting history from bucket brigades to modern fire engines. This little gem of a museum is housed in the former San Diego Fire Station No. 6 and features a host of old equipment and memorabilia, including pumps, hand-crank sirens, fire nozzles, and more.

The museum is run by the fire department, which encourages its firefighters to volunteer as docents in order to keep the history and lore of the department alive and well in the public eye.

San Diego Chinese Historical Museum

Don't blink or you'll miss it, but as you travel between Little Italy and the Gaslamp you'll pass through Chinatown. Not much more than a few historic buildings, this area is home to the San Diego Chinese Historical Museum (404 3rd Ave., 619/338-9888, www.sdchm.org, 10:30 A.M.–4 P.M. Tues.–Sat., noon–4 P.M. Sun., $2), which chronicles the Chinese American experience in San Diego and the rest of the West Coast and offers an interesting perspective on Chinese history, culture, and art.

SAN DIEGO

© AVALON TRAVEL

Marine Corps Recruit Depot Command Museum

I don't know but I've been told, those Devil Dogs are mighty bold. And San Diego's got them in spades. Not only is the county home to Camp Pendleton and Marine Corps Air Station Miramar, but it also plays host to the Marine Corps Recruit Depot, one of two Marine boot camps in the nation. Located right next to the airport, the MCRD is generally closed to the public at large so you probably won't be able to get in to watch the drill sergeants go all R. Lee Ermey on the recruits. But if you'd like to learn about the making of a marine, drop by the Marine Corps Recruit Depot Command Museum (Marine Corps Recruit Depot, 1600 Henderson Ave., Bldg. 26, www.mcrdmuseumhistoricalsociety.org, 8 A.M.–4 P.M. Mon.–Sat., free) on base. This patriotic museum pays tribute to the thousands of recruits who have thrown their hats up in the air following graduation from the grueling 13-week training program. Be prepared to show your driver's license and proof of insurance or your rental car contract when driving onto base.

GASLAMP QUARTER AND EAST VILLAGE

Like Little Italy, the Gaslamp Quarter has experienced a renaissance after spending many decades as a seedy area populated by porno theaters, low-rent hotels, and boarded-up buildings.

Named for the gas lanterns that lit area streets during downtown's formative years, the Gaslamp Quarter now enjoys the distinction of being the epicenter of downtown's ritzy club and lounge scene. Today the streets are lit with neon and if you walk them at night you'll hear the clink of glasses, the pounding bass, and the hoots and whistles emanating from the bars that blanket the district. On any given night throughout the year, smartly dressed couples and groups of singles on the prowl climb out of taxis and scurry into the throng of revelers that line up to gain access into some of the highest-profile clubs south of Hollywood.

In spite of the partying, the area hasn't lost touch with its heritage and actually affords the quiet artsy type a lot to see during the day. Art galleries, boutiques, and fine restaurants are

The Louis Bank of Commerce and the Nesmith-Greely Building are two stunning examples of the Gaslamp's Victorian-era commercial architecture.

SAN DIEGO

GASLAMP QUARTER

COPLEY SYMPHONY HALL

B ST

4TH AND B

KARL STRAUSS ▼ BREWERY

San Diego Trolly (blue)

C ST

DAISY'S BISTRO ▼
GREYHOUND BUS STATION ■

HOUSE OF ▼ BLUES

THE BRISTOL HOTEL

THE TRANSIT ■ STORE

US GRANT HOTEL ▼

WESTIN EMERALD PLAZA ●

WEST   BROADWAY

ON BROADWAY ▼

BROADWAY

SAN DIEGO CHINESE ★ ★SPRECKLES
HISTORICAL MUSEUM   THEATRE

REI DO GADO ▼
BRAZILLIAN
STEAK HOUSE

Horton

Plaza Park

LIBRARY ■

LOUIS BANK OF COMMERCE ■

E ST

POST OFFICE ■

E ST

Horton

BELO ▼ STAR ▼ BAR

GEORGE'S ■ ON 5TH

NESMITH- ■ GREELY BUILDING

ANDAZ SAN DIEGO ●

TRATTORIA LA STRADA ▼

F ST

CROCE'S JAZZ BAR ▼

F ST

Plaza

DECO'S ▼

SAN DIEGO
REPERTORY THEATRE ★

MONSOON ▼

PACIFIC GASLAMP ALL STADIUM CINEMA ■

LLEWELYN BUILDING ■

G ST

G ST

OLD CITY HALL ■

NOBLE ▼ EXPERIMENT

YUMA ■ BUILDING

ST

MARKET

HI-SD DOWNTOWN ● HOSTEL

TAKA ▼

ISLAND ● INN

HORTON GRAND HOTEL ★

CAFÉ ▼ SEVILLA

STINGAREE ▼

ISLAND   AVE

CANDELAS LOUNGE ▼

WILLIAM HEATH DAVIS HISTORIC HOUSE MUSEUM ●

HOTEL SOLAMAR ●

JSIX/JBAR ▼

J ST

MOLLY'S RESTAURANT ▼

ACQUA12 ▼

DIZZY'S ▼

Outfield Park

0   200 yds

0   200 m

K ST

PETCO PARK

Marina

HARBOR DR

L ST

SAN DIEGO CONVENTION CENTER

© AVALON TRAVEL

FRONT ST 1ST ST STATE ST UNION ST 4TH AVE 5TH AVE 6TH AVE 7TH AVE 8TH AVE TONY GWYNN DR sprinkled in between the clubs. And of course, a relaxing afternoon drink can be had at many places without mortgaging your home to pay a cover charge.

The real show-stealers are the buildings that house all of these establishments. Within the nearly 17-block neighborhood there are over 90 buildings listed on the National Register of Historic Places. Some of the most stunning structures in this neighborhood are between the 600 and 800 block of 5th Avenue. The neighborhood architecture is best experienced via a casual walking tour, but there is also a weekly guided walking tour ($10 for adults, $8 for seniors, students, and military) starting at the William Heath Davis Historic House Museum on Saturdays at 11 A.M.

William Heath Davis Historic House

Start on the south end at Island street to take a gander at the oldest of the buildings in the city, the William Heath Davis Historic House (410 Island Ave., 619/233 4692, www.gaslampquarter.org, 10 A.M.–6 P.M. Tue.–Sat., 9 A.M.–3 P.M. Sun., $5). This saltbox-style home was one of 14 prefabricated houses that were hauled all the way from New England and around Cape Horn by William Heath Davis in 1850 in order to jumpstart the development of New Town San Diego. At the time, the bay-front property was completely devoid of trees (and fresh water for that matter), making it necessary to import "modern" wood houses for potential buyers.

Unfortunately, Davis's initiative wasn't matched by his promotional skills and it took seventeen years and the brash salesmanship of Alonzo Horton to make New Town a reality. The house on Island Avenue is the last remaining home imported by Davis and stands today as a symbol of the groundwork he laid to make today's downtown a possibility.

Horton Grand Hotel

Kitty-corner to the Davis House is the Horton Grand Hotel (311 Island Ave., 619/544-1886, www.hortongrand.com), which is actually made up of two historic hotels that were moved to

this spot in the 1980s to avoid demolition. Both constructed in 1886, they were two very different establishments. The Grand Horton was an elegant structure built as a replica of Innsbruck Inn in Vienna, Austria. The Brooklyn Hotel was casual, and eventually became known as the Kahle Saddlery Hotel for the saddle and harness shop that did business in the ground floor. They were painstakingly dismantled from what is now Horton Plaza and stored in a warehouse by the city until the opportunity arose to rebuild them together on their current lot.

Yuma Building

The Yuma Building (631 5th Ave.), an Italianate-baroque beauty that was one of downtown's first brick structures when it was built in 1888. At that time it was used for legitimate business, but by 1901 its upstairs "offices" had been transformed into dens of debauchery. When the police were pressured to crack down on prostitution in the area in 1912, the Yuma was the first building they raided.

Old City Hall and Llewelyn Building

Across the street from the Yuma on the corner of G and 5th stands Old City Hall. Built originally as a bank in 1874, this Florentine-Italianate structure was purchased by the city 1891 and housed City Hall until 1938. During the early years here, city leaders gave a wink and a nod to the illicit activities across the street at the Yuma and at many more prostitution parlors, opium dens, and gambling halls that flanked City Hall to comprise what was known widely as the Stingaree District.

Keeping to the west side of 5th and crossing G, halfway down the block you'll stumble across the Llewelyn Building (722 5th Ave.), which is probably one of the best examples of commercial Victorian architecture in the Gaslamp.

Nesmith-Greely Building and the Louis Bank of Commerce

The Romanesque Revival–style Nesmith-Greely Building (825 5th Ave.) displays a delightful combination of brick coursing and columns. Next door is the intricate and ornate Victorian-style Louis Bank of Commerce (835 5th Ave.). The twin mansard roof towers of the baroque revival Louis Bank of Commerce are the most recognizable features in the entire Gaslamp.

There are dozens of other historic buildings just like these scattered throughout the Gaslamp. Keep a lookout for the bronze placards that are affixed to buildings at street level. They'll give you the date of construction and perhaps a tidbit or two on what makes that structure unique. And don't forget to point that camera upward—you just might capture a one-of-a-kind architectural flourish that can't be found anywhere else.

LITTLE ITALY

The Italian American tradition is strong in San Diego, where in the 1920s a large community of Italians established themselves and helped to build the region into a tuna fishing juggernaut.

They came primarily from Sicily and Genoa, building homes just north of downtown and close to the water for easy access to the docks and the city center. According to some old-timers, this was the kind of neighborhood you could walk through and pick up on the scents of various delicious meals wafting out the windows.

In the mid-20th century, the community suffered multiple setbacks. In the 1940s, many Italians lost their jobs as the tuna industry shrank in response to the war and increased mechanization of the fishing fleet. And in the late 1950s, Little Italy itself was ravaged by the construction of I-5, which cut directly through the district.

As a result, many Italian families moved out and the neighborhood became the type of area where fathers wouldn't want their daughters walking alone. However, there were still a few stubborn stalwarts who continued to operate their businesses through the bad times.

In the early 1990s they led the charge to revitalize the district. Small restaurant and retail store openings were followed by civic projects and street beautifications. This paved the way for larger building redevelopments, including a number of high-profile condo towers.

Little Italy has completely remade itself, while maintaining the flair and culture of its original residents. The colorful buildings reflect the area's Italian heritage and there are still plenty of buildings from the old guard that were lovingly restored by community members who take pride in the neighborhood's roots. The delicious smells now waft out of the restaurants that have opened up in and around these historic buildings, particularly on the main drag on India Street.

Piazza Basilone

While you stroll along India Street be sure to take a moment at Piazza Basilone on the corner of West Fir, which pays tribute to naval and marine heroes from San Diego. The piazza is named after Gunnery Sergeant John Basilone, an Italian American marine who won both the Navy Cross and the

Congressional Medal of Honor for his service during World War II.

Amici Park

North of India Street, on the corner of State and Date Streets, lies a tribute to Italian heroism on a completely different "battlefield"— the kitchen. Among its other features, Amici Park is dotted with decorative tables festooned with traditional white-and-red-checkered tablecloths and engraved with Italian recipes donated by local community members. The park serves as a hub of activity for the district, with its playgrounds, bocci ball courts, and a small open-air amphitheater.

If the bocci courts aren't hopping, it might be because the athletic types are just a block away playing stickball. In operation for over a decade, the **West Coast Stickball League** (www.westcoaststickball.com) was created by some kids at heart with fond memories of their stickball sessions on the streets of another Little Italy, in New York City. The league usually stages matches on Columbia and State Streets; if you are lucky enough to pass by during a game you'll be entertained by the mix of competitive, sometimes overweight, middle-aged *paisans* huffing and puffing to vie with some of the younger participants.

Our Lady of the Rosary Church

Also in the neighborhood is Our Lady of the Rosary Church (1629 Columbia St., 619/233-7039, www.olrsd.org, 8 A.M.–4:30 P.M. Mon.–Fri., 11 A.M.–2 P.M. Sat., 8 A.M.–1 P.M. Sun.), which offers fine examples of art for those who favor religious depictions. This Italian national parish was consecrated on November 15, 1925, to serve the thriving population that yearned for a church that reminded them of the old country. Particularly beautiful are the oil paintings on the ceiling and walls that were painted by Fausto Tasca, a Venetian artist living in Los Angeles who was recruited by the church's founding priest. Also of note are the colorful stained-glass windows and the statues of Mary, St. Anne, and St. Joseph. Our Lady is an active Catholic parish today, so be

aware that on Sundays you might have to wait for services to conclude before whipping out your camera.

WATERFRONT
San Diego Embarcadero

San Diego has long lived and died by the sea, so it is no surprise that much of the city's hubbub still surrounds the waterfront. San Diego Bay, or the "Big Bay" as locals call it, is sheltered from open water by Coronado Island and Point Loma. The easily defendable inlet and calm waters created by these land masses make it an ideal harbor, one which San Diegans have taken advantage of for centuries.

The Big Bay's present still echoes its past. Naval steamers have been replaced by aircraft carriers. The tuna fleet has largely been replaced by sport fisherman. Lumbering cruise ships tower over the pleasure craft that still zip around the bay to this day.

With a dazzling view of the bay and Coronado Island, the Embarcadero is one of the perfect places to soak up the flavor of San Diego's maritime tradition. This bayfront path is dotted with parks, museums, shops, and restaurants. Along the way, the salty air is permeated with the scent of waffle cones and fried fish. Here the jingle of pedicab bells is occasionally interrupted by deep-bass cruise ship horns, giggling children, and the call of the seagulls.

Seaport Village

Dominating the waterfront on the south end is Seaport Village (849 W. Harbor Dr., #D, 619/235-4014, www.seaportvillage.com, 10 A.M.–9 P.M. daily), a 14-acre shopping and dining complex. With its cutesy shops filled with clever T-shirts, 101 varieties of hot sauces, and precious little kitten figurines, this place is the prototypical tourist trap. But it manages to rise above the whimsy thanks to its sublime setting and scenic grounds. Plus, visitors hardly need to spend the whole day at the village.

But there is enough to see and do here to provide a good intergenerational afternoon or morning of fun. Mom and Dad can snap photos of the little ones on the circa-1895 carousel designed by Charles Looff; Gram and Gramps can browse through the shops' tchotchkes to their hearts' content; and teenagers can sullenly pretend they aren't with their parents while walking the waterfront and plunking quarters into the binoculars facing the bay.

With ample parking and several good restaurants, the village makes a good point of embarkation toward the rest of the Embarcadero. Parking isn't free, but if you pick up a souvenir or a bite to eat in the village you can get your ticket validated for some free time.

Embarcadero Marina Park

Really two parks in one, Embarcadero Marina Park (North Embarcadero Marina Park: Kettner at the Embarcadero, South Embarcadero Marina Park: Marina Park Way at the Embarcadero, 6 A.M.–10:30 P.M. daily, parking free) juts out into the bay like two green pinkies embracing the south end of the Embarcadero.

The north and south parks border Seaport Village and the San Diego Convention Center. The two peninsulas feature a fishing pier, basketball courts, gazebos, and a concession stand that sells food and bait.

◖ USS *Midway* Museum

A few blocks north of Seaport Village is the USS *Midway* Museum (937 N. Harbor Dr., 619/544-9600, www.midway.org, 10 A.M.–5 P.M. daily, $18 adults, $15 seniors, $10 students, military, and youth 6–17, free children 5 and under and active-duty military in uniform), a floating monument that honors San Diego's naval tradition.

One of the longest-serving carriers in the nation's history, the *Midway* welcomed several generations of sailors aboard her decks during her 47 years of service. She was commissioned during World War II and went on to be a major contributor during the Korean War and the Vietnam conflict, and even served as the navy's flagship during the Gulf War.

This floating fortress has been lovingly restored by a crew of staff and volunteers who kept it from rusting into the ocean when it was mothballed in 1992. Visitors traverse the gangplanks to explore dozens of restored sections open for tours, including engineering, the mess

© ERICKA CHICKOWSKI

the USS *Midway* Museum and San Diego Bay

deck, berthing spaces, the hangar and flight decks, and the island superstructure.

The audio tour is remarkably good (and worth trying even if you're someone who usually hates wearing those goofy headphones). You'll not only hear commentary, but also sounds similar to what you would have heard back in the day in each area you visit.

As an added bonus, there are over two dozen different aircraft featured on the flight deck. If you visit during the weekend or during summertime, be sure to spend some time listening to former pilots and crew members explain the complicated and dangerous tasks of landing and taking off from a postage stamp–sized runway in the middle of an ocean. Most of these volunteers are still full of the spit and vinegar that made them flight-worthy, making these talks a lively highlight.

◖ Maritime Museum of San Diego

Those who have already found their sea legs aboard the *Midway* should wobble two

blocks north to the Maritime Museum of San Diego (1492 N. Harbor Dr., 619/234-9153, www.sdmaritime.com, 9 A.M.–8 P.M. daily Labor Day–Memorial Day, 9 A.M.–9 P.M. daily Memorial Day–Labor Day, $14 adults, $11 seniors and active military, $8 children 6–17, kids under 5 free). Similar to the USS *Midway* Museum, the Maritime Museum's exhibits float dockside. The museum owns a fleet of historic ships that include an ex-Soviet submarine, an 1898 steam ferry, and a 1904 luxury yacht.

The pride and joy of the museum is the *Star of India,* the world's oldest active ship. This full-rigged iron windjammer was built at Ramsey Shipyards in the Isle of Man in 1863. Another highlight is the HMS *Surprise,* a replica 24-gun frigate of Great Britain's Nelson-era Royal Navy. Russell Crowe fans may recognize her—she was the boat used in the hit movie *Master and Commander.*

In addition to exploring the museum's collection of ships, consider paying the extra fee for the Adventure Package, which buys you a

© PAUL CHICKOWSKI

The Maritime Museum of San Diego allows visitors to tour seven historic ships, including this B-39 Russian submarine.

three-hour sail aboard a replica of a mid-19th-century revenue cutter.

Harbor Island

Away from the hustle of the Embarcadero, Harbor Island offers similar views of San Diego Bay with a lot less competition for legroom. The west side of the island is lined by the appropriately named **Harbor Island Park,** a shoreline park that offers lots of green space in which to throw down a blanket or a towel. It is also bisected by a nice flat sidewalk for strolling or rolling along the bay.

On a typical day, this is a pretty quiet park compared to some others. However, it does get crowded when an event is on. For example, the Big Bay's Fourth of July fireworks are usually based on the island.

Though not actually on Harbor Island, **Spanish Landing Park** is very close by. It runs on the mainland parallel to the island's northern half. This park commemorates the 1769 meeting in San Diego between the Serra-Portola overland expedition and Spanish ships making the simultaneous journey north from La Paz in order to settle the area.

Also parallel to the island, just on the southern half, is **Cancer Survivor's Park,** a bright piece of public green space designed to provide hope to those diagnosed with the disease. The park is decorated with optimistic artwork and sculptures and is a pleasant place for all.

This trio of parks is conveniently located right across the street from Lindbergh Field, where San Diego International Airport is located. Any one of them can be a great place to lounge in the sun while killing time before a flight.

CORONADO ISLAND
◖ Silver Strand State Beach

Frequently rated as a Blue Wave Beach by the Clean Beaches Council, Silver Strand State Beach features seven miles of sugar-sand beaches and undulating sand dunes. The strand is at the base of the spit that makes up Coronado Island, stretching from Imperial Beach all the way up to Naval Air Station

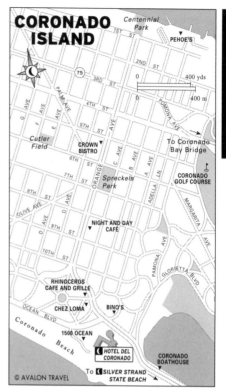

Coronado. Fans of wild and remote beaches would do well to cross the Coronado Bridge or drive up from Imperial Beach in the winter to spend some time here. Though the beach is not far from downtown as the crow flies, its position on the island makes it a bit out of the way compared to other beaches in town. It rests on the narrowest part of the island and there are no restaurants or stores nearby. As a result, there is a good chance that you can have a whole stretch of beach to yourself on certain days during the off-season.

The beach parking lot is open to RV camping, so during the summer it may be crowded with out-of-towners, and it is also a favorite spot of area residents all summer long. As a result, it is not going to be nearly as private as it is during the winter. However, the crowd is perhaps one of the most family-friendly among San Diego's beaches and the beach can still offer a relaxing day during peak season.

Hotel del Coronado

The grand dame of San Diego architecture is Hotel del Coronado (1500 Orange Ave., Coronado, 619/435-6611, www.hoteldel.com), a stunning Victorian masterpiece whose red-hued turrets, gables, and cupolas have beckoned upscale guests for more than 115 years.

Known simply as "The Del," this hotel has hosted every kind of rich and famous caller imaginable: statesmen and royalty, Hollywood starlets and country singers, railroad barons and technology magnates. Eight U.S. presidents have stayed here during their terms and several movies have been filmed on the property, including the 1958 Marilyn Monroe classic *Some Like it Hot.*

Its staying power and iconic status would make its founders Elisha Babcock and H. L. Story proud. In 1885 the two Midwestern entrepreneurs bought up Coronado Island for $110,000 with the intention of building an ocean resort that would be "the talk of the Western world." Three years later their dream was realized when the hotel opened its doors. Even today the Western world hasn't stopped talking about it.

Docents from the **Coronado Historical Association** lead one-hour tours (619/437-8788, www.coronadohistory.org, $15, children 6 and under free) through the hotel on Tuesdays at 10:30 A.M. and Fridays, Saturdays, and Sundays at 2 P.M. You'll learn about the architecture and the history of this San Diego landmark. Tour groups meet at the Coronado Museum of History and Art at 1100 Orange Avenue.

Coronado Bay Bridge

Coronado Bay Bridge is as integral to the San Diego waterfront view as the aircraft carriers and sailboats. The simple arching curves of this clean-lined beauty are meant to pay homage to the Spanish Revival architecture found locally. The design earned it the Most Beautiful

Hotel del Coronado has drawn statesmen and celebrities to the region since 1888.

Bridge Award of Merit from the American Institute of Steel Construction in 1970. Its high towers are made to accommodate tall naval ships passing through. Depending on how you feel about heights, a trip across can either be harrowing or breathtaking, but either way it is the easiest way to cross over to the island from downtown.

Orange Avenue

Coronado's shopping and recreational activity pivots around tree-lined Orange Avenue, the main thoroughfare that seems to link every "here" to "there" on the island. And just as any journey is more important than the destination, the sum of Orange Avenue is more than its parts. So be sure to stay long enough to soak it all in: the shops, the restaurants, the museums, and the parks.

Glorietta Bay Park

Glorietta Bay Park sits bayside just where Orange Avenue begins transitioning into Route 75. With fantastic views of the downtown skyline, grass galore, picnic tables, benches, and grills, this is a primo spot for a summertime barbecues. The park is also an excellent departure point to walk, jog, or ride along the Silver Strand bike path.

Coronado Cays and Grand Caribe Park

Near the Loews Resort there's another grassy bayside park called Coronado Cays that is ideal for picnicking and family relaxation. This six-acre park has playgrounds and ball fields and is adjacent to Grand Caribe Park, which features a nature path with native plants and outdoor art. Either park can be a good place to cap off a day spent on the sands of Silver Strand, which is just across the highway.

The Gondola Company (4000 Coronado Bay Rd., Coronado, 619/429-6317, www.gondolacompany.com, 3 P.M.–midnight Mon.–Fri., 11 A.M.–midnight Sat.–Sun., $85 for two, $20 additional persons, maximum six per boat) offers a bit of Venetian-style touring on its gondola boat rides through the tony

© ERICKA CHICKOWSKI

Orange Avenue in downtown Coronado

Coronado Cays. Munch on the hors d'oeuvres or dessert plate served with the ride and imagine you're Robin Leach as you glide past some of the region's most exclusive estates.

BALBOA PARK AND BANKERS HILL
◖ Balboa Park

As early as 1789, Spain's King Carlos III ordered the present-day site of Balboa Park (open daily 24 hours) to be reserved for "pasturage or for recreational purposes" and the land has remained a recreational reserve ever since.

The jewel of San Diego, Balboa Park epitomizes the dual nature of San Diego. Athletes sweat it out on the ball fields and courts of the park, while nearby museumgoers nod their heads thoughtfully at works of art. At more than 1,200 acres, the park hosts more than 85 different cultural and recreational organizations, including the world-famous San Diego Zoo. The park also features hundreds of species of flora, many of them planted near the turn

of the 20th century by the city's first official gardener, Kate O. Sessions.

The offerings can be a bit overwhelming, so it might make sense to make your first stop at the **Balboa Park Visitors Center** (1549 El Prado, 619/239-0512, www.balboapark.org, 9:30 A.M.–4:30 P.M. daily, free). Tucked away into a building along El Prado, the visitors center is staffed by a number of knowledgeable volunteers who can point you to the best spots based on your needs for the day. They can also arm you with informative books and maps to enrich your stay.

The visitors center also sells the Passport to Balboa Park, a special pass that can be a great bargain for those who wish to fully experience the museums and attractions within the park. The deal offers admission to thirteen different museums at the park and is valid for seven days after purchase. The passport costs $45 for adults and $24 for kids. You can also add zoo admission to the mix, making it $75 for adults and $39 for children.

◖ San Diego Zoo

Arguably the most famous zoo in the world, the San Diego Zoo (2920 Zoo Dr., 619/234-3153, www.sandiegozoo.com, 9 A.M.–9 P.M. daily summer, 9 A.M.–5 P.M. daily fall–spring, $37 adults, $27 children 3–11) has long been the standard-bearer for displaying animals from around the world. Zoo visitors come face to face with creatures great and small and also learn about the efforts that zookeepers and researchers are making to save endangered species and their habitats.

The grounds are almost as impressive as the menagerie of animals, with a lush jungle of exotic plants serving as the setting for the roars of lions and screeches of monkeys. The property is extremely expansive compared to the typical city zoo. There are over 100 acres to explore, so be prepared with sturdy walking shoes and at least three or four hours of time. If attempting this with a screaming toddler in tow sounds nightmarish, you might have more fun exploring the zoo in shorter sessions. A two-day pass for adults runs $70

© ERICKA CHICKOWSKI

Balboa Park

and for kids costs $50. Those with limited mobility will be happy to find that there are a number of options to quickly peruse the park, including a tour bus, a sky tram, and shuttle service for those in wheelchairs.

In the summer, one of the highlights of the park is Nighttime Zoo, when the zoo is open through 9 P.M. Visiting during evening hours allows animal lovers to catch a glimpse of nocturnal animals who might spend most daylight hours holed up in their caves.

Timken Museum of Art

The Timken Museum of Art (1500 El Prado, 619/239-5548, www.timkenmuseum.org, 10 A.M.–4:30 P.M. Tues.–Sat. Oct.–Aug., 1:30–4:30 P.M. Sun. Oct.–Aug., closed Mon., closed Sept., free) is probably one of the best deals in the city for museumgoers. This intimate art gallery offers a collection of very well-known works of art free to the public. The trick is visiting while the museum is open, as hours are more limited than other museums in the park.

KATE O. SESSIONS: MOTHER OF BALBOA PARK

San Diego wasn't always as lush and floral as it is today. Very little except low scrubs and succulents grow naturally here. The city owes a great deal of gratitude for the greenery to Kate O. Sessions, an enterprising botanist that many consider the first lady of gardening in San Diego. Many of the trees and gardens she planted over 100 years ago still grow strong, providing shade and shelter today.

An independent and progressive woman, Sessions was a feminist ahead of her time. While studying for her science degree at University of California-Berkeley in 1881, she wrote an essay titled "The Natural Sciences as a Field for Woman's Labor." This was about 100 years before Women's Studies was established as an academic discipline at Berkeley.

She moved to San Diego a few years after graduation, part of the tidal wave of San Franciscans headed south due to Alonzo Horton's promotion of the area, and started her love affair with horticulture when she partnered with some friends in 1885 to buy the San Diego Nursery.

From there Sessions threw herself into the business of growing plants, owning a number of nurseries all over the city and corresponding with many horticulturalists around the state and the country through published articles and letters. Her studies helped her pinpoint flora that would work in this clime and she introduced many of the popular plants that remain in San Diego today: the bright red bougainvillea, fragrant star jasmine, bird of paradise, and numerous shady trees such as the Brazilian pepper tree, banyan, and Italian cypress.

In 1892, she brokered a deal with the city to take on the role of city gardener. The city agreed to lease her land for a nursery within Balboa Park, then called "City Park," if she would plant 100 trees per year on park land and supply the city with 300 more to plant around town. Sessions more than lived up to her end of the bargain and she personally worked the soil to lay the groundwork for Balboa's amazing gardens.

Together with Mary B. Coulston and George Marston (whose gorgeous Arts and Crafts home is a museum at the park today), Sessions formed the Park Improvement Committee in order to take her stewardship one step farther. This civic work, combined with her gardening, earned her the title "Mother of Balboa Park" in the annals of San Diego history. A statue in her honor can be found just in front of the Cabrillo Bridge at the Laurel Avenue entrance to the park.

Sessions was determined to leave a legacy of a green San Diego. After garnering the appointment to be supervisor of agriculture and landscaper for city schools in 1915, she went about educating the next generation of gardeners by teaching students about horticulture. Together with the children she helped develop gardens at schools throughout the city.

Sessions's work in the city and her involvement in the horticulture world at large made the scientific community take notice of her achievements. Just a year before her death in 1940, she was given the Frank N. Meyer Medal from the American Genetic Association, becoming the first female recipient of the honor.

It is home to the Putnam Foundation Collection of artwork from European old masters, early American artists, and Russian iconographers. This collection is so well regarded that many museums around the world beg to borrow numerous pieces from Timken—but don't worry, this small museum rarely consents, so you'll likely get to see every piece when you visit. Included in the collection are masterpieces by Rembrandt, Rubens, Petrus Christus, Fragonard, Jacques-Louis David, Veronese, John Singleton Copley, and Eastman Johnson.

Two of my particular favorites are Rembrandt's "Saint Bartholomew" and "The Cranberry Harvest, Island of Nantucket" by Eastman Johnson.

The Timken has a very active docent program.

Visit Tuesday through Friday between 10 A.M. and noon to ask for a docent to lead you on a 30- to 60-minute tour of the art here. Docents are also available every second and third Saturday 11 A.M.–1 P.M.

San Diego Museum of Art

San Diego County's oldest and largest art institution is the San Diego Museum of Art (1450 El Prado, 619/232-7931, www.sdmart. org, 10 A.M.–6 P.M. Tues.–Sat., noon–5 P.M. Sun., 10 A.M.–9 P.M. Thurs. during summer, closed Mon., $12 adults, $4.50 children ages 7–17, $10 military, $9 seniors, free children under 7), which features a collection that is particularly strong in representing the works of Spanish masters such as Murillo, Rivera, and El Greco. There are also many other examples from the French Impressionists, the Barbizon School, and French Academic painters. In addition, the collection of American art spans from the colonial period to early 20th century, with work by Durand, Cassatt, Inness, Eakins, Chase, and O'Keeffe. Docent-led tours are held at 11 A.M., 1 P.M., and 2 P.M. Tuesday through Sunday.

San Diego Natural History Museum

One of the region's most esteemed institutes for cultivating archeological, geological, and biological discovery and learning is the San Diego Natural History Museum (1788 El Prado, 619/232-3821, www.sdnhm.org, 10 A.M.–5 P.M. daily, closed Thanksgiving and Christmas, $17 adults, $15 seniors, $12 military, $11 children ages 3–12, children under 3 free). This institution is the leading local scientific research organization studying the geology and biology of San Diego County and Baja Norte and has amassed an amazing collection of specimens throughout 100 years of field work. Selected samples are displayed in a variety of permanent and temporary exhibits throughout the year. Best known for attracting first-rate traveling exhibits, the museum has been intent in recent years to do better justice to its permanent collections

of fossils, rocks, and other natural curiosities. The most evident result is the impressive "Fossil Mysteries" exhibit on the second floor, highlighted by an enormous model of a Giant "Mega-Tooth" Shark hanging over the museum atrium.

San Diego Air and Space Museum

While there are numerous museums around town that offer a peek into some pristine restored aircraft, none offer the same depth and breadth of aeronautical history as the San Diego Air and Space Museum (2001 Pan American Plaza, 619/234-8291, www.aerospacemuseum.org, 10 A.M.–4:30 P.M. daily Labor Day–Memorial Day, 10 A.M.–5:30 P.M. daily Memorial Day–Labor Day, $24.75 adults, $21.75 seniors, students and military, $12.75 children ages 3–11, $8.75 active-duty military, free children under 3). The museum takes you through the annals of human flight with hundreds of models, photos, and restored airplanes, from the Montgolfier brothers' hot-air-balloon ride in 1783 to today's space-exploring astronauts.

Spreckels Organ Pavilion

Home to the world's largest outdoor instrument, Spreckels Organ Pavilion (near the Japanese Friendship Garden south of El Prado) was gifted to San Diego by brothers John D. and Adolf Spreckels in preparation for the 1915 Panama-California Exposition. This impressive musical behemoth, built by the Austin Organ Company, is made up of more than 4,500 pipes. It sits protected from the elements by the ornate Italian Renaissance–style pavilion and surrounded by bench seating for 2,400 listeners. The organ is played regularly for park visitors; free concerts are held every Sunday at 2 P.M. and on summer Mondays at 7:30 P.M. seats are filled for the annual International Organ Festival.

In addition, the stage hosts a Twilight in the Park Concert Series in the summer on Tuesday, Wednesday, and Thursday at 6:15 P.M. Visit the Balboa Park website (www.balboapark.org) for specifics.

Botanical Building

Balboa Park is replete with plant life of all shapes, sizes, and colors. The flora here is so verdant it seems that the park has its own little ecological system, especially in contrast to the native scrubs that cling to surrounding hillsides and mesas. In addition to the abundance of decorative plants that surround the park's structures, there are over fifteen official gardens.

Most famous among them is the collection of plants in the Botanical Building (10 A.M.–4 P.M. Fri.–Wed., free), which sits behind the park's renowned Lily Pond. If you've got a taste for ironic humor, step back and snap a shot of the throngs of photographers that line up on the weekends to capture the beauty of the pond and building—this is one of the most photographed landscapes in the entire park. It is no wonder; this really is a lovely spot.

Kids will love to watch the koi float lazily through the pond, couples can cuddle on the expansive lawn nearby, and garden lovers will enjoy a walk through the building, which is home to more than 2,100 permanent plants. Some of the highlights include an impressive orchid collection, numerous ferns and palms, and a really fun touch-and-smell herbal garden. My favorite scent is the chocolate basil.

Japanese Friendship Garden

Those in a meditative mood can escape the crowds at the Japanese Friendship Garden (619/232-2721, www.niwa.org, 10 A.M.–5 P.M. Mon.–Fri., 10 A.M.–4 P.M. Sat.–Sun., $4 adults, $3 seniors, students, military, free children under 6) Sitting at the edge of a canyon near the Spreckels Organ Pavilion grounds, this garden charges a nominal $3 fee, which tends to keep traffic down a bit. The garden path is lined with bamboo, Japanese ornamentals, a koi pond, and bonsai. The centerpiece of the grounds is a serene Zen Garden. The garden is viewable from the exhibit house, which features a collection of Japanese art. The gardens also have a *shishi odoshi,* a traditional Japanese fountain made of bamboo

tubes that pivot up and down as they fill up and empty themselves through the effects of water flow and gravity. Located at the entrance, this can be a particular favorite for curious toddlers.

From the friendship garden, cross the organ pavilion grounds to find a living oasis right in the park. **Palm Canyon** contains more than 58 species of palm trees—nearly 500 trees in all. Many of them were the original Mexican fan palms planted by Kate Sessions in 1912.

There's a nice trail there that links the canyon to a small cactus garden, but for a real succulent treat, you'll have to venture over the pedestrian bridge that arches over Park Boulevard. There you'll be greeted by the sight of an amazing collection of desert flora. This two-and-a-half-acre park, **Desert Garden,** has over 1,300 succulents and cacti.

For a more traditional form of beauty, **Inez Grant Parker Memorial Rose Garden** is right next to Desert Garden. San Diego's weather is ideal for many varieties of roses, and this particular garden features over 200 variations. The groundskeepers take excellent care of the plants and they've been honored by having the garden distinguished as an All America Rose Selection Display Garden. The roses bloom nearly all year, but the peak time to visit is in April and May. You don't even have to stop and smell the flowers then—the scent surrounds you as you crunch along the gravel paths.

Reuben H. Fleet Science Center

The Reuben H. Fleet Science Center (1875 El Prado, 619/238-1233, www.rhfleet.org, 9:30 A.M.–5 P.M. Mon.–Thurs., 9:30 A.M.–9 P.M. Fri., 9:30 A.M.–8 P.M. Sat., 9:30 A.M.–6 P.M. Sun., $10 adults, $8.75 seniors and children 3–12) gives weary parents a break from yelling out "Don't touch that!" every five seconds. The hands-on science exhibits here encourage visitors to learn through interaction. One of the special favorites in the permanent exhibit is the Tornado, a mini wind funnel that visitors can put their hands through and experiment with to learn about the larger natural phenomenon.

Museum of Photographic Arts

Located right next to the visitors center along El Prado, the Museum of Photographic Arts (1649 El Prado, 619/238-7559, www.mopa. org, 10 A.M.–5 P.M. Tues.–Sun., 10 A.M.–9 P.M. Thurs. during summer, $6 adults, $4 students, seniors, and military, free kids under 12) holds a diverse collection of 4,000 photographs that span the spectrum of photographic media, including daguerreotypes, salt prints, Woodbury types, albumen prints, ambrotypes, and tintypes, through such contemporary processes as 20- by 24-inch Polaroid photographs and laser holograms. This permanent collection is augmented by an always inspirational rotation of traveling exhibits.

Mingei International Museum

A product of the Japanese words *min* (all people) and *gei* (art), *mingei* is a term used to describe "arts of the people." The Mingei International Museum (1439 El Prado, 619/239-0003, www. mingei.org, 10 A.M.–4 P.M. Tues.–Sun., $7 adults, $5 seniors, $4 students, military, and children ages 6–17) features revolving exhibitions of folk arts and crafts that reflect cultures from around the world and throughout time.

California Building

Across El Prado from the Mingei is one of the architectural highlights of the park, the colorful and ornate California Building. Punctuated by the 200-foot California Tower and the dome decorated in blue and white floral tiling, the building has been described as architecturally impure because of its jumble of styles, with elements of Spanish plateresque, baroque, rococo, and Mexican ultrabaroque (or churrigueresque) adorning the cornices and crevices of the building's facade. I say, "Churri-what?" Whatever the mishmash style is, the building is a masterpiece.

When the building opened in 1915 for the Panama-California Exposition it housed an exhibit called "The Story of Man." Today the tradition of anthropological exhibits within the building continues with the **San Diego Museum of Man** (1350 El Prado, 619/239-2001, www.museumofman.org, 10 A.M.–4:30 P.M. daily, $10 adults, $7.50 students, seniors, and military, $5 ages 6–17, free kids under 6).

San Diego Model Railroad Museum

The San Diego Model Railroad Museum (1649 El Prado, 619/696-0199, www.sdmodelrailroadm.com, 11 A.M.–4 P.M. Tues.–Fri., 11 A.M.–5 P.M. Sat.–Sun., $7 adults, $6 seniors, $3 students, free children under 15) is a secret little treasure that offers a fascinating and comprehensive collection. There are very realistic train models in several scales, as well as miniature landscapes of San Diego County to run them on. It is a well-curated setup that is a pleasure even for museumgoers who have had absolutely zero experience with model trains.

San Diego Automotive Museum

Beware—drop a car buff inside the San Diego Automotive Museum (2080 Pan American Plaza, 619/231-2886, www.sdautomuseum.org, 10 A.M.–5 P.M. daily, $8 adults, $6 seniors and military, $4 children 6–15, free under age 6) and they might disappear forever. This amazing collection of restored vehicles and memorabilia covers seemingly every trend in auto history, from Model T Speedsters to high-octane muscle cars.

Veterans Museum and Memorial Center

Housed in the old chapel of the Naval Hospital on Inspiration Point, the Veterans Museum and Memorial Center (2115 Park Blvd., 619/239-2300, www.sdvmc.org, 10 A.M.–4 P.M. Tues.–Sun., $5 adults, $4 veterans, $2 students, free children under 13 and active-duty military and dependents) pays tribute to men and women of all branches of the armed forces who have served the United States in time of war. The setting is fitting considering how many in the military remember San Diego only for its hospital, which has continuously operated from its facilities next to Balboa Park for more than 80 years. The museum's collection dates from the Civil War through the present, with exhibits on World War I, World War II and Pearl Harbor, the Korea and Vietnam conflicts, Desert Storm, and women in the military. It also displays a number of very evocative military paintings by local artists and veterans.

Marston House

If you make the trek to the northwest corner of the park you'll find a pristine example of the Arts and Crafts architectural movement that swept the city at the turn of the 20th century. The Marston House (3525 7th Ave., 619/298-3142, http://sohosandiego.org/marston, tours every half hour 10 A.M.–5 P.M. Fri.–Sun., $8 adult, $6 seniors, $4 children ages 6–12, free under 6) is a Craftsman mansion built in 1905 for prominent San Diego civic leader George Marston and his wife, Anna. A progressive innovator, Marston was a founder and the first president of the San Diego Historical Society, an important supporter of Balboa Park development, and even could be called the city's first environmentalist politician. In 1917 he ran for mayor under the "Smokestacks vs. Geraniums" platform, rallying to balance industrial and environmental concerns. These ideals were probably what attracted him to the Arts and Crafts philosophy, which was a backlash against the lavish excesses of the gilded Victorian era. The architect Marston commissioned for this house was a young Irving Gill, who went on to become one of Southern California's most well-regarded modern architects. The house is run by the Save Our Heritage Organization and is only open through guided tours held Friday through Sunday.

MISSION VALLEY AND OLD TOWN
◖ Old Town State Historic Park

Before Alonzo Horton managed to swing development three miles west to tracts of land and a new wharf on San Diego Bay, the town wasn't much more than a dusty pueblo at the foot of Presidio Hill. Horton's movement to transplant the town from this area led to the creation of "New Town" San Diego, now downtown San Diego.

What was left behind is still called Old Town, an area whose history is commemorated by many reconstructed buildings and a few originals within Old Town State Historic Park (San Diego Ave. at Twiggs St., 619/220-5422, www.parks.ca.gov, 10 A.M.–5 P.M. daily, free). The complex celebrates the town's Californio and early American heritage through museum displays and old-timey shops.

Most of the park's buildings are clustered around grassy Washington Square. To get your bearings and to bone up on the history of Old Town, stop by **Robinson-Rose House Visitor Center** (10 A.M.–5 P.M. daily, free) at the northeast edge of the square. Directly across the square from the visitors center is **Casa de Estudillo** (10 A.M.–5 P.M. daily, free), a classic adobe hacienda. If you are short on time, or if you are in the company of children who get antsy after one too many historic sites, make a visit to Casa de Estudillo your highest priority. This building was rebuilt in 1910 and features rooms with period furnishings and an authentic garden to give visitors a feel for how Old Town's first Californio residents lived.

Other historic buildings that surround the square include the **Colorado House,** which is home to the fascinating **Wells Fargo Museum,** a replica of the first **San Diego Courthouse and Jail,** and the **Mason Street Schoolhouse,** a one-room shack that was built in 1865 as the area's first public school.

Be sure to cap off your tour of Old Town with a visit to the **Seeley Stables Museum** (10 A.M.–5 P.M. daily, free). This is a reconstruction of an 1850 stage stop in the San Diego to Los Angeles Stage Line, run by Albert Seely until it was put out of business by the railroad in 1887. The museum sports a collection of antique carriages and other odds and ends related to stage travel.

The state park runs free guided tours of Old Town State Historic Park at 11 A.M. and 2 P.M. every day. The tour departs from the Robinson-Rose House Visitor Center and will give you a rich understanding of the cultural

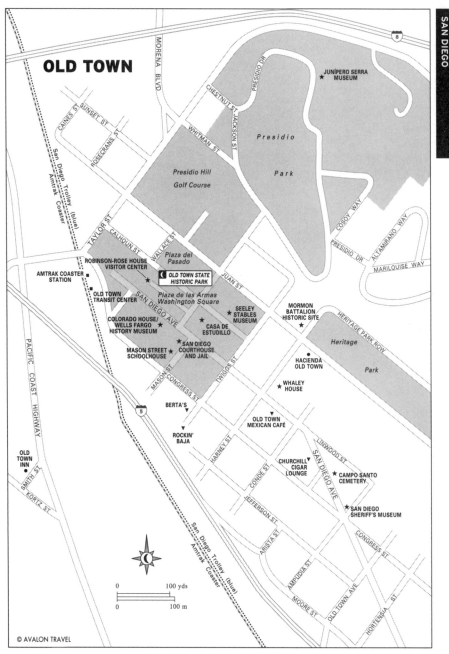

OLD TOWN

MORENA BLVD

CHESTNUT ST

PRESIDIO DR

JACKSON ST

WHITMAN ST

JUNÍPERO SERRA MUSEUM ★

Presidio

Park

CAINES ST

SUNSET ST

ROSECRANS ST

Presidio Hill Golf Course

San Diego Trolley (blue)
Amtrak Coaster

TAYLOR ST

CALHOUN ST

WALLACE ST

Plaza del Pasado

JUAN ST

COSOY WAY

PRESIDIO DR

ALTAMIRANO WAY

MARILOUISE WAY

ROBINSON-ROSE HOUSE VISITOR CENTER ★

■ AMTRAK COASTER STATION

OLD TOWN STATE HISTORIC PARK

HERITAGE PARK ROW

Heritage

Park

■ OLD TOWN TRANSIT CENTER

SAN DIEGO AVE

Plaza de las Armas
Washington Square

SEELEY ★ STABLES MUSEUM

MORMON BATTALION HISTORIC SITE ★

COLORADO HOUSE/ WELLS FARGO ★ HISTORY MUSEUM

CASA DE ESTUDILLO ★

MASON STREET SCHOOLHOUSE ★

★ SAN DIEGO COURTHOUSE AND JAIL

TWIGGS ST

● HACIENDA OLD TOWN

PACIFIC COAST HIGHWAY

MASON ST

CONGRESS ST

★ WHALEY HOUSE

5

BERTA'S ▾

▾ OLD TOWN MEXICAN CAFÉ

LINWOOD ST

SAN DIEGO AVE

▾ ROCKIN' BAJA

HARNEY ST

CHURCHILL ▾ CIGAR LOUNGE

OLD TOWN INN ●

SMITH ST

CONDE ST

CAMPO SANTO CEMETERY ★

KORTZ ST

JEFFERSON ST

★ SAN DIEGO SHERIFF'S MUSEUM

CONGRESS ST

San Diego Trolley (blue)
Amtrak Coaster

ARISTA ST

AMPUDIA ST

MOORE ST

OLD TOWN AVE

HORTENSIA ST

0   100 yds
0   100 m

© AVALON TRAVEL

© ERICKA CHICKOWSKI

Casa de Estudillo in Old Town

and historical background of San Diego's oldest community.

Presidio Park

Though the Spanish had discovered San Diego first in 1542 by way of Portuguese explorer Juan Cabrillo, and then by Sebastián Vizcaíno in 1602, their preoccupation with the settlement of mainland Mexico and Baja California kept newcomers from establishing roots farther north for more than a century after that.

By 1769, though, Spanish leaders worried about the encroachment of Russian fur traders from Alaska down the west coast of the continent. As English colonies thrived on the East Coast, the Spanish feared that they would lose possession of the West Coast if they did not establish settlements quickly. That year the king of Spain ordered four expeditions up to San Diego in order to start the development of missions and settlements in Alta California.

Two expeditions were by sea, the other two by land. The most famous of the four was that of Gaspar de Portolá, who eventually became the first governor of Alta California, and Father Junípero Serra, the priest responsible for establishing a system of missions that would form the backbone of Spanish colonies in Alta California. The pair led a party that journeyed through the desert and scrubland of Baja California from La Paz up to San Diego; this was the first group to make it to the area.

Serra officially established San Diego's first mission by planting a cross atop Presidio Hill and saying Mass. Overlooking San Diego Bay, the hill would become the main military installation for early San Diego as well as the mission's first home.

Today the site is a public park that honors these first Spanish settlers. The 49-acre Presidio Park (2811 Jackson St., 619/692-4918) still has great views of the bay on clear days and plenty of grassy spots to sit and look out.

It is also home to the **Junípero Serra Museum** (2727 Presidio Dr., www.sandiego-history.org, 619/297-3258, 10 A.M.–5 P.M. Sat.–Sun., $5), a historical museum run by the San Diego Historical Society that displays artifacts from Native American, Spanish, Mexican, and American periods through 1929. The museum is housed in a distinctive bright-white mission-style building that can be spotted from I-8 as you drive through Mission Valley.

In addition to cruising through the museum, park visitors can attend an outdoor tour of Presidio Park that is led by park rangers every second Sunday of the month from 1 P.M. to 2 P.M. These tours meet in front of the Serra Museum and are free of charge.

Whaley House

The Whaley House (2476 San Diego Ave., 619/297-7511, www.whaleyhouse.org; 10 A.M.– 10 P.M. daily June–Sept., the first week of Apr., and the last two weeks of Dec.; otherwise 10 A.M.–5 P.M. Mon.–Tues., 10 A.M.–9:30 P.M. Thurs.–Sun.; $6 adults, $5 seniors 55 and over, $4 children ages 3–12, free to kids under 3) is as well known to paranormal investigators as it is to historians. Named the Most Haunted House in America by the Travel Channel, this brick structure is as much a part of the fabric of Old Town as the state park itself.

It was built in 1857 by Thomas Whaley for his wife, Anna, and their young family. Whaley was one of the most prominent entrepreneurs and civic leaders of Old Town and members of the Whaley family lived in the house off and on through 1953. Throughout that time the house also doubled as a granary, a city courthouse, Old Town's first commercial theater, and a polling place.

The house is restored to its late 1860s appearance and the site is said to be haunted by numerous spirits. Prior to the building's construction it was home to Old Town's gallows; the ghosts of some of the area's most notorious criminals are said to be living here. Even early on, the Whaleys were frightened by mysterious heavy footsteps that they believed belonged to a criminal named "Yankee" Jim Robinson whom Thomas had seen hang at the plot years before he bought it.

The home itself saw more than its fair share of tragic deaths under its roof as well. Just a year after the house was built, young Thomas

Jr. died at the age of 18 months. Years later, in 1885, daughter Violet shot herself here after a scandalous divorce. Anna, son Francis, and daughter Lillian also all died while living in the house.

Ghost hunters who would like to visit Whaley House after hours can call ahead to arrange a private tour for $75 per person per hour.

Campo Santo Cemetery

Steps away from the Whaley House is another Old Town site popular with area paranormal investigators. Campo Santo Cemetery (2410 San Diego Ave., 24 hours daily) is San Diego's oldest existing cemetery and is the final resting place for both the prominent and the unknown among original Old Town citizens.

Pay your respects to Yankee Jim, who was buried here after hanging at the Whaley House lot, Antonio Garra, a Cupeño who was actually executed at the cemetery for having led an insurrection over the taxation of local tribes, and numerous members of prominent Californio families such as the Machados, Estudillos, and Aguirres.

On your way in, look down at the sidewalk and street in front of the gate. There you'll see little brass dots scattered around. These are the only markers left to acknowledge the graves that were built over when a streetcar line was built on the site of present-day San Diego Avenue. Rather than re-inter the bodies, city leaders chose to leave them here. The community has tried to make amends with these markers, which were placed after locating burial sites via ground-penetrating radar. Ghost hunters suspect that this token gesture of respect to the dead was not enough to quell the spirits who are rumored to lurk in the area. Legends of misty vapors, cold spots, and car troubles for those parked above the graves have been reported.

San Diego Sheriff's Museum

A few blocks south of the state park stands a museum that chronicles the 150-year history of the San Diego Sheriff's Department. The

SAN DIEGO HAUNTS

No historic city worth its weight in ectoplasm can make it through a few centuries of existence without accumulating its fair share of resident spooks and spirits. Never one to be left out of the hauntings, San Diego bills itself as the home of the "Most Haunted House in America" and enough other paranormal sites to keep both believers and skeptics arguing about their veracity until they become ghosts themselves.

WHALEY HOUSE

Dubbed as the "Most Haunted House in America" by the Travel Channel, this brick structure spooked the Whaley family way back in 1857 when they first moved in. They heard mysterious heavy footsteps upstairs, which they later believed to be the ghost of an outlaw who was hanged on the property before they owned it – the land had served as the town gallows. Since that time, a number of tragic deaths on the site have only added more ghostly stories to the Whaley House mystique.

EL CAMPO SANTO

One of the earliest recorded graveyards in the city, El Campo Santo is believed to be haunted by the spirits of those whose graves were paved over by the adjacent San Diego Avenue. Just a block away from the Whaley House, this is many ghost investigators' second-favorite place to wave around tape recorders and EMF meters on moonless nights.

OLD POINT LOMA LIGHTHOUSE

Perched atop the Point Loma Peninsula at the Cabrillo National Monument, this lighthouse is the site of a controversial haunting – even steadfast paranormal believers quibble over the spirit that supposedly resides here. Skeptics say that the lighthouse was never the site of any kind of tragedy or trauma that would invite a haunting, but others are adamant about seeing the ghost of a forlorn sailor on the property.

HOTEL DEL CORONADO

Like any good old hotel, the Del has its share of hauntings. There are reports of cold spots, flickering lights, a general sense of dread, and even indentations in pillows – like someone's head is resting there – that won't go away even after fluffing. The hotel's best-known ghost is thought to be that of Kate Morgan, an Iowa girl who turned up dead here in 1892. Officially ruled a suicide, her body was found on the steps leading to the beach, a bullet wound in her head.

STAR OF INDIA

Sitting on the docks of the Embarcadero as a part of the Maritime Museum of San Diego, *Star of India* is the world's oldest active ship

---

San Diego Sheriff's Museum (2384 San Diego Ave., 619/260-1850, www.sheriffmuseum.org, 10 A.M.–4 P.M. Tues.–Sat., free) is located at the site of Old Town's first cobblestone jail, which was replaced early on by the iron cage behind the first courthouse after a high-profile escape. Now the Sheriff's Department runs the museum, harboring an assortment of guns, badges, communication equipment, a patrol car, helicopter, and other mementos of law enforcement history.

Mormon Battalion Historic Site

Those looking for another interesting side trip from the state park should take a short walk over to the Mormon Battalion Historic Site (2510 Juan St., 619/298-3317, http://historicmormonbatallion.net, 9 A.M.–9 P.M. daily, free), which honors 500 Mormon men who marched 2,000 miles from Iowa to San Diego in order to help fight in the Mexican American War. This was the only religious unit to ever be formed by the U.S. military and was one of the longest marches in military history. By the time they arrived in San Diego, the tide of war had turned in favor of the Americans, but the band of troops stayed to carry out a number of civic improvement

© ERICKA CHICKOWSKI

Whaley House

and her sometimes tragic history is studded with deaths on the high seas. For example, in 1868 her captain died while the ship was at sea. Some visitors say they've smelled phantom scents and seen apparitions while aboard.

HORTON GRAND HOTEL

Guests who have stayed in room 309 at Horton Grand have reported the bed shaking, unexplained opening and closing of armoire doors, and unearthly movement of objects. The paranormal activity is believed to be the work of Robert Whitaker. Legend has it that this cheating gambler of the mid-1800s was caught one night and his accuser followed him to his room at what was then the Kale Saddlery Hotel and shot him over the dispute. Guests in other rooms have reported hearing the sound of shuffling cards coming from inside room 309 when it was unoccupied.

projects in Southern California in the months after their arrival.

🄲 Mission San Diego de Alcalá

California's very first mission, Mission San Diego de Alcalá (10818 San Diego Mission Rd., 619/283-7319, www.missionsandiego. com, 9 A.M.–4:45 P.M. daily, free), stands along the San Diego River basin in the heart of Mission Valley. The buildings were reconstructed in 1931, when the mission was but a whisper of its former self after years of disuse and neglect.

The exterior is white-washed adobe, accented by a distinctive five-bell *campañario* and a surrounding complex that includes gardens, a rectory, and a smaller chapel. Inside the main church are high wooden ceilings supported by timber beams decorated with delicate hand paintings. The ornate altar and many of the walls also have these hand-painted embellishments and are decorated with recessed reredos holding beautiful sculptures of holy figures.

Visitors are invited to walk the grounds any time and to visit the church interior when Mass is not being held. There is also a small museum and a gift shop on the property.

NORST CITY
◖ Mission Trails Regional Park

At over 5,800 acres, Mission Trails Regional Park is one of the largest urban parks in the country and offers visitors a taste of what San Diego was like before the metropolitan areas were built up and out into the surrounding mountains.

Rocky crags and chaparral sprawl across the hills and valleys of Mission Trails and there are plenty of opportunities to explore by foot, bike, or horseback. Before heading out, learn a little about the nature and history of the park at the **visitors center** (1 Fr. Junipero Serra Tr., 619/668-3281, www.mtrp.org, 9 A.M.–5 P.M. daily).

If time is limited, the signature expedition in Mission Trails is a trek up **Cowles Mountain,** the highest peak within city limits at 1,591 feet. The way to the top is steep but the reward for bagging this peak is a panoramic view of the city that on a clear day will grant you vistas of Point Loma, downtown San Diego, and even Mexico to the south. Remember which trail you hiked up—there are two trails and if you don't take the same one back you are in for a boring walk back to the car through surrounding neighborhoods.

Flying Leathernecks Museum

Flying to give close support to grunts on the ground, the squadrons of the Marine Aircraft Wings have a long tradition of heroism that dates back to World War I. San Diego has a special link with these flying leathernecks as the home of the Marine Corps Air Bases Western Area headquarters at Marine Corps Air Station (MCAS) Miramar.

Those interested in the history of the aviators and the aircraft that built the marine flight program should definitely wander over to Miramar to take a look at the Flying Leathernecks Museum (T-4203 Anderson Ave., 877/359-8762, www.flyingleathernecks. org, 9 A.M.–3:30 P.M. Tues.–Sun., free). This is the only museum in the country dedicated to Marine Corps Aviation and it features a patriotic collection of memorabilia, uniforms, and documents highlighting the rise of the flying leatherneck. Be sure to check out the more than 20 restored helicopters, fighter planes, and jets on display, as well as the museum's unique exhibit on women in the marines.

SOUTH BAY
U.S. Olympic Training Center

You're bound to feel guilty about all those sumptuous vacation dinners when you watch the athletes sweat it out on the grounds of the U.S. Olympic Training Center (2800 Olympic Pkwy., Chula Vista, 619/656-1500, 10 A.M.–5 P.M. daily, free). Located next to Lower Otay Lake, this 155-acre complex is where athletes in field hockey, soccer, paddling, tennis, track, and cycling come to sharpen their skills and perfect their physiques in order to compete for medals in the summer games.

Visitors are welcome to view the facilities from an elevated platform at the Copley Visitor Center; free guided tours of the grounds are conducted at 1:30 P.M. Tuesday through Saturday.

Knott's Berry Soak City

If the sand is rubbing you the wrong way, Knott's Berry Soak City (2052 Entertainment Cir., Chula Vista, 619/661-7373, 10 A.M.–6 P.M. or 7 P.M. daily June–Aug., 10 A.M.–6 P.M. or 7 P.M. weekends May and Sept., call to confirm hours, $27.95 adults, and $16.95 children and seniors) offers a chlorinated alternative in the summer months. This 32-acre water park has a wave pool, a rafting river, and slides galore. There's the winding and twisting kind, the kind that'll make your stomach drop, and the itty-bitty ones for the tykes.

◖ Chula Vista Nature Center

Located on the 316-acre Sweetwater Marsh National Wildlife Refuge, the Chula Vista Nature Center (1000 Gunpowder Point Dr., Chula Vista, 619/409-5900, www.chulavista-naturecenter.org, 10 A.M.–5 P.M. Tues.–Sun., $6) is a regional zoo and aquarium that educates visitors about the fragile wetland ecosystem and its significance in light of the disappearing estuaries and marshes along the Southern California coastline.

Indoor and outdoor exhibits put the spotlight on the web of animals and plants that keep the San Diego Bay and Sweetwater Marsh in a healthy state of balance. Come one on one with an American Kestrel or a Hooded Merganser at the raptor and shorebird aviaries. Or make fish faces at a spotfin croaker or a kelp bass at one of the many aquariums.

There are a number of outdoor gardens onsite and a 1.5-mile nature trail winds through the marsh next to the center.

Bayfront Park

After a morning or afternoon at the nature center, Bayfront Park (J St. and Marina Pkwy., Chula Vista, 6 A.M.–10:30 P.M. daily, parking free) on Chula Vista Harbor is a nice place to relax witht a picnic lunch or dinner. This peninsular park is situated across from Coronado Cays on the south end of San Diego Bay. The well-manicured greens here

look over the fleet of sailboats moored at the Chula Vista Marina. In the breeze the trees that dot the lawns swish in time with the rhythmic pinging of rigging against mast. If you didn't bring anything to munch on there is a concession stand at the park, along with picnic tables, a gazebo, playground equipment, and fire rings.

Imperial Beach

Imperial Beach is presided over by the 1,491-foot long **Imperial Beach Pier** (910 Seacoast Dr., Imperial Beach, 24 hours daily, parking free) at the Portwood Pier Plaza. The plaza is decked out with reminders of IB's pioneering watermen, sporting vintage surfboard benches and a giant board-inspired sculpture called *Surfhenge* that arcs over the entrance to the pier. In the summer, visitors flock to the sand like seagulls to fast-food wrappers. They also gather at Dunes Park, a grassy beachfront area with picnic tables, a jungle gym, and horseshoe pits and volleyball courts.

© ERICKA CHICKOWSKI

The sculpture *Surfhenge* welcomes visitors to the Imperial Beach Pier.

Border Field State Park

Situated on the southwesternmost stretch of sand in the United States, Border Field State Park (Tijuana River National Estuarine Research Reserve, 619/575-3613, 9:30 A.M.–5 P.M. daily, $5 per vehicle) offers respite from the crowds. The beach is located across the Tijuana Estuary from Imperial Beach—which is more popular and crowded—and requires a circuitous route from the town of Imperial Beach's main drags to reach it. (To reach the park by car, take I-5 south and exit at Dairy Mart Road, then head west on Monument Road.) Walk south down this shore and you'll eventually come across the rusty corrugated metal border fence that runs all the way out in the ocean to keep immigrants from sneaking across the border.

Border Field State Park is also home to the **Tijuana Slough National Wildlife Reserve,** a sensitive wetland that has in the past been plagued by toxic sewage and garbage dumped into the Tijuana River further upstream. This waterway mainly runs through Mexican soil until it takes a lazy turn north of the border to deposit itself into the ocean on the American side of the fence. Environmentalists on both sides of the border have been working hard to fix the pollution problem facing the Tijuana River and the U.S. Department of Fish and Wildlife has made incredible strides in rehabilitating the Tijuana Slough since the reserve was founded 25 years ago. Those who take a hike or ride horseback through the trails here will see evidence of that in the hundreds of species of birds that come here to hunt and nest.

The park's award-winning **Tijuana Estuary Visitors Center** (301 Caspian Way, Imperial Beach, 619/575-2704, 10 A.M.–5 P.M. Wed.–Sun.) features interactive activities that educate visitors about watersheds and estuaries.

Entertainment and Events

The velvet rope of San Diego extends mostly around the Gaslamp Quarter, but there are plenty of bars and cafés for all temperaments throughout the city. San Diego also has a thriving music scene (particularly punk). Notable bands to make their start in San Diego include Blink-182, Rocket from the Crypt, Pinback, Jason Mraz, and Jewel. Visitors can check out the next big thing at one of the city's many intimate venues.

NIGHTLIFE
Live Music

If you're the type of music fan who likes to brag about having seen a famous band back in the day, then the **Casbah** (2501 Kettner Blvd., 619/232-4355, www.casbahmusic.com, for tickets visit www.casbahtickets.com or call 888/512-7469) is your kind of place. This spot has been welcoming up-and-comers and cult favorites since Nirvana was cutting its teeth on the small-venue circuit. Grunge's flannel has been replaced by emo's skinny jeans, but Casbah remains as relevant now as it was nearly two decades ago.

Music purists hate it for the corporate influence, but **House of Blues** (1055 5th Ave., 619/299-2583, www.hob.com) really is one of the better venues in the city. The main hall has two stories in order to keep the drinkers happy and still include the under-21 crowd. There's also a side-stage room that features many of the city's emerging rockers. Both have the best sound quality in the city.

If your favorite band is coming to **4th and B** (345 B St., 619/299-2583, www.4thandbevents.com), then by all means attend the show. But don't bother taking a gamble on an unknown band for the sake of this so-so venue. Also owned by House of Blues, this facility is the inferior cousin to the main HOB venue. The one major upside is that it brings in a pretty eclectic lineup of acts, from comedy to "Xtreme" cage fighting and every genre of music in between.

Located in a humble space within a former warehouse near the Gaslamp, **Dizzy's** (344 7th Ave., 858/270-7467, www.dizzysjazz.com) is focused on one thing and one thing only: the music. There is no bar or restaurant or fancy lighting. Just a stage, intimate seating, and a soft spot for jazz and blues.

Croce's Jazz Bar (802 5th Ave., 619/232-2891, www.croces.com) is another spot in the Gaslamp for those hoping to sit in on a good jam session. Located within the popular restaurant run by Ingrid, the widow of folk legend Jim Croce, this venue has been welcoming nightly acts since the 1980s. Traditional, contemporary, and Latin jazz are all part of the scene here, with a little blues thrown in for good measure. Shows usually start at 8:30 P.M. and run through 1:30 A.M.

With such a healthy contingent of hardcore skaters and surfers, this town has always been a hotbed of creativity for the punk, ska, and hardcore metal community. You can catch punk shows in all of the mainstream venues around town, but one particular underground favorite for these kinds of performances is **Brick by Brick** (1130 Buenos Ave., 619/275-5483, www.brickbybrick.com).

One of the largest live music venues in the county, **Cox Arena** (5500 Campanile Dr., 619/594-6947, www.cox-arena.com) is the place to go for big-name artists and music festivals. The arena is on campus at San Diego State University, so parking and traffic can be a real nightmare—try taking the trolley, which has a large station right on campus. SDSU also plays host to smaller acts on the more intimate stage in its **Open Air Theatre** (5500 Campanile Dr., 619/594-6947).

Comedy Clubs

Making its home in a little Mission Hills theater, **National Comedy Theatre** (3717 India St., 619/295-4999, www.nationalcomedy.com, 7:30 and 9:45 P.M. Fri.–Sat., $15 adults, $12 students, seniors, and military) is the place in San Diego for theater sports and improv comedy sets. Consistent with improv tradition, the audience helps pick games and rules as

performers come up with hilarious scenarios on the spot. Performances are clean and there's no age limit, so families can bring the kiddos to join in the laughter.

Located in the northern outpost of Kearny Mesa, **Comedy Palace** (8878 Clairemont Mesa Blvd., 858/344-6981, www.thecomedypalace. com) has quickly become a haven for stand-up comedy in San Diego. The venue draws talent from LA for headlining weekend performances and also offers local up-and-comers the opportunity to try new material during the week.

If you'd prefer not to drive all the way to Kearny Mesa from downtown and are around on the appointed night, opt instead for **The Gaslamp Comedy Show** (770 5th Ave., www. malhall.com, $10), put on at **The Tipsy Crow** on the last Thursday of the month.

Dance Clubs and Lounges

Stingaree was the not-so-nice nickname city residents had for the district of bordellos located within the Gaslamp during the late 1800s. Today, the club **Stingaree** (454 6th Ave., 619/544-9500, www.stingsandiego.com, 9:30 P.M.–2 A.M. Fri. and Sat., 1–9 P.M. Sun.) has taken the same name to pay homage to the saucy ladies that first rouged their cheeks and flaunted themselves on nearby streets. Far classier than the red-light district the building sat in so long ago, this place still offers the ghost of debauchery to modern clientele. Skirts are short, rouge still abounds, and booze flows freely. Ask how much a girl costs for the night, though, and risk a drink to the face. The club offers three levels of entertainment and dancing, but some of its most notable amenities are the rooftop cabanas, which can be rented for the evening along with bottle service—if you are willing to part with upwards of $350.

Right across the street from Stingaree within the Hotel Solamar is **Jbar** (616 J St., 619/531-8744, noon–2 A.M. daily), a trendy rooftop watering hole that attracts a similar set of hipsters who might be a little more intent on lounging than dancing for the evening. The bar is set alongside a pool; lush, padded lounge chairs and patio tables are scattered about for those

FAMOUS SAN DIEGO BANDS

San Diegans love their music. Their loyalty – and eclectic tastes – has helped support a homegrown crop of performers who keep venues large and small thumping with a healthy mix of tunes.

The scene here is best known for its punk and ska influences – this is where Blink-182 got its start as a hard-edged punk band before toning it down for mainstream popularity, and where cult favorite Rocket from the Crypt kept true to those roots for fifteen years of sold-out shows until retirement in 2005. But San Diego is far from a one-trick pony. It is also where singer-songwriter Jewel made her big break – story goes that she was living in her van in the town's beach communities just to keep things going between coffeehouse shows.

When you are in town, check the *San Diego Reader* or *CityBeat* for upcoming shows from the following bands.

B-SIDE PLAYERS

Best described as Latin reggae, the music of B-Side Players throbs with the thumping rhythm of percussion, horns, and throaty vocals belting a mix of English and Spanish lyrics. The crew can be seen at a range of small and large venues while on their own turf and are a particular favorite at local music festivals.

BUCK-OH-NINE

Now that Rocket from the Crypt has called it quits, Buck-Oh-Nine has taken over as the granddaddy of San Diego's punk scene. This band verges more toward the ska end of the spectrum, though. Shows put up a frenetic field of energy – be prepared with some closed-toe shoes and the resignation that your ears will ring the next morning.

A. J. CROCE

Son of folk legend Jim Croce, this eclectic musician has made a name for himself with his diverse mix of jazz, blues, and funk. He's opened for a number of headliners such as Dave Matthews, James Brown, and Carlos Santana on the worldwide circuit, but his most comfortable and welcoming shows are still held where he first soaked up the limelight – on the small stage at Croce's, his mom's venue in the Gaslamp Quarter.

LOUIS XIV

Think "Ziggy Stardust"-era David Bowie and you've got this band's M.O. in a nutshell. Its worship at the altar of '70s-era British glam rock eccentricity extends down all the way to the tight pants and heavy eyeliner. The group regularly plays arena shows around the country, but will pay tribute to its local roots by playing a few smaller venues while in town.

ANYA MARINA

Known simply as Anya to the thousands of listeners who tune in every afternoon to hear her spin tunes on the popular alternative station KBTZ (FM 94.9), Marina is a solid musician in her own right. Her girlish voice

looking for a leisurely drink and an appetizer while the night is still young.

The parties aren't all on rooftops, either. The subterranean hot spot **Belo** (919 4th Ave., 619/231-9200, www.belosandiego.com, 7 p.m.–4 a.m. Fri., 7 p.m.–2 a.m. Sat.), a super-swank club with retro 1960s decorative accents, is a haven for fans of trance and house music. It regularly brings in big-name DJs such as Paul Oakenfold to spin for the night.

On Broadway (615 Broadway, 619/231-0011, www.obec.tv, 9 p.m.–2 a.m. Thurs.–Sat.)

offers clubgoers a little less pretension and a lot of space to kick up their heels. The multiroom disco features a wide array of music, so that fickle clubgoers can spend hours hopping from room to room in search of the right atmosphere. The club is located within a former bank. Be sure to check out the huge vault door that acts as the centerpiece of the club's lower level. Like many clubs in the Gaslamp, the major downside to this place is the cover charge—$20 or more on some nights—but you can often dodge the bullet by either arriving charms the socks off of her avid fans, who are partial to her smart lyrics and proficiency with a guitar pick.

JASON MRAZ

An East Coast native, Jason Mraz was adopted by San Diegans long before his honey-sweet voice, crackling acoustic guitar licks, and cheeky stage persona stormed into the mainstream music community. Mraz made his name playing coffee shops and tiny venues in town. Even touched by fame, he still thanks the region that helped vault him to stardom by frequently playing local festivals and smaller shows when he's back relaxing at his pad in North County.

PINBACK

This two-man indie rock band is still building nationwide appeal, but in its hometown Pinback is frequently greeted by sold-out crowds full of loyal followers. Its music is known for complex bass lines and captivating hooks. The group fleshes out its sound during live shows by adding a few extra bandmates.

SPRUNG MONKEY

This band flirted with serious national attention with a couple of memorable radio-friendly singles in the late '90s. Music-label bungles and promotional limbo held the group back from major exposure, but it still kept doing its own thing here in San Diego. Since then its influences have made a sharp turn toward more hard-core influences, with an equal measure of punk and metal working its way into its small-venue showings.

REEVE OLIVER

This trio is a San Diego darling on an ascending star that keeps rising by the minute. Self-described as indie rock, the band is now signed to a major label (Capitol). Its success is based in part on the tunes (a bit of Weezer meets Jimmy Eat World) and the band members' incredible work ethic. It seems like they play damned near every weekend at some venue or another around the county. If you get a chance, go. Their music plays well in front of a crowd.

ROOKIE CARD

A blend of funky new-wave country, alternative rock, and a little something you can't put your finger on, Rookie Card has been flummoxing band labelers since they busted onto the local scene in 2003. Whatever it is, it's good stuff and very much worth the cheap entrance to the typical small venues the band plays around town.

SWITCHFOOT

This alternative band has managed to make it big without alienating fans, with an accessible pop rhythm balanced with just enough of an edge to keep the music snobs from branding it a "sell-out." These days Switchfoot's shows are mostly at the arenas.

---

early or dropping some greenbacks at the very tasty sushi restaurant, Zen, on the premises.

Named for its architecture, **Deco's** (731 5th Ave., 619/696-3326, 9 p.m.–1:30 a.m. Thurs., 6 p.m.–1:30 a.m. Fri.–Sat.) was built to resemble the South Beach clubs in Miami. Though this place aspires to achieve the same upscale vibe as some of its Gaslamp neighbors, the crowd is more hip-hop than hipster. This is evidenced by the combination of current and old-school rap that plays in heavy rotation on all of the dance floors. This unpretentious club

can be a relief when your neighbors are putting on airs somewhere else.

Bring your dancing shoes, because at **Café Sevilla** (555 4th Ave., 619/233-5979, www.ca-fesevilla.com, 5 p.m.–midnight Sun.–Thurs., 5 p.m.–1 a.m. Fri.–Sat.) you're probably gonna need 'em. This club is the best place in town to shake those hips to the beat of salsa and merengue, featuring live Latin bands at least three nights a week. If spectating is more your style, then consider coming out to the café's restaurant on Friday and Sunday nights, when it features a dinner show that includes a three-course Spanish meal and an authentic flamenco dance performance.

Lace up your heavy black platform boots, slap on some dark eye makeup and get ready to rock with the goth crowd at **Club Sabbat** (www.clubsabbat.net), open the second and fourth Saturdays of the month at **The Flame** (3780 Park Blvd.) in Hillcrest. Drinks are stiff and the mix of industrial and house music will satisfy anyone with a taste for the hardcore scene.

Candelas Lounge (416 3rd Ave., 619/702-4455, www.candelas-sd.com, 5 P.M.–1:30 A.M. daily) offers classy ambience with its flickering lighting and thumping house techno. The place has DJs spinning many nights, but it avoids the typical sweaty, meat-market vibe that many Gaslamp clubs are guilty of cultivating. It is possible to find a cozy nook and just relax with a drink and friendly conversation with friends, or good-looking people you hope will soon be friends.

Impress a date with your "connections" by snagging a reservation at **Noble Experiment** (777 G St., 619/888-4713, www.nobleexperimentsd.com, 7 P.M.–2 A.M. Wed.–Sun.) an open secret among lounge lovers in the know. The only way to get a seat here is to send a text message to the bar's phone number to set a reservation well in advance of the visit. Obscured by a false facade of beer kegs, the door opens into a quirky speakeasy adorned with a whole wall of skulls and a chandeliered ceiling decorated with paintings in gilded frames. The setting is intimate, perfect for a nightcap after a long evening in Gaslamp's louder clubs.

Over in Old Town, **Churchill Cigar Lounge** (2415 San Diego Ave., Ste. 102, 619/546-7758, www.churchillcigarlounge. com, 11 A.M.–10 P.M. Mon.–Thurs., 11 A.M.–midnight Fri.–Sat.) caters to tobacco fans with a smoke-friendly environment and a floor-to-ceiling humidor filled with fine cigars and a bar serving an exemplary selection of craft beers and wine. The staff is very knowledgeable about them all and are the ready to suggest

a good cigar and beverage pairing, which you are likely to enjoy most while lounging on the outdoor patio.

Bars

A San Diego institution, **The Waterfront Bar and Grill** (2044 Kettner Blvd., 619/232-9656, 6 A.M.–2 A.M. daily) has offered no-frills sustenance and spirits since the 1930s, when the Italian Americans in the surrounding community would gather there to share stories from the sea. It's now San Diego's longest continually operating bar. High-rises block the path to the waterfront these days, but you can still sit at the open windows along the sidewalk and smell the hint of salt water that blows with the breeze.

Like a well-appointed eagle's aerie atop one of San Diego's most distinctive waterfront towers, **Top of the Hyatt** (1 Market Pl., 619/232-1234, 3 P.M.–1:30 A.M. daily) offers unparalleled views of San Diego Bay, Coronado Island, Point Loma, the ocean, and, it seems, even Asia if you've had enough to drink. This swanky spot is an ideal destination if you're out to impress your companions. Many a high-value business deal and wedding proposal have been made as the sun sets in time with the rhythm of the bar's tinkling piano.

It's a name, it's an advertisement, it's **Air Conditioned Lounge** (4673 30th St., 619/501-9831, www.airconditionedbar. com, 4 P.M.–2 A.M. Mon.–Fri., 7 P.M.–2 A.M. Sat.–Sun.). Housed in a former warehouse in University Heights, this bar looks like a seedy, underground spot from the exterior but is actually pretty lush inside.

An everyman's local bar, **Bluefoot** (3404 30th St., 619/756-7891, 3 P.M.–2 A.M. daily) is a great place to mingle into the local scene—it really does offer a little something for every man (and woman too!). Stack your quarters along the pool table rails in the main room to challenge the bar's loyal regulars, hop on a stool and order one of the 20 different beers on draft, or get your groove on in the back room alongside the live DJ booth. Be sure to look up—Bluefoot hosts a monthly rotation of artists who work in a loft studio visible above the bar.

A sports bar and bowling alley rolled into one, **East Village Tavern + Bowl** (930 Market St., 619/677-2695, www.bowlevt.com, 11 A.M.–2 A.M. Mon.–Fri., 10 A.M.–2 A.M. Sat.–Sun.) is a perfect evening destination for those who hate to be cooped up on a bar stool all night long, but would rather not venture into the dance club scene. This isn't your old man's bowling alley. The place is moodily lit, with hip graphics adorning the walls over the lanes, and, thankfully, an absence of the bowling alley funk that lingers in the air at many older pin palaces.

If you're a sucker for bars that double as geographical novelties, **IB Forum Sports Bar & Grill** (1079 Seacoast Dr., 619/429-7507, 11 A.M.–11:30 P.M. Sun.–Thurs., 11 A.M.–12:30 P.M. Fri., 8 A.M.–12:30 P.M. Sat.) in Imperial Beach likes to trumpet its position as the most southwesterly bar and grill in the United States. It also happens to be a relaxing post-beach place to grab a longneck and enjoy a ballgame on one of the numerous TV screens scattered about the bar.

Wine and Martini Bars

Many of the city's best wine bars are located in the chic Hillcrest neighborhood, including the perennial favorite, **Wine Lover** (3968 5th Ave., 619/294-9200, www.thewinelover.us, 4:30–10 P.M. Sun.–Mon., 4:30 P.M.–midnight Tues.–Sat.). Approaching the place, you might wonder if you bumped your head and woke up in Paris. The vibrant garden patio is ringed with ornate wrought-iron railings and furniture to match. Brightly colored canopies over the entryway practically beg you to enter. Inside, the ambience is extended with romantic overhead lighting and a beautifully underlit marble bar. The wine flights are the stars here, but they just barely beat out the selection of cheeses, meats, and olives.

Those who prefer their beverages in more angular glasses needn't go far, either. **Martinis Above Fourth** (3940 4th Ave., 619/400-4500, www.martinisabovefourth.com, 5–11 P.M.

Tues.–Thurs., 4 P.M.–midnight Fri.–Sat., closed Mon.) is a hip cabaret that can serve a classic martini with the best of 'em, but will oblige if you insist on a froofy specialty drink. The tinkling piano completes the swanky scene, making this a very enjoyable spot to unwind.

Dive Bars

As far as holes-in-the-wall go, **Star Bar** (423 E St., 619/234-5575, 6 A.M.–2 A.M. daily) has divey ambience by the pintful. Just a stone's throw away from some of the hottest clubs in the glitzy Gaslamp district, Star Bar offers a different kind of sparkle. Namely, what's reflected from the tacky Christmas decorations and lights that adorn the bar all year long.

Let's see, a bar that is right next to the airport? Check. So close to the freeway that it's practically beneath it? Check. Has a decades-old neon sign that practically buzzes with stories of drinks long since drained? Check. **AeroClub** (3365 India St., 619/297-7211, 2 P.M.–2 A.M. daily) has all of the makings of a classic hole-in-the-wall, and a quick look inside confirms its authenticity as a "contagiously fun" dive, rather than an "afraid I might catch something" hole. Along the bar, tattooed elbows rub against Oxford-shirted ones, and old-timers mingle with just-turned-21 youngsters. The bar is the draw here, with a full selection of liquors and more than 20 beers on tap.

Thick-rimmed glasses and skinny jeans are de rigueur at **Tower Bar** (4757 University Ave., 619/284-0158, www.thetowerbar.com, 2 P.M.–2 A.M. Wed.–Sun., 7 P.M.–2 A.M. Mon.–Tues.), a favorite among the hipsters who flock to its somewhat sketchy neighborhood to strut their stuff and pound Pabst Smears—a variation of a Black and Tan with Guinness and Pabst Blue Ribbon. The bar serves booze as well, including absinthe served with sugar and all. Be sure to bring your tweezers—the drinks here are strong enough to put hair on your chest.

Pubs and Taverns

A friendly neighborhood joint just a few blocks from the southeast corner of Balboa

Park, **Hamilton Tavern** (1521 30th St., 619/238-5460, www.hamiltonstavern.com, 3 P.M.–2 A.M. Mon.–Fri., 1 P.M.–2 A.M. Sat.–Sun.) does beer every which way without any bit of snobbery. Pick through a wide selection of brews on tap, in bottles, or cans, everything from highbrow stouts to pedestrian Bud Light, and enjoy it 'neath a ceiling sprouting dozens of tap handles dangling as decorations. Like any respectable local hangout, Ham's has pool tables and shuffleboard for your amusement, plus a standard bar menu to soak up the suds.

A working-class Irish pub with the Black and Tans to prove it, **The Ould Sod** (3373 Adams Ave., 619/284-6594, www.theouldsod.com, 2 P.M.–2 A.M. Mon.–Fri., 10 A.M.–2 A.M. Sat.–Sun.) embraces its identity, decking itself out with vintage Guinness adverts, old Irish newspapers, Irish movie posters and the like, plus live Irish music on Tuesdays. The place is also well known for its Thursday and Saturday karaoke nights, attracting microphone hogs from well outside its Normal Heights neighborhood.

Located in its trademark yellow-washed building in Little Italy for over 25 years, the **Princess Pub and Grille** (1665 India St., 619/702-3021, www.princesspubandgrille.com, 11 A.M.–midnight Mon–Thurs., 11 A.M.–1 A.M. Fri., 10 A.M.–1 A.M. Sat., 10 A.M.–midnight Sun.) is a favorite destination for soccer fans, who flock to this British Pub to watch their favorite European footy teams duke it out on Princess's big screens. Be aware, though, that there's usually a steep cover on days that a big soccer game is on. The traditional British food is decent, though other places like Shakespeare's do it better. What you're paying for is the atmosphere. The brick building is done up with loads of Brit paraphernalia and a crackling fireplace toward the rear.

Late-Night Cafés

When the urge to hang out with friends into the wee hours of the morning is strong and the itch for boozing it up is inversely proportional to that urge, nothing hits the spot like a café open late.

The social environment is warm and inviting at **Café Bassam** (3088 5th Ave., 619/808-3714, 8 A.M.–midnight Sun.–Thurs., 8 A.M.–1 A.M. Fri.–Sat.), thanks to the touch of its owner, Bassam. He can often be seen in his trademark fedora sitting and chatting with customers into the wee hours. This cozy Bankers Hill establishment has an especially good selection of teas and serves a mean Mexican hot chocolate, all the better enjoyed among the vintage knickknacks Bassam has collected over the years.

If the sweet tooth strikes in the middle of the night, pass up that crusty piece of Denny's pie and hurry over to **Lestat's** (3343 Adams Ave., 619/282-0437, 24 hours daily) in Normal Heights. This 24-hour café has some tasty desserts along with plenty of strong coffee to match. Right next door it runs Lestat's West, a small venue that caters to local bands, comedy acts, and open-mic sessions.

Quite possibly the most irreverently named coffeehouse on the planet, **Hot Monkey Love** (5960 El Cajon Blvd., 619/582-5908, 9 A.M.–midnight daily) packs enough cheeky spontaneity into its atmosphere to live up to curious expectations. The café is a hotbed of creativity, hosting some form of live performance, dance session, or artistic endeavor nearly every night of the week. The bohemian vibe cultivated here fits in with its college-area setting. Like the apartment of your college friends who followed their passions instead of a steady paycheck, the interior here is all about function over form. But that's ok, because this place really does what it loves to do.

PERFORMING ARTS
Theater

Initially founded in 1935 in order to stage abridged Shakespearean productions for the California Pacific International Exposition, **Old Globe Theatre** (1363 Old Globe Way, 619/238-0043, www.oldglobe.org) is one of the best-regarded regional theater companies in the country. Though productions have branched out considerably since the 1930s, Old Globe is still well known for its interpretations of The Bard's work. The annual Summer Shakespeare Festival is a highlight in the season's schedule.

Today's Old Globe is actually a complex of three theaters: Old Globe Theatre, Cassius Carter Centre Stage, and Lowell Davies Festival Theatre. As a result, patrons can choose between a number of productions during the season.

Downtown, the **San Diego REP** (79 Horton Plaza, 619/544-1000, www.sdrep.org) stages contemporary productions at Lyceum Theatre within Horton Plaza.

Let **Broadway San Diego** (3666 4th Ave., 619/564-3000, www.broadwaysd.com) give you the ol' song and dance with its renditions of the most popular Broadway musicals. The company puts on shows at two venues downtown, the **San Diego Civic Center** (1100 3rd Ave.) and **Spreckels Theater** (121 Broadway Ave.). Named after the sugar magnate, Spreckels is also one of the top downtown venues for big-name comedy acts and a range of music sets.

Music and Dance

San Diego Symphony (750 B St., 619/235-0804, www.sandiegosymphony.com) plays a range of classical music at Copley Music Hall, a 1929 French rococo building that is one of the West Coast's premier classical music venues. The symphony plays over 100 performances per year, including some very accessible sets through its well-received Summer Pops series. This annual concert series is typically held at Embarcadero Marina Park, rather than Copley Music Hall.

The **San Diego Chamber Orchestra** (858/350-0290, ext. 7, www.sdco.org) primarily performs in venues scattered about North County, but on Friday nights the group often performs at St. Paul's Cathedral downtown. The church has incredible acoustics and the setting is perfect to enjoy the classics.

Acclaimed as one of the top 10 opera companies in the United States by *Opera America,* **San Diego Opera** (1200 3rd Ave., 18th Floor, Civic Center Plaza, 619/533-7000, www. sdopera.com) usually undertakes about five

productions per season. Its solid reputation and the long-term stability of its management staff helps it attract some of the most respected guest performers and conductors in the world. The opera is well known for its rich, opulent sets—the in-house studio is so well respected that it is often contracted by other major opera companies across the country to create their sets.

Watch the dancers of the **San Diego Ballet** (2650 Truxtun Rd., 619/294-7378, www. sandiegoballet.org) pirouette and plié their way across the stage during one of the troupe's performances. The intimate venue at the ballet's training and studio complex gives patrons a very close and personal connection to the movements of the dancers.

CINEMAS

Like most major metropolitan areas, San Diego is home to dozens of movie theaters of all sizes. In Mission Valley, close to the lodging of Hotel Circle, **Mission Valley AMC** (1640 Camino Del Rio N., 858/558-2262) offers the typical googolplex experience. This place has 20 screens packed with the latest blockbusters. Similarly, **Pacific Gaslamp All-Stadium** (701 5th Ave., 619/232-0400) screens Hollywood megaproductions at its downtown location. The tiered stadium seating ensures that you won't have to crane your neck around the eight-foot giant with a cowboy hat that may claim the seat in front of you.

If indie movies are more your thing, **Hillcrest Cinemas** (3965 5th Ave., 619/819-0236) plays one of the best selections of independent and foreign films in the city.

San Diego County is also home to a pair of drive-in theaters that have managed to elude the wrecking ball. One of them is just east of the city, the **Santee Drive-In Theatre** (10990 Woodside Ave. N., Santee, 619/448-7447). If you've never been to a drive-in, this one will likely fulfill all of your expectations. It has two huge screens and a snack shop in the middle. Sound is provided on the FM band of your radio, so the sound is as good as your stereo system. The cost of admission covers a whole night of entertainment, as it includes two movies for the price of one.

FESTIVALS AND EVENTS

San Diegans are a social bunch, so it is no surprise that they look for any excuse to gather for a little organized fun now and again.

Every February and September **San Diego Restaurant Week** makes a splash with penny-pinching gourmands. All week diners can visit some of the best restaurants in town for a three-course meal at an unbelievable price.

Also in February is **Little Italy Carnevale,** a joyful celebration of food and fun that culminates in an authentic Venetian masked costume ball.

In early May, **Fiesta Cinco de Mayo** in Old Town is the biggest party in town to celebrate the Mexican holiday. It is also the most family friendly, with food and craft booths set around Washington Square.

Streets are cordoned off in June for the **Rock and Roll Marathon,** which winds its way through downtown and Balboa Park. This unique running event features bands along the way and a concert for all (even non-athletes) to enjoy once the course has been shut down.

The **Fourth of July** is a very big deal in this patriotic town. During the day there is usually something going on at the USS *Midway* Museum, and Old Town State Historic Park celebrates by dressing volunteers in period dress and celebrating the holiday 19th-century style. One of the best parades in town is over in Coronado, which swaths itself in bunting and hosts events that last from 10 A.M. through the grand finale of its big fireworks show over the water. The biggest San Diego Bay fireworks show comes from the San Diego side; the **Big Bay Firework Show** on Spanish Island is one of the best in the county.

The last weekend in July brings hordes of comic book, sci-fi, and fantasy fans to the San Diego Convention Center for **Comic-Con.** This colorful convention packs the days with a full slate of speakers, but the real action is on the showroom floor, where hundreds of vendors convene to sell comic books, movies, toys, and more.

September is when the events season really heats up. Early in the month the **San Diego Film Festival** pits filmmakers against one another in a competition for viewer and critic popularity.

San Diego Street Scene is another September favorite. This musical event hosts dozens of nationally recognized bands on numerous open stages in the Gaslamp for a raucous party. The music tends to be pretty heavy, with a focus on punk, metal, and rap.

Adams Avenue Street Fair is a lighter music alternative that happens right around the same time as Street Scene. This Normal Heights event is Southern California's largest free music festival and it features over 80 acts that play blues, roots rock, Latin jazz, reggae, alt-country, and zydeco for a family-friendly crowd.

Fleet Week caps off the fall with a series of events that honor those San Diegans who serve in the U.S. Navy, Marine Corps, and Coast Guard. The event's name is a bit of a misnomer—it actually lasts over a month with numerous parades, concerts, charity events, and air shows filling the schedule.

Things stay a bit quiet until the holiday season, when the city really pulls out all of the stops with some of the year's best events. In Balboa Park, buildings and walkways are bedecked in lights and a full-size nativity is set up around the Spreckels Organ Pavilion. The park welcomes visitors in early December for the annual **December Nights** celebration, which features an international food fair, music, and entertainment all beneath the glittering lights.

Those who can't get enough pretty lights should head across the water to Coronado Island, whose well-decorated Orange Avenue leads you to the best display of them all, at the Hotel del Coronado. **Christmas at Hotel del Coronado** has always been a production. The lighting ceremony in early December officially begins the holiday season for many locals; imagine 60,000 lights illuminating the Victorian

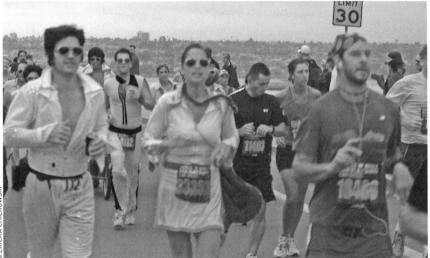

© ERICKA CHICKOWSKI

The Rock and Roll Marathon draws endurance athletes and Elvis impersonators from around the world.

beauty's best architectural features, all aglow at the flip of a switch. The hotel also erects an enormous Christmas tree on its lawn.

Another holiday treat is the **San Diego Harbor Parade of Lights.** Hundreds of boat owners decorate their watercraft for the big event, putt-putting along the bay for the benefit of the happy audience along the shore.

The **Big Bay Balloon Parade** usually starts the holiday season wrap-up. This downtown parade of large balloons usually falls a couple of days after Christmas.

Shopping

San Diego's shopping scene is enough to challenge even those with a black belt in shopping. In Mission Valley the malls extend for miles, making it a prime spot for shoppers that need to find something specific.

Downtown there are plenty of great boutiques and art galleries meant for meandering. That's also where you'll find the towering Horton Plaza, a giant center with hundreds of establishments to choose from.

If you run away at the mere mention of a mall, then continue your sprint to Hillcrest. This neighborhood is a sanctuary for shoppers who prefer to spend their cash at local and independent shops.

Along the waterfront is the place to go to get a little trinket for that special someone back home. Same goes for Old Town, which offers bath salts and candies by the bushel.

And those with a love of the rustic and the rusted should venture north of Balboa Park to Normal Heights, which has a quiet little antique row that can make the time fly.

MALLS

In some respects **Mission Valley** is just one long shopping mall with roads and a freeway running through it. Just about every big-box chain retailer has set up shop in the valley. With the big stores comes traffic, though, and a trip to shop anywhere in Mission Valley can quickly turn aggravating to those with little tolerance for sitting in backups, circling parking lots, and dodging space cadets walking out the stores' doors.

On the northwest end of the valley along Friar's road, **Fashion Valley** (7007 Friars Rd., 619/297-3381, 10 A.M.–9 P.M. Mon.–Sat., 11 A.M.–7 P.M. Sun.) is one of the highest-end malls in all of Mission Valley. This open-air mall is anchored by Nordstrom, Saks Fifth Avenue, and Bloomingdale's, among others. It also has a number of upscale chain eateries such as The Cheesecake Factory.

Running alongside I-8, **Westfield Mission Valley** (1640 Camino del Rio N., 619/296-6375) is the most visible jumble of stores from the freeway. The mall has a movie theater and is anchored by Target, Macy's, Bed Bath & Beyond, and Sports Chalet. Across Mission Center Road is its West Annex, which features a large Borders, Old Navy, DSW, and an assortment of sit-down chain restaurants such as Gordon Biersch.

Hazard Center (7510–7610 Hazard Center Dr., 619/543-8111) may be hazardous to your driving health—tucked away in the north end of the valley, this plaza is one of the valley's most difficult to navigate. Once you are there, though, it is pretty nice, boasting two coffee shops, a movie theater, and five restaurants, including the well-regarded Prego Ristorante. It is also home to a handful of stores, including a small Barnes & Noble, Relax the Back, and Stuart Benjamin and Co. Jewelry Designs.

Horton Plaza (324 Horton Plaza, 619/238-1596, 10 A.M.–9 P.M. Mon.–Fri., 10 A.M.–8 P.M. Sat., 11 A.M.–7 P.M. Sun.) is plopped down right in the thick of the activity of the Gaslamp Quarter. Like the bustling neighborhood, this mall's design is a jumble of frenetic energy. The labyrinthine mazes created by the stairs and ramps and elevators leading up and down the fractured multistory levels are the stuff of legends. Rumor has it that whole families have been lost for days, subsisting only on Cinnabon and Hot Dog on a Stick. The stores are pretty standard mall chains (Nordstrom, Macy's, Gap), but what the selection lacks in creativity it makes up in quantity. There are nearly 200 shops in total. Also on premises is the Lyceum Theater, home to San Diego REP, and a couple dozen food-court restaurants.

Many San Diego locals drive down to San Ysidro just north of the border to score brand-name clothes for cheap at the outlets there. The largest concentration is at **The Shops at Las Americas** (4211 Camino de la Plaza, 619/934-8400, 10 A.M.–9 P.M. Mon.–Fri., 10 A.M.–8 P.M. Sat., 10 A.M.–5 P.M. Sun.). This stylish plaza features over 100 stores, including bargain shops from Adidas, Guess, Calvin Klein, and American Eagle Outfitters.

Right across the street is the smaller **San Diego Factory Outlet Center** (4498 Camino de la Plaza, 619/690-2999, 10 A.M.–8 P.M. Mon.–Fri., 10 A.M.–7 P.M. Sat., 10 A.M.–6 P.M. Sun.) which also has a handful of shops. Here you can find outlets from OshKosh B'Gosh, Sunglass Hut, and Carter's Childrenswear.

ART GALLERIES

Downtown some of the best art galleries are concentrated in Little Italy's **Kettner Art and**

Fashion Valley offers shoppers an open-air mall experience.

Design District (www.taddsd.com), centered around Kettner Boulevard. The multifaceted collections of galleries here feature many mediums and styles. Some of the highlights in the district include **Perry L. Meyer Fine Art** (2400 Kettner Blvd., Ste. 251, 619/358-9512, www.plmeyerfineart.com, 11 A.M.–5 P.M. Tues.–Thurs., 11 A.M.–6 P.M. Fri.–Sat., or by appointment) with 18th-century to contemporary paintings and drawings; **Scott White Contemporary Art** (939 W. Kalmia St., 619/501-5689, www.scottwhiteart.com, 9 A.M.–5 P.M. Tues.–Fri., 11 A.M.–5 P.M. Sat.) featuring contemporary and modern paintings, sculpture, and photography; and contemporary art and furniture at **David Zapf Gallery** (2400 Kettner Blvd., #104, 619/232-5004, noon–5 P.M. Thurs.–Sat.).

The Gaslamp also has a few gallery finds, including the collection of work from emerging artists at **Michael J. Wolf Fine Arts** (363 5th Ave., 619/702-5388, www.mjfinearts. com, noon–8 P.M. daily) and the assemblage of sculpture and jewelry at **Shorelines Gallery** (411 Market St., 619/231-6151, www.slsdgallery.com, 10 A.M.–8 P.M. Sun.–Thurs., 10 A.M.–10 P.M. Fri. and Sat.). Another unique and captivating collection is inside the Gaslamp's **Ashby Galleries** (527 4th Ave., 619/235-6990, noon–2 P.M. and 6–10 P.M. Wed.–Sun.), which features the captivating and ethereal work of Tim Cantor.

BOUTIQUES

For more unique shops just strike out in any direction from Horton Plaza. The Gaslamp side streets are a great place to pick up new designer threads. Ladies can check out the wardrobe options at places like **Le Bijou** (557 4th Ave., 619/232-1454) or **Jacques LeLong** (635 5th Ave., 619/234-2583, 10 A.M.–11 P.M. Sun.–Thurs., 10 A.M.–midnight Fri.–Sat.), maybe stopping by **Poz** (228 5th Ave., 619/234-5625, 1–6 P.M. daily) afterward to pick out a new pair of shoes and a purse to match all those clothes. And guys can unleash their inner metrosexual at the slick Italian shop **Boutique Voss** (946 5th Ave., 619/233-4830) or the ultra-designer "jeanery" **G Star** (946 5th Ave., 619/233-4830, www.g-star.com).

Little Italy is the best neighborhood for trendy knickknacks and furnishings to deck out home sweet home. It has a number of cutting-edge boutiques and studios that are a part of the Kettner Art and Design District. There you can find shabby-chic furnishings at **Dear Prudence** (1644 India St., 619/234-9595, 11 A.M.–5 P.M. Tues.–Sat.), vintage handblown glass at **Vetro** (1760 Kettner Blvd., 619/546-5120, www.vetrocollections.com, 10 A.M.–6 P.M. Tues.–Sat.), and sleek modern furniture and art at **ADORN** (2400 Kettner Blvd., Ste. 105, 619/794-2729, www.adornsd.com, 10 A.M.–6 P.M. daily).

Hillcrest takes the cake in the individuality department. That goes for shopping, too. This offbeat neighborhood is a refuge for the independent-minded shopper. Many of the boutiques and shops here are mom-and-pops (sometimes pop-and-pop, too) that are stocked to the gills with unique items.

Take **Wear It Again Sam** (3823 5th Ave., 619/299-0185, 11 A.M.–7 P.M. Mon.–Sat., 11 A.M.–6 P.M. Sun.), for instance. This used apparel store sells only vintage clothes from the 1940s, '50s, and '60s. We're talking cashmere sweaters, pinstripe suits, fedoras—the works. Shop here and you'll never worry about seeing your outfit on somebody else.

Another one-of-a-kind favorite is **Co-Habitat** (1433 University Ave., 619/688-1390, 11 A.M.–8 P.M. daily), which sells rich and colorful Indian and Southeast Asian furnishings.

Tag for Dogs and Cats (142 University Ave., Ste. D, 619/497-0180, 10 A.M.–8 P.M. daily) is a must visit for anyone who's ever considered buying their pets a massage. This ritzy pet store has plenty of items waiting to help you cross the line from "pet lover" to "one of *those* people." Don't worry, I'm as guilty as the rest of 'em.

SOUVENIR SHOPS

Seaport Village (849 W. Harbor Dr., 619/235-4014, www.seaportvillage.com, 10 A.M.–9 P.M. daily) tends to grow on you. Sure, this shopping center along the waterfront sometimes feels a little manufactured and the souvenirs here are on the pricey side. The thing is, it knows what it is and it does it well. Those expensive souvenirs are the best in town and the atmosphere is fun, especially on the weekends when musicians play in the public spaces. In addition to the T-shirt shops, camera stores, and trinket boutiques, there are also a few stores that break the souvenir-shop mold. For example, the **Kite Store** sells a colorful selection of windsocks and kites for the experienced flyer and the beginner. **The Toy Cottage** offers an array of quality toys that are often one of a kind. And **Whitt/Krauss** has an amazing collection of sculptures, paintings, and fine art on display.

Many of the historic buildings in Old Town double as shops. There you can find an apothecary and bath-salts shop, a coffee house, a gem store, a tobacconist, a pottery shop, and a milliner. The park is also home to **Plaza del Pasado** (2754 Calhoun St., 619/296-3161), a Mexican-inspired *mercado* that has a book store, more pottery, and other souvenirs.

The space there was for decades the home of **Bazaar del Mundo** (4133 Taylor St., 619/296-3161, 10 A.M.–6 P.M. daily), a collection of authentic Latin American shops that was eventually booted out of the park when the state decided it wanted to go in a different direction with the space. It was well-loved by locals, who know to continue their knickknack shopping at the new location just a few blocks away on Taylor Street.

Don't forget to save a little cash for the other shops outside of the park. Some highlights east of the park include **Made in San Diego Chocolates** (3941 Mason St., #1, 619/299-9830) for sweets, **Ye Olde Soap Shoppe** (2497 San Diego Ave., 619/390-3525) for handmade soaps, and **Jarabe Tapatio** (2607 Congress St., 619/574-0039) for fine women's apparel. Another favorite is **Captain Fitch's Mercantile** (2627 San Diego Ave., 619/298-3944, 10 A.M.–9 P.M. daily), which sells books, cards, and sundries.

ANTIQUES

Antique Row in Normal Heights is a nice, neighborly lineup of mom-and-pops set in

© ERICKA CHICKOWSKI

Antique Row Café is best known for its ample breakfasts, but it can also be a tasty lunchtime rest stop for shoppers on Adams Avenue in Normal Heights.

historic homes and quaint little commercial buildings along Adams Avenue. Start from the corner of Adams Avenue and 30th Street and head west on Adams to explore your way through these stores.

You'll encounter a varied collection of furniture, paintings, old photos, license plates, kitchenware, and more at **Zac's Attic** (2922 Adams Ave., 619/284-0400, 10 A.M.–4:30 P.M. Thurs.–Mon.), one of the largest of the shops on this row. It is set in a lovely Craftsman-style building that is accented with river-rock support pillars.

Nostalgic music collectors love **Folk Arts Rare Records** (2881 Adams Ave., 619/282-7833, www.folkartsrarerecords.com, 9 A.M.–5 P.M. Mon.–Fri., 10 A.M.–6 P.M. Sat.–Sun.). This musty shop absolutely crams its little rooms from floor to ceiling with old records.

Resurrected Furniture (2814 Adams Ave., 619/283-3318, 10 A.M.–6 P.M. Mon.–Sat., 10 A.M.–5 P.M. Sun.) is a lot less crowded with inventory and there are also books, knickknacks, and works of art here. This is a good store for those who like Asian antiques.

Jewelry shoppers should drop in on **Abigail's Antiques and Curios** (2831 Adams Ave., 619/563-5490, 10 A.M.–5 P.M. Mon.–Sat.), which carries antique costume pieces as well as assorted gold and silver jewelry.

BOOKSTORES

San Diego is home to lots of quirky booksellers who welcome browsers as heartily as buyers. In Seaport Village, **Upstart Crow Book Store and Coffee House** (835 W. Harbor Dr., 619/232-4855, www.upstartcrowtrading.com, 9 A.M.–10 P.M. Sun.–Thurs., 9 A.M.–11 P.M. Fri.–Sat.) brews up a good blend of one-of-a-kind tomes, kitchy souvenirs, and caffeine. Climb up the creaky steps to find a spot overlooking the coffee bar while you comb through their selection.

On the Orange Avenue strip in Coronado, **Bay Books** (1029 Orange Ave., 619/435-0070, www.baybookscoronado.com, 9 A.M.–8 P.M. Mon.–Sat., 9 A.M.–6 P.M. Sun.) is a good spot to come pick out a summer read before hitting the Silver Strand. This little family-owned shop offers a nice variety of genres, with a special emphasis on children's books and military history and fiction (it is just blocks away from a naval air station, after all).

Comic-Con occurs but once a year, but that doesn't mean we can't dork out over the latest issues the rest of the time. **San Diego Comics** (6937 El Cajon Blvd., 619/698-1177, www.san-diego-comics.com) is one of the most established comic book stores in town. Just remember fellas, reading comics on the beach is a real mood killer for those bikini-clad ladies.

Sports and Recreation

Shoehorned between sparkling water and mountainous backcountry, San Diego is a well-placed headquarters for those who like to get out and sweat a little. Unsurprisingly, there are many occasions to strap on some boat shoes and pick up the old rod and reel. The bay and numerous lakes in town make that a no-brainer. The city also lives up to its reputation when it comes to golf, hosting some of the best public courses on the West Coast.

Many of the best rugged recreation options are outside of city limits in the outer edges of the county's consciousness. But it really doesn't take a long drive to satisfy an appetite for sport. There are oodles of wild and seemingly rural pockets right in town that are ready to surprise the unacquainted with opportunities for rock climbing, mountain biking, and hiking.

SURFING AND BOOGIE BOARDING

You'll need to drive to the city beaches or up to North County to find the really good surfing breaks, but occasionally Coronado Island will

FIDO SURFS AT LOEWS

Everyone in San Diego surfs during the dog days of summer, even, well, the dogs. **Loews Coronado Bay Resort** (619/424-4000) has a surf instruction program designed just for canine companions. Participants in the Su'ruff Camp receive instruction in the long-lost art of dog surfing for $75 per hour. Your fluffy pal will learn how to stay calm atop a longboard in the gentle waves that wash up to Coronado Island.

If Fido is good enough, maybe think about entering him in the annual Surf Dog Competition held by the resort on Imperial Beach in May or June.

see some swells that are decent for a little longboard action. The best bets are usually within **Silver Strand State Beach.**

Boogie boarders can usually get lucky in the mild waves that lap along **Coronado Beach,** close to Hotel del Coronado and downtown Coronado.

CYCLING
Downtown and Mission Valley

With a very extensive selection of bikes and a central location in the Gaslamp Quarter, **Bike Tours San Diego** (509 5th Ave., 619/238-2444, www.bike-tours.com, 8 A.M.–7 P.M. daily, $35 per day for road or mountain bikes) is a great place for the true cycling enthusiast to rent two wheels for one day or even a week. This is one of the only places in the city that rents proper road bikes to out-of-towners. It also has a stock of high-quality mountain bikes that are capable of taking to the county's more extreme back-country trails. The business also runs bike tours all over San Diego for multiple skill levels.

If you are cruising on your own, you can take off directly from the Gaslamp and head along the Embarcadero Waterfront. Serious cyclists can continue along Harbor Drive when it turns into Pacific Highway. There is a signed bicycling route along the highway that skirts around the northeastern curve of the airport all the way to the San Diego River, but there are no bike lanes drawn and it can be really hairy in certain places. Exercise extreme caution on this route.

© ERICKA CHICKOWSKI

the Silver Strand Bike Path along San Diego Bay

From there it is possible to take the southern path along the river until it hits Friars' Road and take the right on Friars' to head into Mission Valley. Friars' Road has a bike lane that stretches on for many miles, continuing on through its transition to Mission Gorge. It is possible to take this route through Mission Valley and head all the way past city limits into the bedroom community of Santee. There is, however, one very dangerous spot a couple miles into the route at the Friars' Road interchange with Route 163. The bike lane is interrupted by the on-ramps and impatient and speedy drivers do little to heed the "Share the Road" signage that was futilely erected here. To bypass this mess, hang a right on Fashion Valley Road and a left on the San Diego River Trail that runs beneath the trolley line. This continues for about two miles until Qualcomm Way. There you can take a left and it will spit you back onto Friars' Road, where you can take a right and continue your eastward journey.

Silver Strand State Beach

In Coronado, **Holland's Bicycles** (977 Orange Ave., Coronado, 619/435-3153, 10 A.M.–6 P.M. Mon.–Sat., 10 A.M.–7 P.M. Sun.) has been in the business of pedals and spokes since 1924. This long-standing company offers rentals out of two locations on Coronado Island. The first is its mail location on Orange Avenue and the second is **Bikes and Beyond** at the Coronado Ferry Landing (1201 1st St., Coronado, 619/435-7180, 10 A.M.–6 P.M. Mon.–Sat., 11 A.M.–5 P.M. Sun., $10 per hour, $30 for four hours, $50 per day).

Once you've been outfitted at either location, pedal south along the **Silver Strand Bike Path** and see how far you can make it. The path is paved and rolling to flat for 8.5 miles all the way down to Imperial Beach, but the wind can create quite a bit of resistance. Just be sure to watch out for cars turning in at the intersections, as drivers can be inattentive to traffic on the trail and the laws of physics dictate that they'll win every time no matter who has the right of way.

Balboa Park

The **Morley Field Velodrome** (2221 Morley Field Dr., www.sdvelodrome.com) is a hit with track cyclists and those who enjoy this fast-paced sport. The velodrome is open for free to all cyclists on road or track bikes on Saturdays from 9 A.M. to noon. On Tuesday nights the facility holds a multi-tiered racing event. The cost to race is $10 and it is free to watch.

BOATING

On a busy day you'll have to navigate around other pleasure craft and naval ships, but beyond this inconvenience San Diego Bay makes for an ideal body of water to glide along by sail or motor. From downtown, rentals can be found at **Seaforth** (333 West Harbor Dr., Gate 1, 619/239-2628, 9 A.M.–30 minutes prior to sunset daily), which is based out of the Marriott Marina. There you can pick up a range of craft, from small rowboats to large sailboats. Seaforth also runs a shop out of Coronado Island (1715 Strand Way, Coronado, 619/437-1514, 9 A.M.–30 min prior to sunset Mon.–Fri., 8 A.M.–30 minutes prior to sunset Sat.–Sun.) that has a similar selection and slightly extended hours on the weekend.

Most of the local saltwater fishing is best found outside of the bay's waters in the open ocean. The majority of the experienced tour guides are based out of America Cup Harbor in Point Loma. This is also where the tackle shops closest to downtown are located.

However, if you are looking to go it alone from a rental boat or from your own craft and are seeking a local shop without any touristy vibe, you can venture up to the strip malls of Clairemont Mesa to shop some of the stores there. A favorites among anglers, **JP's Bait and Tackle** (4488 Convoy St., #C, 858/277-7417) can also help equip and advise those who wish to shore-fish from the waterfront, which can be done from the **Embarcadero Marina Park Pier.** This structure juts from the southern side of the park and provides anglers with the opportunity to hook bass, croaker, and halibut.

FISHING

Most traditional fly fishers wouldn't think of San Diego County as a great spot to wave that wand around, but it actually has a host of opportunities for the open-minded. In the high mountains near Palomar there are a couple of crystal-clear lakes for traditional trout fly-fishing. Beyond that, the weather is usually too hot for those cold water–loving species. But the angler who can think of fly-fishing beyond the strict definition of fishing for trout can have a blast on any number of the county's watery sites.

Lower elevation lakes provide a place to cast out to a range of warm-water species such as bass, crappie, and bluegill. And along the coast and the flats of the bays and lagoons there are opportunities to catch a number of saltwater species who would be lured by the dance of the right fly.

In town, you can stock up on flys, leaders, and local knowledge at **Stroud Tackle** (1457 Morena Blvd., 619/276-4822, www.stroud-tackle.com, 10 A.M.–6 P.M. Mon.–Sat.), which happens to be headquarters for the San Diego Fly Fishers Club.

The **San Diego Fly Fishers** (www.sandiegoflyfishers.com) club also offers free fly casting lessons at Lake Murray every Sunday from 9 A.M. to noon.

Located within Mission Trails Regional Park, **Murray Reservoir** (5540 Kiowa Dr., La Mesa, 619/668-2050, sunrise–sunset daily) is an ideal place to unwind with a fishing pole in hand. It is stocked from November through May with a range of species that include largemouth bass, bluegill, catfish, black crappie, and trout. There's plenty of shoreline to cast into this 171-acre reservoir, but if you prefer to bob along in a boat, rentals are available on Wednesdays, Saturdays, and Sundays. Don't forget to buy a fishing permit. You can pick them up from the electronic pay station next to the concession building.

WALKING AND RUNNING

The abundance of public open spaces and walkways makes San Diego an ideal town

El Prado in Balboa Park is one of the finest spots in the city for a stroll.

© ERICKA CHICKOWSKI

for walkers and runners. For a flat and scenic stroll, the **Embarcadero** along the bay offers exercise and people-watching all at once. Be mindful that the sidewalk can be pretty packed on summer afternoons, so running through the crowd may be frustrating to some. But in mornings, evenings, or in the winter, you can pound the pavement without fear of collision. A good alternative on those busy days is to park and run along the water at Harbor Island Park. Just north of the Embarcadero, this park offers a three-mile walkway that extends along the length of the park. Those with the motivation can actually combine the two together into a longer course, as there is a wide and safe sidewalk that runs all the way from the Embarcadero into Harbor Island.

If you are looking for a little motivation, tie your laces and head over to the **Silver Strand** on Coronado for a little jog. This beach borders the Navy SEAL training facility and if you hit the sand early enough you just might have the pleasure of being lapped by a SEAL out for his morning run.

If the beach is too much for your burning calves, Coronado also has a paved pedestrian path that runs the length of the strand all the way down to Imperial Beach.

Balboa Park is definitely one of the best places in the city to take a stroll, with its level walkways, lush gardens, and beautiful architecture. The park also offers a number of undeveloped canyon trails that are great for exploring leisurely and can also offer a softer surface to pick up the pace a little.

HIKING
San Pasqual-Clevenger Canyon Open Space Park

Just east of Escondido at the northern edge of the city lies San Pasqual and Clevenger Canyon Open Space Park (trailhead on San Pasqual Valley Rd., 5.3 miles past San Diego Zoo Safari Park, 858/538-8082) whose trails wind up and down the area mountains and offer fine views of San Pasqual Valley, a rural area that is currently home to avocado, citrus, and palm farmers. The trails are dotted with oak and sycamore and in the late spring hikers will likely encounter a display of wildflowers including the white chamise and the fragrant purple ceanothus. Hikers are able to enjoy the beauty in peace, as bikes and horses are restricted from this trail.

Mission Trails Regional Park

The trip up Cowles Mountain is the definitive hike within Mission Trails Regional Park Park (Mission Gorge Road and State Route 52, 24 hours daily), but the paths up this peak are just a small part of the trail system here. In fact, the majority of the trails in the park are across Mission Gorge from Cowles on the park's other peak, **Fortuna Mountain.** All of these hikes are moderate to challenging hauls with plenty of elevation change, and the views to match. They run through the chaparral and coastal sage scrub habitats that are so prevalent in this part of the county.

For more information about hiking trails here try the parks' **visitors center** (One Father Junipero Serra Trail, 619/668-3281, 9 A.M.–5 P.M. daily).

MOUNTAIN BIKING

One of the most popular mashing grounds for fat-tire enthusiasts within city limits is **Mission Trails Regional Park,** which offers a trail system of over 40 miles that is open to mountain bikers. The trails range from challenging single-track to more mild fire roads. Climbs and quick descents are abundant. So are hikers, so please ensure the future of mountain biking in the park by being courteous to pedestrians. Similarly, take heed of bike restrictions posted at certain trails. With so many miles of great terrain to roll through, there is no need to sneak onto forbidden trails.

The elevation gain at Mission Trails may be too much for those faint of heart (and lungs). A flatter alternative is the wildly popular trail in **Los Peñasquitos Canyon Preserve.** This nearly six-mile round-trip can be attacked from either of the trailheads, one at each end of the trail. The trail runs through oak canopies, swaying grasslands, and a resplendent springtime mix of California poppies, wild radish mustard, and bush mallow flowers. The real highlight of the trail is the scenic set of waterfalls that cascade down a canyon hillside about halfway along the trail. The water flow is best viewed in winter and early spring.

If this trail is not long enough for you, consider starting at the western trailhead and extending the ride by crossing Mercy Road and continuing down Knott Grove Trail, a 1.5-mile path that edges near and crisscrosses over Penasquitos Canyon creek several times and is shaded by willow, sycamore, and toyon.

Only a couple miles away from Penasquitos is another short lung burner on **Black Mountain.** The way up runs over an old jeep road now called Nighthawk Trail (trailhead at 9711 Oviedo Way), a part of the Black Mountain Open Space Park that the city planners wisely carved out of housing development zones that have all but swallowed what was just recently a rural part of the county. The trail is 1.8 miles to the top, which affords a 360-degree view of the ocean and regional mountain ranges.

ROCK CLIMBING

In town, climbers can limber up at one of several climbing gyms scattered around the city. The most centrally located among them is Old Town's **Solid Rock** (2074 Hancock St., 619/299-1124, www.solidrockgym.com, 11 A.M.–10 P.M. Mon.–Fri., 9 A.M.–9 P.M. Sat., 11 A.M.–7 P.M. Sun., $12 weekday, $15 weekend adults, $13 weekend youth). The biggest is **Vertical Hold** (9580 Distribution Ave., 858/586-7572, www.verticalhold.com, 11:30 A.M.–10 P.M. Mon. & Fri., 11:30 A.M.–11 P.M. Tues.–Thurs., 10 A.M.–9 P.M. Sat., 10 A.M.–8 P.M. Sun., $15 day pass) in Mira Mesa. Both offer rental equipment and hold classes for climbing newbies.

Fans of bouldering will fall in love with the **Santee Boulders,** located just over the city line near the town of the same name. The field here holds popular routes such as Moby Dick, Dog Pile, and the Bullet Hole.

For traditional and top-rope climbing, head over to the granite cliffs of **Mission Gorge** in Mission Trails Regional Park. Here you'll encounter lines like Rock, Rock On, Knob Job, and Lunch Rock.

In addition to running its gym, Vertical Hold also organizes outings to these and other sites across the county. Visit www.verticalhold.com for details.

GOLF

San Diego is heaven for scratch golfers and duffers alike. Most of the world-class links are located north of the city, but there are still a number of very good, centrally located courses to get your swing on without breaking the bank.

Running through some of the best real estate in Mission Valley, **Riverwalk Golf Club** (1150 Fashion Valley Rd., 619/296-4653, www.riverwalkgc.com, $89 Mon.–Thurs., $99 Fri.–Sun. and holidays) ripples along the banks of the San Diego River. The riparian setting makes for some challenging golf, with water playing as a factor on 13 of the 27 holes. If you can, make it a point to play the Mission course. The third hole there is the course's showpiece with a lake

and a waterfall surrounding the green. Just do yourself a favor and play that one conservatively or you'll watch your ball supply dwindle.

The links at **Balboa Golf Course** (2600 Golf Course Dr., 619/235-1184, reservations 619/570-1234, 6 A.M.–sunset daily, $40 Mon.–Fri., $50 Sat.–Sun.) are actually two golf courses in one. There is the 9-hole executive course ($18) that plays pretty straightforward and there's the 18-hole championship course that winds through mesas and canyons and can confound the best golfers. This muni is a great course but be prepared: It gets crowded and plays very slowly, especially on the weekends.

It is hard to believe that **Mission Trails Golf Course** (7380 Golfcrest Pl., 619/460-5400, www.americangolf.com, $22 Mon.–Fri., $38 Sat.–Sun., $13 cart) is still within city limits. Set along the banks of Lake Murray and at the foot of Cowles Mountain, the course has natural vistas aplenty. Owned by the city, this course is privately operated so the grounds are less scrubby than many munis. Watch out for the brush on hole 17. The fairway is short but the scrubs and trees that run across it seem to magnetically attract those dimply fliers.

With glorious views of Glorietta Bay and downtown, **Coronado Golf Course** (2000 Visalia Row, Coronado, 619/435-3121, www.golfcoronado.com, $30 weekdays, $35 weekends, $15 cart) is another great municipal course. The problem is that everybody knows it, so tee times are tricky to book.

Wedged between Old Town State Historic Park and Presidio Hill, **Presidio Golf Course** (4136 Wallace St., 619/295-9476, $10) is a laid-back and fun pitch-and-putt course that is ideal for families with kids just learning to golf. The small facility is well maintained for its size and on weekdays it is usually quiet enough for serious golfers to fine-tune their short games before heading out for a round at the more challenging courses in town.

Finally, those with military connections may want to use them to gain access for a round at **Admiral Baker Golf Course** (Friars Rd. and Admiral Baker Rd., 619/556-5521). The 36 holes here are regarded by many as the best military links in the country. If you're a civvy, you'll need to be in the company of a navy friend or relative to play.

SKATING

Washington Skatepark (www.washington-streetskateboardpark.org, 9 A.M.–dark daily, free) was built in the true antiestablishment spirit of skating. Back in 1999 when the city had no skate parks at all and city police were encouraged to clamp down hard on those skating in public areas, a few enterprising souls decided to take matters into their own hands and pour concrete ramps away from the scrutiny of authority figures. The spot was below the I-5 Washington Street Bridge.

While the parks founders got quite a few heavy sessions on the setup, the clandestine park was eventually ferreted out by the city and was shut down despite the howls of unhappy skaters.

They remained persistent, though, and decided to go through official channels to have the park legitimized. The city agreed to let these citizens take over the park if they could wade through a maze of red tape. It took several years, but in 2002 they accomplished their mission and now what stands is one of the most popular free skate parks in SoCal, designed and built by skaters for skaters. The park is directly under I-5 over Washington Street. From I-5 south, exit on Washington Street and go two blocks south until you see the park.

Bill and Maxine Wilson Skate Park (702 South 30th St., 619/527-3596, 2 P.M.–8 P.M. Mon.–Fri., 11 A.M.–7 P.M. Sat.–Sun.) has a good mixture of street, vert, and pool skating, featuring railings, stairs, and a 90-foot-long snake run. It also has a ten-foot key hole and a beginner's bowl for the youngsters. While entrance is free, parents of smaller kids should be aware that recent cuts by the city have eliminated supervision at the park.

LAWN BOWLING

Members of the **San Diego Lawn Bowling Club** (1549 El Prado, 619/238-5457, www.sandiegolawnbowling.com, $2) regularly don

their dress whites and take to the grass of Balboa Park for a bit of friendly competition. The club maintains grounds at the park and offers free lessons to any interested bowling novice on Tuesday, Friday, and Sunday at 11 A.M.

It also welcomes guests from bowling clubs around the world to join its members in regularly held fixtures. Even those with no interest in playing might enjoy stopping by to watch a match. Visit the website for times and dates and don't forget to bring your whites.

SPECTATOR SPORTS

Some cities are football towns and some ain't. San Diego is unequivocally a skip church on Sunday, dye your dog team colors, and scream out loud at the TV kind of football town. **San Diego Charger games** are played in Mission Valley at **Qualcomm Stadium** (9449 Friars Rd., 619/641-3100, www.chargers.com, tickets $61–106), a 70,000-seat venue that absolutely roars with excitement when the Chargers (also known as the Bolts, as in lightning bolts) score a touchdown. Tickets can be purchased at any Ticketmaster location or online at www.stubhub.com.

The **San Diego Padres** also have their fair share of loyal baseball fans, but the team has a bit more of a fair-weather friendship with its fan base. When the Pads are tearing it up, the hordes throng to cheer them on at **Petco Park** (100 Park Blvd., 619/795-5000, tickets $15–170), but a slump will empty the seats. Whether the Friars are winning or losing, Petco Park is a beautiful ball field and is worth the cost of admission for any baseball junkie who can't get enough of the smell of green grass, leather gloves, and sizzling stadium dogs. Completed in 2004, the park is a stunning visual centerpiece of the Gaslamp Quarter and has done a lot to continue the revitalization of this entertainment district.

OUTDOOR OUTFITTERS

With so many opportunities for outdoor adventure within the city and the region at large, San Diego has plenty of places to pick up gear for rent or purchase that can have you happily

© ERICKA CHICKOWSKI

The iconic Petco Park is home to the San Diego Padres.

wandering the trails, waterways, and cliffsides in no time.

Adventure 16 (4620 Alvarado Canyon Rd., 619/283-2362, www.adventure16.com) is local SoCal chain that specializes in hiking, camping, climbing, and outdoor survival gear.

REI (5556 Copley Dr., 858/279-4400) is one of the largest outdoor outfitters in the county. This is your best bet for rental gear.

Road Runner Sports (5553 Copley Dr., 858/974-4475, www.roadrunnersports.com) is the largest running-shoe store in the country and is a runner's paradise for clothes and accessories. The knowledgeable staff can also clue you in on the best routes in town.

Road cyclists and mountain bikers will be pleased at the selection of bikes and accessories at **Trek Superstore** (4240 Kearny Mesa Rd., #108, 858/974-8735, www.treksandiego.com), a major outlet for America's most prolific bicycle maker.

C & C Outdoor Store (3231 Sports Arena Blvd., 619/222-2326, www.ccoutdoorstore.com) is a smaller hiking and camping shop with a particularly good selection of clothes and shoes suited for exploration in the wild.

Aqua Tech Dive Center (1800 Logan Ave., 619/237-1800, www.divecenter.com) is a well-respected dive shop with a good selection of wet and dry dive equipment for rent, as well as a number of dive classes.

Accommodations

As would be expected from a city that sprawls out nearly 73 square miles, there are dozens of lodging options in every neighborhood. Some visitors might find prices to be a bit of a shock, as even cheap chain hotels and motels charge at least $125 during high season. Downtown and Mission Valley are the best bets for bargain hunters. Those willing to pay a premium can find plenty of quaint inns on Coronado Island and near Balboa Park. The high-rise and penthouse set can look to downtown and the waterfront for their digs. The northern part of the city, in addition to being home to one of the very few tent campsites within city limits, also plays host to several exclusive resorts.

DOWNTOWN
Under $150

Like a hostel for grown-ups, **(500 West** (500 W. Broadway, 619/234-5252, www.500westhotel.com, $109 s, $139 d) rents out small rooms with twin and double beds that are well decorated, comfortable, and clean. You pay slightly more than a hostel, but shoot, you don't have to bring your own sheets, you'll never get locked out at night, and you sure as heck don't have to do any chores! Seriously, though, this place offers a chic room and a more mature atmosphere for those who don't need a large footprint to be comfy. A dorm room for four is $84.

$150-250

Traveling with pets can really limit your lodging options, especially in a busy city center. Often, the only hotels within downtown metropolitan areas that accept furry companions are expensive boutiques or absolute dumps. **Harborview Inn and Suites** (550 W. Grape St., 619/233-7799, www.sdharborview.com,, $159 d) is a happy exception. It offers clean and decent rooms that you don't have to sneak Rover into.

Clad in bright modern furniture and pop art, **The Bristol Hotel** (1055 1st Ave., 619/232-6141, www.thebristolsandiego.com, $149 d) is what you'd get if Andy Warhol did hotels. There's function in the form, too. The hotel is right in the Gaslamp, offers free Internet, and has great big desks for all you sticks-in-the-mud who insist on working while on vacation.

$250-350

Located right next to the House of Blues in a modern restoration of the historic Jessop & Son's Jewelry building, **Se San Diego** (1047 5th Ave., 619/515-3000, www.sesandiego.com, $259) is a hotel destination in which to see and be seen. With a rooftop pool bar thumping bass into the wee hours, Se is the perfect base of operations for a party-hopper's weekend of downtown clubbing—not so perfect for the family or business traveler hoping to get a lot of shut-eye. The hotel's chic design with Asian influence starts at the front door, a 900-pound bronze pivot door that opens into a lobby accented with black ebony columns, Nepali carpets, and shagreen upholstery. Guest rooms are wide open and airy with 10-foot ceilings and sleek furnishing dressed in chocolate and silver with hints of jade and blue. Sleepers are pampered with a pillow menu offering choice of fabric and plumpness, while pet lovers can request a room on a special floor just for them.

Over $350

Lavish, splendid, sumptuous, luxurious, resplendent...there are only so many words in the thesaurus associated with "opulence," and they're all appropriate to describe the **(US Grant Hotel** (326 Broadway, 619/232-3121 or 866/837-4270, www.usgrant.net, $569 d), a 100-year-old historic hotel in the middle of the Gaslamp. It makes its first impression count with a grand marble lobby and enormous glass chandeliers, and it never stops impressing. Rooms are decorated with French art specially commissioned for the hotel and marble bathrooms and 300-thread-count linens. Public spaces are decorated with silk carpets, gilded accents, and original paintings and bronze sculptures. Plus, the service is absolutely on par with the environs and the room rate, which is more than some pay for a whole month's rent.

The **Westin Emerald Plaza** (400 W. Broadway, 619/239-4500, $389 d) is hard to miss in the city skyline. The hexagonal roof-tops on this cluster of sleek black towers are rimmed with green lights at night. This is an ideal place for city sophisticates to rest their heads. The rooftop pool area presents a fantastic skyline and bay view to enjoy from the facility's whirlpool tub.

GASLAMP QUARTER AND EAST VILLAGE
Under $150

Those who prefer a true hostel experience can still find it downtown at the **HI-SD Downtown Hostel** (521 Market St., 619/525-1531, www.sandiegohostels.org, dorm bed $19–24, $47–54 d, family room $64–82), which is located in ground zero of Gaslamp Quarter partying. This typical hostel offers 4-, 6-, and 10-person dormitories, as well as a couple of private rooms.

$150-250

The lobby at the **Horton Grand** (311 Island Ave., 619/544-1886, www.hortongrand.com, $179 s, $199 d) is decorated in Victorian furnishings accented by a 100-year-old oak staircase. Rooms also feature period furniture and each comes with a fireplace to complete the effect. The flickerings you see may not just come from the hearth, though. Legend has it that this hotel is haunted by several ghosts. One of the notables is Roger Whitaker, said to occupy room 309.

Just a stone's throw away from all of the Gaslamp action, **Andaz San Diego** (600 F St., 619/849-1234, www.sandiego.andaz. hyatt.com, $209 d) is trendy enough to keep the bottle service crowd pleased, but has the pedigree necessary to satisfy business travelers in town to visit the Convention Center a few blocks away. Behind all that marketing glitz, this hotel is actually a Hyatt-run establishment.

So, get those last-minute printouts for tomorrow's presentation finished up in the business center, loosen up that tie, and hit the elevator button for the top-floor pool bar.

Spunky, airy, and fresh, the **Hotel Indigo** (509 9th Ave., 619/727-4000, www.hotel-sandiegodowntown.com, $179 d) is so pet-friendly that the darned place has its very own resident hotel dog, Sandy the lovable mutt. Decked out in subtle floral linens that pay homage to the California poppy, the rooms here are as cheerfully SoCal as the designers could possibly make them. That nature theme goes all the way to the hotel's very core—when it opened in 2009 it was San Diego's first LEED-certified hotel, so it's eco-friendly from top to bottom. One of the best amenities has to do with the view: Indigo's rooftop bar hangs over Petco Park so closely that it's possible to watch a Padres game without ever buying a ticket.

A cozy, personable inn that eschews the typical hotel clap-trap, **Mudville Flats** (747 Tenth Ave., 619/232-4045, www.mudvilleflats.com, $189 d) offers well-appointed rooms paneled with rich woods and thick oriental rugs within a beautifully restored Craftsman home. Units come with full kitchens, rooms are spotless, and the atmosphere is everything that the chains are not: quirky, homey, comfortable, and quiet. The place is just outside the Gaslamp. Close enough to walk after a raucous evening, but far enough to leave the noise behind when you retire for the night.

$250-350

When it comes to **⟨ Hotel Solamar** (453 6th Ave., 619/531-8740, www.hotelsolamar.com, king $220 d, suite $320 d), I've got two words for you: leopard-print robes. This boutique hotel cozies up well with its hip and trendy Gaslamp Quarter neighborhood. Bedspreads are bedecked in spunky polka dots and the hotel offers in-room yoga accessories along with a special TV channel to lead you through a session. Plus, the lobby is fresh and modern without being prickly. It is comfortable enough to hang around to read the paper while enjoying the communal coffee service offered gratis each morning.

LITTLE ITALY
Under $150
La Pensione (606 W. Date St., 619/236-8000, www.lapensionehotel.com, $99 d) is one of the better hotel bargains in the city. The European-style hotel offers accommodations in Little Italy for a fraction of what most neighboring hotels charge. The hotel is close to the trolley, which is great for fans of public transport but could be a potential disaster for light sleepers who can't snore through late-night train noise.

$150-250
Little Italy Inn (505 W. Grape St., 619/230-1600, www.littleitalyhotel.com, $179–224 d, 2-br suite $269 d) likes to tout itself as European-style, but one advantage it has over those types of places is the option for a room with the comfort of its own porcelain palace. Some even have bathrooms with jetted tubs. Otherwise, this place is as much a throwback to the old country as the neighborhood it's in, and features subtle architectural flourishes throughout the interior and an elegant decor.

WATERFRONT
Under $150
On-the-go bargain hunters might find **Marina Inn and Hotel Suites** (1943 Pacific Hwy., 619/232-7551, www.marinainnsd.com, $85 s, $105 d) a good buy if they don't plan on spending much time there. Located on a busy thoroughfare, this motel offers humble digs that are centrally located next to the airport, downtown, and the waterfront. Those going on a cruise or using San Diego as a point of departure might consider one of the stay-and-park packages this place offers. Stay a couple of nights and park for seven days while you do your thing elsewhere.

Honestly, though, **Island Inn** (202 Island Ave., 619/232-4138, www.islandinn.net, $90 d) is a better bargain. The location is still pretty central—right across the street from the Convention Center and the water—and rooms

are a little less threadbare. Plus, if you plan on staying three weeks or longer you can negotiate a rock-bottom weekly rate of $183 per week. Just remember that you get what you pay for.

$150-250
The views of San Diego are top-notch at **Holiday Inn on the Bay** (4610 De Soto St., 619/232-3861, $231 d) and the location is within easy walking distance of all of the waterfront sights. Rooms are clean and services are what you'd expect from a chain hotel. Come with an appetite—rooms come with coupons for a free breakfast downstairs.

$250-350
Even if you don't stay at the **Manchester Grand Hyatt** (1 Market Pl., 619/232-1234, www.manchestergrand.hyatt.com, $229 d, suites start at $450), the lobby alone is worth a look during a walk along the San Diego waterfront. The entrance is imposing, with windows that creep up four stories, all the way to the top of the towering ceilings. The sun streams through to bathe the marble floors and pillars with sunlight and further illuminate the floor-to-ceiling Spanish Colonial Revival murals.

Rooms and beds are comfortable and even though the two-towered hotel was designed with the business traveler in mind, it is a nice place for families due to its waterfront location, the large and welcoming pool and tennis courts, the full-service spa, and the on-site babysitting offered to guests.

Over $350
Sidled up right next to the Big Bay, the 30-story **Hilton San Diego Bayfront** (1 Park Blvd., 619/564-3333, $359 d) affords plenty of views of the sailboats, navy ships, and pleasure craft puttering around San Diego Bay. Awash in blues and crisp whites, the interior is clean and stylish. The hotel particularly caters to the business crowd due to its state-of-the-art conference center facilities that often act as overflow for the nearby Convention Center and are big enough to accommodate smaller trade shows. The hotel is prepped and ready to help

out family-minded business-people hoping to mix a little pleasure with business. It allows dogs up to 75 pounds, offers babysitting services, and has a swimming pool and elaborate workout facilities that include a jogging and walking track.

CORONADO ISLAND
Under $150

Crown City Inn (520 Orange Ave., Coronado, 800/422-1173, www.crowncityinn.com, $139 d, $199 suite) is a warm and inviting establishment that welcomes travelers with pets and children. Every room comes outfitted with a microwave and refrigerator and each afternoon the innkeepers set out a spread of cookies, shortbread, and iced tea in the lobby.

$150-250

Just one street removed from the commotion of Coronado's Orange Avenue, **Cherokee Lodge** (964 D Ave., Coronado, 619/437-1967, www. cherokeelodge.com, $125 s, $175 d) offers one of the island's most affordable lodging options. The simple rooms are designed to appeal to visitors on government and navy business, so this bed-and-breakfast avoids the explosion of Laura Ashley patterns that too often plague the decor of bed-and-breakfasts. Instead, visitors can get in touch with their masculinity as they are greeted with solid-colored bedding, wood-paneled walls, paintings of seafaring adventures, and mahogany-hued furniture.

Located close to the Coronado Ferry Landing, **Coronado Inn** (266 Orange Ave., Coronado, 619/435-4121, www.coronadoinn. com, $169 d, with kitchen $209 d) and nearby sister property **Coronado Island Inn** (301 Orange Ave., Coronado, 619/435-0935, www.coronadoinn.com, $149 d) are moderately priced and designed to suit the typical traveler. Rooms are average and both establishments offer free parking and complimentary continental breakfasts. On the whole, the property at Coronado Inn is slightly nicer, with the added bonus of a pool and gas barbecues.

Right across the street from the Hotel del Coronado, **El Cordova Hotel** (1351 Orange Ave., Coronado, 619/435-4131, www.elcordovahotel.com, $215 d) is a pleasantly modest hotel built to resemble a small Spanish village. Around the perimeter of the hotel are a number of boutiques and restaurants, while the room entrances surround the center pool and courtyard–barbecue area to create a cozy community atmosphere. The exterior is decorated with fluted roof tiles, the interior with hand-fired Mexican tile from Tecate. Rooms are small, even the suites, but that is just part of the appeal at this charming little inn.

Villa Capri by the Sea (1417 Orange Ave., Coronado, 619/435-4137, www.villacapribythesea.com, $219 d, with kitchen $349 d) is an endearing midcentury-modern hotel that has aged reasonably well since it opened in the late 1950s. The well-cared-for rooms surround the itty-bitty pool in the courtyard. Its major attraction can also be its biggest downside, as it is right on a busy stretch of Orange Avenue. Coronado shuts down early, though, so nighttime traffic noise isn't too bad.

$250-350

Fans of historic inns should book a room in **The Mansion at Glorietta Bay Inn** (1630 Glorietta Blvd., Coronado, 619/435-3101, www.gloriettabayinn.com, $249 d, mansion room $295 d) in Coronado. The beautifully restored Edwardian home was built by sugar baron John D. Spreckels in 1908 and is slavishly faithful about keeping architectural and decorative details as authentic as possible. Only 11 of the inn's 100 rooms are in the mansion itself, so be sure to book early to get a special room.

Hidden away from downtown Coronado, **Loews Coronado Bay Resort** (4000 Coronado Bay Rd., Coronado, 619/424-4000, $309 d) has long played second fiddle to the reputation of the legendary Del. But this "other" resort on Coronado deserves more respect than it gets. The property features three heated swimming pools and three bayside tennis courts, a full-service spa, pet-friendly policies, an 80-slip marina, and a secluded atmosphere. Guests can access Silver Strand State Beach via an underpass beneath Route 75 and they'll have amazing views of the downtown skyline and the Coronado Bay Bridge.

Over $350

The red gable roofs of the **❰** **Hotel del Coronado** (1500 Orange Ave., Coronado, 619/435-6611, www.hoteldel.com, $380 d) are as vibrant as the day she opened in 1888. Even after more than a century of use, this landmark hotel remains one of the most prominent luxury spots in California. Guests here can stroll the adjacent beach, whack a few rounds of balls on the tennis courts, have themselves rubbed down at the full-service spa, or simply sit with a drink at one of the oceanfront pools. The resort has modernized a bit, with contemporary ocean-themed rooms in its cabana and ocean-tower expansion buildings. But in the main building itself, rooms match the Victorian architecture, with traditional furnishings and elegant linens. The resort is designed to be extremely family-friendly, in fact running a number of summertime kids camps. It also hosts special programs and a game room for teens.

RV Camping

Camping options are sparse near the city, but RV owners can find shelter on Coronado Island at **Silver Strand State Beach** (5000 Rte. 75, Coronado, 619/435-5184, $50 per night per site). The park allows RV campers to stay overnight for "en route" camping. There are no hookups and campers are required to sleep in their RVs at night, as the park bans tent camping of any kind. The park is pretty strict about this policy and it will turn away any vehicles that aren't completely self-contained. Also be mindful of the fact that the gates close early—at 7 P.M. in winter, 8 P.M. in spring and fall, and 9 P.M. in summer—so don't be late or you won't get in for the evening.

Beyond the strict rules, the campground makes an excellent base from which to explore the dunes of Silver Strand.

BALBOA PARK AND BANKERS HILL
Under $150

Hotel Occidental (410 Elm St., 619/232-1336, www.hoteloccidental-sandiego.com, twin beds $94 d, double bed $104 d, queen suite $139 d) tries to follow a similar model to 500 West. The rooms are not quite as nice as 500 West, however, and the location is slightly less central to downtown and waterfront attractions. It is close to Balboa Park, however, and the neighborhood is safe.

$150-250

Literally right across the street from Balboa Park's northern edge, **Balboa Park Inn** (3402 Park Blvd., 619/298-0823, www.balboaparkinn.com, $99 d, suite $149–249 d) is a quiet alternative to the typical downtown lodging options. Set in a complex of four Spanish Colonials, the inn has a quiet patio that can be mighty inviting after a crowded day at the zoo. Be sure to take a walk around the surrounding neighborhood, which was home to San Diego's affluent families in the early 20th century.

$250-350

As the name suggests, all of the rooms at **Park Manor Suites** (3167 5th Ave., 619/296-0057, www.parkmanorsuites.com, $199 s, $219 d) feature full kitchens and dining areas. Located on the west edge of Balboa Park, this stately 80-year-old brick structure has a hint of neoclassical in its exterior accents and its interior is decorated with a European flair. Marble floors, ornate chandeliers, bronze sculptures, and damask arm chairs welcome guests in the lobby. Located in Hillcrest, this hotel is a particular favorite among gay and lesbian travelers. On Friday evenings between 5 and 10 P.M. the rooftop bar here hosts a gay cocktail party.

Over $350

The opulent rooms at **❰** **Britt Scripps Inn** (406 Maple St., 619/230-1991 or 888/881-1991, www.brittscripps.com, $371–511 d) are an example of Victorian extravagance, with ornate floral bedspreads, rich tapestry, and elegant furniture. Built in 1888 by a man named James Britt for the Scripps family, this gorgeous Queen Anne served as a townhouse for San Diego's favorite benefactors when they ventured from La Jolla to do business in the city. Breakfast is served daily on the wraparound porch and an afternoon wine and cheese service is laid out in the parlor.

HILLCREST AND NORTH PARK
Under $150

Set in the neighborly district of North Park, **Carole's Bed and Breakfast** (3227 Grim Ave., 619/280-5258, www.carolesbnb.com, $119–149 d and up) has most of the elements that make a good bed-and-breakfast great. It is set in a historic 1904 Craftsman, it is run by a little old lady who is as cute as a button, and the prices are extremely reasonable. The only downside is that breakfast is only an extended continental. But considering the rates, this is really just a minor setback. You can take those hundreds of dollars you'd have spent at a more gourmet bed-and-breakfast and go blow them on a dozen nice meals downtown. Or you can shell out a few extra dollars for a one-bedroom casita ($159 d) or two-bedroom suite ($259 d), both of which come with full kitchens, and whip up a breakfast in your room.

Lafayette Inn and Suites (2223 El Cajon Blvd., 619/296-2101, www.lafayettehotelsd.com, $129 d, more for poolside rooms) is a last-resort kind of hotel. Rooms could be better maintained and the old building doesn't hide its age in spite of recent renovations. But the neighborhood is safe and it is close to Balboa Park and Hillcrest.

Head east of to find the best bargains in San Diego's city limits. Less than a mile away from San Diego State University, **Best Western Lamplighter Inn** (6474 El Cajon Blvd., 800/545-0778, www.lamplighter-inn.com, $129 d) is a good value for family members in town to visit students, or music fans staying the night for a big concert at Cox Arena. The facility and rooms are absolutely spic-and-span, and

the grounds include a modestly sized heated pool. An expanded continental breakfast, including a make-your-own-waffle station, is included in the room rate. In addition to fostering a kid-friendly atmosphere, Lamplighter also accepts pets.

Just over the edge of city limits, **Rodeway Inn Santee** (10135 Mission Gorge Rd., 619/258-2020, www.thesanteeinn.com, $118 d) is an average motel in the little town of Santee. The inn is close enough to the freeway to make the drive downtown reasonable and it has a small kidney bean–shaped pool. It is also pet friendly and includes a limited continental breakfast.

$150-250

Sommerset Suites Hotel (606 Washington St., 619/692-5200, www.sommersetsuites.com, studio suite $214 d, one-bedroom suite $234 d) offers bare-bones rooms that are large enough to give a big family the space it needs to peaceably survive a vacation. One-bedroom suites come with a fully equipped kitchen and a pull-out sofa bed. The rate includes a continental breakfast each morning.

MISSION VALLEY AND OLD TOWN

Located a few minutes away from the partiers at the beach and the hustle and bustle of downtown and Balboa Park, the Mission Valley and Old Town corridor is the epicenter of affordable, family-oriented hotels and motels. This is especially true in Mission Valley, which is home to Hotel Circle, a cluster of hotels and motels that line a stretch of I-8. Chain hotels are usually the name of the game here, but there are a few independent establishments as well.

Under $150

Other than Motel 6 and its ilk, **Old Town Inn** (4444 Pacific Hwy., 800/643-3025, www.old-town-inn.com $79 d, efficiency $125 d) is one of the least expensive establishments in this area. Accommodations are Spartan, but clean. Staff is friendly. And the location is pretty hard to beat, as it is located just a short walk away from Old Town State Historic Park and the Old Town Transit Center. This is a great choice for budget-conscious families or starving students who plan on taking advantage of the public transit system.

$150-250

Two of the nicer places along Hotel Circle are on the north side of the freeway, abutting the lush greenery of Riverwalk Golf Club. The largest of the two is the 1,000-room **Town and Country Resort** (500 Hotel Circle N., 619/291-7131, www.towncountry.com, $159 d). This locally owned resort has a large convention center on-site, so its amenities are designed to keep business folk satisfied. The big bonus from this setup is the fact that when there are no large events happening, rates go down. The downside is that the rooms are inconsistent here. Some are new and others look worn. If you can, try to snag one of the Royal Palm Tower rooms, which are some of the better of the bunch.

Next door, the **Crowne Plaza San Diego** (2270 Hotel Circle N., 619/297-1101, www.cp-sandiego.com, $125 d) is decidedly tourist friendly. The hotel's schtick is its Polynesian theme, so waterfalls, tropical foliage, and tiki decorations abound. The atmosphere borders on the edge of cheesiness without completely teetering over to the tacky side, and honestly kids will love it, especially the pool area. Some of the rooms can be a little dated, and those inexperienced in San Diego hotel rates might think they aren't getting the best deal during high season. Trust me, the rates are fair for the area—especially if you catch a good deal with a third-party online seller.

Across the freeway from the Crowne Plaza on the south side of the hotel circle is **Kings Inn** (1333 Hotel Circle S., 619/297-2231, www.kingsinnsandiego.com, $160 d), a motel that is sufficient when you just can't find a reservation anywhere else in town. Rooms are adequate but lack much of anything beyond a bed, a TV, and a tiny little bathroom. As a plus, it does offer guests free Wi-Fi, the staff is nice, and

you get vouchers to eat at the Amigo Spot and Waffle Spot located on the premises.

Nearby **C Hacienda Old Town** (4041 Harney St., 619/298-4707, www.haciendahotel-oldtown.com, $175 s/d) is a cute place that has a number of Spanish-style buildings scattered over a hillside that overlooks Old Town and the downtown skyline. The hotel is centrally located in Old Town—in fact it is hard to miss from the shopping district due to the distinctive architecture—which makes it a great base of operation for sampling the margaritas at all of the nearby Mexican joints without worrying about a drive back to the hotel. Don't expect to get too rowdy, though, as the Hacienda is still very family-oriented.

NORTH CITY
Under $150

The northern outposts of town tend to either be bedroom communities or open spaces, limiting lodging options more than within city limits. Most of the available accommodations up here are luxury resorts, but the **Best Western Inn Miramar** (9310 Kearny Mesa Rd., 858/578-6600 or 800/827-2635, $129 d) does have affordable rooms that can work in a pinch for those in the neighborhood on business or to visit family.

Another option for a golf retreat is **Doubletree Golf Resort** (14455 Penasquitos Dr., 858/672-9100, $139 d), which is not nearly as nice as some of the more expensive golf resorts and lacks a spa but still sports an Arnold Palmer–managed golf course, tennis courts, and a more kid-friendly pool area.

$150-250

Rancho Bernardo Inn (17550 Bernardo Oaks Dr., 858/675-8500, www.ranchobernardoinn.com, $229 d) manages to dazzle guests with the amenities of a large resort—golf course, spa, gardens, and tennis courts—while maintaining the intimate atmosphere of a small inn. Rooms and suites are decorated in an elegant but casual Spanish Revival motif and are all equipped with huge 42-inch plasma TVs, deep soaking tubs and Aveda bath products, and a private patio overlooking some type of greenery, be it gardens or the on-site golf course. The room rate includes a full breakfast at the resort's patio restaurant, the Veranda.

Camping

Tent campers will typically need to drive out of the city in order to find a decent campsite, but there is a notable exception in the north part of the city. **Kumeyaay Lake Campground** (2 Father Junipero Serra Tr., 619/668-2748, www.mtrp.org/campground) in Mission Trails Regional Park offers 46 primitive sites with picnic tables, a firebox, tent pad, and bathrooms with hot-water showers on premises. First-come, first-served camping is available, but online reservations are highly recommended for visits during the high season. Camping costs $14 per site per night with one vehicle; $4 each additional vehicle. One camping unit per site; pets are $3 each.

SOUTH BAY
Under $150

Finding a place to rest one's head in South Bay can be a tricky proposition, as some areas are less safe than others. If you're interested in staying in the South Bay, try looking in downtown Chula Vista near Third Street. One of the best places to stay in this revitalized commercial district is **El Primero Boutique** (416 Third Ave., 619/425-4486, $125 d). This zigzag-moderne building has a lot of art deco flair, both inside and out. The lobby is accented with diamond-pattern marble tiling, potted palms, and comfy modern furnishings that evoke the feeling of old Havana-style entrances in South Beach. Rooms are comfortable, bright, and clean. Each morning guest is treated to a healthy continental breakfast out in the center courtyard.

Those in town for the sandcastle competition in Imperial Beach can get a good view of the action from a beachfront room at **Seacoast Inn** (800 Seacoast Dr., 619/424-5183, $75 d). This motel is a little worse for wear and the rooms are basic, but it makes up the difference with its beachfront location and reasonable prices.

Camping

Those planning on rumbling their RV down I-5 toward Baja California should make plans to stop off at the **Chula Vista RV Resort** (460 Sandpiper Way, 619/422-0111, www.chulavistarv.com, $52 per night). This well-cared-for property is as ritzy as an RV park gets. Backed up against the San Diego Bay, 237 full hookup sites are only about 50 yards from the Chula Vista Marina. Each one comes with a cozy shaded picnic table with cushioned benches. The property has two waterfront restaurants, a heated pool and spa, putting green, free Wi-Fi access, and a general store. Pets are allowed, as well.

Sweetwater Regional Park (3218 Summit Meadow Rd., Bonita, 619/472-7572, $20 per site) on the Sweetwater Reservoir is one of the few natural spaces in South Bay appropriate for tent campers. All sites are also RV friendly and come with the standard fire grate and picnic table. The campground has a large picnic pavilion, making it an ideal spot for a trip with extended family. It also features a separate equestrian camping facility that can be a good headquarters for those bringing their horses to explore the Tijuana River Slough Wildlife Reserve.

Food

Even a couple of decades ago, San Diego wasn't well known for its culinary lineup. Things have changed, as the city has attracted many a top-notch chef to lead the new era of dining in San Diego. In addition to many new (and not-so-new) fine dining establishments, there are plenty of casual spots to find a messy burger, barbecue, or a simple sandwich.

DOWNTOWN

With its close proximity to the courthouse and office complexes, downtown is a haven for midweek lunchtime eateries. Though there are a few fine-dining exceptions, the core downtown area is somewhat bereft of those options. Gourmands need to walk just a little farther to Little Italy, the Gaslamp, or Bankers Hill for white-glove service.

Barbecue

If Maverick, Goose, and Iceman are names that mean something to you, then you better plan on making a landing at **Kansas City Barbeque** (610 W. Market St., 619/231-9680, www.kcbbq.net, 11 A.M.–1 A.M. daily, $12). This long-running establishment was an on-location set for the piano scene and the final jukebox scene in the 1986 schmaltz classic *Top Gun*. The bar still sports a collection of *Top Gun* memorabilia, including the fighter helmet worn by Tom Cruise as Maverick. Come for the movie memorabilia, but be sure to stay for some barbecue, which is sweet and smoky—if a little mediocre.

Cafés and Diners

Serving up café favorites with a Cajun flair, **Indigo Café Downtown** (1435 Sixth Ave., 619/702-6478, 7 A.M.–9 P.M. Mon.–Fri., 8 A.M.–9 P.M. Sat., 8 A.M.–8 P.M. Sun., $13) fills a perfect gap between make-do trips to Denny's and wallet-draining visits to some of the more expensive lunch and breakfast joints downtown and in the Gaslamp. Try the eggs Benedict for breakfast, or the shrimp po'boy for lunch. Old classics are melded with Cajun flavors to create dinner dishes like cajun pesto pasta with andouille sausage.

Run by a friendly Italian family, **Al Teatro Panini Grill** (1254 3rd Ave., 619/230-1485, www.alteatropaninigrill.com, 7 A.M.–4 P.M. Mon., 7 A.M.–5 P.M. Tue.–Fri., 11 A.M.–7 P.M. Sat.–Sun., $8) is close to Civic Theatre San Diego, making it a superb place to catch an early dinner before a show. Choose between panini sandwiches—each named after a famous composer—informal Italian comfort food such as lasagna, or a fresh salad during lunch and dinner hours. On a cold day their Italian wedding soup really hits the spot. This café is also an excellent breakfast spot. Coffee is head and shoulders above the chain coffee shops, and all of the pastries and muffins are made from scratch in the restaurant.

Sneak in with the busy business crowd and experience a locals' secret lunch favorite, **Daisy's Bistro** (1055 First Ave., 619/232-6141, 6:30 A.M.–2 P.M. and 5–10 P.M. Mon.–Fri., 7–11 A.M. and 5–10 P.M. Sat.–Sun., $13), a quiet and comfortable little eatery featuring satisfying and affordable sandwiches, wraps, and salads. The soups are particularly tasty here, especially the house special, the cream of mushroom sherry soup.

Bursting out from a petite little brick building on the corner of Kettner and West G St., **Brickyard Coffee and Tea** (675 W. G St., 619/616-7220, 6 A.M.–3 P.M. weekdays, 7 A.M.–P>3 P.M. weekends, $7) accommodates patrons with a spacious pet-friendly patio perfect for lingering over its flavorful breakfast and lunch dishes. Like any good coffeehouse, Brickyard has a fine balance of friendly regulars, personable staff, and rich coffee drinks to complement the tasty grub.

Brewhouses and Gastropubs

San Diego's biggest name in beer is Karl Strauss Brewery, which has produced its craft beer since the infancy of the microbrew craze

MEXICAN GRUB GUIDE

Many of us have the basic Spanish food terms down pat: *cerveza* for beer, *arroz con frijoles* for rice and beans, *pollo* for chicken, and so on. But this is only the tip of the iceberg in the Spanish-speaking lexicon for foodies in search of gastronomic adventure while down in San Diego.

If you're interested in trying new flavors but would like to know what you are in for before ordering, the following list is a good cheat sheet for understanding Mexican food terminology.

- *adobada:* spicy pork, also referred to as *al pastor*
- *agua fresca:* lightly mashed fruit in sugar water
- *barbacoa:* barbecue
- *birria:* spicy stew, often made with goat, lamb, or mutton
- *buches:* pork belly
- *cabeza:* literally cow head, but usually just the cheek
- *caldo:* soup
- *carnitas:* shredded pork
- *cesos:* brains
- *chilaquiles:* fried tortillas in mole or ranchero sauce, typically served for breakfast
- *chorizo:* Mexican sausage
- *churro:* fried pastry stick, similar in taste to a sugar donut
- *elote:* fresh corn
- *empanada:* pastry turnovers, usually stuffed with meat
- *langosta:* lobster
- *lengua:* cow tongue
- *mariscos:* seafood
- *menudo:* a traditional spicy soup made with tripe and hominy
- *molcajete:* a bowl made from lava rock designed for grinding food mortar-and-pestle style; on a menu it is usually filled with grilled meats
- *mole:* a rich sauce traditionally using chocolate and ground chiles, typically served over meats
- *nopalito:* cactus
- *parrilla:* grill
- *telera:* a tasty roll used to make *tortas*
- *torta:* a Mexican sandwich
- *tripas:* tripe

in 1989. The lineup consists of seven core beers and a number of seasonal specialties that can be found on tap at a number of bars around town and are usually stocked by the bottle at local liquor stores.

One of the best places to sip on a pint of Karl Strauss, though, is at **Karl Strauss Brewery and Grill** (1157 Columbia St., 619/234-2739, www.karlstrauss.com, 10 A.M.–11 P.M. Mon.–Thurs., 11 A.M.–midnight Fri., 11:30 A.M.–midnight Sat., 11:30 A.M.–10 P.M. Sun.), located at the business's first brewery location downtown. The restaurant serves everything

you'd expect, like burgers, pizza, sandwiches, and steaks. Be aware that the kitchen shuts down an hour before closing on every night but Sunday.

Beer snobs have plenty of options to choose from when looking for the perfect pairing to match with the renowned lobster tacos at **The Local** (1065 4th Ave., 619/231-4447, www.thelocalsandiego.com, 11 A.M.–midnight Mon.–Wed., 11 A.M.–1 A.M. Thurs., 11 A.M.–2 A.M. Fri., 10 A.M.–2 A.M. Sat., 9 A.M.–2 A.M. Sun., $10). Regulars who crave this crustacean concoction make a habit of showing up for happy hour on Thursdays, when special prices are in effect. Food here is a notch above the typical bar menu, with unique dishes like a fondue made with house-made Stone Smoked Porter cheese, beer and spicy chorizo, a jalepeno tuna melt, and a tasty teriyaki platter.

Seafood

Serving up fresh and tasty seafood in an unpretentious order-at-the-counter atmosphere, **Downtown Fish Joint** (407 C St., 619/239-3506, 10:30 A.M.–5 P.M. daily, $10) delivers up freshly battered or grilled fish served up in traditional fish 'n' chips platters, tacos, and burritos. The tacos are particularly tasty, as long as you're not a purist—these ones are served on flour instead of corn tortillas.

GASLAMP QUARTER AND EAST VILLAGE

The gastronomic heart of San Diego, the Gaslamp and East Village are as close to culinary nirvana as you'll get in San Diego County. It's block after block of good eats waiting for exploration inside the historic structures that stand tall in these neighborhoods.

Contemporary California

Many long-time San Diegans agree that Ingrid Croce was one of the most instrumental pioneers in the Gaslamp Quarter revitalization. Wife of folk crooner Jim Croce, Ingrid opened **Croce's** (802 5th Ave., 619/233-4355, www.croces.com, 5:30 P.M.–midnight Mon.–Fri., 10 A.M.–midnight Sat.–Sun., $28) in 1985 when the Gaslamp was still a bad part of town. This fine-dining restaurant is now at the core of the area's food and entertainment scene, serving a mix of pastas, steaks, seafood, and salads to the diners who come just as much for the food as they do for the nightly jazz shows.

Also in the Gaslamp is **JSix** (616 J St., 619/531-8744, www.jsixsandiego.com, 11:30 A.M.–10 P.M. Sun.–Wed., 11:30 A.M.–11 P.M. Thurs.–Sat., $16–32), which serves a coastal California menu that's heavy on seafood and fresh produce. Its chef is a big proponent of sourcing ingredients from local and sustainable farms, ranches, and fisheries, so the only thing you'll feel guilty about after a meal here is your bulging waistline. The extended hours and eclectic atmosphere also make it a nice hangout for an appetizer and a glass of wine in the late afternoon, while the rest of the Gaslamp's fine-dining establishments take a break between lunch and dinner.

Steak and Seafood

Carnivores will leave **Rei Do Gado Brazilian Steak House** (939 4th Ave., 619/702-8464, www.reidogado.net, 11 A.M.–10 P.M. Sun.–Thurs., 11 A.M.–11 P.M. Fri.–Sat., $40) more than sated. This Brazilian restaurant serves customers an all-you-can-eat feast of savory meats supplemented by a large selection of salads and hot sides from its buffet spread. The choices are unbelievable—17 different kinds of meats, from filet mignon to leg of lamb, are sliced off of the skewer on which they've just been roasting and placed on your plate for as long as your stomach can take it. At $40 per person, it is on the pricey side, but you can save a few dollars by eating here in the middle of the day for the largely unchanged $15 lunch feast.

Those craving a traditional steakhouse dinner should check out **Georges on 5th** (835 5th Ave., 619/702-0444, www.georgesonfifth.com, 5–10 P.M. daily, $35)—or G5, as some of the locals like to call it. The ambience is livened up with a bit of Wyatt Earp memorabilia spread around the dining room and the steak is as good as the prices suggest. This is one of the last remaining holdouts in this rumpled town to enforce a dress code, so men need to be sure to bring a dinner jacket. Please be kind to the chefs and do yourself a favor in the process: Don't order anything well-done. Nobody likes to see a tender piece of prime mangled that way.

At **Turf Supper Club** (1116 25th St., 619/234-6363, www.turfsupperclub.com, 5 P.M.–midnight Mon.–Tues., 5 P.M.–2 A.M. Wed.–Fri., 1 P.M.–2 A.M. Sat.–Sun., $9), you can cook your meat any way you want it. This trendy establishment lets patrons put the sizzle in their own steak at the communal grill. The buzz of cooking around the grill stimulates a lot of social action, making the scene a blast for groups of singles looking to hit it off with a potential Mr. or Ms. Right.

Italian

Venture out of Little Italy for some of the city's better Italian fine-dining experiences. In the Gaslamp are two of the best Tuscan restaurants in the city. Right in the middle of the Gaslamp excitement is **AcquaAL2** (322 5th Ave., 619/230-0382, www.acquaaL2.com, lunch 11:30 A.M.–2 P.M. Mon.–Fri., dinner 5 P.M.–2 A.M. daily, $14–32), the sister restaurant to a popular restaurant in Florence that has been frequented by international stars for almost 30 years. Opened in 2000, the American version imported many of the restaurant's signature dishes, including Fileno al Mirtilio, filet mignon topped with a blueberry sauce, a surprisingly complementary pair.

Like a woman who knows she's beautiful without needing to constantly preen in front of the mirror, **Trattoria La Strada** (702 5th Ave., 619/239-3400, www.trattorialastrada. com, 11 A.M.–11 P.M. Sun.–Thurs., 11 A.M.–12:30 A.M. Fri.–Sat., $23) is a little less pretentious than AquaAl2. The food is just as rich, though, with veal, chicken, and seafood playing the starring role in the best entrées here. If you really want to taste the quality of the meats, the restaurant serves a well-rounded selection of carpaccio.

Asian

For a West Coast town, San Diego is sadly a bit bereft of a well-rounded mix of Asian cuisine. It is possible to find it; you just have to search a lot harder than you should have to.

Most of the town's very best Far Eastern restaurants are located north of I-8 on Kearny Mesa, but the Gaslamp does have the best Indian. One of the perennial favorites is **Monsoon** (729 4th Ave., 619/234-5555, www. monsoonrestaurant.com, 11 A.M.–2:30 P.M.

daily, 11 A.M.–9:30 P.M. Mon.–Fri., 11 A.M.–10:30 P.M. Sat.–Sun., $18), an upscale restaurant that elevates Indian cuisine beyond the simple pleasures of tandoori and vindaloo. The selection on the six-page menu is staggering. Before you even start your meal you'll have to choose between eight different kinds of naan (leavened flat bread) and an equal number of chutneys and pickles. If you don't think you'll be able to choose between the mint curry or the mango ($15.95 for vegetarian, more with meats), the *roghan ghosht* (lamb with spiced yogurt, mint, and mustard seeds) or the Calcutta shrimp simmered in spiced cream and cardamom pods, consider coming during a weekday lunch ($13.95) or Monday dinner ($19.95), when a self-serve buffet is laid out.

Trendy sushi bars are quite plentiful in the Gaslamp, but beware—there are a few stinkers out there that try to skate by on decor alone. Not so at **Taka** (555 5th Ave., 619/338-0555, www.takasushi.com, 5:30 P.M.–9:30 P.M. Sun.–Thurs., 5:30 P.M.–10:30 P.M. Fri.–Sat., $17), where the sashimi is fresh and delicate and the wasabi is nose-clearingly spicy. The place has killer *anmitsu* ($5) for dessert; that's green-tea ice cream with sweet red beans and fruit jelly covered with black sugar syrup.

LITTLE ITALY
Italian

Little Italy is an obvious choice to find *cibo Italiano*. There are a number of restaurants that offer a range of dining experiences, but the informal trattorias are where Little Italy excels.

One excellent choice in this category is **Mimmo's** (1743 India St., 619/239-3710, www.mimmos.biz, lunch 10 A.M.–3 P.M. Mon.–Sat., dinner 5–9 P.M. Mon.–Thurs., 5–11 P.M. Fri.–Sat., noon–9 P.M. Sun., $12). Lunch is served deli-style, while dinner is served on the patio or in the informal dining room. The food rivals some of the more expensive Italian joints in town, without the stuffy atmosphere or the earth-shattering bill at the end.

Slightly higher up the formality scale, but still unpretentiously tasty, **Bencotto Italian Kitchen** (750 W. Fir St., 619/450-4786, www.lovebencotto.com, 11 A.M.–10:30 P.M. Tues.–Sun., $20) is a haven for traditional meals, its signature menu selection being *pasta a modo tuo*, or "pasta your way." You'll be able to choose between eleven different house-made pastas and eight different fragrant sauces to suit your palate. Finish it off with a little creativity. Forget the staid tiramisu and instead go for *sbrisolona con cioccolato fuso*, a biscotto cake with almonds and warm melted chocolate.

Those looking to impress their friends with a slightly more upscale Little Italy experience like to choose **Buon Appetito** (1609 India St., 619/238-9880, www.buonappetito.signonsandiego.com, 11 A.M.–10 P.M. Mon.–Thurs., 11 A.M.–11 P.M. Fri.–Sat., noon–10 P.M. Sun., $15) a quality establishment that's lighter on the pasta in favor of meat and seafood dishes with risotto and potato accompaniments. The boisterous and crowded atmosphere lends itself more to double-date territory than intimate moments, but the food is well worth the sacrifice if you're the quiet type.

Cafés and Delis

Stock up to make your own homemade Italian meal at **Assenti's Pasta** (2044 India St., 619/239-5117, www.assentispasta.com, 9 A.M.–6 P.M. Mon.–Fri., 10 A.M.–5 P.M. Sat., closed Sun.), which sells the genuine article when it comes to fresh pasta. On weekend afternoons you'll see little old ladies streaming in and out of the shop in preparation for their family feasts.

Complement the pasta with some fine imported meats and cheeses from **Mona Lisa Italian Foods** (2061 India St., 619/234-4893, www.monalisalittleitaly.com, 9 A.M.–10 P.M. Mon.–Thurs., 9 A.M.–11 P.M. Fri.–Sat., 10 A.M.–10 P.M. Sun., $10). Fresh balls of mozzarella, delectable burrata, sharp pecorino, plus cured stashes of capicola, soprasetta, and Genoa salami are all available for patrons to swoop in and pick up. If you don't have time to whip up your own meal, Mona Lisa also prepares sandwiches to go. Stop in and grab a number for the privilege of ordering a Caprese

and don't forget to add some amaretto cookies to your order. They're delicious.

If it's a hot sandwich you've got a hankering for, take the time to walk over to **Pete's Quality Meat** (1742 India St., 619/234-1684, 10 A.M.–5 P.M. Mon.–Sat., $7). The stand's specialty is its simple sausage sandwiches, made with the best Italian links you'll find in town. You'll also find steak hoagies, meatball subs, and chicken sandwiches.

When it comes to gelato, **Pappalecco** (1602 State St., 619/238-4590, www.pappalecco.com, 7 A.M.–9:30 P.M. Mon.–Fri., 8 A.M.–10:30 P.M. Sat.–Sun., $5) serves up the real deal here: creamy, dense, and intensely flavorful. The flavors vary by the day but choices abound, with the standards such as pistachio and Nutella and uniquely delicious options such as pear. Put it in a cup or cone, or opt for something special. Pappalecco offers gelato-stuffed croissants and affogato, an espresso float that is worth a stop alone given the high quality of coffee at this shop. This is also a full-service café, too, with lots of pre-dessert meals available. The panini and salad menus are bursting with fresh and affordable selections.

Brewhouses and Gastropubs

Intent on coming up with some of the most creative food and drink concepts in town, **Craft and Commerce** (675 W Beech St., 619/269-2202, www.craft-commerce.com, 5 P.M.–11 P.M. daily, bar open until 1 A.M., $14) sets out a menu full of options you'll certainly not find at any other bar and grill in town. Wash down your order of bacon Cracker Jacks with marcona almonds with a specialty cocktail. Or order one of more than two dozen craft beers along with a hot dog that's anything but standard, served with heirloom tomato relish, chicharrones, chives, and spicy fondue. Buckle up and come ready for quite the culinary ride.

WATERFRONT
Seafood

Tucked in between Embarcadero Marina Park and Seaport Village, **Top of the Market**

(750 N. Harbor Dr., 619/234-4867, www. thefishmarket.com, 5 P.M.–10 P.M. daily, $35) offers some of the best waterfront seafood dining outside of Coronado. Watch sailboats tack lazily around the bay from your second-story perch as you nosh on a menu that changes with the catch of the day in an intimate environment. Set just above The Fish Market, a more informal and unremarkable sister restaurant, Top of the Market excels where its sibling and a lot of tourist traps do not. Service is prompt, the dishes are prepared with care, and the view is perfect for a romantic night out.

Not to be confused with the one on Coronado, **The Boathouse** on Harbor Island (1220 El Carmel Pl., 858/488-6242, www. boathouserestaurant.com, 11 A.M.–10 P.M. Mon.–Fri., 9 A.M.–10 P.M. Sat.–Sun., $21) offers traditional seafood and steak, with a healthy dose of pasta as well, convenient to Harbor Island's lineup of hotels and very close to the airport for a pre-flight feast.

Also on the mainland side of the bay are a pair of eateries over at Seaport Village worth sticking around for post-souvenir shopping. Set on stilts over the bay, **San Diego Pier Café** (885 W. Harbor Dr., 619/239-3968, www. piercafe.com, 11 A.M.–9 P.M. daily, $20) wins out in terms of nautical ambience. The restaurant is set in a Coastal New England–style building, with a menu to match. But **Harbor House** (831 W. Harbor Dr., 619/232-1141, www.harborhousesd.com, 11 A.M.–10 P.M. daily, $25) has it beat in terms of food. While you are there, make your taste buds tingle with one of their beer oyster shooters, served with local suds made by Karl Strauss Brewery.

Cafés and Diners

After several hours of poking your head through hatches and minding the knee-knockers aboard the *Midway* Museum, the **Fantail Café** (910 N. Harbor Dr., 619/398-8258, www.fantailcafe.com, 10 A.M.–5 P.M. daily, $9) presents an inviting respite for a cup of coffee and a quick bite to eat. Neither is exemplary, but the location can't be beat. The museum's set right on the old aircraft carrier's fantail,

overlooking a park-like patch of greenery and Harbor Drive. It's also one of the few establishments remotely resembling a coffeehouse along the waterfront.

Over in Seaport Village, hungry families not in the mood for seafood can satisfy those tummy grumbles at **Greek Islands Cafe** (879 W. Harbor Dr., 619/239-5216, www.greekislandscafe.com, 10:30 A.M.–9 P.M. daily, $9), a surprisingly authentic eatery given the locale. Choose between mounds of freshly sliced gyro meat, dolmas wrapped in grape leaves, and kabobs with rice. And don't forget the baklava— it's flaky and dense with nuts and honey, just the way it's supposed to be.

CORONADO ISLAND
Cafés and Diners

Coronado village is filled with great little cafés from which you can sip coffee, munch on sandwiches, and watch a streaming procession of amblers poke and prod their way through adjoining gift shops and boutiques.

For prime people-watching, nothing beats the patio at **Tent City** (1100 Orange Ave., Coronado, 619/435-4611, www.tentcityrestaurant.com, 8 A.M.–9 P.M. Tues.–Sun., 8 A.M.–4 P.M. Mon., $15). Named for the candy-striped canvas tents that were pitched at the foot of Hotel del Coronado each summer in the early 20th century, this café is run by the Coronado Historical Association and abuts their quaint history museum. It is situated on a well-traveled section of Orange Avenue and there are lots of places to pull up a chair outside. The patio is also dog friendly—if they aren't busy, the nice staffers might even bring your pooch a bit of water to lap up while you eat.

Occupying that culinary ground somewhere between a bistro and a fine restaurant, **Rhinocerous Cafe and Grille** (1166 Orange Ave., Coronado, 619/435-2121, www.rhinocafe.com, lunch 11 A.M.–2:30 P.M. daily, dinner 5 P.M. to close daily, $17) takes its food a bit more seriously than the average café—it must be that extra "e" that they tacked on to the end of "grill." Casual diners will feel most comfortable during lunch, but at dinnertime

Nibble on a sandwich and watch the people stream by from the patio at Tent City in Coronado village.

rumpled beachwear is discouraged and reservations are recommended.

No such formalities are required at **Night and Day Café** (847 Orange Ave., Coronado, 619/435-9776, 24 hours daily, $7), which is the closest thing to a dive-y diner you'll find in Coronado. It is actually quite nice and the food is less heavy than most all-night greasy spoons.

After the kind of night that might require a stop in Night and Day Café, a little restorative grub might be in order once the sun shines again. **Bino's** (120 Adella St., Coronado, 619/522-0612, www.binosbistro. com, 7 A.M.–5 P.M. Mon.–Wed., 7 A.M.–8 P.M. Thurs.–Sun., $8) is the perfect kind of out-of-the-way café to nurse a hangover on one of those dreaded mornings-after. Nestled away from the rush of Orange Avenue, this little coffee shop specializes in scrumptious crepes.

Seafood

San Diego has a cornucopia of waterfront-view restaurants, but none tops the skyline sight lines of **Peohe's** (1201 1st St., Coronado, 619/437-4474, www.peohes.com, 11:30 A.M.–2:30 P.M. and 5 P.M.–10 P.M. Mon.–Sat., 11 A.M.–2:30 P.M. and 4:30 P.M.–9:30 P.M. Sun., $26). This Coronado favorite serves up sea critters tropical style, with Polynesian decor and indoor waterfalls to match. Be sure to ask your server to bring over one of their signature Pupu platters.

Those who'd like their seafood with a heaping helping of history should visit **Coronado Boathouse** (1701 Strand Way, Coronado, 619/435-0155, www.coronado-boathouse. com, 5–10 P.M. Sun.–Thurs., 5–11 P.M. Fri.–Sat., $25–47). It's the distinctive Victorian set on Glorietta Bay that looks a bit like a "mini Del." Some make the mistake of fingering the boathouse as a send-up of the famous hotel, but the building was actually erected a year before Hotel del Coronado. The restaurant lives up to its splendid setting with a fresh and flavorful selection of seafood.

Speaking of the Del, the famous hotel also hosts its own lineup of fine seafood at **1500 Ocean** (1500 Orange Ave., Coronado, 619/435-6611, www.dine1500ocean.com, 5:30–10:30 P.M. daily, bar 5:30–midnight daily, $26). The restaurant overlooks the resort's beachfront and serves a menu that relies on local Southern Californian ingredients.

French

There are several charming French restaurants to choose from in the heart of downtown Coronado. Right along the main drag, **Crown Bistro** (520 Orange Ave., Coronado, 619/435-3678, www.crownbistro.com, breakfast 8 A.M.–2 P.M. daily, lunch 11 A.M.–2 P.M. daily, dinner 5–9 P.M. Mon.–Sat., champagne brunch 8 A.M.–2 P.M. Sun., $20) serves a heavily Americanized version of French food. On Sundays the bistro cancels lunch altogether in favor of its champagne brunch, served until 2 P.M. Reservations are recommended for this weekly event, as well as for dinner.

Set within a cute little Victorian on a village side street, **C Chez Loma** (1132 Loma Ave.,

Coronado, 619/435-0661, www.chezloma.com, $27) offers more traditional French cuisine. If you go, be sure to supplement your meal with a cup of the onion soup—it is some of the best I've ever tasted, with big, delicious cuts of onion that taste as if they've been caramelizing for days. Bargain hunters may want to go early: Chez Loma offers an early-bird three-course prix fixe menu for $24.95 between 5 and 6 P.M. every day. The special also stands all evening on Tuesday.

Brewhouses and Gastropubs
A relatively young upstart in the San Diego brewhouse scene is **Coronado Brewing Company** (170 Orange Ave., Coronado, 619/437-4452, www.coronadobrewingcompany.com, 11 A.M.–2 A.M. daily, $20), which runs a microbrewery and restaurant in the middle of Coronado Island's village. All the usual pub grub is there, but the menu also has quite a few gourmet pastas, seafood, and salads thrown into the mix.

BALBOA PARK AND BANKERS HILL
Contemporary California
Toast to the service, toast to the food, but most of all, toast to the views at **Bertrand at Mister A's** (2550 5th Ave., #406, 619/239-1377, www.bertrandatmisteras.com, lunch 11:30 A.M.–2:30 P.M. Mon.–Fri., dinner 5:30 P.M.–close Mon.–Fri., 5 P.M.–close Sat.–Sun., $30), one of San Diego's finest rooftop eateries with views of the glittering San Diego skyline and the waterfront. The menu is California cuisine at its best, a touch of French flavor here, a dash of Japanese inspiration there, and a supreme respect for fresh meat and seafood throughout. Don't dare leaving without dipping your spoon through the glassy crust of the house's crème brûlée ($12), a must-have dessert. Brick walls lined with banquettes and exposed, high ceilings invite a casual crowd in for a classy meal at **Avenue 5** (2760 5th Ave., Ste. 100, 619/542-0394, www.avenue5restaurant.com, lunch 11 A.M.–2 P.M. Tues.–Fri., dinner 5 P.M.–close

Tues.–Sun., brunch 10 A.M.–2 P.M. Sun., closed Mon., $20), an upscale but unpretentious restaurant serving French-inspired California dishes. The menu changes with the seasons and ingredients, but some past favorites include delectable lamb burgers, prosciutto-wrapped monkfish, and tender halibut served with mussels and clams in a saffron reduction sauce to die for. The house specialty is a homemade mushroom tortellini the chef prepares every day. The atmosphere is lively; when it gets crowded the din will echo around the exposed walls and ceilings so brace yourself for a potentially noisy dinner.

Asian
Mandarin House (2604 5th Ave., 619/232-1101, 11 A.M.–10 P.M. Mon.–Thurs., 11 A.M.–11 P.M. Fri., noon–11 P.M. Sat., 2 P.M.–10 P.M. Sun., $8) on Bankers Hill serves up very good, albeit slightly Americanized, Chinese food. The house specialty is the must-have: salt-and-pepper chicken dredged in seasoned flour and pan-fried with mounds of garlic, green onion, and spicy red peppers.

Cafés and Diners
Right in the center of Balboa Park, the **Tea Pavilion at the Japanese Friendship Garden** (2215 Pan American Plaza, 619/231-0048, 10 A.M.–4 P.M. daily, 10 A.M.–5 P.M. summer weekends) is a great place to rest between museum tours and garden walks. The café serves a light menu of sushi, rice bowls, noodles, and salads.

Within easy walking distance to the park, the concept behind **Evolution Fast Food** (2965 5th Ave., 619/550-1818, http://evolutionfastfood.com, 11 A.M.–8 P.M. Mon.–Thurs., 11 A.M.–9 P.M. Fri.–Sat., brunch 11 A.M.–2 P.M. Sat.–Sun., drive-thru open 11 A.M.–9 P.M. daily, $5) is simple. The owners here have created a healthy fast food joint built on a menu of vegetarian and vegan dishes meant to put Mickey D's to shame. The restaurant serves black bean burgers, vegan pizza, and wraps made especially for raw food aficionados. If you've come by car and really want it quick, Evolution even has a drive-thru.

Southern

Those headed to Balboa Park for an afternoon should make time for a leisurely lunch at **Gulf Coast Grill** (4130 Park Blvd., 619/295-2244, www.gulfcoastgrill.com, lunch 11 A.M.–2 P.M. Mon.–Sat., brunch 9 A.M.–2 P.M. Sun., $18) before they hit the museums. Just blocks away from the park, this eatery fuses flavors of the South and the Southwest to create a happy blend of fresh and spicy flavors. Their blackened seafood is tops on the menu. Try the shrimp atop their Gulf Greens Salad ($9.95) for a refreshing midday meal.

Spanish

Set amid the flourishes of Balboa Park's Spanish Revival architecture, **The Prado** (1549 El Prado, 619/557-9441, dinner 5–9 P.M. Tues.–Thurs., 5–10 P.M. Fri.–Sat., and 4–8 P.M. Sun., $23) delivers food to match the surrounding ambience. As an added bonus, the restaurant operates a food and wine school for nonprofessionals, with observational cooking classes and wine seminars.

Dessert

There's probably no dessert joint in town that can match the atmosphere and the selection of **Extraordinary Desserts** (www.extraordinarydesserts.com). It's the secret weapon of many a local Casanova, a place where you'll be seated in a quiet nook and waited on hand and foot by servers clad all in black who seem to be able to produce just about any sugary concoction that has ever been dreamed up. The menu has tortes, tarts, custards, cookies, ice cream, iced cakes, and cupcakes galore. This café runs two locations: The original is on Bankers Hill (2929 5th Ave., 619/294-2132, 8:30 A.M.–11 P.M. Sun.–Thurs., 10 A.M.–midnight Fri.–Sat.) and the second spot is in Little Italy (1430 Union St., 619/294-7001, 8:30 A.M.–11 P.M. Mon.–Thurs., 8:30 A.M.–midnight Fri., 10 A.M.–midnight Sat., 10 A.M.–11 P.M. Sun.).

HILLCREST AND NORTH PARK
Brewhouses and Gastropubs

The fish-and-chips at **Shakespeare Pub** (3701 India St., 619/299-0230, www.shakespearepub.com, 11 A.M.–midnight Mon.–Thurs., 11 A.M.–1 A.M. Fri., 7 A.M.–1 A.M. Sat., 8 A.M.–midnight Sun., $8) come with a chunk of cod the size of a log. With a splash of vinegar this crispy treat is to die for, but if fried seafood isn't your thing, Shakespeare also plates a number of other English favorites such as bangers and mash and steak-and-kidney pie. The bar is a favorite with soccer fans, who often crowd in to watch the football matches streamed via satellite here.

Contemporary California

I hesitate to write about **Adams Avenue Grill** (2201 Adams Ave., 619/298-8440, www.adamsavenuegrill.com, breakfast from 9 A.M. Sat.–Sun., lunch 11 A.M.–2 P.M. daily,, dinner from 5 P.M. daily, $19) because I feel like this little spot is my own personal dining room and I'd hate to wait for a seat—but for you, dear reader, I have an obligation. Hidden away in a non-commercial stretch of Adams Avenue, this intimate restaurant serves a mixture of home-style dishes, such as the daily pot roast ($16.95) and daring experimental meals such as the saffron-infused poached salmon with peach chutney ($19.95). This is the type of place that warrants a full meal: appetizers through dessert and a wheelbarrow to roll you out in. Be sure to get a taste of the goat-cheese-and-walnut fritters ($8.25) before filling up on dinner, and save room for desserts such as the pecan caramel triangle ($5.95).

Another neighborhood fave, farther southeast in North Park, is **The Linkery** (3794 30th St., 619/255-8778, www.thelinkery.com, 5–11 P.M. daily, $10), which makes up a fresh menu of gourmet homemade sausages each day. You can order them in a tasty picnic plate along with cheese and a spinach salad, in tacos, or as an add-on to one of their other entrée items. This progressive eatery is serious about buying meats and produce from organic and sustainable sources—a list of its vendors is printed on the menu. It is also unique in that waiters work for a higher salary and do not accept tips. If you leave behind a gratuity it will be donated to a charity selected from the owners' rotating list.

Asian

Consistently voted as the best Thai food in San Diego in local publications, **Lotus Thai** (3761 6th Ave., 619/299-8272, www.lotusthaisd.com, 11 A.M.–3 P.M. Mon.–Fri., noon–3 P.M. Sat.–Sun., 5 P.M.–10 P.M. Mon.–Thurs., 5 P.M.–11 P.M. Fri.–Sat.) in Hillcrest has some of the lightest, crispiest spring rolls on the planet and its pad Thai is the perfect blend of sweet and spicy that too many other places are unable to balance.

If Asian fusion cuisine is your kind of thing, **Kemo Sabe** (3958 5th Ave., 619/220-6802, www.cohnrestaurants.com/restaurants/kemosabe/, 5:30 P.M.–10 P.M. Tue.–Sun., $20) is a fun option in Hillcrest. The chef here unites Pacific Rim and Southwestern flavors in combinations that are surprisingly complementary. For example, blackened *satay* chicken breasts are served with chile corn cakes and melon salsa, and onion cake enchiladas are stuffed with *moo shu* pork and Szechwan plum salsa.

Cafés

The popular **Antique Row Café** (3002 Adams Ave., 619/282-9750, 6 A.M.–9 P.M. Mon.–Fri., 6 A.M.–3 P.M. Sat.–Sun., $8) is a quaint little breakfast spot right in the middle of Antique Row in Normal Heights and is itself awash in old bric-a-brac and curios. Servings are huge and known to have cured more than one hangover over the years. Just get there early on the weekend or you'll encounter a long line. On the plus side, the diner offers coffee and cinnamon roll bites for those patient enough to wait.

Painted in the bright red, green, and white colors of the Mexican flag, **Frutilandia** (3647 University Ave., 619/282-0774, 7 A.M.–8 P.M. Mon.–Fri., 8 A.M.–8 P.M. Sat., 8 A.M.–7 P.M. Sun., $6) is what those south of the border call a *frutería*. It specializes in drinks, dishes, and treats made with fruits of all stripes. Fill up on a fruit salad made with a mix of standard and exotic fruits, quench your thirst with an *agua fresca*—fruit mashed into water with a splash of lemon or lime and a dash of sugar—or satisfy both urges with a *licuado*—a milkshake made with fresh fruit and milk.

If you are planning a romantic picnic at any of the hundreds of green spots in town and you like cheese, stop—do not pass Go, do not collect $200—and immediately head to **Venissimo Cheese** (754 W. Washington St., 619/491-0708, www.venissimo.com, 11 A.M.–6:30 P.M. Mon.–Fri., 10 A.M.–6 P.M. Sat., 11 A.M.–4 P.M. Sun., $10). This is the temple at which cheese worshippers of San Diego prostrate themselves. It sells cheddars, Bries, Stiltons, chèvres, and everything in between from all over the world. To complete that picnic basket it also has a selection of fruits, nuts, olives, and crackers, plus a few selected aged meats. You'll have to go elsewhere for the wine, though.

My suggestion for wine to complement your picnic is **Wine Steals** (1243 University Ave., 619/295-1188, www.winestealssd.com, 4–11 P.M. Mon., 11 A.M.–11 P.M. Tues.–Wed., Sun., 11 A.M.–midnight Thurs.–Fri., $10), which is only about a mile away from Venissimo—take Washington Street east and veer right where the road forks into University Avenue. The store has a varied selection of nibbles and vino that suits just about any budget and taste. If you ask nicely, the knowledgeable staff can probably even help you pair with your cheeses.

The **Egyptian Tearoom** (4644 College Ave., 619/265-7287, www.egyptiantearoom.com, 11 A.M.–midnight Sun.–Thurs., 8 A.M.–3 A.M. Fri.–Sat.) provides sustenance and relaxation for SDSU students starved for both. Not far from campus, the Tearoom is usually a quiet spot in the afternoons and early evenings, doling out hummus and pita ($4.95), vegetarian couscous ($4.95), and gyro sandwiches ($5.95) to customers as they work on their homework. In the evening the social butterflies drop in to share a hookah packed with tobacco flavored with fruity aromas.

Diners

By day **Rudford's** (2900 El Cajon Blvd., 619/282-8423, www.rudfords.com, 24 hours daily, $7) is the kind of place where you can get a filling breakfast even when the sun has risen well above its highest point. By night you can still get that breakfast, or your choice of a host of other American diner faves such as chicken-fried steak and patty melts with fries.

The lighting is dim, the plates are industrial grade, and food is served off a cart, but the **Chicken Pie Shop** (2633 El Cajon Blvd., 619/295-0156, 10 A.M.–8 P.M. daily) is still a great place. For $6 you get a chicken or beef pie served up with soup, potatoes, veggies, coleslaw, a roll, a slice of fruit pie, and bit of friendly banter from the waitresses that roll those carts up and down the dining room. The menu also offers fried chicken, sandwiches, and other such sundries, but trust me and order the pie meal—it's what everyone else is having.

Slightly east over in the college area, **DZ Akins** (6930 Alvarado Rd., 619/265-0218, www.dzakinsdeli.com, 7 A.M.–9 P.M. Sun.–Thurs., 7 A.M.–10 P.M. Fri.–Sat., $12) is one of the few delis in town that can satisfy someone with a hankering for a true New York–style corned-beef sandwich. DZ has all of the morning-through-night traditional deli fare many East Coasters miss out on in SoCal, including blintzes, bagels and lox, and matzo-ball soup.

Vegetarian and Vegan

As would be expected in health-conscious Southern California, most restaurants in town offer something tasty for vegetarians. But if you are looking for a restaurant or store that caters strictly to the vegetarian and vegan palate, your best bet is probably the Hillcrest and North Park area.

One well-known spot is Spread (2879 University Ave., 619/543-0406, www. spreadtherestaurant.com, 6–10 P.M. Tues.–Sun., $12), a North Park eatery that bills its fare as "Nouveau Comfort Food." It is completely organic, with offerings for both vegans and vegetarians, and an emphasis on creativity. Because the menu changes based on the local produce offerings, the menu varies. Some past items include macadamia rosemary grits, Thai veggie pizza, and wild-mushroom ragu.

Another spot in nearby Normal Heights is **Jyoti-Bihanga** (3351 Adams Ave., 619/282-4116, www.jyotibihanga.com, 11 A.M.–9 P.M. Mon.–Tues. and Thurs.–Fri.,11 A.M.–3 P.M. Wed., noon–9 P.M. Sat., $9), which is run by the students of the spiritual leader Sri Chinmoy. The menu features a variety of salads, sandwiches, and wraps that rely on fresh produce and house-made veggie protein patties.

Vegans who'd like to pick up a few snacks would do well to visit **All Vegan Store** (4669 Park Blvd., 619/299-4669, www.allveganshopping.com, 11 A.M.–7 P.M. Tues., 11 A.M.–8 P.M. Wed., 2–8 P.M. Thurs.–Fri., 10 A.M.–9 P.M. Sat., 1–6 P.M. Sun.) in University Heights. Similarly, vegetarians and vegans especially appreciate the organic produce and healthy packaged food offered at the specialty grocer **Henry's** (4175 Park Blvd., 619/291-8287, www.henrysmarkets.com, 7 A.M.–10 P.M. daily). This local chain is a subsidiary of Whole Foods and can be found throughout the city. There is a location in North Park that is very close to Balboa Park.

Dessert

Gelato is easy to find in Little Italy, but some of the best in town is served in Mission Hills at **Gelato Vero Caffe** (3753 India St., 619/295-9269, www.gelatovero.net, 6 A.M.–midnight Mon.–Thurs., 6 A.M.–1 A.M. Fri., 7 A.M.–1 A.M. Sat., 7 A.M.–midnight Sun., $5). Try the spumoni—its rich and creamy base is studded with pistachios, cherries, and chocolate and is heavenly on a summer day.

Speaking of divinity, **Heaven Sent Desserts** (3001 University Ave., 619/793-4758, www.heavensentdesserts.net, 11 A.M.–11 P.M. Tues.–Thurs., 11 A.M.–midnight Fri.–Sat., 11 A.M.–10 P.M. Sun., $8) offers a number of desserts that transcend earthly delights. The house's strong suit is its cakes.

MISSION VALLEY AND OLD TOWN

Cafés and Diners

Step into a time warp at **Perry's** (4620 Pacific Hwy., 619/291-7121, 6 A.M.–2 P.M. daily, $9), a 1960s-era breakfast joint that for decades has countered California health consciousness by serving classic greasy-spoon goodness. Mexican and American breakfasts are equally good here and the cups of coffee are strong and bottomless. Don't be scared off by the wait on the weekends. The staff is swarming the place to efficiently usher customers toward gluttonous satisfaction. Just step up to the register, scribble your name on the notepad, and it'll be no time at all before you're elbows-deep in a hearty breakfast.

Steak and Burgers

The vibe at **Hunter Steakhouse** (2445 Hotel Circle N., 619/291-8074, www.paragonsteak.com, 11:30 A.M.–9 P.M. Mon.–Fri., 11:30 A.M.–10 P.M. Sat., 4–9 P.M. Sun., $21) is that of an old college club or the well-appointed den of a stately manor. You'll sink down into the comfortable plush booths and relax under the diffuse lighting that glows around the dark woods that accent the walls. The steaks are prime cuts and sides are as thoughtfully prepared as the main courses.

Listen up, pilgrim. **Longhorn Café** (6519 Mission Gorge Rd., 619/283-0831, $9) has some manly size burgers—if you are lucky you can eat them under the squinty gaze of the Duke himself. This divey burger gem in Mission Valley has a whole room dedicated to John Wayne memorabilia for those who are into his films. In addition to burgers with all the fixin's, you can sink your teeth into the juicy steak sandwiches.

For some of the best pub grub in Mission Valley, head over to **McGregor's** (10475 San Diego Mission Rd., 619/282-9797, 11 A.M.–2 A.M. Mon.–Fri., 10 A.M.–2 A.M.

Sat.–Sun., $9). Set in an inauspicious strip mall, this restaurant and bar is a favorite watering hole for locals. It is located very close to Qualcomm Stadium, making it a good place to continue the festivities after the Chargers hit the gridiron.

Mexican

The stars of **Old Town Mexican Café** (2489 San Diego Ave., 619/297-4330, www.oldtownmexcafe.com, 7 A.M.–2 A.M. daily, $10) are the "Tortilla Ladies of Old Town" who pat and form over 7,000 corn and flour tortillas every day. Passersby can watch them do their thing through the big picture windows that face the street. So can expectant diners, who line up in an eager crowd—the wait is an hour or longer at dinnertime in the summer and during the Christmas to New Year's rush. To beat the crowds try to plan a visit at lunchtime or even in the morning for a filling Mexican breakfast. In the morning, the huevos rancheros or the *machaca* (eggs scrambled with shredded beef, onions, and bell peppers) are best. Tops on the lunch and dinner menu is the *carnitas* feast that can be shared among everyone at the table.

Rockin' Baja (3890 Twiggs St., 619/260-0305, 11 A.M.–9 P.M. Sun.–Thurs., 11 A.M.–10:30 P.M. Fri.–Sat., $20) buzzes with fun. This Mexican seafood restaurant specializes in Baja-style slipper lobster tails, which are flash-fried and served up in the place's signature tin pails. These buckets can also come with shrimp, chicken, and carne asada. All of the meals here come with rice, beans, and tortillas, as well as unlimited rights to pile your plate with the green stuff over at the salad and salsa bar.

Those interested in practicing their Spanish without eating yet another taco can saunter over to **Berta's** (3928 Twiggs St., 619/295-2343, www.bertasinoldtown.com, 11 A.M.–10 P.M. Tues.–Sun., $15). This restaurant dishes out flavors from all over Latin America and beyond, and the menu bursts with empanadas, paellas, fricassees, and flans.

© ERICKA CHICKOWSKI

Watch corn and flour tortillas being made through the window of Old Town Mexican Café.

NORTH CITY
Breakfast and Brunch

TV geeks should insist on stopping by **Studio Diner** (4701 Ruffin Rd., 858/715-6400, www.studiodiner.com, 24 hours daily, $10), set on the lot of Stu Segall Productions, a working movie and TV studio that has produced shows like *Terriers, Renegade, Silk Stockings,* and *Veronica Mars.* This nostalgic restaurant is decorated inside with film memorabilia and the shiny chrome exterior adds an impressive touch of authenticity. The fare here is typical diner grub, served up around the clock.

94th Aero Squadron (8885 Balboa Ave., 858/560-6771 or 858/560-6953, www.94thaerosquadron.signonsandiego.com, 11 A.M.–4 P.M. Mon.–Fri., 9 A.M.–3 P.M. Sun., 4–9 P.M. Sun.–Thurs., 4–11 P.M. Fri., 4–10 P.M. Sat., $25), re-creates the feel of a World War I–era French farmhouse in its architecture and decor. The ambience is enhanced by the fact that the restaurant borders the airstrip at Montgomery Field, so you can watch small aircraft take off and land as you sip mimosas and listen to period music piped through the sound system. The spread at the Sunday brunch has enough food to keep you full for a whole week. The buffet includes prime rib, ham, peel-n-eat shrimp, crab legs, salads, breads and pastries, an omelet and waffle station, and a whole smorgasbord of desserts. The place is packed during brunch, so be sure to make reservations well in advance.

French

If you've been exploring the northern reaches of the county, there is no reason to stick out the traffic on I-15 south in order to enjoy a fine meal. Barely within the northernmost fingers of city limits, Rancho Bernardo has several venerable French establishments worth stopping for.

Just off the Rancho Bernardo Road exit, **Bernard'O** (12457 Rancho Bernardo Rd., 858/487-7171, www.bernardorestaurant.com, lunch 11:30 A.M.–2 P.M. Wed.–Fri., dinner

5:30–9 P.M. Mon.–Thurs., 5–9:30 P.M. Fri.–Sat., 5–8:30 P.M. Sun., $25) serves a California French menu that mixes French cooking traditions with fresh California ingredients. A particular favorite is the California Bouillabaisse, a medley of seafood in a rouille lobster sauce.

About a mile away in the posh Rancho Bernardo Inn, (El Bizcocho (17550 Bernardo Oaks Dr., 858/675-8550, www.ranchobernardoinn.com/bizcocho, 6–9 P.M. Tues.–Sat., 10 A.M.–1 P.M. Sun., $35) is regarded by many critics as one of San Diego's best. An adherent of the molecular cuisine movement, chef Ryan Grant was voted best new chef of 2010 by San Diego Modern Luxury magazine. Entrust your taste buds—and your wallet—to the chef for a $120-per-person, seven-course tasting menu.

The neighborhood around **WineSellar & Brasserie** (9550 Waples St., #115, 858/450-9557, www.winesellar.com, lunch 11:30 A.M.–2 P.M. Thurs.–Sat., dinner from 5:30 P.M. Tues.–Fri., from 6 P.M. Sat., $35) is hardly anything to speak of—in fact it is more of an office park than a neighborhood—but this North City restaurant draws a crowd with its incredibly diverse wine selection and expert food pairings. Located just north of Marine Air Station Miramar on Sorrento Mesa, it frequently changes the menu to match the whims of the chef and the wine.

Asian

San Diego's Asian residents are well assimilated into the general citizenry so there are very few neighborhoods with concentrated Asian populations the way there are in other California cities such as Los Angeles or San Francisco. However, San Diego's thriving Korean community is particularly active amid the strip malls of Clairemont and Mira Mesa. Adventurous diners can't do wrong picking their way through the restaurants here that sometimes are not even labeled in English.

Many of the best restaurants are on Convoy Street. Here you can find **Korea House** (4620 Convoy St., #A, 858/560-0080, http://koreahousemenu.info, 11 A.M.–3 P.M. Mon.–Fri., $18), one of the best of the Korean barbecue places south of L.A. Also nearby is **Noodle Town** (4647 Convoy St., #105, 858/565-0403, 10 A.M.–midnight Mon.–Wed., 10 A.M.–2 A.M. Thurs.–Sun., $15), which specializes in every variety of Korean noodles from cold buckwheat *nehngnyum* to spicy *jam-bong.*

The Convoy area isn't exclusively Korean, either. **Emerald Chinese Seafood** (3709 Convoy St., #101, 858/565-6888, www.emeraldrestaurant.com, 11 A.M.–11 P.M. Mon.–Thurs., 11 A.M.–midnight Fri., 9 A.M.–midnight Sat., 9 A.M.–11 P.M. Sun., $13) offers the most authentic Cantonese cuisine in the county. Visit Sunday for dim sum, but be prepared to open the wallet wide as those little morsels add up.

The best Japanese is on Convoy, too. (**Izakaya Sakura** (3904 Convoy St., #121, 858/569-6151, 11 A.M.–10 P.M. daily, $10) is a hidden place that doesn't even have a sign out front, but it is well worth the hunt. It is located in the same shopping center as Wings and Things and the Original Pancake House. Step inside and see if you can find one of the few English menus floating around the place. Izakaya is like Japanese tapas, small entrées ordered as you go. Don't forget the beverages—the place has an assortment of sake that rivals a fine steakhouse's wine selection.

SOUTH BAY
Mexican

This close to the border it is difficult to go wrong when searching for delicious Mexican eats. If you insist on finding the "best" Mexican *comida* in South Bay on your own you might just find yourself eating through a lifetime's worth of *chilaquiles,* tacos, tamales, and burritos.

I'll help with a little crib sheet. In Chula Vista, **Tacos El Gordo** (689 H St., 619/691-8848, 10 A.M.–2 P.M. Sun.–Thurs., 10 A.M.–4 P.M. Sat.–Sun., $5) serves up some of the most authentic Tijuana-style street tacos this side of the *frontera.* Simplicity is this street taco's key: a small round disc of corn tortilla topped with meat still sizzling from the grill and garnished with a little bit of cilantro, onion, and salsa. The attraction of this particular place is its dazzling array of meats, from carne asada to spicy *adobada* pork, and from chorizo to *tripas*. You'll be able to bone up on the Mexican ingredient dictionary right from the counter.

A block away from the waves of Imperial Beach, **El Tapatio Mexican Food** (260 Palm Ave., Imperial Beach, 619/423-3443, 6 A.M.–9 P.M. daily, $6) is favored by surfers for its juicy carne asada burritos, but it also has other staples like fish tacos and *taquitos*.

Also in this neck of the woods is a place suited for family members who can't agree exactly on the type of Mexican food they crave: **Victoria's Mexican Food** (1912 Coronado Ave., Ste. 107, Imperial Beach, 619/429-1109, 24 hours daily,

$5). The menu is huge, with *tortas,* tacos, burritos, and soups rounding out the list.

Cafés and Diners
Just a little stand on the road to the Silver Strand from Imperial Beach, the much-loved **◖ Stardust Donut Shop** (698 Hwy. 75, 619/424-6200, 8:30 A.M.–2 P.M. Tues.–Fri., 9:30 A.M.–2 P.M. Sat., closed Sun., $3) draws faithful fans with its house specialty, the cinnamon roll. This pastry glazed with sticky icing is a secret that the late-waking regulars hope to keep under wraps for fear of stumbling up to the window after the shop has run out for the day. If you don't make it in time, the donuts are still a fine consolation.

Information and Services

MAPS AND TOURIST INFORMATION
Visitors Centers
The International Visitor Information Center (1040 ⅓ W. Broadway at Harbor Dr., 619/236-1212 or 619/230-7084, 9 A.M.–5 P.M. daily June–Sept., 9 A.M.–4 P.M. daily Oct.–May) along the Embarcadero is one of two major visitors centers run by the San Diego Convention and Visitors Bureau within San Diego County. Staff members at the center can provide visitors with a stack of useful guides and maps and should be able to answer questions or suggest activities based on individual needs. This location also has attraction and tour tickets available, sometimes at reduced rates.

In Coronado, the local chamber of commerce runs a **visitors center** (1110 Orange Ave., Coronado, 619/437-8788, 9 A.M.–5 P.M. Mon.–Fri., 10 A.M.–5 P.M. Sat.–Sun.) that is geared specifically to island activities.

Maps
Members of AAA can find service at two **Auto Club** locations: one in Mission Valley (2440 Hotel Circle N., 619/233-1000) and the other

in Clairemont (4973 Clairemont Dr., Ste. C, 858/483-4960).

EMERGENCY SERVICES
San Diego's central police department is located northeast of downtown. It operates numerous community stations, including a **Balboa Park station** (non-emergency 619/685-8206, 9 A.M.–4 P.M. Mon.–Thurs.) at 1549 El Prado.

As a separate municipality, Coronado Island has its own police force. Coronado police headquarters are at 700 Orange Avenue.

There are two major hospitals in the core of the city. **Scripps Mercy Hospital** (4020 5th Ave., 619/260-7022) is in Hillcrest. The **University of California-San Diego Medical Center** (200 W. Arbor Dr., 619/543-6222) is in Mission Valley.

MONEY AND COMMUNICATIONS
Banks
Downtown there are a number of banks west of 4th Avenue along West Broadway. In Hillcrest near Balboa Park, the largest and most convenient is **Bank of America** (737 University Ave.,

858/452-8400). Coronado visitors can look to the local **Coronado First Bank** (801 Orange Ave, Ste. 101, 619/437-1000) for service.

Post Offices

On Coronado Island, you can mail your postcards from the post office (1320 Ynez Pl.) in the village. Across the bay, there are several post offices downtown, including one inside of Horton Plaza (51 Horton Plaza) and a freestanding post office at 815 E Street. North of I-8, try the post office (5052 Clairemont Dr.) on Clairemont Mesa.

Internet Access

San Diego is very friendly to roaming computer users, with lots of free Wi-Fi hotspots across the city. Tourists armed with laptops can start looking for access at any of the libraries, all of which offer free wireless Internet. Those without their own computers can also take advantage of the free computer access provided at all of these public branches. Another very convenient option for those traveling without a laptop is **The Internet Place** (193 Horton Plaza, 619/702-4643, http:// tipsd.weebly.com, 10 A.M.–9 P.M.), which offers computers for $5.50 per hour. Those downtown can also wander anywhere on India Street from Cedar to Fir in Little Italy. The business district there beams out free wireless from an antenna on India and Date Streets.

Similarly, Normal Heights is constantly working on its NHWiFi Project (www.nhwifi. org) to provide free wireless Internet access to as much of the neighborhood as possible. The most reliable free hotspot here is at the corner of Adams and Bancroft Avenues.

For Balboa Park explorers, stop off near the Plaza de Balboa on the east side near the fountain. The Reuben H. Fleet Science Center's Galileo Café has a free hotspot there, and if it isn't busy they won't chase you away from their tables in the plaza outside.

Libraries

The facilities at San Diego's **Central Library** (820 E St., 619/236-5800, www.sandiego.gov/ public-library, noon–8 P.M. Mon. and Wed.,

9:30 A.M.–5:30 P.M. Tues. and Thurs.–Sat., 1–5 P.M. Sun.) can hardly compete with some of the municipal showpiece buildings that other cities boast. But the collection is decent and it is a good central spot for free computer and Internet access. Where the San Diego library system excels is in its wide network of branch libraries—there are 33 in all. Some of the smaller libraries have spotty hours of operation, but there are still plenty that are open nearly every day.

The **University Heights branch** (4193 Park Blvd., 619/692-4912, 12:30–8 P.M. Mon. and Wed., 9:30 A.M.–5:30 P.M. Tues. and Thurs.–Fri., 9:30 A.M.–2:30 P.M. Sat.) serves the area near Balboa Park. The **Mission Valley branch** (2123 Fenton Pkwy., 858/573-5007, 12:30–8 P.M.Mon. and Wed., 9:30 A.M.–5:30 P.M. Tues. and Thurs.–Fri., 9:30 A.M.–2:30 P.M. Sat., 1–5 P.M. Sun.) is convenient to Hotel Circle. And those in the north end of the city will feel comfortable in the well-appointed **Rancho Bernardo branch** (17110 Bernardo Center Dr., 858/538-8163, 12:30–8 P.M. Mon. and Wed., 9:30 A.M.–5:30 P.M. Tues. and Thurs.–Fri., 9:30 A.M.–2:30 P.M. Sat., 1–5 P.M. Sun.).

Newspapers

The *San Diego Union-Tribune* is the paper of record in town. For information on upcoming concerts and activities, your best bet is to find a copy of either the *San Diego Reader* or *San Diego CityBeat,* both of which are free alternative weeklies that offer comprehensive entertainment calendars.

LAUNDRY

Tending to a laundry emergency is twice as tedious when the San Diego sun is shining. Those looking for full-service laundry or dry cleaning should consider **Continental Cleaners and Laundry** (450 10th Ave., 619/232-3598), which offers cheap and fast full-service dry cleaning and laundering.

If you'd rather not have someone else handle your unmentionables, **Lucky Launderland** (4009 30th St., 619/280-8183) has one of the cleanest and friendliest self-serve facilities in the city.

Getting There and Around

BY AIR

San Diego's major airport is San Diego International Airport (SAN), right in the middle of downtown. The centralized location makes it easy to find a suitable transportation option to relay you to your hotel from here. The airport is small, with only two international terminals and one commuter terminal. The international terminals are adjacent to one another and the airport operates a short shuttle called the Red Bus from both of them over to the commuter terminal. These run punctually every 10 minutes and can be caught at the curb near the big red signs marked "The Red Bus Stops Here."

Airport Transportation

The San Diego public transit system operates the Airport Flyer (Rte. #992) between all three terminals to downtown. This bus takes approximately ten minutes to make the route one-way, for which the one-way fare is $2.25.

Taxis are available at the airport's Transportation Plaza. Follow the signs and wait in line for the transportation coordinator on-site to direct you to the next available taxi. Numerous private shuttle services also offer van pickup from both terminals. These include **Xpress Shuttle** (800/900-7433) and **Cloud 9 Shuttle** (800/974-8885).

Airport Car Rental

Because of its central location, San Diego International has limited real estate, so there are no car rentals on site. However, most major rental companies have lots within a mile of the airport and they all run convenient and very frequent shuttles from the transportation islands located at each terminal. Phone kiosks are located in the baggage terminals in order to call ahead.

Rental companies located nearby include **Alamo** (2942 Kettner Blvd., 619/297-0311), **Avis** (3180 N. Harbor Dr., 619/231-7171), **Dollar** (2499 Pacific Hwy., 619/234-3389),

Enterprise (1691 Hancock St., 619/225-8881), **Hertz** (3202 N. Harbor Dr., 619/220-5222), and **National** (3280 N. Harbor Dr., 619/497-6777).

Airport Parking

Compared to many major international airports, parking at this one is cheap. Short-term parking in the main lots is only $1 per hour and there are free "cell phone" lots available to those who are meeting friends or family at the airport. Drivers simply pull into the lot and can wait there for up to an hour until they make contact with arriving passengers and agree on a spot for pick-up on the main terminal drive.

There are three major long-term parking lots around the airport, but the largest and the cheapest is **SAN Park Pacific Highway** (3302 Pacific Hwy.), which costs $10 per day. Be sure to arrive at least ten minutes earlier than you normally would in order to account for the shuttle ride to the terminal.

BY TRAIN AND TROLLEY

San Diego is serviced by Amtrak at the downtown **Santa Fe Depot** (1050 Kettner Blvd., 619/239-9021, 5:15 A.M.–10 P.M. daily).

Before you rush off to the beaches, museums, or the waterfront, take a look around the station. The depot is an amazing Mission Revival building that is in the Historic American Buildings Survey, San Diego's Historical Site Board Register, and the National Register of Historic Places. Like Balboa Park, it was built for the Panama-California Exposition in 1915–1916.

This busy station is also the southernmost stop for San Diego Northern's Coaster commuter train. Validated Coaster tickets can be used for a free transfer to the **Airport Flyer** (city bus #992) to the San Diego International Airport, which departs from the station at the northeast corner of Kettner and Broadway every 12 to 15 minutes between 5 A.M. and

12:52 A.M. It should take 10 minutes to get to the airport from the train station.

In addition, the depot is home to the hub of the San Diego Trolley System, which can provide transport to other areas in the city upon arrival at the station.

BY BUS

Those arriving by Greyhound bus will find themselves dumped at the downtown **bus station** (120 W. Broadway, 619/239-6737). Unlike many a metropolitan Greyhound station, this is in a pretty safe neighborhood. Gaslamp hostels and other lodging options are within walking distance and there is usually a queue of taxis waiting to whisk you off to wherever you choose.

Mexicoach (619/428-9517, www.mexicoach.com) bus lines are an option for those traveling to and from Mexico. The downtown Mexicoach station is at the Santa Fe Depot.

DRIVING

Like most of Southern California's cities, San Diego is undeniably a driving town. The city is very easy to navigate, though sometimes difficult to explain due to its geographical size. Major freeways running north–south are I-5, I-805, and I-15. I-5 and I-805 run parallel to one another between La Jolla in the north and San Ysidro to the south, at which points they merge together. I-15 begins at the interchange with I-8 in Mission Valley.

Other minor freeways running north–south are Route 163 (running from an I-5 interchange in Balboa Park until it crosses paths with I-15 in Miramar), Route 15 (from I-5 downtown until it transitions into I-15 at I-8), and Route 75, of which the Coronado Bridge is a part and which runs the length of the Silver Strand down to Imperial Beach.

East to west the major freeway is I-8, which rolls along from the ocean at Ocean Beach, through Mission Valley, and all the way across the county and the rest of the state. Other lesser freeways include Route 52 from I-5 at La Jolla, past Miramar and through the town of Santee, and Route 94 running through Midcity.

Parking

Parking is usually ample in areas such as Mission Valley and North City. Spots are scarce downtown on any given day, and during tourist season Balboa Park and Old Town can be a nightmare.

One of the best bets downtown for an open stall is the expansive garage servicing Horton Plaza. Save yourself the aggravation and cough up the $6 per hour to park here, rather than circling the block and worrying about feeding quarters into the streetside meters. Not that I've ever done this, but I hear the cheapskate trick is to park in this lot and stop by Longs Drugs in the plaza to pick up a candy bar and a three-hour parking validation for your troubles.

In Old Town the lots directly surrounding the state park fill up first. One lot that many tourists miss is the large parking area that services Old Town Transit Center. Park here and venture through the underpass tunnel that takes you directly to the park's boundaries.

Most days you'll be able to find a spot in one of Balboa Park's numerous lots, but when there is an event going on, things can get hairy. Unfortunately, during the daytime, what you see here is what you get. Keep circling the lots, as people come and go frequently. Perhaps one of the least utilized lots is the one at Inspiration Point, just across Park Boulevard on the southeast side of the park. From this location it's a trek into the center of the park, but it is serviced by a tram that runs along President's Way all the way to Plaza de Panama. At night, if you're willing to spare $10 plus tip the park offers valet service at the House of Hospitality. Service runs Tuesday–Thursday 5–10 P.M., Friday 5 P.M.–midnight, Saturday 10 A.M.–midnight, and Sunday 10 A.M.–10 P.M. There is no valet parking on Mondays.

PUBLIC TRANSIT

Though it probably has some of the best public transit in the region, there are still often quite a few concessions and compromises that will need to be made when traveling without a set of wheels. Those who plan to stay in the city center and stick to attractions along the waterfront, downtown, and around Balboa Park may find that they can get away with skipping a car rental and rely on buses and trolleys instead. Rather than paying full fare each time you ride, it might make sense to pick up a transit pass. For $5 you can ride unlimited for one day, $9 for two days, $12 for three days, and $15 for four. Passes can be purchased at the **Transit Store** (102 Broadway, 619/234-1060, www.sdcommute.com).

Bus

Downtown most of the major routes run along Broadway between Front Street and 9th Avenue. This is also where the Transit Store is located. Go there for timetables and maps and unlimited-ride passes.

The major bus hub is located at the Old Town Transit Center, which acts as a transfer point between the trolley, many of the buses that shuttle from downtown and parts south to those in the northern part of the city, and the beach communities. This center also has ample parking, making it a good option for park-and-ride users who may want to avoid parking hassles in high-traffic areas such as the beaches.

Trolley

The San Diego Trolley system has over 55 trolley stations throughout city limits and more beyond, reaching south all the way down to the border. This light rail system is by no means as complete as the New York subway system, but it does act as a decent means of conveyance between centrally located sights, lodging, and spectator sports venues such as Petco Park and Qualcomm Stadium.

The one missing link in the trolley system is its lack of service to the city beach communities. In order to get there via public transport you'll have to catch the trolley to Old Town Transit Center and transfer to a bus headed northwest.

For more information and maps, visit www.sdcommute.com or stop by the Transit Store (102 Broadway, 619/234-1060).

Ferry

Coronado Island has been easily reachable from downtown by car since the construction of the Coronado Bridge in 1969. However, it is still possible to take to the water the old-fashioned way and ride over on a ferry (619/234-4111, www.sdhe.com, $3.75 one-way, with or without a bicycle). The ferry leaves downtown at the Broadway Pier (1050 N. Harbor Dr.) every hour on the hour starting at 9 A.M. and arrives at Coronado's Ferry Landing Marketplace (1st St. and B Ave.) about a half hour later. Similarly, the ferry departs from Coronado on the half hour every hour starting at 9:30 A.M. During the week, the last ferry departs from downtown at 9 P.M. and from Coronado at 9:30 P.M. Operation is extended by one hour on Fridays and Saturdays.

TOURS
Bus and Trolley Tours

Old Town Trolley Tours (4010 Twiggs St., 800/213-2474, $30 adults, $15 children 4–12, free under 4) is one of the most complete guided trips in the city. These bright-orange trolley buses start from Old Town and wind their way along the waterfront, through downtown and the Gaslamp, over the Coronado Bay Bridge and into downtown Coronado, back over the bridge and up to Balboa Park, returning to Old Town after two hours. The dandy part about the arrangement is that there are eight stops along the way at key tourist destinations and riders are encouraged to hop off their current bus to eat or sightsee and hop back on any of the other buses that come by every half hour. Tours run daily between 9 A.M. and 4 P.M., until 5 P.M. in the summer.

It's corny, it's fun, and your teenagers will hate you for taking them on a **SEAL Tour** (619/298-8687, www.sandiegoseals.com, 10 A.M.–4 P.M. Oct.–May, 10 A.M.–5 P.M. June–Sept.). These off-the-wall land and sea tours are taken aboard a colorfully painted amphibious bus that guides you through the nature, history, and culture of San Diego's Big Bay. The tours start from Seaport Village and go along the Embarcadero and up through Point Loma to take to the water from Shelter Island. In total you'll be exploring for about 90 minutes. A lightweight jacket is recommended.

Boat Tours

The San Diego shoreline is a beautiful sight from the water. There are a number of boat tours on the Big Bay to choose from.

San Diego Harbor Excursions (www.sdhe. com) offers a number of different kinds of trips from its dock on the Embarcadero. Its signature boat ride is the Dinner Cruise ($66.50 adults, $37.50 children ages 4–12), a two-and-a-half-hour trip around the bay that departs at 7:30 P.M. daily, even on holidays. In addition the company offers whale-watching trips hosted by naturalists from the Birch Aquarium, nature trips to the uninhabited Los Coronados Islands off the Mexican coast, and one- to two-hour harbor tours.

Boat lovers can also choose to take similar tours with **Hornblower Cruises** (1066 N. Harbor Dr., 888/467-6256, www.hornblower. com), which offers nightly dinner dance cruises for $65 as well as its very own whale watching cruises.

To feel the wind in your hair, hop aboard the **Maritime Museum of San Diego's Californian** (1492 North Harbor Dr., 619/234-9153), a topsail schooner that is designated the official Tall Ship of the State of California. The museum runs daily sailing trips at 1 P.M. These four-hour trips can be as interactive as you want them to be, as the ship's skipper allows riders young and old to help sail the boat if they are interested.

Walking Tours

Learn about the booms and busts of the Gaslamp Quarter on Saturdays at 11 A.M., when the **Gaslamp Foundation** (www. gaslampquarter.org) runs a walking tour that starts at the William Heath Davis Historic House Museum and passes by some of the best examples of Victorian-style commercial buildings that still stand in the district. The walk costs $10, $8 for seniors, students, and members of the military.

The Black Historical Society of San Diego also runs its own Gaslamp walking tour called the **Harlem of the West Tour** (520 E. St., www.harlemofthewest.com, $5, free 16 and younger), which departs from the lobby of the Gaslamp Plaza Suites Hotel every Saturday at 11 A.M. This 45-minute tour will take you to sites of some of the most historic black businesses, jazz and blues establishments, and community gathering spots.

An informative pre-recorded audio guide can be rented from the **Balboa Park Visitors Center** (1549 El Prado, 619/239-0512, 9:30 A.M.–4:30 P.M. daily, $5 adults, $4 seniors, students, and active military, $3 children 3–11). The hour-and-a-half walking tour offers a breezy and fun look at the park's architectural, horticultural, and cultural attractions.

The state park runs free guided tours of Old Town State Historic Park at 11 A.M. and 2 P.M. every day. The tour departs from the Robinson-Rose House Visitor Center and will give you a rich understanding of the cultural and historical background of San Diego's oldest community.

CITY BEACHES AND POINT LOMA

In just a few short miles of ocean shoreline, the city beaches of San Diego offer varied landscapes that appeal to a variety of sensibilities. Hidden cove beaches provide a space for solitude and private meditation, while open sandy shores attract crowds and bring out the social animal in all of us. Sandstone cliffs encourage pensive thought. Rocky tide pools delight curiosity.

The diverse scenery is reflected in the assortment of people it attracts. In a beachside café you're just as likely to cross paths with a fisherman as you are with a yacht owner. Buzz-cut Marines are as likely to toss their blanket on the sand next to yours as dreadlocked hippies. At a stoplight it is possible to see a Rolls Royce pull up behind a rusted-out pickup with a surfboard hanging out of the tailgate. Look over to the sidewalk while you wait and you just might see a middle-aged skateboarder rolling side-by-side with his teenaged son.

All of these disparate characters create the fabric of a community that celebrates its differences. The diversity doesn't create friction; instead it is a testament to the welcoming atmosphere found here.

PLANNING YOUR TIME

You can easily drive through all of the city beach neighborhoods in under an hour, but as many transplant residents will tell you, it can take a lifetime to explore the beaches and the streets that surround them. Because of the accessibility between each neighborhood, plan your itinerary around your interests rather than

© NATALIA BRATSLAVSKY/123RF.COM

HIGHLIGHTS

◖ **The Strand:** Find the quintessential Southern California beach along this two-mile length of sandy seashore (page 114).

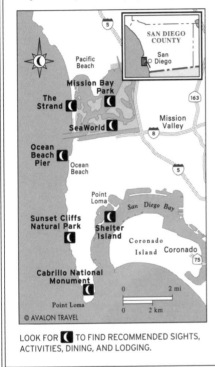

LOOK FOR ◖ TO FIND RECOMMENDED SIGHTS, ACTIVITIES, DINING, AND LODGING.

◖ **Mission Bay Park:** What was once mudflats is now a little slice of heaven for boaters and picnickers at the largest artificially constructed aquatic park in the country (page 116).

◖ **SeaWorld:** Parked on the shores of Mission Bay, this adventure park has something for animal lovers and thrill-seekers alike (page 117).

◖ **Ocean Beach Pier:** The longest concrete pier on the West Coast, this is a good spot from which to cast a line, soak in the sunset, or watch surfers threading the pylons aboard their rides (page 134).

◖ **Sunset Cliffs Natural Park:** The scenic and sheer sandstone formations along Point Loma's eastern face reflect the light in a majestic fashion during sundown (page 134).

◖ **Cabrillo National Monument:** Perched on top of the very tip of Point Loma, the views of San Diego Bay and the ocean are unparalleled here. Named after the first explorer to discover the area, it is also home to several historical curiosities and a national cemetery (page 135).

◖ **Shelter Island:** Shimmied up next to the eastern side of the Point Loma peninsula, this island is home to marinas, hotels, and restaurants. Unwind in the city-view park that stretches along its entire length (page 136).

worrying about sticking to a particular area of town on any given day.

There are innumerable opportunities for adventure seekers. Learn to surf at **Tourmaline Surfing Park** or near the Ocean Beach Pier. Or zip around **Mission Bay** on a personal watercraft. Scramble around the precipices that make up **Sunset Cliffs Natural Park.** Or simply take a stroll along the Mission Bay Boardwalk. All of these activities are in such close proximity that it is easy to hit several in a single day and still leave time to venture to **Point Loma,** which acts as a complementary

southern bookend to the beach neighborhoods. As one of the oldest neighborhoods in the city, this area features highlights of San Diego's past. Be sure to visit **Cabrillo National Monument,** which features historic coastal gun emplacements and the **Old Point Loma Lighthouse.** If you are an antique hunter, stop off at the **Ocean Beach Antique District** on your drive south.

Just try not to cram too much in, or you won't fit in with the locals. No matter which beach you're near, stress should never be on the schedule.

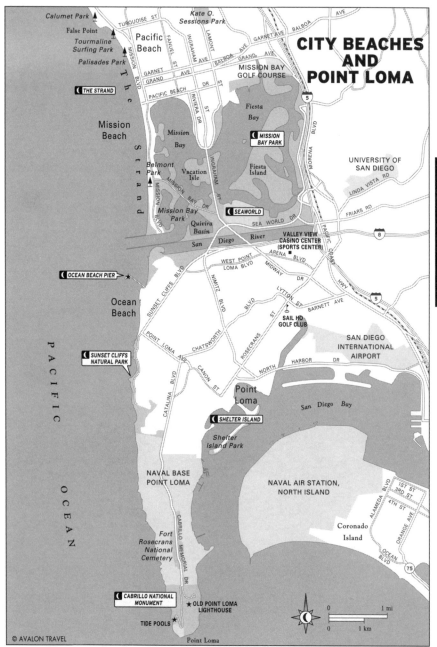

CITY BEACHES AND POINT LOMA

CITY BEACHES

Pacific Beach and Mission Beach

Sandwiched between the ocean's swells and Mission Bay's glassy waters are two prototypical California neighborhoods that draw an eclectic crowd of locals, transplants, and wayfarers with one common bond: love of sand, surf, and sun. The combination of these three magic ingredients seems to be the perfect cocktail to lull visitors into the easy frame of mind so typical of the locals in Mission Beach and Pacific Beach.

Cruising down Mission Boulevard, the main drag that strings the two beach neighborhoods together, you'll see all the things you expect to see in coastal Southern California: sun-bleached surfer dudes, Royal Palms reaching skyward, and a glimpse out to sea at every cross street. But it's the things—and the people—you don't expect that really define the area: a hotel perched up on a pier, paunchy old men skipping across the street with longboards under-arm, couples riding skateboards side-by-side holding hands, and toddlers swinging playfully from Mom and Dad's tattoo-covered arms.

Driving south from La Jolla, you'll hit Pacific Beach first. Affectionately called "PB" by the locals, it's larger than its neighbor Mission Beach, and is generally where beach residents rest their heads each night. Consequently, there are many more hidden restaurants and bars to be found on quiet streets out of the main commercial districts.

Mission Beach, on the other hand, is hardly more than water and sand with Mission Boulevard running through both elements. The neighborhood is long and skinny on the map, at some points only a couple of blocks wide. The narrow grid of streets between bay and ocean are organized chaos—a collection of beach shacks and luxury rentals, restaurants and bars, all built upon one another with no seeming borders. The funny thing is, it doesn't seem cluttered. The coexistence just adds to the charm and vitality of the area.

Pacific Beach shoreline

© ERICKA CHICKOWSKI

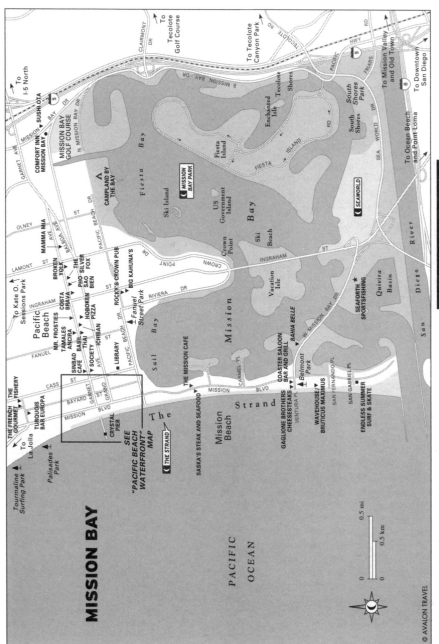

CITY BEACHES

© AVALON TRAVEL

SIGHTS
Belmont Park

The seaside rides at Belmont Park (3146 Mission Blvd., 619/491-2988, 11 A.M.–8 P.M. Mon.–Thurs., 11 A.M.–10 P.M. Fri.–Sun. Oct.–Apr.; 11 A.M.–11 P.M. Sun.–Thurs., 11 A.M.–midnight Fri.–Sun. May–Sept.) are a blend of old-school carnival thrills and newer rides. Its longtime jewel is the Giant Dipper roller coaster. Originally built in 1925, the wooden coaster still packs enough punch to keep most adventure-seekers happy.

Prices on rides vary, but visitors can buy unlimited-ride wristbands to avoid the hassle and expense of ride tickets. Those under 50 inches in height pay $13.95, while taller riders pay $19.85.

Also within Belmont Park are two stationary wave machines operated by **Wavehouse** (3127 ½ Ocean Front Walk, 858/228-9283, www.wavehousesandiego.com), including **Bruticus Maximus** (11 A.M.–8 P.M. daily). Bruticus simulates some of the sickest tube waves that have challenged and bested the most talented surfers in the world. A crack at Bruticus's beginner wave requires a one-time registration fee of $10

and costs $20 per hour. Advanced waves are double that: $20 initially and $40 per hour.

Crystal Pier

Sitting like a sentry at the terminus of the happening Garnet Avenue, Crystal Pier (sunrise–sunset, free) is a good place to break out a rod and reel or to just look seaward in contemplation. Some of the more talented local surfers like to stake out a spot in the water just north of the pier, so this PB landmark also makes a good vantage point to watch their snaps, floaters, and cutbacks when big swells roll in.

◖ The Strand

Spanning several miles through both Mission Beach and Pacific Beach, the Strand is San Diego's quintessential stretch of sand. In the summer you can just let your nose carry you through the sights. The smells of brine, hot asphalt, lighter fluid, sizzling burgers, football leather—they all mix with the sweet tropical scent of SPF collectively rising off sunbathers' lotioned bodies.

Typically, families and couples will head down the steep wooden steps from the streets

Giant Dipper at Belmont Park

© ERICKA CHICKOWSKI

PACIFIC BEACH WATERFRONT

PACIFIC SHORES INN
BAYARD ST
MISSOURI ST
BEACH HAVEN INN
DIAMOND ST
PACIFIC TERRACE HOTEL
EMERALD ST
POST OFFICE
CASS STREET
MAD DOGS CAFÉ
THRUSTERS'S LOUNGE
CASS STREET BAR & GRILL
PACIFIC OCEAN
JRDN TACO SURF
FELSPAR ST
CAFÉ 976
PB BAR & GRILL
SULLY'S ST
TOWERR 23
GARNET
OLDE CITY GRILL
710 BEACH CLUB
MOONDOGGIES
CRYSTAL PIER
BAR WEST
CRYSTAL PIER HOTEL & COTTAGES
PACIFIC BEACH SHORE CLUB
GRAND
RALPH'S
THOMAS AVE
OPEN BAR
BLVD
THE BANANA BUNGALOW
MISSION BAY MOTEL
LAHAINA
OLIVER AVE
THE EGGERY
RED'S SALOON
PACIFIC BEACH DR
WORLD FAMOUS
PACIFIC BEACH SURF SHOP

0   200 yds
0   200 m

© AVALON TRAVEL

© CITY BEACHES

up right to street level, making it easy to drag a keg out to the beach. During the summer the volleyball courts south of the pier are always hopping, and you can usually find at least a few college kids playing football in board shorts and backwards caps nearby.

Even farther south, close to Belmont Park, the scene calms down again. This is an excellent spot for families who aren't staying in the beaches area, as it is close to the only free public parking lot along the Strand.

Mission Beach Boardwalk

One of the best places to soak in the character of San Diego's beaches isn't on the sand, but instead the paved walkway of the Mission Beach Boardwalk. Winding three miles from **Palisades Park** in Pacific Beach down to the jetty at Mission Bay's inlet, the boardwalk is lined by vacation rentals and little motels, and occasionally peppered with restaurants, coffee stands, and beach vendors.

Heading south from Palisades, the walkway starts on a cliff overlooking the beach. After about a half a mile you'll pass Crystal Pier and get a peek up Garnet Avenue before

of Pacific Beach to find a spot out on the sand north of Crystal Pier. The atmosphere is more subdued here.

Head south for crazier fun closer to Mission Beach. At about Grand Avenue the beach slopes

© ERICKA CHICKOWSKI

A cyclist cruises the Mission Beach Boardwalk.

reaching a point where the terrain levels out and the boardwalk is even with the sand on the beach. Meandering farther, the walkway will likely be more congested with revelers as you reach the bars and restaurants near Oliver and Reed Streets. From there it is full-steam ahead until you reach Belmont Park, which is the last concentration of commerce along the walkway before reaching its final point at the jetty.

The walk is populated with a diverse cast of characters, including some amusing regulars that you should keep your eyes peeled for. This includes Slo-Mo, an older man who goes so slowly on his inline skates it's a marvel he doesn't fall over. He's usually carrying an old boom box with him to share his tunes with the rest of the boardwalk—shout out his nickname and he'll give you a wave. For years a man known as The Flash has streaked by on the holidays in inappropriately appropriate garb—one Easter he was roller-skating in a bunny get-up of costume ears, a thong bikini bottom, and '80s-style roller skates. Sandman, as he's known locally, is a little more G-rated and far more stationary. He'll use his broom to design cool sketches in the sand that blows onto the boardwalk.

Tourmaline Surfing Park

If you want to learn a little bit about the spirit of surfing, spend some time in the parking lot at Tourmaline Surfing Park (Tourmaline St. and La Jolla Blvd.), just north of the Strand. The asphalt is a staging ground for the park's beach, but it's almost a social scene in its own right. There you'll find old-timers and "kooks" (new surfers) chatting while waxing their boards, dancing their way into wetsuits, and scanning the horizon to figure out a good paddle-in route.

Here new arrivals mingle with their dripping-wet "bros" in arms, who skip back toward the lot's bathrooms and shower off after a good session. The whole area has the electricity of a schoolyard at lunchtime, only without the bullies. Old friends crack jokes, newcomers make

small talk, and it seems like the good times will never end.

◖ Mission Bay Park

At 4,600 acres, Mission Bay Park (best access from E. Mission Bay Dr., Ingraham St., and W. Mission Bay Dr.) is the largest man-made aquatic park in the country. Once a salt marsh consisting primarily of mudflats, the bay was dredged in 1944 to create the palm-lined recreational paradise that it is today. Most of the 27 miles of shoreline along this irregularly shaped bay is beach with adjacent grass, giving picnickers, kite flyers, and sunbathers plenty of room to spread out. The bay itself has a number of little inlets and coves, and even a couple of islands that are navigated by an endless stream of boats and personal watercraft.

One of those islands, **Fiesta Island,** is particularly noteworthy. This 485-acre mass of land was created with the extra soil acquired from dredging the bay. The land has a paved road looping through it, but it has largely been left unimproved, giving visitors a less manicured but more natural space to visit. All of Fiesta Island is leash free, and in one corner of the island there is a large area fenced for dogs, making this a particularly great stop for those traveling with pets. Access is easy: Take Fiesta Island Road from East Mission Bay Drive.

The well-manicured beaches around the bay are easily toured via **Bayside Walk,** a wide and largely wheelchair-accessible path that leads around much of the park. Easiest access to the walkway is at the Crown Point lot along Crown Point Drive with ample free parking.

By water, the bay can also be explored by the boatless aboard the *Bahia Belle* (3999 Mission Blvd., 858/539-7779, www.sternwheeler.com, $10 adults, $3 children 12 and under), a Mississippi-style sternwheeler that hosts evening cruises around the bay. Cruises shuttle between the Bahia and Catamaran hotels, with round-trips lasting one hour. Kids and teens under the age of 21 are allowed on the early boats until 9:30 P.M. when the cocktail cruises commence.

◖ SeaWorld

Perhaps San Diego's most recognized attraction, SeaWorld (500 SeaWorld Dr., 800/257-4268, www.seaworld.com, from 9 A.M. daily mid-summer through fall, 10 A.M. daily the rest of year, closing times vary, general admission $69, kids 3–9 $59, kids 2 and under free) offers families a mix of animal fun and amusement-park action. This 189-acre park on the shores of Mission Bay offers smaller kids a chance to see Shamu, has a couple of heart-thumping rides for teens, and even has a beer-tasting pavilion for adults looking for a little refreshment.

Kate O. Sessions Park

Hidden away in one of PB's quieter neighborhoods, the hillside Kate O. Sessions Park (Lamont St. and Soledad Rd.) offers incredible views of Mission Bay and the beaches. Picnic tables and barbecues are scattered, but the best spots are on the oft-blanketed lawn.

The park also features a more natural section on its north side, with a short but satisfying little trail that winds through native chaparral.

Palisades Park

Palisades Park (btwn. Crystal Dr. and Law St. along the boardwalk) is a scenic little park perched atop the cliffs overlooking the Pacific Beach shoreline. The park is the northernmost point on the boardwalk and is a great spot to cuddle with a loved one while watching the sunset.

Fanuel Street Park

Near Mission Bay, Fanuel Street Park (Fanuel St. and Bayfront Walk along the bay) is a good place to start a stroll down Bayside Walk. The park is right next to the path and has a small parking lot. The park also features a fun jungle gym for the kids, a large lawn for picnicking, restrooms, and a fish-cleaning station for lucky anglers fishing the bay.

ENTERTAINMENT AND EVENTS
Nightlife
BARS

The singles scene in Pacific Beach is legendary among college-aged kids in Southern California and beyond. Walking through the area, it sometimes seems as if the entire local economy is fueled by bars, tattoo parlors, and smoke shops. Much of the partying is centered in the commercial district of Garnet Avenue, though there are also plenty of watering holes along the beach and scattered over side streets as well.

On Garnet, **PB Bar and Grill** (860 Garnet Ave., 858/272-4745, www.pbbarandgrill.com, 11 A.M.–1:45 A.M. Mon.–Sat., 9 A.M.–1:45 A.M. Sun.) is a popular stop for those celebrating their 21st birthdays. Undeniably the most aggressive "meat market" in the entire city, it can be fun if you just loosen up and embrace it for what it is, cheesy pick-up lines and all.

Right next door, **Moondoggies** (832 Garnet Ave., 858/483-6550, www.moondoggies.com, 11 A.M.–2 A.M. daily) has its fair share of

SeaWorld's orcas are some of San Diego's best-known animal ambassadors.

COURTESY OF SEA WORLD

CITY BEACHES

college co-eds, but the atmosphere is a little more relaxed.

A few blocks farther from the beach, **Sinbad Café** (1050 Garnet Ave., 858/866-6006, www.sinbadcafe.com, 11 A.M.–2 A.M. Sun.–Thurs., 11 A.M.–4 A.M. Fri.–Sat.) not only offers refreshments, but also the opportunity to share a measure of flavored tobacco with your pals in one of its ornate hookah pipes. The tobacco is mild, imbued only with the fruit flavor of choice, so even non-smokers can enjoy this communal activity.

If they were holding red plastic cups you'd think the crowds at **Open Bar** (4302 Mission Blvd., 858/270-3221, 1 P.M.–2 A.M. Mon.–Fri., 10 A.M.–2 A.M. Sat.–Sun.) were at a college kegger. On big nights the young and rowdy crowd absolutely jams the deck for some raucous fun.

WINE BARS

The atmosphere is sultry at **Turquoise Bar Europa** (873 Turquoise St., 858/488-4200, www.cafebareuropa.com, 5 P.M.–midnight Mon.–Wed., 5 P.M.–2 A.M. Thurs.–Fri., 11 A.M.–2 A.M. Sat.–Sun.) an out-of-the-way but popular bar that attracts a packed house most days of the week with its daily evening jazz sets. Come prepared to make an evening out of it and order drinks two at a time if you can. While the bar is a pleasant place to linger over your vino, the service is very slow here.

While Turquoise likes to tout its sangria, if that's your poison you're better off taking a pass and finding a stool at the bar of **Costa Brava** (1653 Garnet Ave., 858/273-1218, www.costabravasd.com, 11 A.M.–midnight daily), a favorite haunt among the Spaniards in town who come for the tapas and the soccer games on the bar's flat-screens.

DIVE BARS

Why settle for the hair of the dog when you can have the fox instead? **The Silver Fox** (1833 Garnet Ave., 858/270-1343, www.silverfoxlounge.com, 6 A.M.–2 A.M. daily) that is. This dodgy little hole is renowned by the locals as one of the earliest opening bars on Garnet and

GETTING INKED

Body art is de rigueur in Mission Beach and Pacific Beach, with tattoo parlors almost as plentiful as the bars that jam the area's storefronts. These establishments are all part of a San Diego culture of acceptance that celebrates the artistry of "tats." No one knows for sure exactly what it is that has made San Diego such an inky city, but it probably has to do with a mix of factors, including the area's long seafaring history and its counterculture surf-and-skate scene.

If you decide to commemorate your trip with something as permanent as a tattoo, be sure to take some time between the trip to the bar and the one to the tattoo seat. Drunken tattoo decisions are rarely good ones, especially considering that the truly professional artists will turn you away if you're inebriated.

Experts recommend that you shop around a little for both the right shop and the right artist. By visiting a couple of shops, you can compare levels of cleanliness and professionalism. Ask to see pictures of an artist's past work to see if their style matches what you have in mind.

Some of the most popular and well-regarded shops are located on Garnet Avenue, including **Chronic Tattoo** (1253 Garnet Ave., #B, 858/274-9140, noon–10 P.M. daily), which only inks original designs, and **Guru Tattoo** (1122 Garnet Ave., 858/270-1070, noon–9 P.M. Sun.-Thurs., noon–10 P.M. Fri.-Sat.).

is a frequent stop-over in the morning after a raging all-nighter. It's also a chill spot to bust out the pool cues or the darts and enjoy a few beers before the next all-nighter. The mix of drinkers varies from crusty old-timers to fun-loving bottle blondes.

Little more than a long bar in a slightly longer hallway, **Red's Saloon** (4190 Mission Blvd., 858/750-2512, http://thebeachwood.com/content/reds-saloon, 11 A.M.–2 A.M. Mon.–Fri., 10 A.M.–2 A.M. Sat.–Sun.) simplicity is its biggest charm. Tucked into the unassuming Promenade strip mall just a few paces from the beach, Red's is a nice dark place to duck into after a little too much sand and sun.

BEACH BARS

By day, probably the most in-demand beach-side property in either PB or Mission Beach is on the deck at **Lahaina** (710 Oliver Ave., 858/270-3888, 9 A.M.–9 P.M. daily). Tacked onto an oceanfront beach shack, this veranda is standing-room-only in the summertime, with crowds often spilling out onto the adjacent boardwalk. Since alcohol was banned at the beach in 2008, the deck here is as close as you can get to drinking on the beach without risking a ticket.

Whether it's a Sunday morning, a Wednesday evening, or a Saturday night on the town, head up the stairs to **Pacific Beach Shore Club** (4343 Ocean Blvd., 858/272-7873, www.pb-shoreclub.com, 11 A.M.–2 A.M. Mon.–Fri., 8 A.M.–2 A.M. Sat.–Sun.) and you're bound to mingle into a crowd. Set on the second story of a building directly abutting the boardwalk at the end of Grand Avenue, this hoppin' bar offers phenomenal sunset views over the ocean and the Pacific Beach lifeguard tower. Locals come to catch NFL games on the big screen, dance a little, or just stand around and flirt a little with the available chicks and dudes that come supplied with coquettish smiles and pat pick-up lines.

Because the Mission Beach neighborhood is situated on such a small amount of land—the bulk of which is taken up by rental properties—the range of watering holes is a little more limited than in Pacific Beach. But there are definitely a couple of notable highlights. Close enough to the beach that you'll track sand over the doorway and right across the street from the Big Dipper, **Coaster Saloon Bar and Grill** (744 Ventura Pl., 858/488-4438, www.coasterssaloon.com, 9 A.M.–2 A.M. Mon.–Fri., 8 A.M.–2 A.M. Sat.–Sun.) absorbs a bit of the carnival atmosphere with a sometimes-rowdy tourist crowd blowing off steam away from home.

If you're looking for something different, visit **Wavehouse Bar and Grill** (3127 ½ Ocean Front Walk, 858/228-9283, 11 A.M.–midnight Sun.–Wed., 11 A.M.–12:30 A.M. Thurs.–Sat.) to watch the waterworks. It's a hoot to watch surfers try their hand on the barrel wave machine, Bruticus Maximus. When they're good it is very exciting, and when they're not, well, sometimes it's kind of funny.

If you'd rather enjoy the ocean view in something a little more formal than board shorts, the snazzy bar at **JRDN** (723 Felspar St., 858/270-5736, www.jrdn.com, 11 A.M.–midnight daily, closing hours may vary) over in Pacific beach is a hip spot to sip a martini and stare over the boardwalk and at the ocean. Lit with a dim kaleidoscope of colors over the sleek bar and the glow of fire pits, the open-air atmosphere here takes the beach bar vibe and dresses it up a little without compromising the relaxation factor.

PUBS AND TAVERNS

Because it is hidden away from the traffic of Garnet Avenue, **Cass Street Bar and Grill** (4612 Cass St., 858/270-1320, 10 A.M.–2 A.M. Mon.–Fri., 9 A.M.–2 A.M. Sat.–Sun.) is frequently missed by tourists. Too bad, because the patrons who frequent this place can be a breath of fresh air compared to the homogenous crowds a few blocks away. Salty old men with their dogs tied up out front, married couples on a night out away from the kids, and young professionals all mingle in this relaxed, open-air establishment. In addition to being a good bar, its food is also head and shoulders above typical pub fare. Bring a wad of bills, though, because the grub is cash only.

DANCE CLUBS AND LOUNGES

Outside of the Gaslamp District downtown, the beaches have the best collection of night-time entertainment in the region.

Visit **Club Tremors** (860 Garnet Ave., 858/272-4745, 9 P.M.–1:30 A.M. Tues., Thurs.–Sat.) to get your groove on. Actually a part of the popular PB Bar and Grill, Tremors plays the typical hip hop and Top 40s tunes you'd expect at a club that caters to the college set. You can either choose to get in for free by waiting in line to get into the bar and migrating over, or jump the line by paying the cover at the Tremors entrance.

For trance, hip-hop, and other thumping tunes mixed by a skilled DJ, **Thruster's Lounge** (4633 Mission Blvd., 858/483-6334, 1 P.M.–2 A.M. daily) is a surprising venue. Little more than a shoebox with mirrors (including a comically small dance floor), Thrusters still has a loyal following of techno enthusiasts who pack the place on weekends.

Just a couple of blocks away from Garnet, **Bar West** (959 Hornblend St., Pacific Beach, 858/273-9378, 9 P.M.–2 A.M. Thurs.–Sat., 9 P.M.–1 A.M. Sun.) caters to the slightly older set who are more accustomed to premium-label liquor and bottle service. Owned by the same folks who run Stingaree over in the Gaslamp, this club delivers the downtown scene without the traffic and parking issues.

It's a musical free-for-all at **710 Beach Club** (710 Garnet Ave., 858/483-7844, www.710bc. com, 1 P.M.–2 A.M. daily) in Pacific Beach, which hosts live music sets nearly every night. Located nearly right on top of Crystal Pier at the end of Garnet Avenue, 710 is also a favorite place to catch Pay-Per-View sporting events, with its massive big screens and impressive sound system.

Finally, those who enjoy a bit of friendly competition can invite their friends out for a little nine-ball action at **Society** (1051 Garnet Ave., 858/272-7665, www.societybilliard.com, noon–2 A.M. Mon.–Fri., 11 A.M.–2 A.M. Sat.–Sun.). This high-class pool hall features well-maintained tables and has a full-service bar and kitchen.

Festivals and Events

San Diegans are awfully proud of the softball-derived sport Over the Line (OTL). Invented right in town, this beach pastime is so popular here that kids learn how to play it in P.E. class. The peak of OTL competition comes each summer at the annual **Over the Line Tournament** that has been organized by the Old Mission Beach Athletic Club (www. ombac.org) for over half a century. Part athletic contest and part toga party, the two weekend-long event in July draws more than 20,000 people at a time to its Fiesta Island digs each year. The event is a bit of a bacchanalia, so parents are strongly encouraged to leave their kids at home.

Fourth of July is the apex of high season in the beach area, one of the few times of the year when almost every square inch of beach is taken up by blankets, bodies, and surfboards. Families tend to converge on the Strand, while singles and the younger set congregate on the bayside beaches to watch the annual fireworks over SeaWorld.

In October, Pacific Beach celebrates its sense of community with **Pacific Beach Fest.** Bring a bundle of single dollars and try a taste from each participating restaurant in the festival's Taste of Pacific Beach.

SHOPPING
Boutiques

Dress to impress in a pair of designer jeans from **Raw Clothing** (940 Garnet Ave., 858/483-9111, www.rawclothing.com, 10 A.M.–7 P.M. Mon.–Sat., 11 A.M.–6 P.M. Sun.) a Garnet Avenue staple for beach area fashionistas. The high-end clothes here aren't cheap, but they will act as a lasting and chic reminder of your San Diego adventure.

Take a detour off of Garnet's shopping bonanza down Cass Street to find **Chillers** (4667 Cass St., 858/274-3112, www.chillersclothing. com, 11 A.M.–7 P.M. Tues.–Fri., 10 A.M.–6 P.M. Sat.–Sun.) a clothing boutique with a very unique collection of clothes, both designed by the shop and lines such as Goddis, Havaianas, and Sanctuary.

Purses, pocketbooks, large handbags, and more can be found at **The Purse Addict** (1815 Garnet Ave., 858/272-8585, www.purseaddictsd.com, 10:30 A.M.–6 P.M. Tues.–Fri., 10 A.M.–5 P.M. Sat., 10 A.M.–3 P.M. Mon.) an accessorizing lady's dream store, featuring bags that run the gamut from classic little black numbers to faux-alligator and leopard-print bags.

Once you've got your purse in order, find a pair of pumps, wedges, or sandals to match at the trendy **Tutto Cuore** (1019 Garnet Ave., 858/490-4685, www.tuttocuoreshoes.com, 10 A.M.–8 P.M. daily), a clearinghouse of fashionable shoes that'll match that cocktail dress you plan to go clubbing in later in the evening. And since comfort is not exactly in the books for that pair, why not find a companion pair of walking shoes for the next day at **Sketchers** (4475 Mission Blvd., Space #A, 858/581-6010, www.sketchers.com, 9 A.M.–9 P.M. Mon.–Sat., 8 A.M.–8 P.M. Sun.)? This outlet shop frequently has fantastic specials and is a great place to pick up sneakers and flip-flops for those casual days around town.

If you're looking to spice up the trip a little bit with your honey, don't forget to make a stop off at **Dr. Love's** (1155 Garnet Ave., 858/270-7861, www.doctorloves.com, 11 A.M.–10 P.M. Mon.–Thurs., 11 A.M.–midnight Fri.–Sat.) a cheeky erotic store with lingerie, costumes, and, ahem, accessories for extending your evening activities beyond the public sphere.

Thrift Shops

Pacific Beach is flush with thrift shops along Garnet Avenue, with none so clean and filled with recycled treasures as the **United Cerebral Palsy Thrift Store** (1454 Garnet Ave., 858/490-6400, 9 A.M.–8 P.M. Mon.–Fri., 9 A.M.–6 P.M. Sat., 10 A.M.–5 P.M. Sun.). The assortment of lightly used clothes here usually has a high concentration of name-brand threads that can be picked up for under $5 a pop.

If you're going to stop there, you may as well saunter a couple doors down to **Goodwill** (1420 Garnet Ave., 858/274-4960. 9 A.M.–8 P.M. Mon.–Fri., 10 A.M.–6 P.M. Sat., 10 A.M.–5 P.M. Sun.), which has a decent selection as well, though it isn't quite as organized.

A step above the standard thrift shop goods, **Buffalo Exchange's** (1007 Garnet Ave., 858/273-6227, www.buffaloexchange.com, 10 A.M.–8 P.M. Mon.–Sat., 11 A.M.–6 P.M. Sun.) racks are usually full of the cutest used clothes on Garnet, but you'll definitely pay a premium for them.

Art Galleries

Step up and become a patron of the local art scene with a purchase at **Surfindian** (4652 Mission Blvd., 858/412-5334, www.surfindian.com, 10 A.M.–5 P.M. Mon., 10 A.M.–8 P.M. Tues.–Sat., 10 A.M.–6 P.M. Sun.), a unique shop that features a lineup of art created by local lovers of all things related to surfing area waves. You'll have your pick between interesting photos, paintings, and even one-of-a-kind surfboards. The shop is worth a stop even if you can't afford the art and you can commemorate the trip with a t-shirt or hat designed by the same artists who sell their goods here.

A sort of indoor bazaar minus the street grime, **Pangea Outpost** (909 Garnet Ave., 858/581-0555, www.pangaeaoutpost.com, 10 A.M.–7 P.M. Mon.–Sat, 11 A.M.–6 P.M. Sun.) offers a lovely collection of art, jewelry, furniture, candles, and decor items created by dozens of artists and craftsmen that rent their own individual slices of floor space here.

Bookstores

If you're in the mood to indulge in a trashy pulp novel while lounging on your towel, **Pennywise** (1331 Garnet Ave., 858/270-1640, www.pennywisebooks.info, 10 A.M.–5 P.M. daily) will hook you up with the goods for entertainment. With a huge collection of used genre fiction such as romances, mysteries, and horror novels, plus a few classics thrown in the mix to keep things balanced, Pennywise is worth the stop before you stake your umbrella in the sand.

Surf Shops and Beach Essentials

If you're looking to pick up a new board for your quiver, or just want to do a little wistful window shopping, the strip along Mission Boulevard has a healthy bounty of surf shops to choose from.

Pacific Beach Surf Shop (747 Pacific Beach Dr., 858/373-1138, 9 A.M.–7 P.M. daily) is one of the best shops on the north end for both beginners and lifelong surfers. The shop is in a plaza with ample underground parking.

The staff is friendly and the store has a good selection of new and used boards, as well as beachwear, sandals, and sunglasses. It also has a wide selection of boards, wetsuits, and other beach toys for rent in the shop and in its nearby rental shack on the boardwalk.

Down in Mission Beach you can also check out **Endless Summer** (2888 Mission Blvd., 858/488-8983, www.surfmissionbeach.com, 9 A.M.–5 P.M. daily). In addition to surf and beach accessories, the store also specializes in skate gear.

Ladies who can't find something girly enough at the surfshops should browse at either **Gone Bananas** (3785 Mission Blvd., 619/488-4900, 10 A.M.–8 P.M. Mon.–Fri., 10 A.M.–6 P.M. Sat.–Sun.) in Mission Beach or **Sun Splash** (979 Garnet Ave., 858/581-3400, www.sunsplashswimwear.com, 10 A.M.–8 P.M. Mon.–Fri., 10 A.M.–7 P.M. Sat.–Sun.) in Pacific Beach. Both are high-end swimsuit boutiques that sell suits designed to attract heaps of attention.

SPORTS AND RECREATION
Beaches and Surfing

Though there are better breaks in the county, the central location and easy access to amenities make the waters along Mission Beach and Pacific Beach very popular with surfers.

At **South Mission** just north of the jetty, the waves are very rideable even on days with the smallest waves. To rent a board nearby, visit **Hamel's Action Sports Center** (704 Ventura Pl., 858/272-2828, 9:30 A.M.–6:30 P.M. daily) across the street from Belmont Park. You can't miss it; it's in the building shaped like a castle right on the boardwalk.

North of the pier is also a popular spot for shredders. Just be aware that, typically, the closer to the pier you get the more aggressive and serious the surfers. If you are a beginner, try not to get in their way.

Another favorite location is **Tourmaline Surfing Park** (Tourmaline St. and La Jolla Blvd.), which is completely closed to swimming and wading. Longboarders especially dig

The protected waters of Mission Bay are ideal for tacking aboard small and midsized sailboats.

SURFING ETIQUETTE

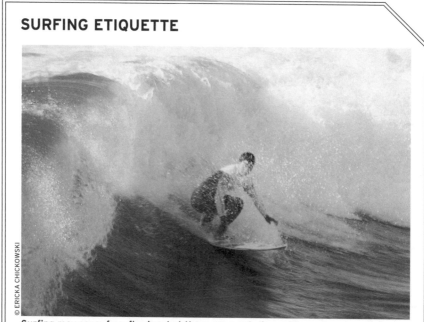

© ERICKA CHICKOWSKI

Surfing may seem free-flowing, but there are a set of unwritten rules.

As free-flowing as surfing is, it might come as a surprise to newcomers that there are a few rules to follow. There aren't many – but the ones that exist are ironclad. Because you aren't likely to find these laws of wave riding on any sign on the beach, I'll lay them out for you.

First, never jump in on a wave that someone else has caught. This sin, called "dropping in," is on par with baby 'napping to a surfer.

The person who is closest to the peak of the wave has right of way, so if you see someone closer than you making an attempt don't bother paddling. Just pull back and wait your turn.

Try not to paddle out right where the waves are rolling in. Spend a moment on shore to see where they are breaking and plan your route on the edges of the breaks to avoid obstructing someone else's ride. Not only is this the polite thing to do, it also makes it a heck of a lot easier to make it out to the line.

the long, languid waves here, which give them plenty of time on deck to practice cross-stepping and hanging a few toes over the nose.

In Pacific Beach there are plenty of places to rent surfing equipment. **Pure Life** (4466 Mission Blvd., 858/274-2468, 10 A.M.–5 P.M. daily) has the best deal on the Mission Boulevard strip, with an all-day board-and-wetsuit combo running you one cool Alexander Hamilton ($20).

Most rental shops will only rent out beginner foamies (boards made entirely of foam) because they are more forgiving and buoyant. If you are an advanced surfer who would rather have the maneuverability of a traditional fiberglass board, you can rent one from **Pacific Beach Surf Shop** (4150 Mission Blvd., #161, 858/373-1138, 9 A.M.–7 P.M. daily) in the Pacific Beach Promenade mall.

© ERICKA CHICKOWSKI

CITY BEACHES

No need to learn surfing. Ride a wave using a boogie board.

Swimming

The shore along the strand is obviously one of the best places to go for a dip. In the summer be sure to keep your eyes peeled for the sandwich boards set out on the beach by the lifeguards; they'll tell you which areas are for surfers and which areas are for swimmers. They'll typically have a yellow-and-black checkered flag flying on them.

For calmer waters, Mission Bay is another good bet. Lifeguards staff swimming beaches around the bay in the spring and summer, including those at **Sail Bay** (4000 Fanuel St.), **Crown Point** (3700 Crown Point Dr.), and **Tecolote Shores** (1600 East Mission Bay Dr.).

If the thought of sea creatures creeps you out a little, you can doggie paddle through the clear and chlorinated water at **The Plunge,** an indoor pool at the Wavehouse (3146 Mission Blvd., 858/228-9283) whose deck has hosted more than its fair share of children's birthday parties during the more than eight decades it has been open.

Boating and Fishing

Situated at the entrance to Mission Bay, **Quivira Basin** is the hub of boating activity in the area. Visitors can rent a range of motorized craft at the docks of **Seaforth Boat Rentals** (1641 Quivira Rd., 619/223-1681, www.seaforthboatrental.com, 8 A.M.–30 minutes before sunset Mon.–Fri., 7 A.M.–30 minutes before sunset Sat.–Sun.) in the marina at Quivira. Next door, the affiliated **Seaforth Sportsfishing** (1717 Quivira Rd., 619/224-5447, www.seaforthlanding.com, 5 A.M.–5 P.M. daily) provides a selection of frozen and live bait, as well as tackle designed for bay fishing.

Anglers with a sense of adventure can also depart from Quivira with either Seaforth's chartered trips or with the boats of **Islandia Sportfishing** (1551 West Mission Bay Dr., 619/222-1164, www.islandiasportfishing.com), which runs overnight trips in the spring and summer that start at $150.

To splash down in the water, there are six boat ramps circling Mission Bay Park. The two with the best access and parking are at **South Shores** (Mission Bay Pkwy. and SeaWorld Dr.) and **Ski Beach** (Ingraham St. and Vacation Rd.). These spots are also a good place to launch personal watercraft, which are a popular form of propulsion on the waters of Mission Bay. To rent your own for the day, visit **San Diego Jet Ski Rentals** (2830 Grand Ave., 858/272-6161, www.sdjetski.com, 8 A.M.–5 P.M. daily May–Oct., $200 per day).

Cycling and Running

The three-mile **Mission Beach Boardwalk** is an excellent spot to steer a beach cruiser if you don't mind using your feet to slow you a little when the crowds occasionally get in the way. It shouldn't bother you, because this ride is more about seeing the sights than working up a sweat.

To continue the ride, try cutting over on one of Mission Beach's surface streets to the bay and ride north on **Bayside Walk.** Except on very busy days, this path is less crowded and more easily navigated on wheels. It continues for five miles before coming to an end at the

© ERICKA CHICKOWSKI

California doesn't require fishing licenses for pier fishing.

nature preserve on the northeast corner of the bay. It is possible to ride all the way around the park by hanging a right on Pacific Beach Drive, a left on Olney Street, and a right on Grand Avenue. Continue along Grand as it curves toward the northeast entrance of the park. There you can recommence on the bayside path.

Much of the boardwalk and the bayside path are constructed with concrete, which can be murder on the knees when running long distance. The obvious alternative is taking the sandy beaches, but another low-impact choice is heading a few miles inland to **Tecolote Canyon Park** (5180 Tecolote Rd., 858/581-9944). This park spreads its fingers through the canyons that lie under the mesas overlooking Mission Bay. Follow the main trail for an enjoyable run or walk that'll keep your joints intact.

Golf

The Mission Bay area has a couple of very family-friendly golf courses that can offer a leisurely afternoon for any level of player.

Within Mission Bay Park, the municipal **Mission Bay Golf Course** (2702 N. Mission Bay Dr., 858/581-7880, 18 holes $23, 9 holes $14, carts $10) is an 18-hole executive course that promotes a very friendly environment where few people get stuck on stuffy conventions. You'll be as comfy in board shorts as in khakis, and rarely will you have a pushy party behind you rushing your strokes. Most notably, this course is the only fully lighted course in San Diego, offering night golfing until 10 P.M. every night. The course also has a lighted driving range and a modest practice green and bunker area.

Just up the hill from the bay, **Tecolote Canyon Golf Course** (2755 Snead Ave., 858/279-1600, greens fees $25, carts $12) is a challenging executive course that can sometimes catch even the scratch golfers off guard at first. Don't be fooled by the short yardage; the tricky course winds within canyons, and the scattered hazards force a high level of accuracy to reach par on any given hole. This course also has a nighttime driving range and a practice facility open during daylight hours.

ACCOMMODATIONS

Beach- and bay-area lodging lies on a spectrum from flophouses to the hippest of hotels. Pricing might shock some travelers expecting more for their money—in the end you are paying for location more than anything else.

Under $100

The Banana Bungalow (707 Reed Ave., 858/273-3060, www.bananabungalowsandiego.com, $20–25 dorm bed, $65–105 d) youth hostel bumps right up against the boardwalk and is a favorite for international travelers who would like to mingle with like-minded wanderers. Quarters are tight, with most guests sleeping in the bunk beds that crowd the hostel's dormitories. Private rooms are also available. Most guests don't mind the lack of personal space in the dorms, spending most of their time on the hostel's large deck overlooking the beach.

$100-200

Those looking for a crash pad with more privacy than the hostel can stay at the **Mission Bay Motel** (4221 Mission Blvd., 858/483-6440, www.missionbaymotel.com, $149 d). It is across the street from the beach and the boardwalk and within easy walking distance from Pacific Beach's bar scene. There is a modest pool area and rooms are fairly well kept. The crowd here is fairly young during high season, so come prepared to be put up in a room next to a group of not-so-quiet partiers. These walls, they are thin.

Beach-lovin' families stretching their dollars will be delighted with **Pacific Shores Inn** (4802 Mission Blvd., 858/483-6300, http://pacific-shores-inn.pacificahost.com, $200 d), one of the cheapest and cleanest motels you'll find in Pacific Beach. There's no ocean view, but there is a small pool and it is only a block from the beach. Plus the beds are comfy and the front desk is staffed all night, which is not always the case at competing motels nearby.

Comfort Inn Mission Bay (4540 Mission Bay Dr., 858/274-7888, $134 d) is not in the most scenic part of the neighborhood, but it is an easy drive from SeaWorld and has painless freeway access to reach the rest of the city. This discount motel is designed to be a launching pad for families who will spend most of their time at the beach and SeaWorld anyway and would prefer not to spend a bundle on their room. The pool is a good spot to lounge when there isn't time to hunt for parking on the Strand.

Beach Haven Inn (4740 Mission Blvd., 858/272-3812, www.beachhaveninn.com, $159 d) offers budget-minded travelers a good compromise between weather-beaten motels and über-luxury hotels. The inn is tidy and well cared for, with an appealing pool and spa area with a barbecue for those times when you'd just rather not go out to eat. Plus, it's a stone's throw from the Pacific Beach commercial district, as well as the boardwalk.

$200-300

You can't get any closer to the ocean than in the rooms at ◖ **Crystal Pier Hotel and Cottages** (4500 Ocean Blvd., 858/483-6983, www.crystalpier.com, $300 for four, $500 for six). Stay here and you'll be sleeping right on top of the ocean, as the cottages are actually built on the pier itself. Cottages come equipped with kitchens. One-bedroom units are limited to one car, and two-bedroom units to two cars.

Over $300

Pacific Terrace Hotel (610 Diamond St., 858/581-3500 or 800/344-3370, www.pacificterrace.com, $380 d) has one of the best oceanfront pools in the entire region. The hotel sits atop the bluff that overlooks Pacific Beach, and the pool bumps right up against the boardwalk. Watch the surfers rip it up without even leaving the heated pool. Rooms are spacious and well appointed, and continental breakfast and afternoon refreshments are included in the rate.

Two blocks down along the boardwalk, ◖ **Tower 23** (723 Felspar St., 858/270-2323,

© ERICKA CHICKOWSKI

Crystal Pier in Pacific Beach

www.tower23hotel.com, $389 d) is another scenic option for singles and young couples. The hotel caters to well-manicured partiers with its hip architecture and cheeky atmosphere. Its signature feature is the Tower Deck, from which you can look over the boardwalk and pier while being warmed by the deck's huge open-flame fireplace.

Camping
Campland by the Bay (2211 Pacific Beach Dr., 800/422-9386, www.camplandonthebay. com, $41 no RV hookups, $72 full hookups per site, per night) is centrally located right on Mission Bay in Pacific Beach. This RV-friendly mega-campsite has a full slate of amenities for visitors, including two pools, a whirlpool tub, an arcade, laundry facilities, and a market and deli.

FOOD
Sometimes there's no better way to cap off a trip to the beach than with a salty or sugary treat that would land you in hot water with a nutritionist. Pizzas, burgers, sandwiches, and ice cream are all easy to find, with a few notable eateries that stand out above the crowd.

Cafés and Delis
The coffeehouse-and-café scene thrives in the beach area. Visit **Café 976** (976 Felspar St., 858/272-0976, www.cafe976. com, 7 A.M.–11 P.M. daily, $5–9) and snag a spot in their shady garden. The menu runs from healthy to indulgent at all times of day, with a number of vegetarian choices mixed in throughout. Whether you are a meat eater or not, the breakfast burrito with soy chorizo is darned tasty ($7.95).

If you're still recovering from last night's bender at Garnet's bars, visit **Broken Yolk** (1851 Garnet Ave., 858/270-9655, www.the-brokenyolkcafe.com, 6 A.M.–3 P.M. daily, $7) for a little hair of the dog: Tableside mimosas are served with a jug of freshly squeezed OJ (the best in town), a bottle of champagne, and a brace of flutes. The Broken Yolk is also known for its gustatory challenge. The café serves a

12-egg omelet dish that is only $1.99 if you can finish it yourself in an hour. Winners also walk out the door with a celebratory T-shirt and the honor of having their name engraved on the restaurant's wall-of-fame plaques. Losers leave with a very full stomach and 20 fewer dollars in their pocket for the privilege of trying.

Closer to the beach, the patio at **The Eggery** (4150 Mission Blvd., #121, 858/274-3122, www.theeggery.com, 7 A.M.–2 P.M. daily, $7) affords a view of the river of people streaming by on the nearby boardwalk. The country-style breakfasts will fill you up practically until dinner, making this a good pit stop before going to see Shamu.

The Mission Café (3795 Mission Blvd., 858/488-9060, 7 A.M.–3 P.M. daily, $10) is also steps to the beach, though it only has streetside views. That's OK, though, because it serves what most locals regard as the best-tasting breakfast in either of the beach neighborhoods. If you like rosemary, try the roast beef hash and eggs ($8.95) served with rosemary potatoes. And if you're an adventurous java lover, wash it down with a Vincent Vega. This unique coffee cocktail includes a shot of espresso and a dash of vanilla syrup poured over an icy glass of Coca-Cola.

On a sunny day diners can sit under the shade of the eponymous flora at **Fig Tree Cafe** (5119 Cass St., 858/274-2233, http://figtree-cafepb.com, 8 A.M.–2:30 P.M. and 5–10 P.M. Thurs.–Tues.) a cute eatery set in a tiny bungalow and yard on a quiet part of Cass Street. The setting is this place's strongest selling point, with tables and chairs positioned for prime sidewalk people watching. Service is a bit slow, but the staff is cheerful and who's watching time on a lazy Sunday anyhow?

Specializing in smoothies and salads, **Rum Jungle** (4150 Mission Blvd., #153, 858/273-2227, www.rumjunglecafe.com, 8 A.M.–7 P.M. Mon.–Sat., 8 A.M.–6 P.M. Sun.) makes a dandy pit stop at the Promenade before or after going for a long walk on the boardwalk. The shop itself is tiny, but there are a few scattered tables on the walkway outside and the beach is no more than a two-minute walk away.

Don't let the line wrapping around the building at **Kono's Café** (704 Garnet Ave., 858/483-1669, 7 A.M.–3 P.M. Mon.–Fri., 7 A.M.–4 P.M. Sat.–Sun., $4) scare you off on busy days. The kitchen crew is mighty speedy and the cheap eats are well worth the queue.

Sandwiches

If you're in Mission Beach near Belmont Park, stop by **Gaglione Brothers Cheesesteaks** (724 Ventura Pl., 858/488-1690, 11 A.M.–9 P.M. daily, $7). The steak sandwiches there aren't Philly-style, but they're still smothered in meat and melted cheese. You can top that off with an ice cream cone at Kojacks just two doors down. Just don't forget to ride the Big Dipper *before* you eat.

Near the intersection of Garnet and Cass in PB, **Olde City Grill** (967 Garnet Ave., 858/483-4624, 8:30 A.M.–4 P.M. Mon.–Fri., 8:30 A.M.–5 P.M. Sat.–Sun., $8) is an excellent spot to find authentic Philadelphia cheesesteaks, as well as pizza and Italian ice.

For sandwiches outside the realm of cheesesteaks, saunter around the block to **Sully's** (4508 Cass St., #C, 858/483-3322, 11 A.M.–8 P.M. daily, $6). The shop puts a California twist on old-school deli favorites, the vegetarian Reuben being a good example of some of the bolder interpretations. There are plenty of classics, too, like the meatball sub that practically splits at the seams with sauce and meat.

Pizza and Italian

An inviting little pizza den decked out with pictures of the Brooklyn Bridge and Frank Sinatra, **Hoboken Pizza** (1459 Garnet Ave., 858/270-7766, www.hobokenpizza.com, 4–11 P.M. Mon., 4 P.M.–2 A.M. Tues.–Thurs., 11:30 A.M.–2:30 A.M. Fri.–Sat., 11:30 A.M.–2 A.M. Sun., $18) serves up pie the way that East Coasters crave it. The crust is thin and crunchy, toppings fresh, and sauce imbued with loads of oregano and garlic.

For a more authentic Italian meal, venture to the brightly painted orange bungalow that houses **Mamma Mia** (1932 Balboa Ave., 858/272-2702, www.mammamiaitalianrestaurant.com,

11 A.M.–10 P.M. Tues.–Sun., $11). Tucked into a tiny lot on a busy stretch of Grand Avenue, this spot is difficult to find parking for, but you'll find it is well worth the effort the minute you walk in the door. There you'll meet Francesco, the raspy-voiced half of the power duo that runs the place; he will greet you as an old friend and sit you down for one of his wife Cinzia's well-crafted entrées. Everything is tasty here, but my particular favorite is the gnocci served with shrimp in a delightful pink sauce. Whatever you do, save room for dessert. Cinzia bakes a new cake each day, along with the always-popular tiramisu.

Burgers and Hot Dogs

The folks at **Mad Dogs Café** (746 Emerald St., 858/750-3114, www.maddogscafe.com, 8 A.M.–5 P.M. Mon.–Thurs., 8 A.M.–6 P.M. Fri.–Sun., $7) know their sausages—they serve up more than a dozen on the menu, all of them wrapped up and baked in a homemade roll and served with a choice of plenty more sauces. If I have my druthers I usually pick the tangy and spicy house-made Mad Sauce and I always accompany it with the joint's freshly fried potato chips. Just those choices alone would be enough to carry Mad Dogs, but it also serves fresh crumpets for breakfast, a fantastic array of coffee drinks and loose-leaf teas, and a delicious lineup of gelato.

The Big Kahuna Burger is **Big Kahuna's** (3780 Ingraham St., 858/270-9200, http://bigkahunaspb.com, 11 A.M.–9 P.M. Mon.–Fri., 10 A.M.–9 P.M. Sat.–Sun., $10) claim to fame. Pulp Fiction fans will remember that this was the name of the burger Samuel L. Jackson indulged in while shaking down one of the minor characters in the movie. Now, while the real Big Kahuna Burger didn't actually inspire the movie makers, owners here still like to riff off the connection. Not that they need to— the burger is a juicy combo topped with cabbage instead of lettuce, well spiced and on a Hawaiian sweet roll, worthy of praise no matter its Hollywood chops.

Burger fans heading to Big Kahuna will have a tough choice to make, though. As they walk up the sidewalk in PB's Crown Point neighborhood they'll have to pass **Rocky's Crown Pub** (3786 Ingraham St., 858/273-9140, www.rockyscrownpub.com) literally two doors away. And while it may not look like much, just a divey corner bar packed with folks, there's a reason why it is usually so busy. This place has quite possibly the best burger in all of San Diego—juicy, flavorful and no frills. The menu is simple. You can get a ⅓ pound or ½ pound burger, with or without cheese and with or without fries. Just come prepared with cash and a little patience. They don't take credit cards, it gets crowded, and the place isn't renowned for its great service.

Ice Cream and Dessert

A PB institution, **Mr. Frosties** (1470 Garnet Ave., 858/274-9977, www.mrfrosties.com, 10:30 A.M.–9 P.M. Sun.–Thurs., 10:30 A.M.–10 P.M. Fri.–Sat., $4) has been pleasing lines of soft-serve ice cream fans since 1949. With dependable hours, longevity, and a creative mix of sundaes, cone dips (chocolate, butterscotch, AND cherry!), shakes, and floats, it's just the place to satisfy the old sweet tooth rain or shine.

Contemporary

Pacific Beach isn't exactly known for fine dining, but **JRDN** (723 Felspar St., 858/270-5736, www.jrdn.com, lunch 7 A.M.–4 P.M. daily, dinner 5–10 P.M. Sun.–Thurs., 5–11 P.M. Fri.–Sat., $22) makes a good attempt at breaking the mold. The fresh interior (reminiscent of Miami Beach) and scrumptious menu items are worth the visit. And the setting is hard to beat, with most diners getting at least a little peek at the beach from this boardwalk restaurant. Just be prepared to look oceanward for a long time— the servers are notoriously slow.

Steak

Late at night, pass Denny's by in favor of **Saska's Steak and Seafood** (3768 Mission Blvd., 858/488-7311, www.saskas.com, lunch 11 A.M.–3 P.M. Mon.–Fri., 10 A.M.–3 P.M. Sat.–Sun., dinner 4 P.M.–2 A.M. daily, $17), which serves a full menu every night until the bars close at 2 A.M. Saska's was the first real steakhouse to open in the beach neighborhoods, propping its doors wide open for customers back in 1951. Today the signature steaks are joined on the menu by loads of fresh seafood.

Seafood

Unlike some seafood restaurants on the beach's boardwalk, the food is as good as the view at **World Famous** (711 Pacific Beach Dr., 858/272-3100, www.worldfamous.signonsandiego.com, 7 A.M.–11 P.M. daily, $18–20). The menu here highlights the best in California coastal cuisine, with an emphasis on dishes featuring mahi mahi, shrimp, lobster, and crab. Entrées are reasonably priced, around $18 a pop on average.

There aren't any beach views at **The Fishery** (5040 Cass St., 858/272-9985, 11 A.M.–10 P.M. daily, $23), but the menu does show off the variety of fresh fish displayed and sold in the fish market that is integrated into the restaurant. Tucked into the quiet north end of Pacific Beach, this restaurant is a perfect find for travelers who like to live as the locals do. The market is closed during dinner hours, but during lunch there is a steady procession of neighborhood regulars streaming in and out of this place to pick up tidy white packages of seafood.

Mexican

For authentic Mexican grub with a decidedly local vibe, check out **Taco Surf** (4657 Mission Blvd., 858/272-3877, 9 A.M.–10 P.M. Sun.–Thurs., 9 A.M.–midnight Fri.–Sat., $5). The eats are cheap, tasty, and filling at this paper-plates-and-plastic-forks hole-in-the-wall. Try the fish tacos. In a town that practically made this treat a national phenomenon, these are the best ones served. The fish is battered and fried as you wait and served up on hot corn tortillas with cabbage and a tangy white sauce. While the cooks do their magic, check out the collection of vintage surfboards hanging from the walls and ceiling.

Wrapped up in steaming corn husks, the hearty Mexican bundles of cornmeal and meat that **Tamales Ancira** (1404 Garnet Ave., 858/270-1810, www.tamalesancira.com, 9 A.M.–9 P.M. Mon.–Sat., 10 A.M.–5 P.M. Sun., $5) serves are about as authentic as it gets. Hands down the best tamale shop in the county, Tamales Ancira will tempt you with an impressive collection of flavors. Old favorites such as chicken, beef, and pork are joined on the menu by corn and cheese, raisin and pine nuts, and chiccharones. Each tamale is fairly small, so you'll have the chance to sample a couple of flavors before you fill up.

French

Don't let the delicious desserts waiting for you at **The French Gourmet** (960 Turquoise St., 858/488-1725, www.thefrenchgourmet.com, 10 A.M.–8:30 P.M. Tues.–Thurs., 8 A.M.–9:30 P.M. Fri.–Sat., $23) make you rush through your meal. The food at this tiny restaurant is just as delicious as the dazzling array of breads and pastries baked fresh each day.

Tapas

It is easy to whiz past **Costa Brava** (1653 Garnet Ave., 858/273-1218, www.costabravasd.com, 11 A.M.–midnight daily, $19) when you're driving along Garnet Avenue toward the ocean. The restaurant is about a block away from the main concentration of eateries in PB and its door is camouflaged by a thick set of shrubs that act as a patio border between the restaurant and the street. But if you like paella bursting with seafood and saffron, it is definitely worth slowing down to find. Owned by a restaurateur straight from Madrid, Costa Brava also serves creative tapas dishes and potent sangria. If you have the chance to try the ox tail entrée, a semi-frequent special on the nightly menu, don't hesitate. Braised until the sauce envelops the meat in a velvety finish, this is heaven on a fork.

Thai and Vietnamese

Basil Thai (1315 Garnet Ave., 858/270-8424, 11 A.M.–11 P.M. Sun.–Thurs., 11 A.M.–2 A.M. Fri.–Sat., $9) isn't far behind Thai Village in the taste category and it does win out in one important criteria, particularly for the party goers: it's open 'til 2 A.M. on the weekends. The filling rice dishes and curries will make for a delicious and more stomach-stable alternative to the typical taco shop fare that fills the Garnet Avenue late-night dining void.

Served with the traditional sides of basil leaves, bean sprouts, and lime, the Vietnamese soups at **Pho Sao Bien** (1958 Garnet Ave., 858/272-9612, www.ieatpho.com, 10 A.M.–10 P.M. daily, $6) make for a simple and hearty meal on the cheap. The broth is flavorful and complex and the meats available are varied, the best option being the steak and shrimp combo.

Sushi

Widely regarded by local foodies as the best sushi restaurant in the entire city, **Sushi Ota** (4529 Mission Bay Dr., 858/270-5670, www.sushiotamenu.info, lunch 11:30 A.M.–2 P.M. Tues.–Thurs., 11:30 A.M.–2 P.M. Fri., dinner 5:30–10:30 P.M. Mon.–Thurs., 5–10:30 P.M. Fri.–Sun., $18) stays well disguised from most tourists. Hidden away right behind a 7-Eleven in a nondescript strip mall on a busy thoroughfare, the restaurant envelops diners in Japanese ambiance once they actually get through the front door. With bamboo screens a wide expanse of a sushi bar and plenty of tables scattered throughout the room, this restaurant serves some of the freshest sushi in town.

College kids counting their next semester's book money in pickle jars will still manage to scratch up some coin to grub on tasty rolls and nigiri at **Ichiban** (1441 Garnet Ave., 858/270-5755, 5–9 P.M. Mon.–Sat., $13) one of the best workaday sushi eateries in PB. The nigiri is decent, the rolls are good and the prices are downright irresistible here, where you order at the counter, take a number, and wait for staff to bring a tray full of seafood.

Groceries

There are lots of little markets and liquor stores that sell quick beach snacks, but to really stock up, stop at the **Ralph's** (4315 Mission Blvd., 858/273-0778, 24 hours daily) on Mission Boulevard. The full-service grocery store has ample parking in its underground lot to make it a convenient shopping trip.

INFORMATION

For more information on Pacific Beach restaurants, hotels, and shops, stop by the offices of **Discover Pacific Beach** (1503 Garnet Ave., 858/273-3303, www.pacific-beach.org, 9 A.M.–5 P.M. Mon.–Fri.). Located within Mission Bay Park, the **Mission Bay Information Center** (2688 East Mission Bay Dr., 619/276-8200, 9 A.M.–5 P.M. Mon.–Sat., 9:30 A.M.–4:30 P.M. Sun.) also provides information on establishments and services throughout San Diego.

SERVICES

For non-emergency police issues, there is a neighborhood **police station** (4439 Olney St., 858/581-9920) in Pacific Beach.

If you need to tear yourself away from beach or bay to check your email, or if you're just looking for a good place to nurse a sunburn, the **public library** (4275 Cass St., 858/581-9934, 12:30 P.M.–8 P.M. Mon. and Wed., 9:30 A.M.–5:30 P.M. Tues., Thurs., and Sat., 12:30 P.M.–5:30 P.M. Fri., 1 P.M.–5 P.M. Sun.) is within a few blocks of both. The **post office** (4680 Cass St., 858/272-1948) is a block away from Garnet Avenue.

Pacific Beach Urgent Care (4490 Fanuel St., Ste. 208, 858/274-9116, www.pburgentcare.com, 8 A.M.–8 P.M. Mon.–Fri., 8 A.M.–4 P.M. Sat.–Sun. and holidays) is off of Cass Street and can take care of most non-trauma medical issues.

GETTING THERE AND AROUND

Because of its unusual location, both beach neighborhoods are a bit isolated from the rest of the city with a few arterials over the bay acting as major choke points. When jetting across town to keep a dinner reservation, just remember that it always takes longer than you think to get into and out of the beaches due to traffic and parking concerns.

Speaking of parking, in the summer it can be quite a game of chance to find a good spot near the beach. The only free public parking lot along the strand is at Belmont Park.

If you'd like to forgo a car altogether, the #30 bus services the beach area. If you're staying out of the immediate area, think seriously about public transportation on busy beach days

such as the Fourth of July. For example, you can park at the **Old Town Transit Center** and hitch a ride on the #30 to get to the beach in only about 15 minutes. That is probably at least as long as you'll be walking from your parking spot anyway, unless you're really lucky or willing to pay some college kid $50 to park on his landlady's lawn.

Point Loma and Ocean Beach

Visitors can leave the pretension behind when they travel through Ocean Beach (just call it OB—the locals do) and Point Loma. These funky little communities are home to flower children and military folks alike, all harmoniously united through the same laid-back attitude toward life.

OB sports a unique beach scene at the southwest corner of land where the San Diego River and Pacific Ocean meet. The beachside streets

are a maze of unique local shops and eateries, and the neighborhood attracts bohemians and beatniks with its distinct counterculture vibe.

Point Loma tends to be a little less irreverent, but just as easygoing. Named for the peninsula that juts out at the entrance of San Diego Bay, this area understandably has a long relationship with the sea and a storied naval history. After all, it is surrounded by towering coastal cliffs on one side and a steady procession of boats in the bay on the other.

Nearly five centuries ago it was the landing point for Juan Rodriguez Cabrillo, the first European to set foot on the West Coast, who arrived in 1542. Over the region's history the neighborhood has been home to numerous Navy installations. The area is also a haven for fishing boats and pleasure craft, with marinas crowding the harbors that line the neighborhood on its east side.

SIGHTS
Ocean Beach Park

Keep your ears open for the sound of guitars astrummin' from the dreadlocked denizens at Ocean Beach Park. The mile-long beach extends from the OB Pier all the way to the mouth of the San Diego River. Unlike the bronzed and buff regulars up in Mission Beach and Pacific Beach, the crowd here is more concerned with enjoying the scenery than showing off.

At the north end of the park is **Dog Beach,** an off-leash area that runs next to the river. It is fun to watch the dogs dance like whirling

© ERICKA CHICKOWSKI

Heading down to the tide pools at Cabrillo National Monument.

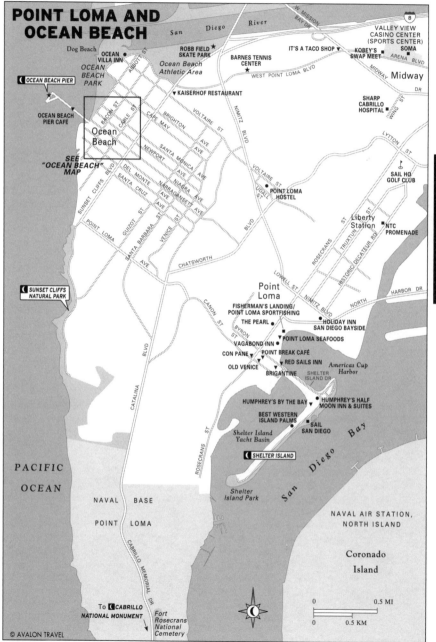

POINT LOMA AND OCEAN BEACH

CITY BEACHES

San Diego River

W. MISSION BAY DR

VALLEY VIEW CASINO CENTER (SPORTS CENTER)

SOMA

KOBEY'S SWAP MEET

SPORTS ARENA BLVD

IT'S A TACO SHOP

Dog Beach

OCEAN VILLA INN

ROBB FIELD SKATE PARK ★

BARNES TENNIS CENTER

OCEAN BEACH PARK

Ocean Beach Athletic Area

WEST POINT LOMA BLVD

MIDWAY DR

Midway

◖ OCEAN BEACH PIER

SHARP CABRILLO HOSPITAL ■

WING ST

OCEAN BEACH PIER CAFÉ

★ KAISERHOF RESTAURANT

BRIGHTON AVE

VOLTAIRE ST

LYTTON ST

Ocean Beach

SEE "OCEAN BEACH" MAP

CAPE MAY AVE

SANTA MONICA AVE

NEWPORT AVE

BACON ST

CABLE ST

ABBOTT ST

NIMITZ BLVD

VOLTAIRE ST

SAIL HO GOLF CLUB

SUNSET CLIFFS BLVD

DEL MONTE AVE

SANTA CRUZ AVE

NIAGRA AVE

NARRAGANSETT AVE

VENICE ST

GUIZOT ST

SANTA BARBARA ST

POINT LOMA AVE

UDALL ST

POINT LOMA HOSTEL

CHATSWORTH

VOLTAIRE BLVD

ROSECRANS ST

TRUXTUN ST

HISTORIC DECATUR RD

Liberty Station

NTC PROMENADE ■

Point Loma

CAMON ST

LOWELL ST

NIMITZ BLVD

NORTH HARBOR DR

HARBOR DR

◖ SUNSET CLIFFS NATURAL PARK

FISHERMAN'S LANDING/ POINT LOMA SPORTFISHING ●

THE PEARL ●

HOLIDAY INN SAN DIEGO BAYSIDE

BYRON ST

▼ POINT LOMA SEAFOODS

VAGABOND INN ●

CON PANE ● ▼ POINT BREAK CAFÉ

OLD VENICE ● ● RED SAILS INN

BRIGANTINE

SHELTER ISLAND DR

Americas Cup Harbor

CATALINA BLVD

HUMPHREY'S BY THE BAY ▼

HUMPHREY'S HALF MOON INN & SUITES

BEST WESTERN ISLAND PALMS ●

● SAIL SAN DIEGO

Shelter Island Yacht Basin

◖ SHELTER ISLAND

San Diego Bay

ROSECRANS ST

PACIFIC OCEAN

NAVAL BASE POINT LOMA

Shelter Island Park

NAVAL AIR STATION, NORTH ISLAND

Coronado Island

CABRILLO MEMORIAL DR

To ◖ CABRILLO NATIONAL MONUMENT

Fort Rosecrans National Cemetery

0   0.5 MI

0   0.5 KM

dervishes in the sand here, dodging and rough-housing with each other while their owners either socialize or watch amusedly. Just be sure to keep your sandals on, as some owners aren't always responsible about picking up messes. If you are a dog owner, be sure not to set that bad example. There are complimentary bags stands and garbage cans scattered over the beach.

Also, remember that Fido can't drink the water here. The river water is brackish once it gets this far downstream. For hangin' tongues, visit the parking lot where there is a water fountain made just for mutts.

◖ Ocean Beach Pier

At 1,971 feet long, Ocean Beach Pier (5091 Niagara Ave., 24 hours daily) is the longest concrete pier on the West Coast. The massive concrete structure extends far enough out to give anglers a chance at deeper waters and fish within the Point Loma kelp beds. And the T-shaped deck at the end of the pier gives passersby enough room to look out to sea without worrying about getting caught in someone's line. On quiet winter days this is a great place for a smooch with your sweetheart.

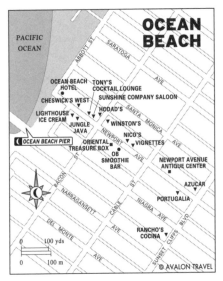

◖ Sunset Cliffs Natural Park

Sunset Cliffs Natural Park (Sunset Cliffs Blvd., 619/235-1169, 24 hours daily) certainly earns its name. When the sun kisses the ocean each day these sandstone cliffs glow orange. The cliffs are unstable, though, so be careful where you

Ocean Beach Pier is a favorite among anglers.

step when you're hunting for a snapshot. There are parking lots sprinkled along Sunset Cliffs Boulevard for access up top. The adventurous can trek from the parking lot at the pier around the cliffside bend farther south to explore the small beaches and tide pools hidden within the cliffs' nooks and crannies. Just be sure to bring a tide chart and be aware of the time so as not to get trapped during high tide.

◖ Cabrillo National Monument

Right on the tip of Point Loma is Cabrillo National Monument (1800 Cabrillo Memorial Dr., 619/557-5450, www.nps.gov/cabr, 9 A.M.–5 P.M. daily, $5 per vehicle, $3 for cyclists), a 144-acre park featuring tide pools teeming with sea life, a historic lighthouse open for tours, a historical museum, and the best view of downtown and San Diego Bay in the city.

The entrance is midway up the steep hill that leads to the top of Cabrillo Monument. As you drive past the gatehouse, you can veer right to wind down to the tide pools that face the Pacific. Put on some sandals with traction and clamber down for a look at the tiny crustaceans, fish, and other sea life that live in the craggy fissures that make up these pools. Just be sure to tread lightly and take only pictures—the ecology here is fragile and will only persevere with your cooperation.

Continue up the main road to the top, which holds the other highlights of the park. Be sure to bring your binoculars in the winter, because this 350-foot peak affords great views of migrating grey whales to the west.

Named after Juan Rodriguez Cabrillo, who discovered San Diego Bay nearly five centuries ago, the park features a 150-foot statue of the explorer at the summit. Steps away is a museum that commemorates his exploration and his interaction with the Kumeyaay natives.

Also within walking distance of the parking lot is the **Old Point Loma Lighthouse.** Towering 422 feet above the sea, the lighthouse opened in 1855 as a major disappointment to the sailors it was intended to guide. Most lighthouses work best when placed on high, but engineers had not factored in the layer of fog that often plagues San Diego in the summertime. After a couple of decades trying to make it work, authorities built another lighthouse farther down the cliffs of the peninsula in order to get the light under the fog. But

© ERICKA CHICKOWSKI

Sunset Cliffs Natural Park is often enjoyed by runners, but it's best appreciated by loungers.

CITY BEACHES

the old lighthouse stands today, restored and opened for visitors to tour at their leisure.

On your way up you will probably notice a cemetery on the left side of the road, a seemingly endless sea of marble gravestones rolling over green grass. The park is also home to **Fort Rosecrans National Cemetery,** where 88,826 souls from armed services are interred. On Memorial Day, the navy works with other branches of the military to hold a moving ceremony on the grounds to pay respects to those who have fallen to protect our freedom.

◖ Shelter Island

Located just north of downtown, right across Harbor Drive from the airport, Shelter Island (2126 Shelter Island Dr., 6 A.M.–10:30 P.M. daily) isn't actually an island anymore, but it has an isolated hideaway feel to it nonetheless. Once nothing more than a shoal off of Point Loma's shores on San Diego Bay, the island's land level was raised and a causeway was added in the 1940s when the Port Authority dredged between the island and mainland to provide better marina space there.

In the 1950s, when GIs returning from the Pacific brought back with them an excitement for all things Polynesian, many resort and restaurant developers decided to take advantage of the newly connected piece of land to build a sanctuary that pays homage to the tropics. Today the decor still persists, with many of the hotels, restaurants, and shops on the west side of the island sporting a tiki motif and lush gardens reminiscent of Hawaii and other far-flung islands. Behind all of this is a forest of sailboat masts in the marinas that sit between the island and the rest of Point Loma.

All of the buildings overlook **Shelter Island Park,** which spreads along the entire east side of the island. The 1.2-mile park has few obstructions, lending an incredible view of San Diego Bay, with downtown San Diego in the distance and north Coronado Island in the more immediate foreground.

ENTERTAINMENT AND EVENTS
Nightlife

The best bars in this neck of the woods are on Ocean Beach's main drag, **Newport Avenue.**

marina at Shelter Island

© ERICKA CHICKOWSKI

Most of them are rowdy affairs, with revelry reaching its peak during football season. **Sunshine Company Saloon** (5028 Newport Ave., 619/222-0722, 11 A.M.–2 A.M. Mon.–Fri., 10 A.M.–2 A.M. Sat.–Sun.) is one of the largest of the bunch, with two stories to mingle through with pint in hand. Clear days are particularly pleasant on the second-story open-air patio, from which you can catch a glimpse of the beach.

Another OB classic is a couple of doors down at **Cheswick's West** (5038 ½ Newport Ave., 619/225-0733, 11 A.M.–midnight Mon.–Sat., 10 A.M.–midnight Sun.), a particular favorite among leather-clad bikers. Snag a stool near the open-shuttered window to watch passersby wander to and from the beach.

For something stronger than beer, swing by **Tony's Cocktail Lounge** (5034 Newport Ave., 619/223-0558, 11 A.M.–2 A.M. Mon.–Fri., 10 A.M.–2 A.M. Sat.–Sun.) for a martini. The drink slingers here pour them stiff. The atmosphere isn't snooty, either. The leather booths are about as formal as it gets in this place.

Performing Arts
The Shelter Island marinas offer a scenic backdrop for the stage at **Humphrey's by the Bay** (2241 Shelter Island Dr., 619/523-1010, www.humphreysconcerts.com). In the summer Humphrey's hosts a perpetually sold-out concert series in its open-air venue of 1,350. It has hosted popular musicians such as Chris Isaak, B. B. King, and Lionel Richie.

For edgier artists and up-and-coming bands from the San Diego music scene, try **SOMA** (3350 Sports Arena Blvd., Ste. I, 619/226-7662, www.somasandiego.com). A smaller venue in this same vein is **Winston's** (1921 Bacon St., 619/222-6822, www.winstonsob.com), which is located near the beach. This popular bar hosts live music every night on its well-equipped, though small, stage.

One of the most unique venues in San Diego, **NTC Promenade** (2640 Historic Decatur Rd., 619/573-9260, www.ntcpromenade.org/events) is made up of a complex of buildings formerly owned by the Navy and now redeveloped as a part of the massive Liberty Station complex of homes, condos, shopping, and restaurants. The Promenade plays host to arts and dance events throughout the year from organizations such as the San Diego Ballet Company, Jean Issacs's San Diego Dance Theatre, and Capoeira Brasil.

Festivals and Events
Come summertime, the biggest festival this side of the San Diego River is the **Ocean Beach Street Fair,** which takes place the last weekend in June. Tents overwhelm the beach's streets with vendors selling arts and crafts by local artists, while bands rock out on the stage near the pier, and pots roil nearby as amateur chefs duke it out for bragging rights at the event's annual chili cook-off.

SHOPPING
Kobey's Swap Meet
On the weekends, bargain hunters take over the parking lot at the Valley View Casino Center for Kobey's Swap Meet (3500 Sports Arena Blvd., 619/226-0650, 7 A.M.–3 P.M. Fri.–Sun, $1). Running continuously since 1976, Kobey's is San Diego's largest market and the third-largest on the West Coast. Each weekend over 1,000 sellers put out their clothing, electronics, fresh produce, and assorted other items for the 30,000 shoppers that come to pick through their wares.

Newport Avenue Antiques
San Diego is a great city for antique hunting, and one of the best strips of antique shops in town is in Ocean Beach. Newport Avenue's 4800 block features an antique district with an assembly of shops that sell treasures from all different time periods and geographies.

The largest and most eclectic selection can be found at **Newport Avenue Antique Center** (4864 Newport Ave., 619/222-8686, 10 A.M.–6 P.M. daily), which offers space to vendors in its warehouse-like space. There you'll be able to find items from the early 1800s all the way up to the mid-20th century. Collectors

CITY BEACHES

© ERICKA CHICKOWSKI

Newport Avenue is the center of Ocean Beach's shopping, nightlife, and food scenes.

of 1950s-era memorabilia will find a visit there particularly fruitful.

The center also features Asian antiquities, but the better bet for these items is across the street at **Oriental Treasure Box** (4847 Newport Ave., 619/221-9071, 11 A.M.–5 P.M. Tues.–Sun., closed Mon.). This smaller shop has a very strong selection of kimonos, hand-carved woodwork, and ceramics, among other Asian curiosities.

Vignettes (4828 Newport Ave., 619/222-9244, 10:30 A.M.–5 P.M. Mon.–Sat., 11 A.M.–5 P.M. Sun.), on the other hand, is better suited for collectors of Western antiques. Its vintage Paris souvenirs are particularly fun to browse through and it has a medley of elegant furnishings and decorative accessories.

SPORTS AND RECREATION
Surfing and Swimming
While swimming is certainly allowed at Ocean Beach, those looking for a place to jump in the water without a board can find cleaner agua at the beaches farther north. The San Diego

River empties out at Ocean Beach, and as a result the water here sometimes catches the dirty runoff that collects during the river's traverse downstream.

Unless it has rained, however, the water is far from dangerous, and because of the good breaks that occur here, the surfers are not deterred. The area south of the pier is good for all levels of surfers. For board rentals, visit **Cheap Rentals** (3689 Mission Blvd., 858/488-9070, 9 A.M.–6 P.M.) just across the West Mission Bay Drive Bridge in Mission Beach. In addition to hourly and daily rentals, this place also loans out equipment by the week.

North of the pier all along **Sunset Cliffs** (Sunset Cliffs Blvd.) there are reef breaks that lifelong surfers dream about. However, this area is only for the advanced surfer. The rocks leading up and down the cliffs are unstable and dangerous, and the tricky tides can easily create conditions that can quickly pin the inexperienced to the cliff sides. The bottom line is this: Don't paddle in here unless you have the chops for it, and always bring a buddy.

Fishing

The rails of the Ocean Beach Pier offer some of the best land-based saltwater fishing in the county. **Ocean Beach Pier Bait Shop** (5091 Niagara Ave., 619/226-3474, 7 A.M.–9 P.M. daily) can help you find something enticing to put on the end of your hook.

To ply deeper waters, wander over to Point Loma, from which a number of deep-sea tours depart. **Point Loma Sportfishing** (1403 Scott St., 619/223-1627, www.pointlomasportfishing.com, $42–95 per person)) offers a range of trips: half-day, three-quarter-day, full-day, overnight, and multi-day outings. For a fishing trip to really brag about back home, try one of the overnight squid fishing trips and hunt giant squid the size of peewee-league linebackers.

Fisherman's Landing (2838 Garrison St., 619/221-8506, $200–400 per person) also offers chartered trips of varying length. In addition, the Fisherman's shop has an extensive line of rods and tackle for those looking to pick up some supplies for a trip out on their own.

Sailing

The well-protected waters of San Diego Bay are a haven for sailing enthusiasts from 'round the world. If you're sailing into San Diego on your own craft, Point Loma's the best bet for guest slips and boating-related amenities. The sanctuary provided by Shelter Island and Harbor Island offers refuge to dozens of private marinas, as well as the **Harbor Police's guest marina** (1401 Shelter Island Dr., 619/686-6227) on the south end of the Shelter.

This facility has 22 slips for boats up to 40 feet and end ties for longer boats, as well as water, shore power, restrooms, and parking. No reservations are taken, but you can reach the Harbor Police on VHF 16 to ask if space is available.

Additionally, if you belong to a yacht club, you may have reciprocal privilege at the numerous clubs that make their home in Point Loma. This includes the granddaddy of them all, the **San Diego Yacht Club** (1011 Anchorage Ln., 619/221-8400, www.sdyc.org). Call ahead for specifics.

For those who don't have their own boat, there is still plenty of opportunity to sail the Big Bay from Point Loma. **Sail San Diego** (955 Harbor Island Dr., Docks A–D, 619/297-7426, www.sailsandiego.com, $85) has morning, afternoon, and sunset sails from Harbor Island each day.

And for a truly unique vacation experience, **Harbor Island Yacht Club** (Marina Cortez, 1880 Harbor Island Dr., 619/291-7245 or 800/553-7245, www.harboryc.com) offers five-day live-aboard, learn-to-sail vacations. For $1,995 you'll stay aboard a Catalina slipped at the yacht club while you learn the art of catching wind.

Golf and Tennis

Originally constructed by the navy in 1925, the **Sail Ho Golf Course** (2960 Truxtun Rd., 619/222-4653, www.sailhogolf.com, greens fees $15) has a long and storied history for such a small course. When it was in the hands of the military, the course was just four holes, used as part of a physical fitness and well-being

Barnes Tennis Center offers some of the nicest tennis facilities available to the public.

© ERICKA CHICKOWSKI

CITY BEACHES

program for recruits. At some point Sam Snead acted as head golf professional there when he served in the navy.

In later years the course was expanded to nine holes and eventually transferred to the city, where it was especially popular for junior tournaments. San Diego natives Craig Stadler and Phil Mickelson both played here as kids. In recent years the course was renovated. As a part of the redesign, a clubhouse with a pro shop and a restaurant was added, making this a comfortable course for all comers.

If you prefer racquets over clubs, **Barnes Tennis Center** (4490 West Point Loma Blvd., 619/221-9000, www.tennissandiego.com) is a world-class tennis facility just a few minutes away from the beach. Catering to the highly competitive youth tennis movement in San Diego, Barnes lets kids hit around for free. Adults can play here too, for a nominal fee. Hard courts are $6 per hour and clay courts are $8.50 per hour, with a $4 light fee at night.

Cycling

For a true test of strength and stamina, turn your quads to jelly on **Cabrillo Memorial Drive,** which climbs steeply up to Cabrillo National Monument. The views are your reward—as is the ride down—and the $3 walk-in and bicyclist entrance fee is lower than if you enter the monument in a car.

A more leisurely (and flat!) ride can be had along **both banks of the San Diego River.** The north-side path leads up to Friars Road, which has a protected bike lane leading into Mission Valley. The south-side path leads to Pacific Highway, which provides easy street access to the haciendas of Old Town.

Bike rentals are difficult to find in Point Loma and Ocean Beach if your hotel doesn't provide them. The closest shop is **Bike Tours San Diego** (509 5th Ave., 619/238-2444, 8 A.M.–7 P.M. daily) in the downtown Gaslamp District.

Skating

To get a taste of the gnarly San Diego skate scene, visit **Robb Field Skate Park** (2525 Bacon St., 619/525-8486, 1 P.M.–sunset Mon.–Fri., noon–sunset Sat.–Sun., day pass $5). The 40,000-square-foot facility was planned with the help of local skate pros and features a street-course design with a number of bowls, handrails, ledges, and blocks. All skaters must wear protective gear, and minors must have a liability waiver signed by their guardians.

Spectator Sports and Concerts

Known by the locals simply as "Sports Arena," **Valley View Casino Center at the San Diego Sports Arena** (3500 Sports Arena Blvd., 619/224-4171, www.sandiegoarena.com) is one of the larger venues in the city for headlining artists making the national tour circuit. The arena is also equipped for sporting events. It is home to ice skating events and tennis tournaments and plays host to the Los Angeles Lakers and Los Angeles Clippers for the occasional pre-season basketball game.

ACCOMMODATIONS
Under $100

International travelers, educators with proper credentials, and those with a current hostel card from any of the big chains are welcome at the **OB International Hostel** (4961 Newport Ave., 619/223-7873 or 800/339-7263, www.californiahostel.com, $25 dorm bed). The friendly rooming house provides dorm rooms with a reservation and offers a couples room on a first-come, first-serve basis. Guests are offered free breakfasts in the morning, featuring eggs, pancakes, and cereal among other items.

A more restrained crowd frequents the **Point Loma Hostel** (3790 Udall St., 619/223-4778, www.sandiegohostels.org, $22 dorm bed, $55 d, $65 t) just a few miles away. Run by Hostelling International, this clean hostel also offers advanced reservations for its private rooms and its special family-size private room.

$100-200

The ho-hum accommodations at **Vagabond Inn** (1325 Scott St., 619/224-3371, reservations

800/522-1555, $150 d) aren't going to spark much excitement, but they'll do the job. The motel is located between Shelter Island and Harbor Island, only two miles from the airport and within walking distance of several good seafood restaurants. The property has a heated pool and room rates include continental breakfast and a morning paper.

Prices might seem a bit high for the state of the rooms at **Ocean Villa Inn** (5142 West Point Loma Blvd., 619/224-3481 or 800/759-0012, www.oceanvillainn.com, $189 d), but dog lovers should be willing to pay the premium. The motel abuts Dog Beach, the only 24-hour off-leash space in San Diego County. For an extra $25 the hotel will let up to two pets stay with you. The property also has a dog comfort station to take your puppy to the bathroom on the property, a dog wash, and a pool (for human comfort only). Families traveling with fido may prefer their suites, which for $300 per night sleep six and feature a wet bar and a fridge. Rates for all rooms include continental breakfast.

Ocean Beach Hotel (5080 Newport Ave., 619/223-7191, www.obhotel.com, $199 d) is positioned on the most happening corner on the beach, Newport Avenue and Abbott Street. Singles and free-spirited couples enjoy this hotel, as it is within stumbling distance of Ocean Beach's best bars. Ocean-facing rooms cost quite a bit extra, but if you spring for one you'll have a fantastic view of the pier and the hippies who frequently stroll on the boardwalk across the street.

Holiday Inn San Diego Bayside (4875 N. Harbor Dr., 619/224-3621 or 800/345-9995, www.holinnbayside.com, $179 d) sits along the gateway arterial to Point Loma from downtown and the airport. Rooms are above average for a franchise hotel and the grounds are so well protected by building placement and foliage that it is hard to tell that it is on a fast-moving thoroughfare. Amenities include a nine-hole putting area, a heated pool, and a deck area that features a billiards table, shuffleboard court, and table tennis. The deck area is home to outdoor movie screenings in the summer.

Bike rentals are complimentary, as is the shuttle to and from the airport.

The Pearl (1410 Rosecrans St., 619/226-6100, www.thepearlsd.com, $176 d) delivers the swanky digs of a boutique hotel at more affordable prices than the fancier hotels downtown. The place is an old roadside motel that was completely refurbished to make use of the midcentury architecture. Furnishings, tapestries, and carpets all pay homage to the building's roots, making this a fab spot for *Mad Men* fans to revel in the retro appeal. Quiet this place is not, though, so families are advised to take a wide berth. The hotel's lounge and poolside bottle service is quite popular on the weekends and the party frequently lasts into the wee hours.

$200-300

The most obvious choice for lodging on Shelter Island is **☾ Humphrey's Half Moon Inn and Suites** (2303 Shelter Island Dr., 619/224-3411 or 800/542-7400, www.halfmooninn.com, $383 d, $460 junior suite for four). Located at the end of the island's causeway, the Polynesian-style architecture, gardens, and pool and spa facilities replete with poolside bar all add to this luxury inn's charm. The open-air concert venue and well-regarded restaurant put things over the top for visitors.

If you are seeking a truly secluded hotel on Shelter Island away from the noise of concerts, partiers, and giddy kids, try **☾ Best Western Island Palms** (2051 Shelter Island Dr., 619/222-0561, www.islandpalms.com, $249 d) for a more relaxed atmosphere. The character of this property is low-key, with a lot of good amenities in its own right, including two pools, tennis courts, and a comfortable bar and grill by the marina.

FOOD
Cafés and Casual Eats

You'll have to weigh your priorities before visiting **Ocean Beach Pier Café** (5091 Niagara Ave., 619/226-3474, 8 A.M.–8 P.M. daily, $8). On one hand, the café is as much a landmark as the pier itself, the view is great, and the food is tasty. On the other hand, cleanliness is not exactly top of mind for the managers here. If you aren't picky, ask for a wet towel to wipe up your sticky table before you chow down. If you like seafood, be sure to try the house's special lobster tacos. These succulent treats are a favorite with adventurous taco fans.

Only a block away from the beach, **Jungle Java** (5047 Newport Ave., 619/224-0249, www.junglejavaofob.com, 7 A.M.–8 P.M. daily Sept.–May, 7 A.M.–10 P.M. daily June–Aug., $3) offers a garden sanctuary to sip a cup or two. While you're there, browse through the unique crafts and handiwork items displayed for sale.

If you're in the beach area but would prefer something cooler, try **OB Smoothie Bar** (5001 Newport Ave., 619/222-0293, 9:30 A.M.–5:50 P.M. Mon.–Sat., 10 A.M.–4:30 P.M. Sun., $6) a few blocks east. This small no-nonsense shop blends up a whole array of frozen and fruity concoctions and also makes healthy sandwiches for those who'd like something solid.

In Point Loma, **Con Pane** (2750 Dewey Rd., Ste. 105, 619/224-4344, 7 A.M.–6 P.M. Mon.–Tues. and Thurs.–Fri., 8 A.M.–6 P.M. Sat., 8 A.M.–4 P.M. Sun., $5) and **Point Break Café** (2907 Shelter Island Dr., 619/758-9870, 6:30 A.M.–3 P.M. daily, $8) are both good choices. Con Pane bakes fresh rustic breads and serves up food in a coffee-shop atmosphere, while Point Break offers hearty and healthy meals made for diners seeking a sit-down type of restaurant.

Dessert

Before you head back from the beach to your hotel or car, be sure to stop off at **Lighthouse Ice Cream** (5059 Newport Ave., #102, 619/222-8600, 11:30 A.M.–10 P.M. daily) for some of the best sweet stuff in town. The shop is less than a block away from the pier. If you're not worried about the waistline, try the fresh waffle sandwich ($2.50). Made with two squares of Belgian waffles sizzled right in front of you, they're so good you'll want to have two.

Indulge in the delectable treats served up at **Azucar** (4820 Newport Ave., 619/523-2020, www.iloveazucar.com, 7 A.M.–7 P.M. Mon.–Sat., 8 A.M.–5 P.M. Sun., $7), a bakery that fuses the tropical flavors of the Caribbean with the sophisticated pastries of Europe to great effect. The Cuban American owner of this shop trained in France as a pastry chef and Azucar is the perfect synthesis of her experiences.

Burgers

If your tummy is grumbling for something more substantial, ◖ **Hodad's** (5010 Newport Ave., 619/224-4623, www.hodadies.com, 11 A.M.–9 P.M. Sun.–Thurs., 11 A.M.–10 P.M. Fri.–Sat., $8) is the ideal place for a giant burger and a plate of onion rings. This place's name is surfer parlance for a poser, someone who dresses and acts the part but can't actually surf very well. The atmosphere is just as silly as a hodad walkin' the beach with a never-used surfboard. There's a table set in a car, License plates, funny pictures, and memorabilia line the walls, and, yes, surfboards are mounted on the ceiling.

© ERICKA CHICKOWSKI

Hodad's juicy burgers and enormous milkshakes hit the spot after a long day at the beach.

Seafood

Point Loma is probably one of San Diego's best neighborhoods for those in search of some tasty creatures of the deep. At America Cup Harbor, stop off for a quickly prepared meal at the fish-market deli **Point Loma Seafoods** (2805 Emerson St., 619/223-1109, www.pointlomaseafoods.com, 9 A.M.–6:30 P.M. Mon.–Thurs., 9 A.M.–7 P.M. Fri.–Sat., 10 A.M.–7 P.M. Fri.–Sun., $9). Fish and seafood is plucked from the huge display cases and fried fresh while you wait.

Near the entrance to Shelter Island, **Brigantine** (2725 Shelter Island Dr., 619/224-2871, www.brigantineseafood.com, lunch 11:30 A.M.–3 P.M. Mon.–Sat., dinner 5–9:30 P.M. Sun.–Thurs., 5–10 P.M. Fri.–Sat., $27) is a Point Loma institution. The restaurant is a local chain now with six locations, but this is the original. Try the signature swordfish, a staple of Brigantine meals since it opened in 1969.

If Brigantine is packed, amble over to **Red Sails Inn** (2614 Shelter Island Dr., 619/223-3030, www.theredsailsinn.com, 7 A.M.–11 P.M. daily, $19) across the street. Also a longtime favorite, this restaurant not only has good seafood selections but also some savory steaks.

Mexican

In the Point Loma area, the brightly colored **It's a Taco Shop** (3910 W. Point Loma Blvd., 619/223-6330, 7 A.M.–1 A.M. Mon.–Fri., 24 hours Sat.–Sun., $6) is honest about its intentions right off the bat. This bright-yellow establishment is all about Mexican fast food, specifically the taco but also burritos and other quick eats. For those who love authentic Mexican comfort food, this place serves *menudo* (tripe stew).

Nico's (4918 Newport Ave., 619/223-0230, 7 A.M.–9:45 P.M. daily, $5) in Ocean Beach is a tasty place to stop for a big and juicy California burrito. Stuffed with carne asada and freshly fried potatoes, these beauties will fill you up for the day.

Healthier Mexican choices can be found at OB's **Rancho's Cocina** (1830 Sunset Cliffs Blvd., Ste. H, 619/226-7619, 8 A.M.–10 P.M. daily, $8), which prepares a number of vegetarian and vegan renditions of typical dishes.

German

There aren't any tubas here, but **Kaiserhof Restaurant** (2253 Sunset Cliffs Blvd., 619/224-0606, www.kaiserhofrestaurant.com, lunch 11:30 A.M.–3 P.M. Fri.–Sun., dinner 5–10 P.M. Tues.–Sat., 4:30–9 P.M. Sun., $15) puts a little oompah on your plate with its authentic German food. Located right at the foot of the Sunset Cliffs Boulevard Bridge as you enter Ocean Beach, this bar serves up schnitzels and sausages in a myriad of different ways. The outdoor *biergarten* is also a very comfortable place to put away a few mugs of the authentic German beer on tap here. It's particularly great for soccer fans, who are invited to watch the week's biggest games on the *biergarten*'s wide-screen television.

Portuguese

Portugalia (4839 Newport Ave., 619/222-7678, www.sdportugalia.com, 11 A.M.–2 A.M. Tues.–Sat., 4 P.M.–midnight Sun., $18) is one of the few eateries in San Diego that serves up Portuguese and Brazilian eats. The location is hard to miss—the exterior is adorned with a two-story-high painted cross. Inside, the restaurant serves such favorites as beef Madeira and *linguica* (Portuguese sausage). It also acts as a social meeting space for the Portuguese-speaking community.

Italian

Good Italian is hard to come by in Point Loma, but there are is one definite diamond in the rough. **Old Venice** (2910 Canon St., 619/222-5888, 11 A.M.–9:30 P.M. Sun.–Thurs., 11 A.M.–10:30 P.M. Fri.–Sat.) is a cozy and elegant place to find dependable favorites like veal saltimbocca ($19) and chicken piccata ($16.75). The interior is lit with elegant sconces and a flickering fireplace, and on the weekend evenings, live piano music keeps things animated.

CITY BEACHES

INFORMATION AND SERVICES

Visit **Ocean Beach Mainstreet Association** (1868 Bacon St., #A, 619/224-4906, www.ocean-beachsandiego.com, 9 A.M.–5 P.M. daily) for the skinny on neighborhood happenings and recommendations on where to eat, drink, or stay.

The headquarters for **San Diego Police Department's Western District** (5215 Gaines St., 619/692-4800) is in Ocean Beach. There is also a storefront neighborhood **police station** (3750 Sports Arena Blvd., Ste. 3, 619/531-1540, 8:30 A.M.–4:30 P.M. Mon.–Fri.) in Point Loma near the Sports Arena.

Several banks can be found along Sunset Cliffs Boulevard, which crosses by Newport Avenue in Ocean Beach. The **public library** (4801 Santa Monica Ave., 619/531-1532, 9:30 A.M.–5:30 P.M. Tues. and Thurs.–Sat., noon–8 P.M. Mon. and Wed., 1 P.M.–5 P.M. Sun.) and the **post office** (4833 Santa Monica Ave., 619/224-3570) are only a block from Newport Avenue.

GETTING THERE

The Ocean Beach and Point Loma areas are accessible from the northern beach areas by two bridges over the San Diego River. However, the area has good access to the rest of the city. On the north end, I-8 reaches its end in Ocean Beach, with easy access to parts east. To the south, North Harbor Drive has quick and painless access to the airport and downtown.

By bus, Ocean Beach is served by routes 35 and 923. Point Loma has access to the 28 A, B, and C lines.

LA JOLLA

Spanish for "The Jewel," La Jolla is one of San Diego's most affluent neighborhoods. It is home to some of the region's best restaurants and most lavish shops. But the area isn't all about flashy cars and expensive jewelry; it features a wealth of natural beauty, too. Tucked away in the northeasternmost corner of San Diego city limits, La Jolla lives up to its sparkling moniker with a breathtaking shoreline that squeezes together a number of different beach landscapes in just a few miles—rocky tide pools, sandstone precipices, and gentle sandy beaches.

The magnificent landscape is a major source of inspiration for the renowned and thriving arts community in the area. La Jolla is home to dozens of galleries, museums, and world-class performing arts organizations.

From a sightseeing perspective, La Jolla is primarily broken up into two distinct areas. To the north and east is La Jolla Shores and University Town Center, which surrounds the University of California–San Diego (UCSD). Farther south and closer to the rest of San Diego is La Jolla Cove and the adjacent La Jolla Village. Along the water the Shores and the Cove are less than a mile apart, but the shoreline between the two beaches is rocky and inaccessible, making it necessary to make the ten-minute drive along Torrey Pines Road to shuttle between them. On the map, the distance is relatively short, but plan on some form of transportation because the road is a busy thoroughfare and very steep.

© FOTO168/123RF.COM

HIGHLIGHTS

◖ **La Jolla Shores Beach:** The traditional white sandy beach you think of when you get your towel ready, this is the epicenter of La Jolla's water sports scene (page 148).

◖ **Birch Aquarium at Scripps Institution of Oceanography:** The ocean research and animals studied by Scripps are put on display here. Be sure to bring the kids to the re-created tide pool to see how it tickles to hold a sea anemone (page 149).

◖ **La Jolla Cove:** This gorgeous little beach sits in a nook tucked into the sea cliffs of San Diego's northernmost beach neighborhood (page 150).

◖ **La Jolla Village:** Mingle with millionaires in this posh district, a magnet for fine cuisine, shopping, and the arts (page 151).

◖ **Museum of Contemporary Art San Diego:** Check out the edgy collection of modern paintings and sculpture at La Jolla's most impressive museum (page 151).

◖ **Children's Pool:** Watch mamma seals take their pups under their flippers along the sand at the protected waters of this beach (page 153).

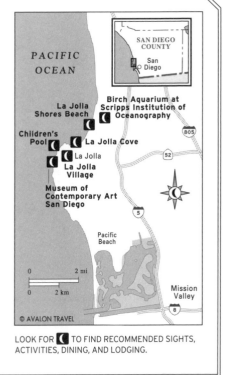

LOOK FOR ◖ TO FIND RECOMMENDED SIGHTS, ACTIVITIES, DINING, AND LODGING.

PLANNING YOUR TIME

Don't don your bathing suit until you've spent some time wandering the high-class storefronts in La Jolla Village. Art lovers will enjoy the dozens of galleries there, as well as the Museum of Contemporary Art San Diego. The Village overlooks La Jolla Cove, a pristine inlet that inspires many of the resident artists who sell their work here. It is also home to some of the only fine-dining restaurants in this casual region that actually require a jacket.

From there you can venture to La Jolla Shores Beach, a sandy beach full of room to spread out a towel and get ready for a full day of surfing, kayaking, swimming, or just diving into a good book.

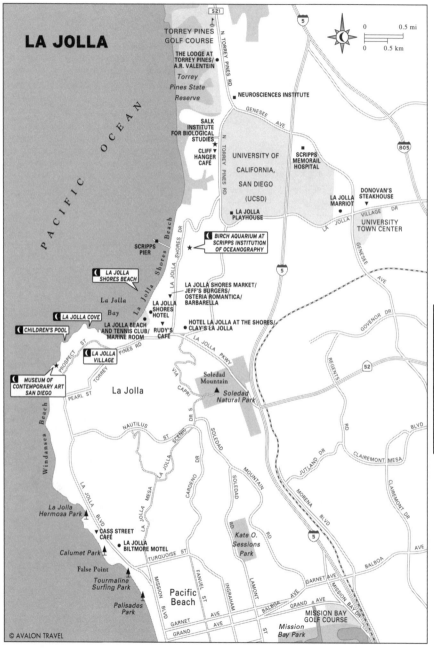

LA JOLLA

TORREY PINES GOLF COURSE

THE LODGE AT TORREY PINES/ A.R. VALENTIEN

Torrey Pines State Reserve

NEUROSCIENCES INSTITUTE

GENESEE AVE

SALK INSTITUTE FOR BIOLOGICAL STUDIES

CLIFF HANGER CAFÉ

UNIVERSITY OF CALIFORNIA, SAN DIEGO (UCSD)

SCRIPPS MEMORAIL HOSPITAL

LA JOLLA MARRIOT

DONOVAN'S STEAKHOUSE

LA JOLLA PLAYHOUSE

UNIVERSITY TOWN CENTER

P A C I F I C   O C E A N

SCRIPPS PIER

BIRCH AQUARIUM AT SCRIPPS INSTITUTION OF OCEANOGRAPHY

LA JOLLA SHORES BEACH

LA JOLLA SHORES MARKET/ JEFF'S BURGERS/ OSTERIA ROMANTICA/ BARBARELLA

La Jolla Bay

LA JOLLA SHORES HOTEL

LA JOLLA COVE

LA JOLLA BEACH AND TENNIS CLUB/ MARINE ROOM

RUDY'S CAFÉ

HOTEL LA JOLLA AT THE SHORES/ CLAV'S LA JOLLA

CHILDREN'S POOL

LA JOLLA VILLAGE

MUSEUM OF CONTEMPORARY ART SAN DIEGO

La Jolla

Windansea Beach

PROSPECT ST

PEARL ST

Soledad Mountain

Soledad Natural Park

NAUTILUS ST

La Jolla Hermosa Park

CASS STREET CAFÉ

LA JOLLA BILTMORE MOTEL

Calumet Park

False Point

Tourmaline Surfing Park

Palisades Park

Pacific Beach

Kate O. Sessions Park

MISSION BAY GOLF COURSE

Mission Bay Park

0   0.5 mi
0   0.5 km

LA JOLLA

© AVALON TRAVEL

Sights

◖ LA JOLLA SHORES BEACH

All of the geological stars aligned to make La Jolla Shores Beach (along Camino del Oro from Ave. de La Playa to El Paseo Grande) an idyllic place for family outings. This particular stretch of coast is protected from the fiercer SoCal waves by a cavernous 500-foot-deep underwater canyon. The canyon ends up deflecting much of the break farther north, which is also likely the reason why the pristine white sand has been able to accumulate over the mile-long section of seashore. All of this adds up to a peaceful beach perfect for sunbathing, building sandcastles, and wading with the little ones.

The beach also shares space with **Scripps Pier.** Built for oceanographic research at the nearby Scripps Institution of Oceanography, the pier is not open to the public. However, it is a landmark structure in La Jolla and makes a great background for vacation snapshots.

If you'd like to get the sand out of your

NAME GAME

While it will certainly always be one of San Diego's finest jewels, La Jolla may not have gained its name from its sparkling beauty. Historians for years have bickered over the origin of the town's name. While the most popular explanation is that it is a perversion of the Spanish phrase La Joya – or "the jewel" – some believe it is actually derived from the local Native American term Woholle – or "hole in the mountains" – a reference to the caves along La Jolla's Shorelines.

shorts without losing sight of the ocean, grassy **Kellogg Park** runs parallel to the beach. The park also features barbecue grills, picnic tables, and a playground for kids to swing and climb on.

La Jolla Shores Beach is one of San Diego's most family-friendly beaches.

LA JOLLA

🄲 BIRCH AQUARIUM AT SCRIPPS INSTITUTION OF OCEANOGRAPHY

San Diego has long been a hub for oceanographic studies, primarily due to the early development of the Scripps Institution of Oceanography in 1903. Now a part of UCSD, Scripps Institution is the one of the world's leading centers for marine studies.

Part of the endowment plans establishing the institute stipulated that the organization operate an aquarium for the public, and since 1905 it has maintained four successive aquarium and museum facilities. Its most recent facility is the Birch Aquarium (2300 Expedition Way, 858/534-3474, www.aquarium.ucsd.edu, 9 A.M.–5 P.M. daily, $12 adults, $9 seniors and students, $8.50 children 3–17, kids under 3 free), which rests on a hillside overlooking the Shores, the institution's campus, and its research facilities on Scripps Pier.

Birch Aquarium's marine and museum exhibits bring to light much of the work that the institute does to protect oceanic ecosystems worldwide. Though the aquarium is designed to be enjoyed by visitors of all ages, it is particularly accessible to the inquisitive minds of the younger set. If you have children, you'll want to check out the facility's centerpiece: three artificially constructed tide pools placed on a patio with a view of **La Jolla Bay.** Kids are encouraged to get their hands wet and touch the sea anemones, starfish, and other tidal creatures on display.

MISS SCRIPPS

Few families made as much of an impact on San Diego development as the Scripps clan did. And among the Scripps, no member was quite as generous or as beloved as Miss Ellen Browning Scripps.

Miss Scripps moved to La Jolla in 1896 after amassing an enormous amount of money through her work to help build her family's national chain of newspapers. In a time when few women had careers, Ellen Scripps worked side by side with her brothers James and Edward Willis ("E. W.") to build a newsmaking empire. She was a talented journalist and to her last days continued to write a syndicated column.

It is said that a journalist provides a voice to those who have none, and renders aid to those who cannot help themselves. It is very possible that the same traits that led her into the trade that would make her a wealthy woman also spurred her on to become one of the greatest philanthropists the city has ever seen.

In 1924 she wrote, "The most important and beautiful gift one human being can give to another is, in some way, to make life a little better to live." She did that by giving money and support to hundreds of civic efforts throughout San Diego. Miss Scripps was responsible for saving the rare Torrey pine tree, found only on the San Diego coast, by buying a parcel of land north of La Jolla and donating it to the state with the condition that it never be developed. She provided funds to Balboa Park for buildings, and to San Diego Zoo to build the world's largest aviary.

Because she firmly believed that there were no two betterments of life than science and art, many of her contributions flowed into organizations that followed these pursuits.

She founded Scripps Memorial Hospital and Scripps Clinic. Her money helped open doors at The Athenaeum Music & Arts Library and La Jolla Public Library. And with her brother E. W., she provided the seed money to start the Scripps Institution of Oceanography.

She wasn't the type to give her money for recognition, and perhaps because of this, Miss Scripps was fondly regarded by her fellow citizens. *Time* called her "the most beloved woman in Southern California" in 1926, when she graced the cover of the magazine at the age of 89.

As her nephew Thomas Scripps wrote in a memoir about her, "Aunt Ellen had the heart of a nurse, the courage of an astronaut and a capacity to give both generously and wisely."

LA JOLLA

La Jolla Cove

© ERICKA CHICKOWSKI

SALK INSTITUTE FOR BIOLOGICAL STUDIES

Less than two miles from Birch Aquarium and the Scripps Institution is another world-class research outfit. Founded by the medical researcher who cured polio, Jonas Salk, the Salk Institute (10010 N. Torrey Pines Rd., 858/453-4100, ext. 1287, www.salk.edu, tours noon Mon.–Fri.) is a private scientific center focused on biological research that can improve the human condition. When Salk first dreamed up his organization, he was determined to build it a home that was as inspiring and creative as the work that would be done there.

In 1959 he teamed up with the already well-known architect Louis Kahn to create what would become one of Kahn's greatest masterpieces. Built on land gifted by the city, the campus centerpiece is its civic plaza, bounded on each side by two angular buildings that mirror one another and point to an expansive blue sky that leads to the ocean.

The free guided tour, offered Monday, Wednesday, and Friday at noon, will offer you an appreciation for the award-winning architecture and the work it has inspired over the years. Call for reservations.

◖ LA JOLLA COVE

Nestled under sandstone cliffs, the beach at La Jolla Cove (along Coast Blvd. northeast of La Jolla Village) is minimal—the winter high tide often washes over the first few steps that lead up to the street. But it isn't the sand that keeps visitors coming. The water that washes up is part of the **San Diego–La Jolla Underwater Park,** a 6,000-acre sanctuary that extends north all the way to Del Mar. Water visibility is usually very good, making the cove a favorite among swimmers, snorkelers, and scuba divers who all vie for a peek at the sea life that teems below. With good visibility it is possible to spot fish such as Garibaldi, rockfish, and sea bass. The 533 acres of the cove's water are also an ecological reserve, so you can look at but not touch the sea life. Taking marine life or rocks from the site is unlawful.

You needn't get wet to enjoy the cove's natural beauty, though. Overlooking the cove is **Ellen Browning Scripps Memorial Park** (1133 Coast Blvd.), a 5.2-acre park that offers lots of grassy space to toss a blanket and watch the hubbub in the water below. Perched on the green at Scripps Park, you'll be able to see the craggy line of San Diego County's northern coast stretch for miles. And in the more immediate distance you can see the crowds of sunbathers at La Jolla Shores Beach.

Just out of view from Scripps Park are a string of hidden jewels tucked into the sandstone that stretches from the Cove to the Shores: the La Jolla Caves. Nearly all of these seven oceanside caves are only accessible by water. The lone exception is open to the public through the **Cave Store** (1325 Cave St., 858/459-0746, www.cavestore.com, 9 A.M.–5 P.M. Mon.–Fri., 9 A.M.–5 P.M. Sat.–Sun., $4 adults, $3 children 16 and under), a short walk away from Scripps Park. Sunny Jim Cave is accessible through a long, steep set of stairs that start in the shop, so keep that in mind if you're traveling with someone with mobility limitations. Hours are extended Memorial Day through Labor Day, when the cave opens at 9 A.M. and closes at 7 P.M. on weekdays and at 8 P.M. on weekends. Visitors are advised to call in advance because hours fluctuate.

◖ LA JOLLA VILLAGE

The beating heart of La Jolla's bustling arts, dining, and shopping scene, La Jolla Village is located right next to La Jolla Cove. Much of the activity is centered around Prospect, Girard, and Herschel Streets, but there are plenty of sites tucked away throughout this 30-block neighborhood.

The Athenaeum Music & Arts Library

Among them is The Athenaeum Music & Arts Library (1008 Wall St., 858/454-5872, www.ljathenaeum.org, 10 A.M.–5:30 P.M. Tues. and Thurs.–Sat., 10 A.M.–8:30 P.M. Wed., free), a private library dedicated solely to the arts. It has one of the largest collections of classical music

Take a stroll underneath the palms around La Jolla Village.

© ERICKA CHICKOWSKI

LA JOLLA

in the United States and hosts art exhibits featuring rising new talent throughout the year.

La Jolla Historical Society

Walk a few blocks south and you can learn how La Jolla became a magnet for the arts at the La Jolla Historical Society (7846 Eads Ave., 858/459-5335, www.lajollahistory.org, 10 A.M.–4 P.M. Mon.–Fri., free). Located in a quaint turn-of-the-20th-century beach cottage, the society's home is packed with memorabilia, photos, and documents that illustrate the area's vibrant past. The cottage is also the jumping-off point for its annual Secret Garden Tour in the spring, which highlights some of the most beautiful private homes and gardens hidden in and around the village. Call in advance for reservations, as this crowd-pleaser sells out every year.

◖ Museum of Contemporary Art San Diego

Also within walking distance is the La Jolla branch of the Museum of Contemporary

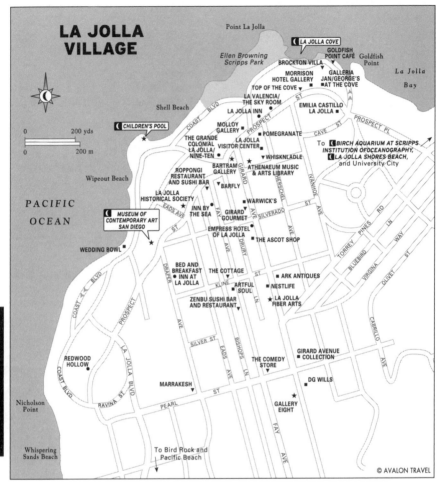

Art San Diego (MCASD, 700 Prospect St., 858/454-3541, www.mcasd.org, 11 A.M.–5 P.M. Fri.–Tues., 11 A.M.–7 P.M. Thurs., $6 adults, $2 students, military, and seniors, kids under 12 free, members free, free to all the third Tues. of the month). Initially established in 1941 as a La Jolla community art center, MCASD boasts a combined collection of more than 3,000 works of art created from 1950 onward. After many decades of success, MCASD La Jolla, housed in the remodeled 1915 home of Ellen Browning

Scripps, is one of two museum locations to feature its collection, which includes works in all different media and genres. Of particular note are its minimalism and pop art pieces, as well as its collection of regional art.

Cuvier Park

Across the street from the museum's back door is Coast Boulevard, which offers an excellent opportunity for strolling alongside the ocean. The promenade along Coast Boulevard winds all the way to the Cove, with plenty of greenery and a couple of notable parks along the way. Directly across the street from MSCAD is Cuvier Park (intersection of Coast Blvd. and Cuvier St.), sometimes called the Wedding Bowl. This grassy spot is sometimes missed because it is a few steps below street level. If there isn't a wedding being held there, it is sometimes possible to have the oceanview lawn to yourself.

◖ Children's Pool

Closer to the Cove along Coast Boulevard is Children's Pool, an artificially protected beach made possible by Ellen Browning Scripps. Miss Scripps donated the money to build a curving wall to protect the area from buffeting waves and create a safe spot for children to swim. However, in the intervening years her plans have been upset by Miss Mother Nature. It seems that some of the local marine mammals took a shine to the protected beach, and they told their friends. Now the sand is a favorite resting spot for local seals and their pups, particularly during pupping season. Seals are very territorial, so it isn't an ideal spot for swimming or sunbathing anymore, but Children's Pool still benefits kids. They love watching the antics of resident seals from the walkways overlooking the beach.

BIRD ROCK

Just out of the hustle of La Jolla's busier neighborhoods is Bird Rock, which acts as a gateway to Pacific Beach farther south. Along the oceanside streets, Bird Rock is home to some of La Jolla's most stunning residences, as well as a few hidden parks worth a stop.

This includes my favorite stretch of shore, **Windansea Beach** (along Neptune Pl. from Bonaire to Westbourne). Windansea has a sandy beach, but it is broken up by numerous sandstone formations that make for good eye candy and can provide secluded spots for sunbathing. Its trademark formation is its Polynesian-style *palapa* hut, called the "sugar shack," first built by surfers in the 1940s and now designated a historical landmark by the San Diego Historical Resources Board.

LA JOLLA

Entertainment and Events

NIGHTLIFE
Comedy Clubs

If it's laughter that you're seeking, **The Comedy Store** (916 Pearl St., 858/454-9176, www.thecomedystore.com, 7 P.M.–midnight Wed.–Sun., $20) is selling it. Operated by Mitzi Shore, mother of the Hollywood flash-in-the-pan Pauly Shore, this comedy lounge features up-and-coming and established talent.

Bars

You'll have to fight the urge to sing a sea shanty when raising your glass at **The Whaling Bar and Grill** (1132 Prospect St., 858/454-0771, 7 P.M.–midnight Wed.–Sun.). Located at La Valencia Hotel, this longtime bar is decked out with harpoons, lanterns, and fishing murals. The cozy pub decor is completed with dark leather banquettes and mahogany accents for an atmosphere that invites you to stay for "just one more round."

For jet-setting hipsters, **Koi Lounge** (7660 Fay Ave., 858/454-4540, 6 P.M.–1 A.M. Thurs.–Sat.) is a spot for the fashionably dressed-down. The raw bar there serves sushi favorites from Zenbu, just two doors down.

Set inside a cute 1904 farmhouse painted blazing red with white trim, **Burgundy Grill and Wine Bar** (830 Kline St., 858/729-9905, www.burgundywinegrill.com, 4–10 P.M. Mon.–Sat.) has cultivated a warm and relaxing atmosphere in its cozy environs. The interior is accented with deep browns and wine-colored tablecloths, while the pleasantly lit patio bar affords a view into the wine cellar. As the name suggests, the bar serves a healthy list of wines from Burgundy, as well as plenty of California favorites. Enjoy a sip from several by imbibing from the robust wine flight menu and don't forget to pair those wines up with one of Burgundy Grill's cheese and meat boards.

Live Music and Dancing

Another stylish location to sip a few is **Clay's La Jolla** (7955 La Jolla Shores Dr., 858/551-3620, www.clayslajolla.com, 5–11 P.M. daily, no cover), which features jazz shows Wednesday through Sunday night, usually starting around 7 P.M.

Those who want to try a little salsa dancing should find the hidden **La Jolla Marriott bar** (4240 La Jolla Village Dr., 858/587-1414, around $10 cover), where the locals flock on Friday and Saturday night for lessons and dancing. Lessons and dancing usually start at 8:30 P.M.

La Jolla is hardly a dance club mecca, but you can find yourself behind a velvet rope at the popular **Barfly** (909 Prospect St., 858/454-2323, www.barflylajolla.com, 11 A.M.–4 A.M. daily), which brings in DJs every weekend to spin some base-thumpin' beats for the diverse 20- and 30-something perfumed crowd that flocks here to get their groove on. Slightly more mature than the crowd down south in PB and less plastic and silicon supported than the divorcées up in Del Mar, the dancers here are a fun and interesting mix of folks.

PERFORMING ARTS

Philanthropist Ellen Browning Scripps set the tone early on for La Jolla generosity. La Jolla's elites play patron to a wide variety of artistic endeavors, particularly in the performing arts. Tops in this category is the Tony Award–winning **La Jolla Playhouse** (2910 La Jolla Village Dr., 858/550-1010, www.lajollaplayhouse.com). Founded in 1947 by Gregory Peck, Dorothy McGuire, and Mel Ferrer, the playhouse operates three facilities to perform an average of six shows each season. The playhouse also shares its stages with the UCSD theater department, an award-winning entity in its own right.

Musically, the **La Jolla Music Society** (858/459-3728, www.ljms.org) is the preeminent classical-music concert producer in San Diego. The Society puts on shows at intimate local venues such as the stage at The **Neurosciences Institute** (10640 John Jay Hopkins Dr., 858/626-2000, www.nsi.edu) and **MCASD La Jolla's auditorium** (700 Prospect St., 858/454-3541), as well as other larger facilities in the county.

Another cozy concert setting is the venue at the **Athenaeum Music & Arts Library** (1008 Wall St., 858/454-5872), which seats only 150 people. The Athenaeum's shows are extremely popular with music enthusiasts due to the snug atmosphere—buy tickets early because shows regularly sell out.

The university also plays host to numerous musical acts throughout the year. **La Jolla Symphony & Chorus Association** (858/534-4637, www.lajollasymphony.com) is a performance ensemble affiliated with the school. It performs six concert weekends each year at **UCSD's Mandeville Auditorium** (UCSD campus on Muir College Dr. near lot 207, 858/534-8497), and the **RIMAC Arena** (9500 Gilman Dr., 858/534-6467) on campus is a frequent stop for big-name artists on their national tours. Check www.ticketmaster.com for updated show calendars and pricing.

FESTIVALS AND EVENTS

Once known as the Buick Invitational until the demise of said automaker, the **Farmers Insurance Open** (www.farmersinsuranceopen. com), held during the last week of January, draws in the best and brightest of the PGA elite each January for one of its first tournaments of the year. Held at the storied Torrey Pines Golf Course, the week-long Farmers Insurance Open allows fans to get up close and personal with golf's greatest from the galleries scattered around the course. The most exciting action is at the end of the week, but your best chance for prime viewing is at the beginning of the week, when crowds are lighter.

In April, Ellen Browning Scripps Park over at La Jolla Cove is a haven for well-burnished chrome, tailfins, and suicide doors during the well-attended **La Jolla Motor Car Classic** (www.lajollamotorcarclassic.com). Hot rods and luxury vehicles gleam in the sunlight, many with popped hoods and doors ajar for car enthusiasts to see the care with which the autos owners have restored and maintained their rides.

For well over a decade now, each May the La Jolla Historical Society hosts an exclusive peek into the private patios and yards of some of the neighborhood's nicest homes during the **La Jolla Secret Garden Tour** (www.lajollahistory.org). Participants are paraded through the gardens—the locations of which are provided on the day of the tour—and treated to classical music performed by local musicians scattered throughout the grounds, as well as whimsical displays designed by area interior decorators.

A blend of the area's love affair with art and cuisine, the **La Jolla Festival of the Arts and Food Faire** (www.lajollaartfestival.org) held in June is a favorite for all San Diegans. Similarly, the **La Jolla Gallery & Wine Walk,** held in early November, is a good chance to get a taste of art, wine, and fine cheeses in one glitzy evening.

During the Fourth of July, festivities are centered around La Jolla Cove, where you'll be able to catch the annual **Lights Over the Cove** fireworks show, which has dazzled fans for decades.

Families are treated to live music on the grassy embankment of the Cove every Sunday afternoon from around mid-July through early September. Musical genres vary wildly, with all sorts of styles performing over the years: rockabilly, mariachi, classical, and jazz.

La Jolla also hosts a number of well-regarded sporting events. Held continually for over three quarters of a century, the **La Jolla Rough Water Swim,** which takes place in mid-September at La Jolla Cove, is the nation's largest rough-water swimming competition. By land, the **La Jolla Half Marathon,** held in mid-April, is another popular test of fitness, renowned among endurance athletes for its grueling ascent up to the top of Torrey Pines State Reserve. The route runs from Del Mar through La Jolla's most scenic roads with the finish at the Cove. Middle-aged tennis aficionados also get the chance every November to try their racquets on the hard courts of the La Jolla Beach and Tennis Club during the **US National Men's and Women's 40's Hard Court Championships,** a well-regarded amateur tourney that draws players from all over the country.

LA JOLLA

Shopping

MALLS

University Town Center (4545 La Jolla Village Dr., 858/546-8858, http://westfield.com/utc, 10 A.M.–9 P.M. Mon.–Fri., 10 A.M.–8 P.M. Sat., 11 A.M.–7 P.M. Sun.) is one of the largest shopping centers in the city. Known simply as UTC by the locals, this mall has 187 stores, a food court, and even an ice-skating rink. The lineup of stores includes Abercrombie & Fitch, Nordstrom, The Limited, and Pottery Barn.

Located just off the 5 at the Nobel Drive exit, **La Jolla Village Square Shopping Center** (8657 Villa La Jolla Dr., 858/455-7550) is home to a lot of the typical chains you'll see at strip malls along freeways around the country: Ross Dress for Less, Marshall's, Best Buy, and Trader Joe's. It's also host to chain restaurants like California Pizza Kitchen and Chipotle. While shopping in downtown La Jolla Village or at UTC may be more fun, this mall is a more convenient and affordable spot to pick up essentials that you may have forgotten to pack.

ART GALLERIES

La Jolla Village's streets are packed with dozens of art galleries that feature collections ranging from the beautiful to the downright bizarre.

© ERICKA CHICKOWSKI

The shopping options are endless at La Jolla Village Square Shopping Center.

Serious art collectors and lookie-loos alike can easily fill an entire afternoon enjoying artwork in the neighborhood.

Much of the action is on Prospect Street and Girard Avenue. On Prospect, **Morrison Hotel Gallery** (1230 Prospect St., 858/551-0835, www.morrisonhotelgallery.com, 11 A.M.–7 P.M. Sun.–Thurs., 11 A.M.–9 P.M. Fri.–Sat.) is named after The Doors' album *Morrison Hotel*. As the name suggests, music is the motif here, with collectible fine-art photography featuring musicians and moments in music. A few steps away is **Galeria JAN** (1250 Prospect St., #B21, 858/551-2053, www.galleriajan.com, 11 A.M.–7 P.M. Sun.–Thurs, 11 A.M.–9 P.M. Fri.–Sat.), which was originally established in Europe in 1986 and moved to La Jolla a decade later. Visitors strolling through over the years have been delighted by originals created by masters such as Max Ernst, Miró, Chagall, Jean Pierre Rousseau, and Roy Lichtenstein. The work at **Emilia Castillo La Jolla** (1273 Prospect St., 858/551-9600, www.emiliacastillolajolla.com, 10 A.M.–6 P.M.

Mon.–Sat., 11 A.M.–5 P.M. Sun.) is only by one master, the great Mexican silversmith Emilia Castillo. Here you'll see the largest exclusive collection of her silver jewelry and houseware, along with work in other mediums such as gold and porcelain.

On Girard, **Molloy Gallery** (8008 Girard Ave., Ste. 190, 858/729-9909, www.molloy-gallery.com, 11 A.M.–6 P.M. Tues.–Sun.) is a unique specialty gallery that sells Australian Aboriginal fine art. **Bartram Gallery** (7874 Girard Ave., 858/459-9797, www.bartram-gallery.com, 10 A.M.–7 P.M. Mon.–Thurs., 10 A.M.–9 P.M. Fri.–Sat., 11 A.M.–6 P.M. Sun.) has a collection of fine photography that captures the natural world. The medium at **La Jolla Fiber Arts** (7644 Girard Ave., 858/454-6732, www.lajollafiberarts.com, 10 A.M.–6 P.M. Tues.–Sat., 11 A.M.–4 P.M. Sun.–Mon.) is anything textile. The collection includes handwoven tapestry, baskets, quilts, and even book arts.

BOUTIQUES

When price is no object, La Jolla Village's boutiques should be the first place you look for apparel, jewelry, and one-of-a-kind items for the home. For those with a lighter pocketbook, these trendy shops are still fun to browse through and dream a little.

Fashionistas should start their spending spree at **Pomegranate** (1152 Prospect St., 858/459-0629, www.pomegranatelajolla.com, 10 A.M.–6 P.M. Mon.–Wed., 10 A.M.–9 P.M. Thurs.–Sat., 11 A.M.–6 P.M. Sun.), which features unique wardrobe items that you'll never see someone else wearing. Pick through the shop's selection of antique jewelry or continue on to **Artful Soul** (7660 Fay Ave., Ste. A, 858/459-2009, www.artfulsoul.com, 10 A.M.–5:30 P.M. Mon.–Sat., 10 A.M.–4 P.M. Sun.), which has a stunning collection of jewelry and handbags created by La Jolla artists. Before making a jewelry decision, be sure to also stop in on **Suzan's Silver & Amber Jewelry** (1298 Prospect St., Ste. 1N, 858/454-9808, noon–5 P.M. daily), which has interesting pieces in its own right.

The men in your party don't have to be left out in the cold. **The Ascot Shop** (7750 Girard Ave., 858/454-4222, www.ascotshop. com, 9 A.M.–6 P.M. Mon.–Sat.) is bound to have the perfect tie to spiff them up for a night on the town.

If your home is your castle, why not choose decor that makes you feel like royalty? Shop at **Nestlife** (7636 Girard Ave., 858/454-4220, www.nestlife.com, 9:30 A.M.–5 P.M. Mon.–Sat., 10 A.M.–5 P.M. Sun.) and you'll likely find something that fits the bill. The shop specializes in fine china, crystal, linens, and well-crafted home accessories.

ANTIQUES

With an assembly of everything from mid-century furnishings to estate china, **Girard Avenue Collection** (7505 Girard Ave., 858/459-7765, 10 A.M.–5:30 P.M. Mon.–Sat.) is an antique fetishist's delight. Pick through the furnishing and decor treasures here and you're bound to find something that suits your style—if not your pocketbook. Run by volunteers to benefit local animal charities, **Ark Antiques** (7643 Girard Ave. C, 858/459-7755, http://arkantiques.org, 10 A.M.–4:30 P.M. Mon.–Sat.) sells a charming assortment of consignment art, furniture, linens, tableware, and everything in between.

BOOKSTORES

A little bit stationary store, a little bit office supply store, and a lot bookstore, **Warwick's** (7812 Girard Ave., 858/454-0347, www. warwicks.com 9 A.M.–6 P.M. Mon.–Sat., 11 A.M.–5 P.M. Sun.) is a reader-friendly shop great for a little poking around with latte in hand. It frequently plays host to author events and book signings and its knowledgeable staff is at the ready to offer suggestions based on your taste and mood.

With books piled, stacked, and squeezed into the shelves all the way up to the rafters, **DG Wills** (7461 Girard Ave., 858/456-1800, www.dgwillsbooks.com, 10 A.M.–7 P.M. Mon.–Sat., 11 A.M.–6 P.M. Sun.) is the type of musty, charismatic bookstore that bibliophiles dream of. Ephemera hangs from said rafters, busts are scattered in the few stray bits of bare shelving, and paintings hang from the sides of shelves because there's hardly even space on the walls for them. Like any respectable intellectual's interests, the collection here is all over the map, and over the years it has welcomed notables from many different fields, including Nobel Laureate DNA discoverers James Watson and Francis Crick, Pulitzer Prize–winning columnist Maureen Dowd, beatnik hero Allen Ginsberg, and novelist Norman Mailer.

Sports and Recreation

SURFING AND SWIMMING

La Jolla Shores' consistently gentle break makes it an ideal place for beginning surfers to test their mettle. If you're the adventurous type, you can paddle right on in and pick it up as you go. Numerous shops on nearby Avenida de la Playa will rent you a beginner's board and a wetsuit, including **La Jolla Surf Systems** (2132 Avenida de la Playa, 858/456-2777, www.lajollasurfsystems. com, 10 A.M.–5 P.M. Mon.–Fri., 9 A.M.–5 P.M. Sat.–Sun.), which will rent a board and a suit for $11 per hour. The shop also offers private

lessons ($60 per hour) for those who would prefer a little guidance.

For even more structure, consider a surf camp. **Surf Diva** (2160 Avenida de la Playa, 858/454-8273, www.surfdiva.com, 9:30 A.M.– 5:30 P.M. Mon.–Thurs., 9:30 A.M.–6 P.M. Fri.–Sun.) specializes in surf instruction for the sport's underrepresented sex. But beginners of either gender (and any age, for that matter) are welcome at many of Surf Diva's camps and clinics. Private lessons start at about $75.

Advanced surfers and those with an appreciation for surf culture have to put **Windansea**

LA JOLLA

© ERICKA CHICKOWSKI

A surfer limbers up before a session at Windansea Beach.

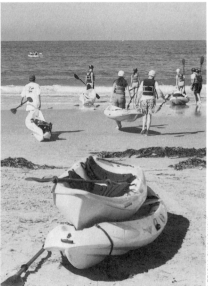

© ERICKA CHICKOWSKI

Rent a kayak or join a tour departing from La Jolla Shores.

Beach (6800 Neptune Pl.) on their must-visit shortlist. A reef just offshore provides a consistent break that has acted as home base for some of Southern California's most renowned surfers. The beach gained lasting literary notoriety when in 1965 Tom Wolfe wrote about some of the local characters that frequented the beach board-in-hand in *The Pumphouse Gang*.

Surfing isn't allowed at La Jolla Cove, but it serves as a major focal point for the purest of water sports: swimming. Competitive swimmers flock from around the world to freestyle in the Cove's clear and scenic waters. The beach serves as prime practice grounds for a close-knit but welcoming community. On any given morning there are usually swimmers out for a dip, but to be safe consider contacting the **La Jolla Cove Swim Club** (www.lajollacoveswimclub.org) or the **Triathlon Club of San Diego** (www.triclubsandiego.com) before your stay to arrange for a local swim buddy to join you. If you have what it takes, earn bonus points with the locals by forgoing the wetsuit in the winter months. The water is so frequented by hard-

core swimmers that it's likely you won't be the only one out there without the neoprene.

KAYAKING

Almost all of the La Jolla Caves are accessible by water, making these secret grottos a paddler's treasure. Several Shores-area touring outfits offer kayak tours of the cliff-side caves, including **La Jolla Kayak** (2199 Avenida de la Playa, 858/459-1114, www.lajollakayak.com, 8 A.M.–sunset daily summer, 9 A.M.–6 P.M. daily fall–spring, single kayak $45, double $70, rentals $28 single, $45 double).

Other specialty firms also offer a twist on the typical kayak experience, teaching anglers the art of fishing on a kayak. **La Jolla Kayak Fishing** (619/461-7172, www.kayak4fish.com) offers an all-day fishing excursion from La Jolla Shores that will teach participants basic kayak skills, surf survival, kayak setup, and fishing techniques—all while hunting for trophy fish such as yellowfin tuna and thresher sharks. The trip is $175 for a single and $300 for a double kayak and includes a kayak and fishing gear. Call ahead to pre-arrange a tour and meet at a pre-arranged push-off spot, usually La Jolla Shores.

SCUBA AND SNORKELING

Some of La Jolla's best features are underwater at the **San Diego–La Jolla Underwater Park** (accessed from La Jolla Shores or La Jolla Cove) in La Jolla Bay. Both experienced and beginning scuba divers can benefit from a trip to **Ocean Express** (2158 Avenida de la Playa, 858/454-6195, www.oexcalifornia.com, 9 A.M.–6 P.M. Mon.–Fri., 8 A.M.–6 P.M. Sat.–Sun., snorkel gear and wetsuit $40 per day, scuba tours $110–180), which offers equipment rentals, instruction, and dive tours of the underwater park.

In the summer some of the best wildlife isn't deep at all. A snorkel, mask, and fins are all that are needed to see the annual influx of leopard sharks in the shallows of La Jolla Bay. These spotted sharks come close to shore in the late summer months to give birth to their young. They are completely harmless to humans and fascinating to watch in their own element. One reliable spot to get the right gear is **Hike Bike Kayak Sports** (2246 Avenida de la Playa, 858/551-9510, www.hikebikekayak.com, 9 A.M.–5 P.M. daily, snorkel gear and wetsuit $25 per day, snorkel tour $40 per person), which offers rentals and also conducts snorkel tours when the sharks come into the bay.

GOLF

One of the nation's finest sets of municipal links is found at **Torrey Pines Golf Course** (11480 N. Torrey Pines Rd., 800/985-4653, www.torreypinesgolfcourse.com, dawn–dusk daily). Built in 1957, this oceanview course is home to the PGA Buick Invitational each January and also hosted to the 2008 U.S. Open.

It features two 18-hole golf courses, North and South, that can challenge even the most experienced player. You'll contend with long yardage, tricky wind patterns, and even sneakier course formations, so pick your tee wisely—the black tees are for pros and masochists only. Realistic golfers should choose the North course, as it is the easier of the two. It is

LA JOLLA

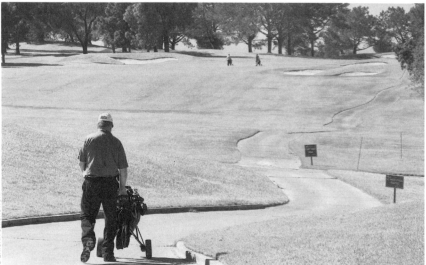

© ERICKA CHICKOWSKI

One of the finest municipal golf courses in the nation, Torrey Pines, played host to the U.S. Open in 2008.

also cheaper, with full greens fees of $125. The South course fees are $229.

BIKING

Touring the streets of La Jolla on a bike can be really rewarding, but the killer hills are a dealbreaker for most casual riders. **Hike Bike Kayak Sports** (2246 Avenida de la Playa, 858/551-9510, www.hikebikekayak.com, 9 A.M.–5 P.M. daily, $50) solves this problem with a bike tour that it likes to call the La Jolla Plunge. Riders are shuttled up to the top of La Jolla's highest peak, Mount Soledad, which features a park with a monument to local veterans and a 360-degree view of San Diego. From there it rolls downhill through La Jolla for 3.5 miles. The two-to-three-hour tour also rides through Pacific Beach and Mission Beach before heading back to Hike Bike Kayak's shop at the Shores.

ICE SKATING

For a cool moment out of the sun, **IceTown** (4545 La Jolla Village Dr., 858/452-9110, www.icetown.com, 10:30 A.M.–5:30 P.M. Mon., 10:30 A.M.–4:30 P.M. Tues., 10:30 A.M.–5 P.M. Wed.–Thurs., 10:30 A.M.–4:15 P.M. and 7–10 P.M. Fri., 12:30–4 P.M. and 8–10:30 P.M. Sat., 1:30–4 P.M. Sun., $11 admission adults, $6 children 5 and under, $2 skate rentals, rentals free to seniors, military, and students, $40 family four-pack) at University Town Center is just the ticket. The Olympic-sized rink is set within the mall's food court, making it a favorite rest stop for families shopping with kids in tow.

PARAGLIDING AND HANG GLIDING

Soar above the Pacific Oceans from the cliffs of La Jolla through the **Torrey Pines Gliderport** (2800 Torrey Pines Scenic Dr., 858/452-9858, http://flytorrey.com, hours vary depending on wind conditions). One of the most well-known gliderports in the state, this one offers beginners the opportunity to pair up with experienced gliders for tandem paragliding ($150) or hang gliding ($200) flights. Because all flights are wind-dependent—especially for hang gliding—the gliderport doesn't take reservations. Call around 10:30 A.M. on the day you're interested in taking to the skies to find out if the conditions are right.

Accommodations

La Jolla lodging ranges from the elegantly simple to the sumptuously opulent. Be prepared to pay for the scenery—and the bragging rights—that come with staying in the area. During high season most accommodations will not be available for less than $200 per night. Beachfront and oceanview properties often charge many times that rate. Travelers who prefer more Spartan beach accommodations or simply wish to save a buck are advised to look a few miles south in Pacific Beach.

UNDER $150

Located in Bird Rock, **La Jolla Biltmore Motel** (5385 La Jolla Blvd., www.biltmoremotel.com, 858/459-6446, $76 d) is reasonably close to both La Jolla and Pacific Beach. Facilities are more "motel" than "Biltmore," but the low price includes a room that will be serviceable and clean.

$150-250

Located within a short walk of the Village's boutiques and restaurants, the **Inn by the Sea** (7830 Fay Ave., 800/526-4545 or 800/462-9732 from California or Canada, www.lajollainnbythesea.com, $179 d) offers an affordable alternative to some of the neighboring luxury hotels. Online reservations are significantly less expensive than reservations by phone.

Built on one of the Village's busiest street corners, **La Jolla Inn** (1110 Prospect St.,

858/454-0133, www.lajollainn.com, $200 d) offers well-appointed European-style accommodations. Rooms either overlook the ocean or the busy shops below. Rates include a continental breakfast served to your room and afternoon refreshments served in the hotel's library. The hotel also offers bike and snorkel rentals to guests.

A ten-minute stroll from the sandy La Jolla Shores Beach, **Hotel La Jolla at the Shores** (7955 La Jolla Shores Dr., 800/666-0261, www.hotellajolla.com, $173 d) gives umbrella-toting families a good value for their vacation dollars. Rooms are spacious, beds soft, linens crisp and clean. The view is excellent from the rooms on the top stories of this eleven-story building, as well as from the heated rooftop pool. The clan can even bring Rover, so long as he's under 60 pounds ($75 fee).

$250-350

Set slightly south of the noise and crowds of La Jolla Village, but still within a stone's skip from La Jolla Cove, **Redwood Hollow** (256 Prospect St., 858/459-8747, http://redwoodhollow-lajolla.com, $189 studio, $239 1-br suite, $299 2-br suite) is a cluster of classic beach cottages built between 1915 and 1940. Designated a historic site, the property binds all those cottages together with little brick-paved patios and walkways and an appealing display of garden florals and greenery. Amenities vary across the seven units, but most have kitchens and many have fireplaces. Most cottages are cozy wood-paneled affairs, with homey furniture that invites you to unwind and hang out a while.

Centered right in the thick of La Jolla Village shopping and dining, **Empress Hotel of La Jolla** (7766 Fay Ave., 858/454-3001, www.empress-hotel.com, $239 d) greets guests in a classy manner from the start, as crisply dressed doormen underneath a nicely lit awning and flapping flags usher you into a dramatic lobby featuring deep navy blue velvet couches and dark wood pillars. Richly appointed, this hotel features spacious rooms decorated in muted tones. You'll not be nickled and dimed at this upscale place, either. Wireless access is

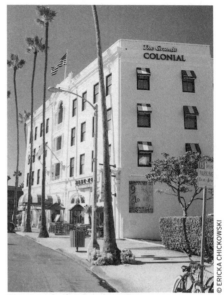

The Grande Colonial La Jolla

complimentary and a tasty continental breakfast is included in the rate.

Frequently voted as the best bed-and-breakfast by national media outlets, **Bed and Breakfast Inn at La Jolla** (7753 Draper Ave., 858/456-2066, www.innlajolla.com, $179–310 d) features fifteen unique rooms in a 1913 home designed by the famous Cubist architect Irving Gill. Each guest's stay includes a gourmet breakfast and a wine-and–hors d'oeuvres reception in the evening.

Another hotel with historical architectural highlights is **ⓒ The Grande Colonial La Jolla** (910 Prospect St., 858/454-2181, www.thegrandecolonial.com, $245 d). Built in 1926, the building's architecture features colonial accents and a colorful palette, highlighted by the front facade's sunburst-style windows. Rooms are European-style and include evening turn-down service.

OVER $350

One of the most architecturally impressive hotels in all of San Diego is **The Lodge at**

Torrey Pines (11480 North Torrey Pines Rd., 858/453-4420, www.lodgeattorreypines.com, $375 d) which sits right along the fairways and greens of the city's most storied golf course. An honest-to-goodness Craftsman structure, the lodge was built in 2002. Authenticity was its designers' number-one goal, as they built up a beautiful complex featuring a post-and-beam structure with authentic clinker brick foundation, metal strap and wedge joinery, expanses of stained glass, and broad roof overhangs with projecting outriggers and raftertails. So even though the lodge maintains the up-to-date and crisp fresh feeling of a newly-minted penny, it manages to exude a aura of historic significance. The whole effect is rendered even more complete by the lodge's impressive collection of Stickley furniture, Oriental rugs and artwork, and landscapes painted *en plein air* by famed California impressionists. These classics line the hallways and the nooks and crannies of the hotel's public spaces, so don't forget to give yourself time to explore the property.

One of the precious few hotels in San Diego that is positioned directly on the beach is (**La Jolla Shores Hotel** (8110 Camino Del Oro, 866/392-8762, www.ljshoreshotel.com, $399 d). The hotel is right next door to Kellogg Park. All the rooms have patios that either overlook the ocean or the hotel's center courtyard, a hacienda-style garden area that features lush greenery, fountains, latticework, and several comfortable spots from which guests can enjoy the scenery.

Referred to as "The Pink Lady" by the locals, (**La Valencia** (1132 Prospect St., 858/454-0771 or 800/451-0772, www.lavalencia.com) is a luxury hotel with a long history of accommodating the rich and famous. The lobby features signed photos with best wishes to the hotel from classic greats such as Lon Chaney and Greta Garbo. The hotel is built into a hill overlooking the ocean. One of the legendary quirks of the place is that the lobby level is referred to as the eighth floor. When the building was constructed in the mid-1920s, the plan was to dig down seven floors below street level. Developers only made it three floors down, but the numbering for the floors lived on. No two rooms are alike at the hotel, making each stay a unique one. The ocean villas by the pool (from $695 d) come with an on-call butler to do your bidding, but many of the rooms and suites (from $350 d) in the other two towers have a better view. Although you're largely paying hefty prices for the beachfront locale, the hotel does have a number of first-class amenities. Facilities include a swimming pool, children's wading pool, spa, and sauna. Beach accessories are also available free of charge.

If you've ever wondered what it is like to belong to an exclusive country club, satisfy your curiosity with a stay at the **La Jolla Beach and Tennis Club** (2000 Spindrift Dr., 800/624-2582, www.ljbtc.com). The 14-acre club is one of the city's most elite, with a four-and-a-half-year waiting list and an initial price tag of $60,000 to join its ranks. As a patron in one of the club's 90 guest rooms, you'll be entitled to all of the perks enjoyed by full-fledged members. This includes access to the club's private beach, championship tennis courts, and nine-hole pitch-and-putt golf course, plus admittance to the club dining room and permission to use club meeting spaces. The property features eight different kinds of rooms with rates from $299 d a night up to $1,179 d per night. The most common, the beachfront two-bedroom suite, runs $879 per night.

Food

La Jolla's fine comestibles are enough to win over even the snobbiest of foodies. Though fine dining is the area's forte, there is no shortage of comfortable spots for a casual meal.

CAFÉS AND DELIS

La Jolla has an abundant supply of quaint cafés. Among the standouts is **Rudy's Café** (2168 Avenida de la Playa, 858/454-5665, www.rudyscafeca.com, 6 A.M.–7 P.M. daily, $5), which is one of the first eateries to open on the Shores' main drag. Stop in for an early cup of joe or enjoy a sandwich or salad later in the day when the people-watching is at its best.

Over in the Village, **Goldfish Point Café** (1255 Coast Blvd., 858/459-7407, 8 A.M.–8:30 P.M. daily, $6) offers a stunning view of the ocean and a friendly atmosphere. Situated across the street from the Cave Store, this little establishment rarely frowns on lingering customers.

If you find yourself in Bird Rock, try the **Cass Street Café** (5550 La Jolla Blvd., 858/454-9094, 7:30 A.M.–9 P.M. Sun.–Mon., 7:30 A.M.–10 P.M. Tues.–Sat., $11). Its pastries and breads are baked daily. They're delicious on their own and can be purchased to go at the counter up front. Or consider trying them with a meal. The café serves hearty breakfasts, fresh salads, and filling sandwiches.

As the name suggests, **The Cottage** (7702 Fay Ave., 858/454-8409, www.cottagelajolla.com, 7:30 A.M.–3 P.M. Sun.–Mon., 7:30 A.M.–9 P.M. Tues.–Thurs., 7:30 A.M.–9:30 P.M. Fri.–Sat., $10) is set in a cute little bungalow and its surrounding patio on a shady street in the Village. Lines are long on the weekend but staffers usually set out a cart with coffee for the patient patrons who linger on the sidewalk. The food that awaits is worth it. Breakfast favorites include the special house-baked granola ($9) and crabcake benedict ($11), while the Waldorf salad is a fresh lunchtime treat during the middle of the day.

Perched high above the La Jolla Cove on a steeply staircased hillside, **Brockton Villa** (1235 Coast Blvd., 858/454-7393, www.brocktonvilla.com, 8 A.M.–3 P.M. and 5–9 P.M. daily, $11) has made for an aerie lookout at the swimmers, kayakers and snorkelers for many brunch diners over the years. While the entire menu is worthy of praise, the Coast Toast ($12) is what keeps people coming back for seconds. Fragrantly orange-flavored, this thick-cut French toast has a crispy exterior and the perfect light and fluffy while still custardy consistency of soufflé.

The breakfast and lunch sandwiches at **Girard Gourmet** (7837 Girard Ave., 858/454-3321, www.girardgourmet.com, 7 A.M.–8 P.M. Mon.–Sat., 7 A.M.–7 P.M. Sun., $7) never fail to please. Piled high with ingredients on top of fresh bread or croissants, this coffee shop's fare can be enjoyed in the little shop or, better yet, wrapped up to be enjoyed on the grass overlooking the Cove. While you're there, you might as well indulge the sweet tooth a little, too. The enormous Cowboy Cookie here is a crumbly treat worth breaking the diet for, chock full of chocolate, pecan, coconut, oats, and cinnamon.

Get an up-close view of the hang gliders and paragliders taking off from the sandy cliffs at the Torrey Pines Gliderport while munching on a sandwich or sipping a cappuccino when you visit the aptly named **Cliff Hanger Café** (2800 Torrey Pines Scenic Dr., 858/452-9858, www.flytorrey.com, 10 A.M.–4 P.M. daily, $8). This simple eatery has one of the best views in town and is a great place to chill out whether you're waiting for your turn to takeoff from the "window" at the gliderport or if you're just there to support a more adventurous companion while keeping two feet firmly planted on the ground.

For those who prefer picnicking on the beach, **La Jolla Shores Market** (2259 Avenida de la Playa, 858/459-3465, 7 A.M.–8 P.M. daily) is a clean, well-stocked spot to pick up groceries, ice, and charcoal.

A TASTE OF THE COAST

Diners flock to the scenic patio of **Brockton Villa** for the sweeping views of La Jolla Cove and a taste of the breakfast haunt's signature dish, the souffle-like Coast Toast, a thick-cut French toast imbued with orange flavor. Your Coast Toast experience doesn't have to be fleeting. Try it at home using this recipe, straight from Brockton Villa's recipe vault.

COAST TOAST

- 1 loaf soft French bread (sliced)
- 1 qt. whipping cream
- 10 eggs
- ¾ cup orange juice
- ½ cup sugar
- a pinch of salt
- 2 tbs. vanilla
- 2 tbs. orange flavoring

Combine liquid ingredients. Pour over bread slices. Cover and refrigerate for at least one hour.

Remove bread and discard liquid. Spread butter on flat grill.

Cook bread until golden brown, then bake at 450 degrees for 5-7 minutes or until bread is puffed up like a soufflé. Dust with powdered sugar.

Serve immediately.
Serves 6.

Recipe courtesy of Brockton Villa Restaurant

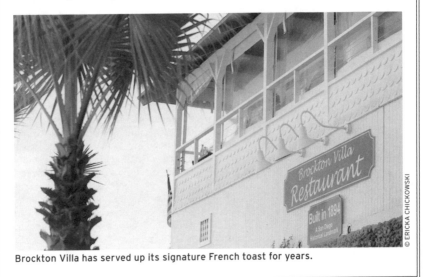

Brockton Villa has served up its signature French toast for years.

LA JOLLA

© ERICKA CHICKOWSKI

CONTEMPORARY CALIFORNIA

Most San Diegans regard the ◖ **Marine Room** (2000 Spindrift Dr., 858/459-7222, www.marineroom.com, 5:30–9 P.M. Sun.–Wed., 5:30–10 P.M. Thurs.–Sat., $35) as the "go-to" place for special events such as birthdays or anniversaries. Situated directly on the beach, this restaurant sets the bar for cuisine across the region. Its award-winning dinner menu never fails to please, but for a really unique experience, try to arrange a reservation for one of its High Tide brunches. Held just a few times a year when the tide crashes against the restaurant's ocean-facing walls, these brunches offer the best tastes of breakfast nibbles, seafood, and desserts.

One of the finest views of the cove can be found at **George's at the Cove** (1250 Prospect St., 858/454-4244, www.georgesatthecove.com, 11 A.M.–9 P.M. Sun.–Thurs., 11 A.M.–10 P.M. Fri.–Sat., $36), which is actually two restaurants in one. George's Ocean Terrace serves fresh and casual fare on a patio facing the cove, while George's Modern California offers a dynamic menu that focuses on seafood and seasonal produce offered locally.

A culinary staple in the La Jolla scene is **Nine-Ten** (910 Prospect St., 858/964-5400, www.nine-ten.com, 11:30 A.M.–2:30 A.M. and 6 P.M.–10 P.M. daily, $30), based out of the Grande Colonial Hotel. Serving classic California cuisine, this restaurant uses produce selected daily from the harvests of local farms to create a fresh menu. For the best of what Nine-Ten has to offer, ask for the Mercy of the Chef ($70, $110 with wine pairings), a multi-course dining experience you won't soon forget.

Overlooking the storied Torrey Pines Golf Course from the wood-paneled Craftsman interior of the Torrey Pines Lodge, **A.R. Valentien** (11480 North Torrey Pines Rd., 858/453-4420, www.lodgetorreypines.com, 7:30 A.M.–11:30 A.M. and noon–2:30 P.M. Sat.–Sun., 11:30 A.M.–2:30 P.M. Mon.–Fri., 5:30 P.M.–10 P.M. daily) presents farm-to-table dining at its best. If you can, try to make a reservation on a Thursday for the chef's weekly Artisan Table, a special meal served family style to a table full of like-minded culinary adventurers—strangers at first but soon friends. You'll be served a few dishes at a time, all of them made with the freshest ingredients offered seasonally by local farmers. The chef comes out to introduce each of his creations, explaining how he prepared the dishes and why he chose the ingredients he picked for each. Convivial and relaxed, this dining experience costs $85 per person.

The laid-back ambiance of **Whisknladle** (1044 Wall St., 858/551-7575, http://whisknladle.com, 11:30 A.M.–9 P.M. Mon.–Thurs., 11:30 A.M.–10 P.M. Fri., 10 A.M.–10 P.M. Sat., 10 A.M.–9 P.M. Sun., $18) belies the quality of the food. An airy bistro with a sprawling patio and simple furniture, this is the place to come for five-star food wearing two-star clothes. If it can be made from scratch, there is a good bet that the kitchen here will make it that way. You'll find that the cured meats, pickled veggies, crispy bread, tender pasta, and even the ice cream are all prepared in-house. Ingredients are sourced from local growers and the menu changes with the harvest.

STEAKHOUSES AND BURGERS

Jeff's Burgers (2152 Avenida de la Playa, 858/454-8038, www.jeffsburgerslajolla.com, 10 A.M.–9 P.M. daily during summer, 10 A.M.–6 P.M. daily during winter, $7) serves typical beach-day treats just a walk away from La Jolla Shores. Its specialty is in the name, with plenty of other sandwich and ice cream choices also available.

Decked out in sleek mod-squad decor with orange and white accents, **Burger Lounge** (1101 Wall St., 858/456-0196, www.burgerlounge.com, 10:30 A.M.–9 P.M. Mon.–Sat., $8) has quickly built itself up as a local San Diego chain phenomenon in recent years. Built around fresh, high-quality grass-feed beef, crisp and fresh veggies, plus a fluffy artisan bun, the burgers here are so juicy they'll drip happily all over your chin. They can be accompanied by fresh-cut fries sprinkled with sea salt and

LA JOLLA

parsley, crispy hand-battered onion rings or an appealing salad that's anything but a cursory menu afterthought. And for desert the restaurant serves cute, soft, red velvet cupcakes donning a dollop of cream cheese frosting. If you are feeding a crowd larger than four, be forewarned. The interior here is tiny, so you may want to order it to-go.

For choice cuts and white-glove service, **Donovan's Steakhouse** (4340 La Jolla Village Dr., 858/450-6666, www.donavanssteakhouse.com, 5–10 P.M. Sun.–Thurs., 5–11 P.M. Fri.–Sat., $38) near UTC is one of the West Coast's finest steakhouses and the only one in La Jolla to win a prestigious Distinguished Restaurants of North America Award. The restaurant also features an award-winning wine selection of over 800 bottles, and a knowledgeable staff and sommelier to help you choose between them. All of the food is first-rate at Donovan's, but the meat easily steals center stage. Donovan's is one of only five restaurants in the country to receive prime-grade beef in every shipment, and every single steak served at the restaurant is prime grade.

FRENCH

The intimate dining room at **The Sky Room** (1132 Prospect St., 858/454-0771, 6:30–10 P.M. daily, $35) only has twelve tables, assuring that each diner will be well attended. Located on the top floor of the La Valencia tower, the restaurant juts up and out of the cliff on Prospect Street and has wraparound windows to give an unobstructed coastal view to the north and south. At night you can see the lights on Scripps Pier twinkle over the water as you savor entrées such as the slow-cooked muscovy duck breast or the Sky bouillabaisse. The Sky Room also offers a sumptuous five-course tasting menu for $85.

ITALIAN

La Jolla Shores features two delicious choices for Italian fare only a couple of doors from one another. Checkered tablecloths and hanging prints depicting Italian villages are meant to evoke the community feeling of a European town square at **Osteria Romantica** (2151 Avenida de la Playa, 858/551-1221, www.osteriaromantica.com, 11:30 A.M.–2:30 P.M. and 5 P.M.–10:30 P.M. Mon.–Fri., 11:30 A.M.–10:30 P.M. Sat.–Sun., $16). This little bistro is informal, but the entrées are not. Try the seafood dishes—particularly good is the bow-tie pasta with salmon, vodka, and asparagus.

Two doors east, **Barbarella** (2171 Avenida de la Playa, 858/454-7373, www.barbarellarestaurant.com, 11:30 A.M.–10 P.M. Sun.–Thurs., 11:30 A.M.–10 P.M. Fri.–Sat., $16) is a chic little spot that adds a touch of French cuisine to its Italian favorites. The French onion soup is, in fact, one of the best items on the menu. The owner is an avowed wine enthusiast and offers a robust selection of vino for very reasonable prices, so don't forget to pair your meal with a glass or two.

FONDUE

Kids will love to dunk their bread, meats, and fruits into the pots at **Forever Fondue** (6110 Friars Rd., 619/295-7792, 5–10 P.M. Sun.–Thurs., 5–11 P.M. Fri.–Sat., $30) in Mission Valley. This classy but casual eatery equips diners with traditional fondue gear and lets them choose their flavors. The all-inclusive meals come with a cheese fondue pot of your choice with breads, veggies, and apples; a salad; and a brothy entrée pot in which to cook one of seven assortment trays of meats and vegetables. It is all capped off with a dessert pot—there are ten chocolatey concoctions to choose from—served with fruit, pound cake, cheesecake, and Rice Krispie treats.

MIDDLE EASTERN

Bring a hearty appetite and a sense of adventure to **Marrakesh** (634 Pearl St., 858/454-2500, www.marrakeshdining.com, 11:30 A.M.–3 P.M. and 5–11 P.M. daily, $24–35). Stepping into the dining room with its brocade and tapestries and the nearly floor-level plush seating you'll feel as if you've been whisked off to a well-appointed North African tent. The vibrant decor is highlighted by an oversized Moroccan mural on its largest wall. The couscous is phenomenal and you'll have a chance to taste it through one of seven five-course feasts. Don't forget to bring some single dollars, too. The restaurant features belly dancing nightly, so you'll want a couple of bucks to tip the dancers.

SUSHI

Styled after the hippest restaurants in Tokyo, **Roppongi Restaurant and Sushi Bar** (875 Prospect St., 858/551-5252, www.roppongiusa.com, 11 A.M.–11 P.M. daily, $25) offers a creative selection of sushi and Asian-fusion cuisine. Adventurous diners should try the Albacore Jalapeño Roll. Made with albacore, jalapeños, cucumber, and garlic ponzu sauce, it is spicy and refreshingly cool at once.

Vying for accolades with Roppongi is the nearby ◖ **Zenbu Sushi Bar and Restaurant** (7660 Fay Ave., Ste. 1, 858/454-4540, 5 P.M.–9:30 P.M. Sun.–Wed., 5 P.M.–1 A.M. Thurs.–Sat., $16), which features sushi so fresh it is practically still wiggling. The restaurant is owned by a family that also owns a local seafood distribution company, giving it exclusive access to the freshest fish in the city. In addition to some traditional sushi rolls, this place makes some off-the-wall concoctions. Those with a slight sweet tooth should definitely try the Wind-N-Sea Roll with freshwater eel, tempura banana, avocado, and cucumber. Another fun item is the Hot Rock, which comes with wafer-thin slices of fresh beef and a steaming-hot chunk of volcanic rock to sear them on.

DESSERT

My advice is to take a picture before you tuck into one of **Michelle Coulon Dessertier's** (7556 Fay Ave., Ste. D, 858/456-5098, www.dessertier.com, 9 A.M.–4 P.M. Mon.–Sun., $6) cakes. Not only are they pretty, but they're so delicious that dessert will disappear off your plate before you've had a chance to remember what it looks like. Any number of her slices, petit fours, or cupcakes will make a worthy finish to a night of dining in the Village—just be sure to pick your treat up before you eat, because the store closes right before dinner hours.

Information and Services

The **La Jolla Visitor Center** (7966 Herschel Ave., 619/236-1212, www.sandiego.org) is one of two regional centers operated by the San Diego Convention and Visitors Bureau. Situated in the middle of La Jolla Village, this location employs a multilingual staff and stocks a complete collection of brochures and maps. It's open daily year-round, but hours vary widely by season. Call for hours.

The local branch of the **public library** (7555 Draper Ave., 858/552-1657, www.lajollalibrary.org, noon–8 P.M. Mon. and Wed., 9:30 A.M.–5:30 P.M. Tues., Thurs., and Fri., 1–5 P.M. Sat.) has free wireless Internet.

Look for both of La Jolla's free weekly newspapers, *The La Jolla Light* and *La Jolla Village News,* at local establishments.

In the Village, the nearest **post office** is at 1140 Wall Street. There is also a post office closer to the Shores and UCSD at 3298 Governor Drive. Numerous banks dot the main Village streets of Girard and Herschel.

Medical services are available at **Scripps Memorial Hospital** (9888 Genesee Ave., 858/626-4123, www.scripps.org).

Getting There and Around

La Jolla is accessible by public transit on bus routes #30, #150, and #50. From downtown San Diego and Old Town, the most scenic bus route is #30, which winds along the coast all the way to UCSD.

From downtown, the easiest driving route is on I-5 north. Take the La Jolla Village Drive exit and turn left on Torrey Pines Road to take you to either La Jolla Shores or La Jolla Village.

If you want to enjoy the area like some locals do, **San Diego Prestige** (7736 Fay Ave., Ste. 200, 858/551-6001, www.sandiegoprestige. com) rents exotic cars such as Lamborghinis, Ferraris, and Lotuses starting at $350 per day. Hourly rates are also available.

NORTH COUNTY

Dubbed North County by resident San Diegans, the territory between northern city limits and the county line is home to an array of quirky sights. Meander the roads here and you're bound to encounter world-class horse racing, marshy lagoons, a couple of secluded nudist beaches, and even a school for trapeze artists.

North County is best known for its coastal communities. These small towns dot the historic Coast Highway 101 (U.S. 101), a notable strip of pavement that was once San Diego's major link to Los Angeles and the rest of the state until I-5 was built in the 1960s.

Each has its own particular flair. Del Mar is home of the ponies as the longtime host of the Del Mar Thoroughbred Club. Solana Beach is a quiet bedroom community with artistic flair.

Encinitas was built by surfers who flocked here during the sport's early days to try their skills on some of the best breaks on the West Coast. Carlsbad also attracts its fair share of surfers, along with loads of families who come for the long stretch of sandy beach at South Carlsbad State Beach and the amusement park fun offered at Legoland California. Sandwiched between Carlsbad and Oceanside, the sprawling Camp Pendleton Marine Corps Base attracts water lovers and anglers who flock to the Oceanside Pier to cast from and surf near what is the longest pier on the West Coast.

North County isn't just about the ocean breezes, either. Heading inland to Escondido, visitors will find hidden in the craggy hillsides the San Diego Zoo Safari Park, one of the West's most impressive zoological preserves.

© ERICKA CHICKOWSKI

HIGHLIGHTS

◖ Torrey Pines State Reserve: Visit this state reserve for a glimpse of the rare Torrey pine tree, ocean vistas from the sandstone cliffs, and beachcombing on secluded beaches (page 171).

◖ Downtown Encinitas: Founded as an enclave for hippies and surfers, this community offers small-town, coastal charm with quaint historic sights and friendly walkways (page 189).

◖ Leo Carrillo Ranch Historic Park: A hidden favorite among local picnickers and strollers, this 10-acre city park is a preserved piece of what was once a sprawling ranch owned by Hollywood actor Leo Carrillo, best known for his role as Pancho in *The Cisco Kid* (page 198).

◖ Legoland California: Any kid who has spent hours on the living room floor in front of a pile of Legos will appreciate this amusement park dedicated to those clickable bricks (page 199).

◖ Mission San Luis Rey: Once known as the King of Missions, Mission San Luis Rey features beautiful gardens, a fascinating museum, and a church painstakingly rebuilt according to historical literature (page 208).

◖ San Diego Zoo Safari Park: This expansive wildlife preserve run by the San Diego Zoological Society is a fun place to check out majestic creatures such as elephants, zebras, rhinoceros, and antelope in environments that best approximate their habitat in the wild (page 214).

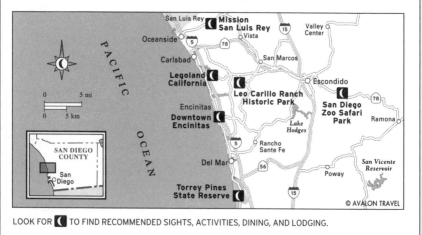

LOOK FOR ◖ TO FIND RECOMMENDED SIGHTS, ACTIVITIES, DINING, AND LODGING.

PLANNING YOUR TIME

Many locations in North County take at least a half-hour to 45 minutes to reach from downtown, and when traffic strikes the drive can stretch out to an hour—especially when trying to reach spots like the Oceanside Pier and the San Diego Zoo Safari Park. Traffic is the worst in the summer during the county fair and race season in Del Mar.

If you decide to visit more than a couple of sights in North County, it might make sense to spend a few nights up there rather than trying to commute from downtown.

The towns in North County can take as little as one day to wander through and up to a week or more to really explore. Many of the biggest draws up here, such as the **San Diego Zoo Safari Park** and **Legoland California** are full-day adventures in and of themselves. If time is limited, be sure to at least plan one day to cruise U.S. 101 through all of coastal towns to really experience the California beach vibe.

Del Mar and Solana Beach

Best known for its horse racetrack, Del Mar boasts a number of natural attractions for visitors. The quaint village of Solana Beach also makes for a fine stop for those heading up U.S. 101, especially shoppers who dig antiques and unique housewares.

Farther inland is Rancho Santa Fe, an enclave of the super-wealthy that is also home to several exclusive resorts.

SIGHTS
◖ Torrey Pines State Reserve
The golden sandstone cliffs of San Diego's wildest natural beachscape ripple by the ocean like earthen corduroy. Chaparral dotted with stands of windswept Torrey pine, the rarest pine native to the United States, clings to the cliffs.

In addition to the pines themselves, the natural wonders of Torrey Pines State Reserve (www.torreypine.org) are plentiful. A series of short oceanview trails wind under the pines, and rabbits are frequently seen scampering through the underbrush and wildflowers that bloom in springtime. Several of these trails lead to the foot of the cliffs, where a wide and peaceful beach sits unmarred by development. Also down at sea level is the marshy Los Penasquitos Lagoon. Here great blue heron swoop by flitting western meadowlark, black-necked stilts, and killdeer.

A stop at the visitors center can yield trail maps and a bit of extra information about local flora and fauna.

Torrey Pines State Reserve and Torrey Pines State Beach is officially in La Jolla, but it is sandwiched between La Jolla and Del Mar in such a way that parking and most access is closer to Del Mar. It is open between 8 A.M. and sunset, and it costs $10 to pass through the access parking gate.

Seagrove Park
Perched on a bluff at the foot of 15th Street and only a few blocks from the Del Mar shopping district, Seagrove Park (Coast Blvd.) has a well-maintained green space from which to watch the dolphins that frequent the breakers just off the shore below. This picturesque spot is a favorite among wedding planners who fall in love with the undulating lawn, the shady pines, and the vibrant brick walkways. Just below the train tracks there is a fenced-in playground area with swings.

Powerhouse Park
Walking north from Seagrove over the railroad crossing, the park transitions into Powerhouse Park, so named for the circa-1928 power station on premises. Originally built to provide heat for the legendary Stratford Inn, the building has been repurposed many times

© AVALON TRAVEL

NORTH COUNTY

over its lifespan and its smokestack serves as a symbol of civic pride for the surrounding community, which is probably why Del Mar converted the building into a community center after acquiring the land for a public park. Visitors can veg out on the expansive lawn or venture down the nearby dirt path to the beach below.

Del Mar City Beach

The Del Mar City Beach is best known for the stretch below Seagrove and Powerhouse, a wide, sandy section that attracts every type of beach denizen due to the convergence of circumstances: a couple of grassy parks, nearby parking lots, and a lifeguard tower staffed from 9 A.M. to dusk. But the beach actually extends all the way from Torrey Pines State Beach up to Solana Beach city limits.

South Beach is a little more secluded due to limited access. Intermittent cliffsides tower over this section of sand, so the easiest way to get here is via a walk on the beach from Torrey Pines or from Seagrove Park.

As the beach meanders north of 29th Street, the shoreline goes to the dogs. Sometimes called North Beach by local residents, most of San Diego calls this stretch **Dog Beach,** in honor of its tolerance of wet and waggin' tails. Rover can romp freely through the surf and the river here between October and May. The rest of the year, dogs are still allowed, but leashes are required. This popular beach is also known as Rivermouth due to the creek estuary on its south edge.

Fletcher Cove

Here's a trick question for you: Where in the so-named town can you find Solana Beach? The answer: It doesn't exist. Unlike similarly named beach towns and neighborhoods in San Diego, Solana doesn't have a corresponding beach.

Oh, sure, it has its fair share of coastal stretches, and even a few nice places to pound an umbrella in the sand. It's just that none of them are actually called Solana Beach.

If locals were forced to name one of their

NORTH COUNTY

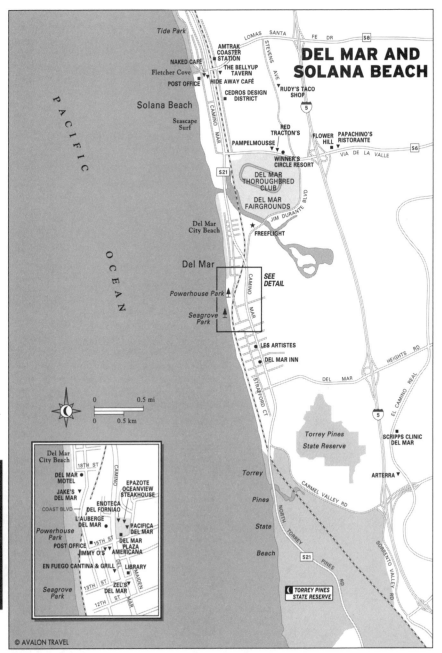

DEL MAR AND SOLANA BEACH

Tide Park

LOMAS SANTA FE DR 58

AMTRAK
COASTER
STATION
NAKED CAFE
Fletcher Cove
POST OFFICE
THE BELLYUP
TAVERN
HIDE AWAY CAFÉ
CEDROS DESIGN
DISTRICT

STEVENS AVE

RUDY'S TACO
SHOP

I 5

Solana Beach

Seascape
Surf

RED
TRACTON'S
PAMPELMOUSSE

FLOWER
HILL
PAPACHINO'S
RISTORANTE

VIA DE LA VALLE

S6

P
A
C
I
F
I
C

CAMINO MAR

S21

WINNER'S
CIRCLE RESORT

DEL MAR
THOROUGHBRED
CLUB

DEL MAR
FAIRGROUNDS

JIM DURANTE BLVD

Del Mar
City Beach

FREEFLIGHT

O
C
E
A
N

Del Mar

SEE
DETAIL

Powerhouse Park

CAMINO MAR

Seagrove
Park

LES ARTISTES

DEL MAR INN

HEIGHTS RD.

DEL MAR

EL CAMINO REAL

STRAFORD CT

I 5

0   0.5 mi
0   0.5 km

Torrey Pines
State Reserve

SCRIPPS CLINIC
DEL MAR

ARTERRA

NORTH COUNTY

Del Mar
City Beach
18TH ST
DEL MAR
MOTEL
JAKE'S
DEL MAR
COAST BLVD
L'AUBERGE
DEL MAR
Powerhouse
Park
POST OFFICE
JIMMY O'S
EN FUEGO CANTINA & GRILL
Seagrove
Park
13TH ST
12TH ST

CAMINO

EPAZOTE
OCEANVIEW
STEAKHOUSE
ENOTECA
DEL FORNIAO
PACIFICA
DEL MAR
15TH ST
DEL MAR
PLAZA
AMERICANA
LIBRARY
ZEL'S
DEL MAR
MADEN ST
MAR ST

Torrey

Pines

State

Beach

CARMEL VALLEY RD

NORTH TORREY PINES RD

SORRENTO VALLEY RD

S21

TORREY PINES
STATE RESERVE

© AVALON TRAVEL

© ERICKA CHICKOWSKI

Fletcher Cove

beaches after the town, it would probably be Fletcher Cove (Lomas Santa Fe Dr., Solana Beach, 858/755-1569, parking lot open 6 A.M.–10 P.M. daily, free parking), a pretty little inlet at the base of Solana's sandstone cliffs. The cove, like all of Solana's beaches, is facing an onslaught of erosion that can sometimes wash almost all the sand away, leaving cobblestones behind. That's OK, though, because the park above can still be a nice green spot to lay out and enjoy views of the surf. The park also has a playground that is usually equipped with at least a few kiddos ready to welcome newcomers for a game of tag.

Seascape Surf

Several of Solana Beach's shoreside parks are hidden at the foot of cliffs topped by houses and condos. Access may be provided via narrow sidewalks shooting between private property and down public stairs to the waterfront below.

This is the case with Seascape Surf, which is a few blocks south of Fletcher Cove. Access is granted through the condos at the 500 and 700 blocks of South Sierra Avenue. This is a nice

secluded beach that is often enjoyed by surf fishers, boogie boarders, and snorkelers.

Tide Beach Park

Tide Beach Park is north of Fletcher at the foot of the stairs leading from Pacific Avenue and Solana Vista Drive. This beach tends to have the least erosion problems of all of the Solana beaches. During low tide here, the tide pools teem with sea life.

During summer months, lifeguards staff both of these beaches between 10 A.M. and 6 P.M. Parking on nearby streets is free.

Freeflight Aviary

If you've been under the sun a little too long and are looking for a shady activity before the races, head over to Freeflight Aviary (2132 Jimmy Durante Blvd., Del Mar, 858/481-3148, www.freeflightbirds.com, 10 A.M.–4 P.M. Thurs.–Tues., 10 A.M.–3 P.M. Wed., $5, $2 children under 14). Run by a local animal hospital, the tropical setting at Freeflight is barrier-free. Parrots, macaws, cockatoos, and other exotics can fly wherever they like within the confines of the aviary.

HISTORIC COAST HIGHWAY

Before city leaders cut the ribbon on I-5 in 1968, there was just one major route from Los Angeles down to San Diego: Pacific Coast Highway, also known as U.S. 101.

Running just a few blocks from the ocean for much of the route in the county, this major arterial was responsible for much of the growth of towns like Carlsbad and Encinitas during the middle part of the 20th century.

Though I-5 supplanted much of the old U.S. 101 in the southern part of the county, it completely bypassed the decommissioned highway for a more inland route in North County. That left behind the two-lane whisper of highway history, one that cruisers and cyclists love to stroll along to this day. Though it isn't the major north-south arterial anymore, it is still an important link between North County's coastal communities. And it is definitely a much more colorful route on this stretch than I-5. If

© ERICKA CHICKOWSKI

The Coast Highway was the main route to San Diego before I-5 opened. Now it is the scenic byway of choice in North County.

you have the time and are traveling up through Del Mar, Solana Beach, Encinitas, Carlsbad, and Oceanside, do yourself a favor and take the detour. Your sense of nostalgia will thank you.

The best part is that visitors are welcome to pet and feed the birds if the animals are willing to allow it.

ENTERTAINMENT AND EVENTS
Nightlife

Del Mar and Solana Beach aren't well-known for a hoppin' bar scene, a fact that makes **The Belly Up Tavern** (143 S. Cedros Ave., Solana Beach, 858/481-9022, www.bellyup.com) such a pleasant surprise for many newcomers. Locals with the inside scoop know this club well—many of them will tell you that it is probably in the top five of all music venues in the county.

Del Mar's nightlife tends to skew toward the middle-aged double-date crowd, but **En Fuego Cantina & Grill** (1342 Camino del Mar, Del Mar, 858/792-6551, www.enfuegocantina. com, 11:30 A.M.–10:30 P.M. Sun.–Thurs., 11:30 A.M.–12:45 A.M. Fri.–Sat.) usually has a boisterous mix of young singles packing the patio on the weekend evenings.

For a younger crowd—if in spirit, if not actual age—head around the corner to **Jimmy O's** (225 W 15th St., 858/350-3735, www. jimmyossportsbar.com, 4 P.M.–2 A.M. daily) a cavernous sports bar festooned in jumbo flat-screen televisions flickering with gnarly surf and skate videos and visited by the flip-flop and board-shorted set that eats up that type of entertainment.

The patio at **Enoteca del Forniao** (1555 Camino del Mar, Del Mar, 858/755-8639, 10 A.M.–10 P.M. Sun.–Thurs., 10 A.M.–11:30 P.M. Fri.–Sat.) makes an excellent spot to sip a glass of wine and puff a fine cigar while watching the sun dip down into the ocean. Set on the second floor of the Del Mar Plaza, this wine and coffee bar stocks a whole cellar full of Northern Italian wines and serves an expertly poured espresso, *crema* and all. In addition to the great views, there is plenty of fun people-watching, with lots of interactions between Del Mar's elite: self-satisfied men hitting on surgically enhanced fortune hunters, Hawaiian-shirted retirees reminiscing, and

NORTH COUNTY

businessmen loosening their ties with prospective clients.

The bar is open until 1 A.M. on Fridays and Saturdays during the summer.

With an open-air patio kissed by salty breezes, a lively bar, and a creative menu, **Zel's Del Mar** (1247 Camino del Mar, Del Mar, 858/755-0076, www.zelsdelmar.com, happy hour 4 P.M.–6:30 P.M., bar open 11 A.M.–2 P.M. Tue.–Sun., 5 P.M.–11 P.M. Tue.–Thurs., 5 P.M.–midnight Fri.–Sat.) is an ideal spot to hang with the happy hour crowd. The patio is a big draw here, set right along Camino del Mar for prime people watching and heated by a crackling outdoor fire pit, it draws in plenty of young professionals looking to unwind over a glass of vino at the end of the day.

For happy hour closer to the racetrack and polo grounds, consider hitting up **Tommy V's** (3790 Via de la Valle, Del Mar, 858/259-3663, http://tommyvdelmar.com, happy hour 5 P.M.–7 P.M. daily, bar open 4:30 P.M.–11 P.M. Mon.–Thurs., 4:30 P.M.–midnight Fri.–Sat. 4:30 P.M.–9 P.M. Sun.), an Italian chophouse with a lively post-work crowd, particularly during race season. The restaurant is operated by the vivacious and sassy Maggiore clan, the stars of the Food Network show *Family Style*. Its piano bar can get loud, so first dates looking for solitude may want to take the getting-to-know-yous elsewhere.

Festivals and Events

The Del Mar Fairgrounds is a complex that holds the **San Diego County Fair** (adults $13, seniors $7, kids 6–12 $7, kids 5 and younger free) every year. Run every year in June, the county fair might seem out of place in such a suburban community as Del Mar. But it really hasn't been more than a decade since this area was built up with luxury homes and condos. If you look east of I-5 you can still see plenty of open space tilled for the flowers and produce that are coveted by people all over the West Coast.

The fair is a good mix of carnival rides, animal shows, and gluttonous eating. Be sure to plan ahead, as the traffic down I-5 can be intense.

SHOPPING

Del Mar's shopping is on par with La Jolla in quality, if not quantity. The action is centered around the corner of 15th and Camino del Mar, which is the unofficial "downtown" of this small community. Meanwhile, Solana Beach's shopping charms are especially apparent along Cedros Avenue.

Stratford Square

On the southwest corner of 15th and Camino del Mar, Stratford Square is the remaining vestige of the famous Stratford Inn. This half-timbered, stucco Tudor square is peppered with local shops that sell curios, clothes, and collectibles. These include **Frustrated Cowboy** (1444 Camino del Mar, Del Mar, 858/755-7963, www.frustrated-cowboy.com, 10:30 A.M.–5:30 P.M. daily), which has all nature of Western knickknacks and doodads; **Earth Song Book Store** (440 Camino Del Mar, Del Mar, 858/755-4254, www.earthsongbooks.com, 10 A.M.–6 P.M. daily), a new-agey purveyor of books, cards, and gifts; and **Marquis Jewelers** (1448 Camino Del Mar, Del Mar, 858/792-1826, 11 A.M.–4 P.M. Mon.–Tues., Thurs.–Sat., closed Wed. and Sun.), a place of many shiny baubles.

Del Mar Plaza

The Del Mar shopping scene's other centerpiece is Del Mar Plaza (1555 Camino Del Mar, www.delmarplaza.com). Diagonal from Stratford Square, this upscale center is a cozy, open-air complex designed to convey a town-center feel. It features three stories that blend into the Del Mar cliffsides with 22 shops and luxury boutiques, designer hair salon and spa facilities, and a number of gourmet restaurants. Most stores at the plaza are open 10 A.M.–9 P.M. Monday–Saturday and 11 A.M.–6 P.M. Sunday.

Some of the designer chain stores include **White House/Black Market** (858/794-4038, www.whiteandblack.com, 10 A.M.–9 P.M. Mon.–Sat., 11 A.M.–6 P.M. Sun.), **Georgiou** (858/481-1964, www.georgioustudio.com), and **Banana Republic** (858/350-0847, www.bananarepublic.com).

The plaza also has several one-of-a-kind boutiques such as **Jolie Femme** (858/792-1222), a lingerie and accessory shop; **Shoetique 101** (858/350-7642, www.shoetique101.com), which features handmade shoes; and **Bayley Boutique** (858/792-9002), a designer store that sells contemporary fashion for twenty- and thirty-somethings.

Del Mar Plaza also has an underground parking lot, a big plus in the parking-deficient Del Mar.

Flower Hill Promenade

Away from the tourist beach zone off the I-5 ramp to the racetrack is the less glamorous Flower Hill Promenade (2720 Via de la Valle, Del Mar, 858/481-7131, 10 a.m.–6 p.m. Mon.–Sat., noon–5 p.m. Sun.), a more weathered shopping mall that actually has an abundance of decent independently owned stores hidden away in that dingy exterior. Notable highlights include a bath and body store, **Bathe** (2670 Via de la Valle, Ste. A220, 858/794-9069, 10 a.m.–6 p.m. Mon.–Sat., noon–6 p.m. Sun.); an upscale kitchen shop, **Silver Skillet** (2690 Via de la Valle, Ste. 150, 858/481-6710, www.silverskillet.com, 10 a.m.–6 p.m. Mon.–Sat., noon–6 p.m. Sun.); and one of the best toy stores in San Diego, **Thinker Things** (2670 Via de la Valle, 858/755-4488, www.thinkerthings.com, 10 a.m.–6 p.m. Mon.–Sat., noon–6 p.m. Sun.).

Bookworms can take a break at **The Bookworks** (2670 Via de la Valle, Del Mar, www.book-works.com, 858/755-3735, 10 a.m.–9 p.m. Sun.–Thurs., 10 a.m.–11 p.m. Fri.–Sat.), and cigar aficionados can take refuge at **Liberty Tobacco** (858/523-9240, www.libertytobacco.com, 10 a.m.–6 p.m. Mon.–Sat., 10 a.m.–5 p.m. Sun.) both also located at the Promenade.

Cedros Design District

Artisan furnishings, handcrafted home accessories, and assorted works of art are the major draws in Solana Beach's Cedros Design District (www.cedrosdesigndistrict.com). This funky strip is checkered with '50s-style homes and old Quonset huts converted into showrooms, studios, and cafés. Pick up a wrought-iron wall accent at **Cokas-Diko** (412 South Cedros, Solana Beach, 858/481-4341, www.cokas-diko.com, 10 a.m.–5 p.m. daily). Or choose between the bouquets of pretty silk flowers at **Flora & Ambiance** (415 S. Cedros Ave., Ste. 140, 858/259-6730, www.flora-ambience.com, 10 a.m.–5 p.m. Tues.–Sat., noon–5 p.m. Sun.). Other notable temptations include the Latin American furniture at **Laura y Laura** (404 N. Cedros Ave., 858/345-1286, www.lauraylaura.com, 10 a.m.–5 p.m. Tues.–Sat.) and the original paintings by local artists that are on display at **Cedros Village Fine Art Gallery** (348-E S. Cedros Ave., 858/720-1838, 11 a.m.–5 p.m. Tues.–Sun.).

If you want some perspective on all that cool stuff you're looking at, stop in at **SoLo** (309 S. Cedros Ave., 858/794-9016, www.solocedros.com, 10 a.m.–6 p.m. Mon.–Sat., 11 a.m.–5 p.m. Sun.) and page through the architecture and design books they sell.

SPORTS AND RECREATION
Surfing

Located on Torrey Pines State Beach, the break off of **Black's Beach** is probably just about the only place in San Diego where it is socially acceptable to surf naked. But the popularity of this surf spot doesn't hang on this novelty factor. It is actually known to be the best beach break in the entire county. The powerful and clean waves here are formed by a deepwater canyon located far offshore. On big days it is an experts' only area, due to dangerously strong rip tides and the isolated nature of the beach. To get there you must hike about a mile down the beach access trail from Torrey Pines State Reserve.

If Black's is closing out or too small to do anything with, chances are luck can be found farther north at **15th Street's reef break.** Accessible from the section of Del Mar City Beach just below Seagrove Park, the reef here is an island of rocky sea floor amid Del Mar's mostly sandy-bottom beaches. This is known as one of the county's very best breaks, producing a long and well-defined left-breaking wave.

Cycle through all of North County's coastal towns via U.S. 101, along the North County shoreline.

Rusty Surfboards (201 15th St., Del Mar, 858/259-3200, Mon.–Fri. 10 A.M.–6 P.M., Sat. 9 A.M.–6 P.M., Sun. 9 A.M.–5 P.M.) is just two blocks away from this break. This is a convenient place to make a pit stop for wax, combs, rashguards, and even a new stick if you've got a wad of cash to burn.

When there's a south swell and the Santa Ana winds blow from the northeast, conditions are ripe for a good session off of the Del Mar sandbars. One popular area known as **Rivermouth** is located on the north end of the beach. Just beware: If it has rained within 72 hours you need to give this spot a wide berth no matter how appealing the waves look. This is a high-pollution area when runoff is flowing out after a storm.

In Solana Beach, **Fletcher Cove** is a fun all-purpose wave that all levels of surfers will paddle out for. The real draw, though, is Seaside. Located to the north of town, this features a reef affectionately known as **Table Tops.** Solana also has a better selection of surf shops, including **Surf Ride Board Shop** (325 N. U.S. 101, Solana Beach, 858/755-0858, www.surfride.com, 10 A.M.–6 P.M. Sun.–Fri.,

9 A.M.–6 P.M. Sat.) and **Mitch's Surf Shop North** (363 N. U.S. 101, Solana Beach, 858/481-1354, 10 A.M.–6 P.M. Mon.–Sat., closed Sun.).

Cycling

Serious cyclists can always be found cruising the bike lanes on U.S. 101 along the North County shoreline. Del Mar is a rational starting point for riders heading north, as the road flattens out at the entrance of Torrey Pines State Reserve after a huge hill that leads down from La Jolla.

Cyclists can pick up spare tubes, apparel, and other accessories in Solana Beach at **B&L Bikes** (211 N. U.S. 101, Solana Beach, 858/481-4148, www.blbikes.com, 10 A.M.–7 P.M. Mon.–Fri., 8 A.M.–6 P.M. Sat., 11 A.M.–5 P.M. Sun.). Due to its very knowledgeable staff of gearheads, this store is popular with the strong contingent of triathletes who train along U.S. 101. B&L also owns a rental shop two doors down called **101 Rentals** ($25–60 per day) that can hook riders up with high-tech steeds that even Lance might be a little jealous of.

Recreational riders who might be intimidated

NORTH COUNTY

by riding along the highway can find refuge on the **Coastal Rail Trail** that starts in Solana Beach. This paved bike path unfolds along an easement provided by the railroad that runs parallel to the highway. The Solana stretch goes 1.7 miles in total and features public art along the way. Further stretches unfold all the way up to Oceanside, along former railway easements.

Balloon Rides

Float over the racetrack, the polo grounds, the palatial estates, and the farms that surround Del Mar on a hot-air-balloon ride from **Panorama Balloon Tours** (800/455-3592, www.gohotair.com). The colorful canopies fill up and lift the baskets away two hours before sunset. You'll sail through the dusky sky and return back to terra firma in the gloaming light. The cost is $195 per person on weekdays and $215 per person on weekends and includes hors d'oeuvres and drinks. Be sure to check the company's website, though, as it often features Web-only pricing specials.

Horse Racing and Polo Matches

Bing Crosby was nothing if not a self-promoter, so it's no surprise that when he partnered with Jimmy Durante, Pat O'Brien, and Charles Howard to open up the **Del Mar Racetrack** (2260 Jimmy Durante Blvd., Del Mar, 858/755-1141, www.delmarracing.com, mid-July–early Sept., $5–25), he wrote a song about his brand-new place:

> *There's a smile on every face and a winner in each race where the turf meets the surf down in old Del Mar.*

Ol' Bing might have been a little biased, but this racetrack where the surf meets the turf really is a special place. The ocean breeze is ever-present and fans get a glimpse of the ocean from the grandstands. The setting is perfect for a place with a storied racing history. This was where Seabiscuit beat Ligaroti in 1938, and it was a magnet for Hollywood stars and wealthy gadflies. Today the diminutive jockeys still sport their colorful garb and gallop over

Horse racing season is the high point of the year in Del Mar.

COURTESY OF DEL MAR THOROUGHBRED CLUB

OPENING DAY AT OL' DEL MAR

Every day of Del Mar Racetrack's short summer race season is special, but if you really want to feel the electricity of beautiful people, social maneuvering, and galloping ponies, battle through the traffic and the crowds to experience the rush of opening day.

The kick-off party for the races, held on a Wednesday in mid-July each year, is a day for pageantry and partying at the track. The locals dust off their finest duds for the event, with the ladies sporting sleek summer dresses and stylish hats, a tradition that is continued in honor of the track's early days. In fact, besides the races themselves, the biggest competition on this day is among these fillies in the annual "One and Only Truly Fabulous Hats Contest."

Opening day also brings a procession of celebrities, a big party in the track's center field, and some of the best gambling action of the season. Be sure to get there early to stake out a seat and consider taking the train if you aren't already staying in Del Mar – traffic from downtown San Diego is brutal.

the track for the benefit of a whole new generation of gamblers and socialites.

The season runs from July to early September. First post is at 2 P.M. every day except Tuesday, when the track goes dark, and Friday, when first post is at 4 P.M. Each week these Friday races are followed by raucous concerts on the center green.

As for Bing, his memory lives on: His tribute song is played every day the ponies run.

The 65-acre **Del Mar Horsepark** (14550 El Camino Real, Del Mar, 858/794-1171, 7 A.M.–4 P.M. daily, entry prices vary) pulls in a lot of visitors enamored with equines. This championship equestrian facility is about three miles away from the racetrack and features a pair of jumping stadiums, four show rings, and

a dressing ring. When there isn't a big event going down, horse enthusiasts are welcome to stop by to watch the riders and horses train.

Even if you can't afford to live there, you can still get a taste of the ritzy Rancho Santa Fe lifestyle at the **San Diego Polo Club** (14555 El Camino Real, Rancho Santa Fe, 858/481-9217, www.sandiegopolo.com, Sun. June–Oct., entry $10, VIP table seat $25). It only costs $5 to watch a whole day of *chukkers,* or match periods, at the polo grounds during the season. These Sunday events are like a picnic at the park, only with galloping ponies and mallets a'swinging amid a churn of flying grass. For an extra $35 you can actually make it a picnic— the club offers a buffet lunch at every match.

ACCOMMODATIONS
Under $150

Each of the 10 rooms at the eccentric **Les Artistes** (944 Camino del Mar, Del Mar, 858/755-4646, www.lesartistesinn.com, $105–250 d) is named for a famous artist and designed using that person's style for inspiration. Remington is done up in rough-hewn pine, cowboys, and cattle skulls; Furo offers Shoji screens and a Japanese-style soaking tub; and O'Keeffe is accented with Santa Fe highlights and floral displays. Many of the rooms offer patios facing the inn's gardens and the entire place is pet-friendly, which can be a real benefit to those who wish to take Fluffy for a short walk down to Dog Beach.

$150-250

There is not much about **Winner's Circle Resort** (550 Via de la Valle, Solana Beach, 858/755-6666, www.winnerscircleresort.com, two-person studio $145, four-person 1-br $195, six-person 2-br $250) that screams luxury other than the price tag. The facilities and rooms are about on par with a suite in a well-cared-for chain hotel with the added bonus of tennis courts and a heated pool. But, and this is a big one for race fans, this property is literally across the street from Del Mar Race Track.

Morgan Run Resort & Club (5690 Cancha De Golf, Rancho Santa Fe, 858/756-2471,

NORTH COUNTY

www.morganrun.com, $169 d, $279 suite) has golf right on the premises. This set of links is a part of the very private, very extravagant Morgan Run Country Club. Guests at the resort are afforded access to club facilities, including a group exercise studio, a spa, championship tennis courts, a lap pool, and private dining facilities.

The Tudor revival stylings of **Del Mar Inn** (720 Camino del Mar, Del Mar, 858/755-9765, www.delmarinn.com, queen $163 d, $203 d) pay homage to the town's legendary but no longer running Stratford Inn, which was also accented by the pitched roofs and half-timbered framework seen here. The interior plays it up further with traditional floral bedspreads over a poster bed frame. Don't bother paying extra for an "ocean view" here; it really is a partial view with buildings obstructing the way. While this is the nicest Clarion Inn I've ever seen, it is still a Clarion nevertheless. The price is for the location, which is easy walking distance to the center of Del Mar's shopping district. Continental breakfast is included.

$250-350

You've got to hand it to (**Del Mar Motel** (1702 Coast Blvd, Del Mar, 858/755-1534, www.delmarmotelonthebeach.com, king $289 d, double $299 d, oceanview $309 d). In a town that is as completely wrapped up in appearances as this one, the temptation had to be high to rename the place an "inn" or a "cottage" or *anything* but the seemingly low-brow title of "motel." The name continues to stick, practicing a little truth in advertising. This white cinderblock motel is a seaside relic from the past and a breath of fresh air amidst all of the fancy resorts in town. The paint is fresh and the linens are new, but these rooms are extremely basic. So why's it so expensive? Well, this place is parked literally right on the beach. Sand drifts over the wooden deck patio and barbecue area that overlooks the ocean not more than a couple yards away. There's a lifeguard shack right there as well, giving a little peace of mind to parents with rambunctious little ones.

© ERICKA CHICKOWSKI

Del Mar Motel is a classic beach motel right on the sand.

Over $350

If your first name is an initial, you frequently tie your cashmere sweaters around your neck, or you carry your dog in a handbag, the help just might let you darken the doorstep at **L'Auberge Del Mar** (1540 Camino del Mar, Del Mar, 858/259-1515 or 800/245-9757, www.laubergedelmar.com, $445 d). This exclusive luxury property is the centerpiece of the Del Mar village. The handsome Tudor buildings hold an even more beautiful interior—dark woods line the lobby and the rooms are accented with marbled bathrooms, plush beds, and artwork framed with gilded edges. Along with the country-club atmosphere comes the attitude as well. Unless you've clearly just inherited a large trust fund you may receive a somewhat aloof reception from the staff.

What's a ritzy enclave without a cream-of-the-crop luxury resort in its backyard? Rancho Santa Fe more than lives up to its tony reputation with two incredible resorts.

Set on a lush 40-acre property, (**Rancho Valencia** (5921 Valencia Cir., Rancho Santa

Fe, 858/756-1123 or 800/548-3664, www. ranchovalencia.com, king $550 d, studio suite $825 d, 1-br suite $975 d) welcomes guests to get a treatment at its full-service spa, take lessons from the staff tennis pro on its pristine courts, or play on its croquet lawn. The resort also features gardens and two heated pools, as well as access to tee times from five of Rancho Santa Fe's most exclusive golf courses.

FOOD

Between Del Mar and Solana Beach, Solana has the lock on the best casual beach grub. There's an ample supply of breakfast cafés, sandwich joints, taco shops, and pizza parlors there that'll never ask you to shake the sand from your shorts before strolling in. Meanwhile, Del Mar is a foodie's paradise. The town plays host to some of the best fine dining establishments in the county.

Cafés and Diners

Before heading out to the beach, fuel up on the home-style breakfasts served at **Hide**

Away Café (150 S. Acacia Ave., Solana Beach, 858/755-3388, 7 A.M.–2 P.M. daily, $6). The name says it, but this ivy-covered little cinderblock building is really easy to miss. It is concealed in a shopping center less than half a block to the northeast of Fletcher Cove.

◖ **Naked Café** (106 S. Sierra Ave., Solana Beach, 858/259-7866, 7:30 A.M.–2:30 P.M. daily, $11) is even closer to Solana's main shoreside haunt, Fletcher Cove—right across the street, in fact. The café's name should probably be preceded by "Feel Good . . ." what with all of the healthy meals served here.

Area surfers will break bread, er...tortillas, at **Rudy's Taco Shop** (524 Stevens Ave., Solana Beach, 858/755-0788, 7 A.M.–8:45 P.M. Mon.–Sat., 7 A.M.–7:45 P.M. Sun., $5) between sessions at Fletcher Cove. Even some of the most voracious among them can't finish the monster carne asada burritos. With a drink this trademark vittle costs about $9 and can probably feed a family of rabid wolverines.

Del Mar beachgoers can find soda, ice cream, and other nibbles at the snack shack

© ERICKA CHICKOWSKI

Solana Beach's secret lunch spot, the Hide Away Café, isn't so hard to find if you know where to look.

in the parking lot adjacent to the 18th Street lifeguard headquarters.

For something a bit more substantial near the Del Mar City Beach, make yourself presentable and head up to the corner of 15th Street and Camino del Mar to **(C Americana** (1454 Camino del Mar, Del Mar, 858/ 794-6838, www.americanarestaurant.com, 7 A.M.–9 P.M. Sun.–Thurs., 7 A.M.–10 P.M. Fri.–Sat., $15), which is shorts-casual, not wet-bathing-suit-and-bare-feet casual. If a classed-up diner and a cute little farmhouse met and had kids, this would be their offspring. Open for breakfast, lunch, and dinner, this place is decorated with black-and-white checkered flooring, petite plants potted in rustic tin, and café curtains. The front room is dominated by a lunch counter lined with chrome and black cushioned chairs and the back has table seating. The menu is California home-style: a mix of rib-sticking classics and healthy meals featuring gourmet greens, meats, and cheeses.

Contemporary Californian

With its proximity to quality local farms and to some of the richest communities in Southern California, Del Mar is a hotbed of haute cuisine.

Situated on a serpentine road that rolls by the estates of rural Rancho Santa Fe, **(C Mille Fleurs** (6009 Paseo Delicias, Rancho Santa Fe, 858/756-3085, www.millefleurs.com, 6–9:30 P.M. Mon.–Fri., 5:30–10 P.M. Sat.–Sun., $35) is probably the most decorated of them all. *Food & Wine* magazine cited it as "Top 25 in America" and the *New York Times* calls it the best restaurant in all of San Diego. The cuisine here is French with California influences, with a frequently changing menu that usually sprinkles exotic dishes featuring ingredients like frog legs and veal tongue in with traditional favorites like lobster and filet mignon. You'll be dining alongside Rancho Santa Fe residents whose net worth is more than some developing countries, so don't embarrass your mom by showing up in anything less than Sunday best.

Pamplemousse Grille (514 Via de la Valle, Del Mar, 858/792-9090, www.pgrille. com, dinner nightly 5 P.M.–10 P.M., lunch 11:30 A.M.–2 P.M. Fri., $39) is as much a restaurant as it is a fashion show during horse-racing season, when the well-heeled come to be seen, dressed in their chic hats and Italian threads. The crowd is drawn by the excellent fare here, a blend of Asian and Continental flavors that generates dishes like nori-crusted seared ahi loin with vegetable hand rolls and glass noodles ($37) or basil-roasted sea bass with sautéed rock shrimp and polenta cakes ($40). The restaurant sits in an unlikely business park across Via de la Valle from the horse track, a location that belies its homey Country French interior. Once summer passes it is actually a much quieter environment conducive to an intimate night out with that special someone.

Further up the road, located in a more chic abode, **(C Market** (3702 Via de la Valle, Del Mar, 858/523-0007, www.marketdelmar.com, 5:30–9:30 P.M. Sun.–Thurs., 5:30–10:30 P.M. Fri.–Sat., $25–35) has quickly become one of Del Mar's culinary treasures. Known best for its tasting menus, Market's dining room pays homage to retro '60s design, replete with patterned and boxy architectural design. The real attraction is the food. The kitchen labors to plate vibrant and creative dishes that allow the freshness of the produce and meat sourced by the chef to really shine through. Diners are advised to spring for the wine pairings with the tasting menu here—the staff often come up with some unexpected but very complementary pairings to further enhance the experience. Best of all, the service is completely on par with what you'd expect of a high-class establishment such as this. Servers are attentive, friendly, and very knowledgeable about the menu and the wine list.

An open secret that some North County foodies would probably hate me for advertising too much, **Arterra** (11966 El Camino Real, Del Mar, 858/369-6032, www.arterrarestaurant.com, breakfast 6:30–9:30 A.M., lunch 11:30 A.M.–2 P.M., dinner 5:30–9:30 P.M. daily, $33, tasting menu $65–72, pairings $45–52) is inauspiciously located at the Del Mar Marriott, which itself is tucked on a side street away from Del Mar's core tourist areas. Once you make it in, though, it is clear that this is not your average hotel restaurant. The spacious dining room's high-backed chairs, oak flooring, and floor-to-ceiling drapes are dressed in a warm palette that echoes the name, which means "art of the earth." The food is the true expression, though—marrying locally grown produce with the best California meat and seafood. The seasonal menu changes to suit the harvest, but the tuna and lamb dishes are almost always stunners no matter how they are prepared.

Steak and Seafood

Red Tracton's (550 Via de la Valle, Del Mar, 858/755-6600, www.theredtractons.com, 11 A.M.–3:30 and 4 P.M.–10 P.M. Mon.–Sat., 4 P.M.–10 P.M. Sun., $27) has been slicing up cuts of its signature prime rib since men wore fedoras and ladies wouldn't be caught dead wearing slacks on a night out. Though this place has the den-like setting, the menu, and the prices of a traditional steakhouse, diners today get away with a more casual look there than they could elsewhere.

Eating at **Jake's Del Mar** (1660 Coast Blvd., Del Mar, 858/755-2002, www.jakesdelmar.com, 11:30 A.M.–3:30 P.M. and 4:30 P.M.–9 P.M. Tues.–Sat., 10 A.M.–2 P.M. and 4:30 P.M.–9 P.M. Sun., $30) is the quintessential Del Mar dining experience. Snuggled up to the Powerhouse, this waterfront restaurant has a bank of windows overlooking the surf and sand. The seats farther away from the windows are elevated so that every seat in the house is a good one for watching the sun set over the water. Seafood is the specialty, but the meat dishes aren't neglected either. Try the osso bucco and you'll find that the tender meat surrenders at the slightest push of a fork tine.

Pacifica del Mar (1555 Camino del Mar, Del Mar, 858/792-0476, www.pacificadelmar.com, 8 A.M.–11 P.M. daily, $30) is an energetic seafood bistro that sits atop Del Mar Plaza's second story. The oceanfront patio affords a great view over the shopping district and the water beyond. This is a lively spot even on the weekends with the din of social chatter punctuated by fork-on-plate clatter as diners dig into dishes like the salt-and-pepper prawns with *udon* noodles and *petrale sole paupiette* stuffed with lobster ($29).

Italian and Pizza

Papachino's Ristorante (2650 Via de la Valle C-210, Del Mar, 858/481-7171, www.papachinos.com, 11 A.M.–10 P.M. Sun.–Thurs., 11 A.M.–11 P.M. Fri.–Sat., $12) is a casual option for dinner after an afternoon at the races. Hidden away in the Flower Hill Promenade, it is convenient to the freeway and to the Del Mar Fairgrounds. This Italian American eatery serves up pasta like ravioli and spaghetti, along with a huge menu of pizzas. Diners have the options to order a pie with traditional ingredients, or to go for others like shrimp, pesto, or barbecue chicken.

The buzzing bistro atmosphere at **Pasta Pronto** (2673 Via de la Valle, Del Mar, 858/481-6017, http://pastaprontodelmar.com, 10:30 A.M.–9 P.M. Mon.–Sat., $13–24) will offer families who eschew frou-frou white-gloved service in favor of a tasty sensible meal. The pasta is fresh and for those with a problem with wheat flours, there is a large array of gluten-free pasta choices. Don't let the loud dining room turn you away—the restaurant has a large take-out menu that might be just the ticket for a picnic at the polo grounds or the beach.

After a long day at the beach, or a tiring drive through Del Mar race traffic, **Pizza Port** (101 N. Hwy. 101, Solana Beach, 858/481-7332, www.pizzaport.com, 11 A.M.–10 P.M. Sun.–Thurs., 11 A.M.–11 P.M. Fri.–Sat., $12) makes an excellent harbor for a melty slice of pie and pint of craft beer. This boisterous canteen is the go-to hot spot when locals want to get the crew together for a casual get-together.

Farmers Markets

East of I-5, Del Mar still clings to its rural identity with a patchwork of farms that produce a bumper crop of plump fruit and vegetables. Most famous of them all is **Chino Farms** (6123 Calzada del Bosque, Rancho Santa Fe, 858/756-3184, 10 A.M.–4 P.M. Tues.–Sat., 10 A.M.–1 P.M. Sun. in fall and winter, 10 A.M.–5 P.M. Tues.–Sat., 10 A.M.–1 P.M. Sun. in spring and summer), a farm stand revered by the high-profile chefs who flock here daily to stock their kitchens for the dinner rush. The flavorful produce here is so delectable that even the titans of L.A.'s dining community will make the one-and-a-half-hour drive every day to get their hands on fresh delicacies like the dainty French strawberries, the Heirloom tomatoes, and the squash blossoms that have made Chino Farms a culinary legend.

INFORMATION AND SERVICES

There's a **police station** (858/565-5200) at 175 N. El Camino Real. **Scripps Clinic Del Mar** (12395 El Camino Real, Ste. 317, 858/794-1250) can handle most nonemergency illnesses and injuries. Probably the most convenient drugstore to get those prescriptions filled is the **CVS** (7 A.M.–midnight daily) on Coast Highway (U.S. 101) in Solana Beach. Emergency medical care can be found one town north in Encinitas at Scripps Memorial Hospital.

In downtown Del Mar, the **post office** (122 15th St., 858/755-1509) is less than a block from Seagrove Park. Within walking district is the **public library** (1309 Camino del Mar, 858/755-1666, 10 A.M.–6 P.M. Tues., 10 A.M.–8 P.M. Wed.–Thurs., 10 A.M.–5 P.M. Fri.–Sun.), which offers free wireless Internet.

GETTING THERE AND AROUND
Public Transit

The North County Transit System operates a commuter train service called **Coaster** that rumbles from Oceanside to downtown San Diego. There is a Coaster station in Solana Beach at 105 North Cedros Avenue, which offers morning and afternoon service both north and south. Riders can park their cars up to 24 hours in the adjacent lot.

Amtrak operates on the same tracks as Coaster, shuttling in passengers on the **Surfliner.** This Amtrak line runs from San Luis Obispo all the way south to downtown and stops at the Solana Beach station.

Solana Beach Train Station is also serviced by two **bus routes** run by the North County Transit Department. The #101 runs north to south from Oceanside to University Town Center in La Jolla. The #308 runs east to west from the station to the Escondido Transit Center.

There is no public transit service to Del Mar, but the city contracts **British Bus Company** (619/251-5074, www.britishbuscompany.com) to operate free shuttles from the Solana Beach station during racing season.

Driving

Car rentals are available in Del Mar from the **Enterprise** (15575 Jimmy Durante Blvd., Del Mar, 858/350-1050, www.enterprise.com) location adjacent to the racetrack. Another company, **Delmartrain.com** (858/481-7099, www.delmartrain.com), offers a third-party service that arranges for rental through one of several major chains and drops the car off at the Solana Beach Train Station.

Those driving from downtown San Diego should be mindful of the Del Mar traffic jams that lock up I-5 in the summertime. The county fair in June and the races from July through September create such an influx of people to the Del Mar Fairgrounds that the freeway frequently backs up all the way to La Jolla. It is not unheard of for it to take two hours to traverse I-5 from Pacific Beach to the Via de la Valle exit.

A potential workaround to bypass this snarl is to drive on North Torrey Pines Road through La Jolla, which will wind down past Torrey Pines onto U.S. 101. Depending on the conditions, this can be a way to sneak into Del Mar and Solana Beach or farther on to the other North County coastal areas. If you are going to the races it may or may not help you, because the side streets are likely to also be a mess as you approach the track.

Encinitas

Encinitas is home to one of the most famous surf breaks on the West Coast, Swami's. Named in honor of the Self-Realization Fellowship spiritual center that rises above the cliffs overlooking the water at the break, Swami's was forever memorialized in the Beach Boy's tune "Surfin' USA." While the water is certainly inviting there and at the eleven other beaches in Encinitas, you can enjoy the town without getting wet. The city is made up of three distinct neighborhoods, surfer-friendly Cardiff-by-the-Sea to the south, downtown Encinitas, and the artist's enclave of Leucadia.

SIGHTS
San Elijo Lagoon
This wetland has long provided natural resources to the people of San Diego County. Archeologists have found ancient landfills known as shell middens that are full of fish bones, shell fragments, and refuse left behind by Native Americans as many as 8,000 years ago. These people came to San Elijo to hunt and fish the marshland and ocean that surrounds this waterway.

Today most of the surrounding land and its wildlife is protected as a part of the San Elijo Lagoon Ecological Reserve (2710 Manchester Ave., Encinitas, www.sanelijo.com), a 1,000-acre plot of protected land. The ecological diversity here is wide. Terns, cormorants, coots, and gulls all scour the water here for fresh and brackish water fish. Trails wind through grasses and the coastal shrub along the lagoon. And the waves crash into the vibrant tidal zone of this wetland.

In addition to the trails, the San Elijo Lagoon Conservancy runs a nature center that celebrates the flora and fauna of San Elijo through interpretive displays and literature.

Even if you don't get a chance to stop at the lagoon, you can witness its beauty as you

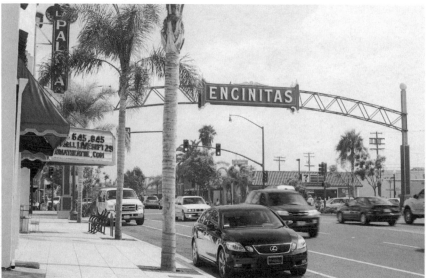

© ERICKA CHICKOWSKI

Part bohemian, part yuppie, Encinitas is united by a sense of community — and the surf.

NORTH COUNTY

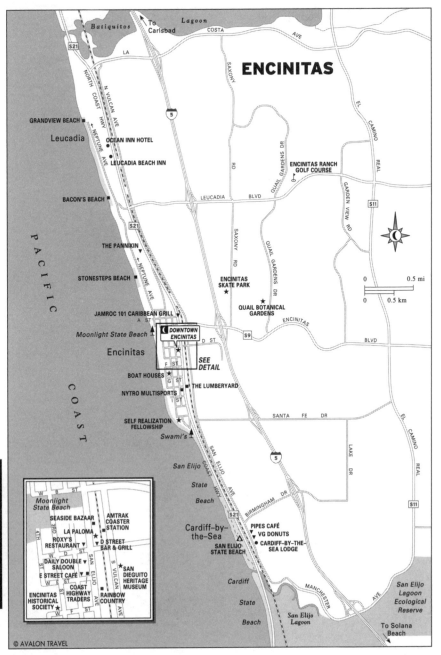

Batiquitos *Lagoon*
To Carlsbad
COSTA AVE
S21
LA
SAXONY
ENCINITAS
EL CAMINO REAL
GRANDVIEW BEACH
Leucadia
OCEAN INN HOTEL
LEUCADIA BEACH INN
ENCINITAS RANCH GOLF COURSE
QUAIL GARDENS DR
GARDEN VIEW RD
S11
BACON'S BEACH
LEUCADIA BLVD
SAXONY RD
THE PANNIKIN
STONESTEPS BEACH
ENCINITAS SKATE PARK
QUAIL BOTANICAL GARDENS
QUAIL GARDENS DR
ENCINITAS
JAMROC 101 CARIBBEAN GRILL
A ST
Moonlight State Beach
DOWNTOWN ENCINITAS
D ST
SEE DETAIL
S9
BLVD
Encinitas
F ST
BOAT HOUSES
G ST
THE LUMBERYARD
NYTRO MULTISPORTS
I ST
SELF REALIZATION FELLOWSHIP
SANTA FE DR
Swami's
LAKE DR
S5
San Elijo State Beach
SAN ELIJO COAST HWY
BIRMINGHAM DR
S21
Cardiff-by-the-Sea
PIPES CAFÉ
VG DONUTS
CARDIFF-BY-THE-SEA LODGE
SAN ELIJO STATE BEACH
Cardiff
EL CAMINO REAL
S11
State Beach
San Elijo Lagoon
MANCHESTER AVE
San Elijo Lagoon Ecological Reserve
To Solana Beach

PACIFIC COAST

N VULCAN AVE
NORTH COAST HWY
NEPTUNE AVE
S21
NEPTUNE AVE

0   0.5 mi
0   0.5 km

Inset (SEE DETAIL):
Moonlight State Beach
W ST
SEASIDE BAZAAR
AMTRAK COASTER STATION
LA PALOMA
ROXY'S RESTAURANT
D STREET BAR & GRILL
DAILY DOUBLE SALOON
E STREET CAFÉ
SAN DIEGUITO HERITAGE MUSEUM
COAST HIGHWAY TRADERS
RAINBOW COUNTRY
ENCINITAS HISTORICAL SOCIETY
W ST
4TH
3RD
SAN ELIJO AVE
S VULCAN AVE

Moonlight Beach in Encinitas is a hot spot for those looking to bump, set, and spike their way to glory.

drive from Solana Beach to Encinitas on Coast Highway (U.S. 101). The road connects the two towns with a bridge that passes through the lagoon just behind the surf zone.

Moonlight Beach and Beacon's Beach

Moonlight Beach (B St. at the ocean) is by far the most popular park in Encinitas, and with good reason. This white-sand beach features volleyball courts, playgrounds, a well-staffed lifeguard station, a snack shack, and beach-toy rental, plus a copious amount of parking in nearby lots and street parking. All of this is located just a few blocks from downtown Encinitas.

North of Moonlight, Beacon's Beach is named for a World War II–era military signal station. The beacon is gone now, but this Leucadia beach still draws surfers who come for the waves.

Cardiff State Beach

The banks, reefs, and cays of Encinitas are her strongest selling points. In Cardiff-by-the-

Sea, the best shoreline is at two state beaches. Farthest south is Cardiff State Beach, which runs adjacent to the San Elijo Lagoon. The sloping sand is good for beachcombing and the shore is frequented by anglers who cast their long surf rods here for ocean fishing. The adjacent reef here is popular among snorkelers and divers as well.

San Elijo State Beach

Just north of Cardiff State Beach, past the lagoon's outlet, is San Elijo State Beach. This beach is similar to Cardiff with the added benefit of a campground that is equipped with a supply store that also rents beach equipment.

◖ Downtown Encinitas

You might not know it from a trip to Encinitas, but surfer dudes are not an indigenous people. Learn about the real locals at the **San Dieguito Heritage Museum** (561 S. Vulcan Ave., 760/632-9711, www.sdheritage.org, noon–4 P.M. Wed. and Fri., $4 adults, $3 seniors, $2 children under 14). It offers a quiet little repository of artifacts and photos that

HEAVEN'S GATE IN RANCHO SANTA FE

The wealth factor of Rancho Santa Fe's elite residents puts them in another world compared to San Diego at large. But that wasn't enough for a certain group of people who called this small town home in the mid-1990s. Tucked away on a quiet street of this serene community, 38 people lived in a mansion as part of a cult that believed they would be taken off the planet and into interdimensional nirvana on the Hale-Bopp Comet.

Led by their wide-eyed leader, Marshall Applewhite, this group called itself Heaven's Gate. It shocked the tightly knit Rancho Santa Fe community when in 1997 almost every single one of its members was found dead in the mansion as part of a mass suicide meant to trigger their ride into the stars.

The town has tried to distance itself from the event. The street that the mansion stood on has changed names, and after being sold several times the mansion itself was torn down. Nevertheless, this bizarre event remains a morbid footnote in the town's mostly unremarkable history.

chronicle the regional heritage of Diegueño, Luiseño, and Kumeyaay tribes, as well as the local history behind the Ranchero period and the transition to U.S. sovereignty.

La Paloma (471 S. U.S. 101, 760/436-7469, www.lapalomatheatre.com) is a historic symbol of Encinitas's thriving art and music scene. The theater was built in 1928, a time when vaudeville acts preceded movies that screened here. Not only does the theater have a rich history of cinema, airing movies from Laurel and Hardy to Warren Miller, but it is also a storied small venue for music concerts and poetry slams. The building itself is visually intriguing with Spanish colonial flourishes and a barrel-tile roof that has inspired many artists to take pen or brush to capture its beauty on paper or canvas.

The oldest structure in town also happens to be the home of the **Encinitas Historical Society** (390 W. F St., 760/753-5726, www.encinitashistoricalsociety.com, noon–4 P.M. Wed., Fri., and Sat., free). This historic school house is located just four blocks from U.S. 101. The society houses a number of events here; on every second Saturday at 10:30 A.M. the house is the starting point of a 90-minute historical walk of downtown.

While you are stopping by the schoolhouse, be sure to turn the corner on 3rd Street heading south. Less than halfway down that first block you'll come across two of the city's most curious structures. There at 726 and 732 3rd Street stand two beautiful boats, blue and white gleaming in the sunlight, looking like they are ready to float down the street and head out to sea momentarily. These craft are "moored" a block away from the ocean and have never had the pleasure of feeling waves lap at their sides. Known simply as **the boat houses,** they were built expressly as dry-land habitation by an eccentric Encinitas native in 1928.

Self-Realization Fellowship

Surfers and locals call it Swami's but this cliffside spiritual compound that is known by its gilded onion-domed towers is really named the Self-Realization Fellowship Ashram Center (215 K St., Encinitas, 760/753-2888, www.yogananda-srf.org). The center was founded in 1937 by Paramahansa Yogananda, a charismatic spiritual leader from West India who taught a blend of Christian, Hindu, and yoga philosophies that continues to captivate followers worldwide today.

The fellowship runs a lovely property that is open to the public regardless of religious belief. Most attractive are the Hermitage (2–5 P.M. Sun.) and meditation gardens (9 A.M.–5 P.M. Tues.–Sat., 11 A.M.–5 P.M. Sun.), a peaceful sanctuary that includes several stunning ocean views, a waterfall, and a koi pond.

Quail Botanical Gardens

Quail Botanical Gardens (230 Quail Gardens

Dr., Encinitas, 760/436-3036, www.qbgardens. org, 9 A.M.–5 P.M. daily, $10 adults, $7 seniors, students, and active military, $5 children 3–12, free 2 and under) is a source of inspiration for any aspiring botanists who are convinced there is no hope for their out-of-season garden. Amid the parched native coastal scrub, these gardens are an oasis of tropical foliage and other plant life from around the world.

The 30-acre grounds are almost like a zoo for plant matter. Trails connect various exhibits that display collections from exotic regions like the Himalayas, the Canary Islands, and South Africa. Other themed gardens include a subtropical fruit garden, two desert gardens, and a bamboo garden. There's even a rain forest here, for crying out loud!

The gardens were first cultivated in the early part of the 20th century by a pair of Boy Scout leaders who grew their plants from clippings and seeds collected during their worldwide travels. The couple left their estate to the county in 1957 in order to continue teaching children about botany in perpetuity. Be sure to bring a little extra change for parking; it'll cost you a dollar here.

ENTERTAINMENT AND EVENTS
Nightlife
Normally you go on vacation to get away from the office, but you should make an exception when visiting Encinitas. **Duke's Cardiff Office** (110 A Aberdeen Dr., Encinitas, 760/753-7766, 10 A.M.–2 A.M.) is a classic windowless dive, hidden away in a tiny strip mall, with a name that offers a ready-made excuse for liquid lunch libations when local spouses ask how their sweetie's day at work went. You're as likely to see the pool tables racked by surfers as you are business peeps, as all types of drinkers are drawn by the easy, breezy atmosphere here.

Competing with the Office for the title of Best Encinitas Dive is **Daily Double Saloon** (546 S. U.S. 101, Encinitas, 760/753-1366, 11 A.M.–2 A.M. daily) in downtown Encinitas. The floors are sticky, the furniture is worn, but the Saloon keeps drawing a rough-and-ready

crowd with its cheap, stiff drinks. Ladies on the prowl will especially dig the eye-candy here. This is a congregating temple of the Holy Order of Hot Surfer Dudes.

D Street Bar and Grill (485 S. U.S. 101, Encinitas, 760/943-9101, www.dstreetbarandgrill.com, 11 A.M.–1:30 A.M. daily) is another all-purpose favorite. This classed-up sports bar is a comfortable spot to enjoy a pitcher or three with a group of friends. The scene is lively, but not so loud that you can't shoot the breeze with pals.

Festivals and Events
The biggest shindig in Encinitas goes down in April, when the roadways are flooded with vendors and artists for the **Encinitas Street Fair.** The event typically features live music and dance scattered on outdoor stages, a special performance at the historic La Paloma Theater, and a beer garden with its own dedicated music stage.

This event also kicks off the annual **Arts Alive Banner Project,** a cooperative effort between city government and local artists to create unique fine-art banners to hang in the city beginning in February until they are auctioned off in late May.

Held on the third Thursday of each month from June through September, the **Rods & Woodies Classic Car Show** series is a tribute to the historic Highway 101 and the cars that used to roll by. The event is a spectacle of vintage vehicles mostly from the 1930s through the '50s, all in mint and shiny condition.

Encinitas is the world's most prolific producer of that scarlet holiday harbinger, the poinsettia. The city honors its leafy flower with at the **Encinitas Fall Festival,** once known as the Poinsettia Festival, a street fair held downtown each year in mid-November.

SHOPPING
Well-heeled shoppers flock to Del Mar's shops and showrooms to express their individuality through a flashy display of conspicuous spending. The frugal and the eccentric go to Encinitas.

NORTH COUNTY

Here they can still convey their style—only through a bargain hunt in and out of the bazaars, thrift shops, and art studios downtown. This is bohemian shopping at its best.

Encinitas's hippie artist roots have flowered with a good crop of new-age shops sprinkled about town. You can smell the patchouli for miles at **Rainbow Country** (633 S. U.S. 101, Encinitas, 760/943-8006), a rasta-reggae affair that is heavy on the incense and tie-dye and none too discreet with the smoking accessories.

Coast Highway Traders (530 S. Coast Hwy. 101, 760/944-1381, 10 A.M.–6 P.M. daily) has an incredible collection of Día de los Muertos (Day of the Dead) skeleton dolls along with folk art from around the world.

Home-spun knitters can spend hours picking through the natural and exotic fibers for sale at **The Black Sheep** (1060 S. Coast Hwy. 101, 760/436-9973, www.theblacksheep.biz, 10 A.M.–6 P.M. Mon.–Sat., noon–5 P.M. Sun.). And **Seaside Bazaar** (459 S. U.S. 101, Encinitas, 760/753-1611, 10 A.M.–4 P.M. Sat.–Sun.) is a weekend open-air market that features antiques, linens, and funky clothes and jewelry.

While Encinitas does maintain strong ties to its nonconformist hippie heritage, the fact of the matter is that the average house here costs well over $500,000 and most hippies here have grown up to live flashier lifestyles than their parents ever dreamed up. If Ben and Jerry didn't have their palaces in Vermont, they'd be in Encinitas. **The Lumberyard** (8525 Gibbs Dr., Ste. 200, Encinitas, 858/292-8989) betrays the real dual nature of Encinitas. In the no-man's-land between Cardiff and downtown Encinitas, this cookie-cutter strip mall has a concentration of 20 or so shops that pretty effectively sum up the confused, sometimes guilty psyche of the locals. On one hand, there are stores like **Magical Child** (967 S. Coast Hwy. 101, 760/633-1326, 10 A.M.–5:30 P.M. Tues.–Sat., 10 A.M.–5 P.M. Sun., closed Mon.) and **SoulScape** (765 South Coast Hwy. 101, Ste 106, 760/753-2345, www.shopsoulscape.

com, 9:30 A.M.–9 P.M. daily), which promise to get shoppers in touch with their inner spirit if only they lay down enough smackers for some nature of cosmic merchandise. Then there are others like **Bella Moda Boutique** (967 S. Coast Hwy. 101. Ste. 104, 760/479-9879, www.shopbellamoda.com, 10 A.M.–5:30 P.M. Mon.–Sat., 11 A.M.–4 P.M. Sun.) and **Chuao Chocolatier** (937 S. Coast Hwy. 101, Ste. C-109, 760/635-1444, 10 A.M.–6 P.M. Mon.–Thurs., 10 A.M.–7 P.M. Fri.–Sat., 10 A.M.–5 P.M. Sun.), which are upscale without even pretending to be in touch with their karmic centers.

SPORTS AND RECREATION
Swimming and Surfing

Besides at Moonlight Beach, the shoreline in Encinitas is typically pocked with ragged reefs or littered with cobblestones, cliffside shores whose beach is mostly submerged come high tide. Not so great for family wading or sunbathing, but perfect for paddling out and tucking into that perfect curl.

The reefs are particularly plentiful on the southern edge of town. At Cardiff State Beach's middle section, **Cardiff reef** offers a consistent set of waves that are enjoyed by kooks and aggro types alike. On the northern part of this state beach near the outlet of San Elijo Lagoon is **Suckouts,** a steep section that can give the experienced surfer an opportunity to get tubed if they don't go over the falls first.

San Elijo State Beach is just north of Cardiff State Beach, right in front of Cardiff-by-the-Sea. Here the best-known break is called **Pipes.** This is another of North County's trademark left-breaking waves, best firing in the winter at low tide with a medium swell.

The most famous of them all, though, is **Swami's,** which is named for the temple with the onion-domed turrets that rise on the cliff above this legendary reef break. Swami's breaks the rules of Encinitas surf spots. The wave breaks right and it doesn't lose its form when the monster swells come in—in fact, that is when this titan really shines, which makes this spot a SoCal magnet in the winter. Even

© ERICKA CHICKOWSKI

the view from Swami's hilltop

on the mellowest days, though, the parking lot above this beach is likely to be buzzin', full of barely running VW busses, sensible Hondas, and snazzy BMWs, all with one thing in common: an empty surf rack.

The lineup at Swami's can become as crowded as that parking lot, so if you get there and feel like you need your space, another nearby alternative is **Boneyards,** a reef break that is only accessible by walking north from Swami's.

The beach break at **Moonlight Beach** is fickle, but it can be cooperative during its fair share of swells. The whitewash here is a friendly spot to bring out a foam board to learn how to surf, which is probably why Encinitas's most popular surf instruction outfit, **Kahuna Bob's** (760/721-7700, www.kahunabob.com), chooses Moonlight as one of two beaches on which to instruct first-timers. The other beach is **Beacon's** farther north.

One of the most popular spots in the northern Leucadia area is **Grandview Beach,** which features a mix of beach and reef break that makes for good all-purpose riding at all ability levels. This particular section of shoreline is home to another popular surf academy, **Leucadia Surf School** (760/685-7873, www. leucadiasurfschool.com, by appointment only, $65 two-hour lessons).

Cycling

Riding south to north on U.S. 101, the first sight as you descend the rise from Solana Beach is a breathtaking vista of Cardiff Beach to the left and San Elijo Lagoon to the right. The views don't let up the rest of the way, which will bring you past the gilded domes of the Self-Realization Fellowship, the slow bustle of downtown Encinitas, and the artists enclaves in Leucadia.

Two of the most convenient spots to pick up supplies or have those derailleurs tuned are **Nytro Multisports** (940 S. U.S. 101, Encinitas, 760/632-0006, www.nytro.com, 10 A.M.–6 P.M. Mon.–Sat., 10 A.M.–5 P.M. Sun.) and **Ride Cyclery** (559 S. U.S. 101, 760/332-8356, www.ridecyclery.com, 10 A.M.–6 P.M. Tues.–Sat., 11 A.M.–4 P.M. Sun.).

Golf

The golf options are thin in Encinitas compared to its neighbors to the north and south. If you are looking to tee up within city limits your best bet is at **Encinitas Ranch** (1275 Quail Gardens Dr., Encinitas, 760/944-1936, $81 weekday, $87 Friday, $103 weekends and holidays), which is set on a plot of former flower fields. The course is designed with the windswept look of a coastal sea ranch. Hole 11 is the signature. Surrounded by a constantly blooming ring of plants, "The Flower Hole" pays tribute to Encinitas's agricultural roots.

Skateboarding

The North County skate scene is as legendary as its surf. In fact, when the swells aren't rolling in, many of the area surf rats will join their brothers in boards at the **Encinitas YMCA Skatepark** (200 Saxony Rd., Encinitas,

NORTH COUNTY

760/942-9622, regular hours 3:30–6 P.M. Mon.–Fri., 10 A.M.–6 P.M. Sat.–Sun., summer hours 2:30–7:45 P.M. Mon.–Fri., 9 A.M.–5 P.M. Sat.–Sun., $10 per 2.5-hour session). The facility gets major props for its 80-foot-wide, 13-foot-tall vert ramp, designed by the Birdman himself, Tony Hawk.

This massive park also has a double-hipped keyhole pool, numerous mini-ramps, and a street course packed with skateable surfaces.

ACCOMMODATIONS
Under $150
A cute little motel by the U.S. 101, ☾ **Leucadia Beach Inn** (1322 N. U.S. 101, Encinitas, 760/943-7461 or 800/706-7461, www.leucadiabeachinn.org, $85–145 d) is reminiscent of your first apartment after college. Sure, the rooms are spartan and the furniture isn't new. But every colorful wall is painted with care, decorations are lovingly placed, and the vibe is friendly and cheerful. The place is spotless; it really has some of the best bargain lodging in all of North County. The downside is that it has only a handful of rooms so vacancy can be hard to come by in the summer months.

$150-250
Nuzzled up against one of the winding cliffside roads leading from the freeway down to the Encinitas coast, **Inn at Moonlight Beach** (105 N. Vulcan, Encinitas, 760/561-1755, www.innatmoonlightbeach.com, $179 d) has four homey rooms and a comfortable oceanview garden with koi pond and waterfall, all in a pet-friendly setting. If you can afford it, try to book the Penthouse Suite ($299 d), which has a private spa on a patio with ocean vistas. During the week breakfast is more limited than what some bed-and-breakfast regulars might expect.

Ocean Inn Hotel (1444 N. Coast Hwy. 101, 760/436-1988 or 800/546-1598, www.oceaninnhotel.com, $199 d) is another Coast Highway hotel popular with beachgoers—it is only a block away from Grandview Beach.

SK8 TOWN

San Diego's anti-establishment board culture has long substituted smooth concrete for watery waves when the inclination or the need arises. The region is a hub for the skateboarding community, an incubation tank for homegrown legends like Tony Hawk and a mecca for dozens of other pros who have come to settle down in the area to have a chance to grind next to likeminded athletes. Especially popular is the North County area, which boasts one of the best public skate parks in the country at the Encinitas YMCA. The following is a roster of some of the skate legends that call the area home:

- Tony Hawk
- Bucky Lasek
- Andy MacDonald
- Rob Lorifice
- Bob Burnquist
- Mathias Ringstrom
- Chad Muska
- Jamie Thomas

Don't be surprised if you see these pros, or any others for that matter, when you shred the rails and ramps at local skate parks. This town is crawling with skate legends.

All rooms come with a microwave and a mini-fridge and the patio has barbecues available for those who'd like to save a bit of cash by grilling up a few meals.

For a more authentic bed-and-breakfast experience, visit **Black Orchid Bed and Breakfast** (653 Requeza St., Encinitas, 760/753-0584, www.bedbreakfastsandiego.com, $185–235 d). This inviting and well-decorated place is located away from the beach, but the quirky and fun-loving innkeepers pour their heart into being gracious hosts. A full breakfast each morning is included.

$250-350

Cardiff-by-the-Sea Lodge (142 Chesterfield, Cardiff-by-the-Sea, 760/944-6474, www.cardifflodge.com, $189–289 d) isn't on the beach, but it is within walking distance. The pretty building is across the railroad tracks from Cardiff State Beach. The rooms here are a bit worn down, though, and the breakfast at this bed-and-breakfast is more of an extended continental than a full meal. However, it does offer a few rooms with whirlpool tubs and it's the lodging option closest to the beach in Cardiff-by-the-Sea.

Camping

You'd better book early if you want to save a spot at the **San Elijo State Beach** (2050 N. U.S. 101, 760/753-5091, $35 tent, $65 full hookup) campground. This is the county's southernmost beachfront campground that allows tent camping and its qualities are hardly a secret. The 30 campsites are shielded from one another by coastal scrubs and accented by the occasional palm tree. The beach is just a quick scamper down the low bluff's wooden staircase.

This is a developed campground that has full restrooms with hot showers, an RV dump station, and cold outdoor showers for rinsing off after a surf. In the summer the park store has supplies, ice, and beach equipment rentals.

FOOD

Just the aroma wafting out of **VG Donuts** (106 Aberdeen Dr., 760/753-2400, www.vgbakery.com, 5 A.M.–9 P.M. Mon.–Thurs., 5 A.M.–10 P.M. Fri.–Sat., 5 A.M.–7 P.M. Sun, $2) is enough to widen your hips, but who can think of that when there are creamy, fresh donuts waiting to be gobbled up? You can munch on your sugary treat and a cuppa joe on the patio that overlooks Cardiff reef's surf break just beyond the railroad tracks.

No café is as revered by the wave-riding set

as ◖ **Pipes Cafe** (121 Liverpool Dr., 760/632-0056, www.pipescafe.com, 7 A.M.–3 P.M. daily, $6), though. This Cardiff eatery has the three essential elements that make up a truly classic breakfast joint: flavorful food, huge portions, and cheap prices.

Surfers famished after a session at the famed surf spot near the Self-Realization Fellowship will often stop for a gorge-fest of healthy grub at **Swami's Café** (1163 S. U.S. 101, 760/944-0612, 7 A.M.–4 P.M. daily, $6). The menu is very veggie-friendly, with lots of salads, options with tofu, and smoothies. Breakfast is hearty, featuring big breakfast burritos, French toast, pancakes, and granola. Don't come here in a hurry, though. The food's good, but it takes a while to get it.

The cookies at **E Street Café** (130 W. E St., 760/230-2038, www.estreetcafe.com, 7 A.M.–10 P.M. daily, $7) make for an excellent pick-me-up after a day of shopping for art and incense in downtown Encinitas. This large coffee house and Internet café has a dizzying selection of teas and coffees to warm those bones on the days that the marine layer never quite burns off, as well as a selection of iced drinks for the real scorchers.

Also downtown is **The Pannikin** (510 N. U.S. 101, Encinitas, 760/436-0033, http://pannikincoffeeandtea.com, 6 A.M.–6 P.M. daily, $5), a distinctive café that makes itself at home in a historic train station from the 1880s. Pannikin is part of a small chain that has two other locations sprinkled in Del Mar and La Jolla, but the location in Encinitas can't be beat for its historic setting and friendly vibe. The place continues the railroad theme with its decor inside. The coffee is robust and full-flavored, the pastries are fresh-made by the store, and the menu also features a slate of quiche, egg steamers, and lunchtime sandwiches.

Eat to the beat of steel drums and Rastafari rhythms at **Jamroc 101 Caribbean Grill** (101 N. U.S. 101, Encinitas, 760/436-3162, www.jamroc101.com, 11 A.M.–8:30 P.M. Mon.–Thurs., 11 A.M.–9:30 P.M. Fri.–Sun., $10), which is probably the only place in North County that you can get your hands on authentic jerk chicken and fried plantains. Open for lunch and dinner, Jamroc features most entrées in two sizes: "Likkle" or "Bigga," making it a good pit stop for a quick family meal without draining vacation coffers.

Roxy's Restaurant (517 S. Coast Hwy. 101, 760/436-5001, 11 A.M.–10 P.M. daily, $14) sounds like the name of a greasy-spoon diner, but this Encinitas eatery is actually a refuge for health-food nuts and vegetarians. The menu here is a blend of Mediterranean and vegetarian classics, with a good dose of salads mixed in with other specialties like homemade spanakopita and a falafel plate.

The glut of cafés and grills can wear on a poor traveler who just wants a restaurant where napkins are folded nicely on the table rather than dispensed from a chrome box. **El Q'ero Restaurant>** (564 S Coast Hwy, 760/753-9050, www.qerorestaurant.com, 11:30 A.M.–3 P.M. Mon.–Sat., 5 P.M.–9 P.M. Mon.–Thurs., 5 P.M.–10 P.M. Fri.–Sat., $27) offers that respite with its refined atmosphere and fine Peruvian cuisine. Settled into a brick-fronted building, the dining room interior is awash in color. Its brightly painted yellow walls are bedecked with South American artwork and its dishes are just as vibrant, with traditional dishes like ceviche with sea bass ($15), braised short ribs ($30), and a *tres leches* cake worth saving room for. Much of the menu is centered around small plates, making this an choice spot for a leisurely, lingering meal with friends or loved ones.

INFORMATION AND SERVICES

Get the skinny on the ins and outs of Cardiff-by-the-Sea, Leucadia, and downtown Encinitas at the **Encinitas Visitor Center** (138 Encinitas Blvd., Encinitas, 760/753-6046, www.encinitaschamber.com, 9 A.M.–5 P.M. Mon.–Fri.), run by the Encinitas Chamber of Commerce.

If you run into problems, there is a **police station** (175 N. El Camino Real, Encinitas, 760/966-3500), and **Scripps Memorial Hospital** (354 Santa Fe Dr., Encinitas, 760/633-6501) has an around-the-clock emergency room.

There are two **public libraries,** one in Cardiff-by-the-Sea (2081 Newcastle Ave., Cardiff-by-the-Sea, 760/753-4027) and another farther north at 540 Cornish Drive (760/753-7376) in Encinitas.

The **post office** (760/753-1415) is located at 1150 Garden View Road in Encinitas.

GETTING THERE AND AROUND

Encinitas is serviced by the **Coaster** commuter train at the station (25 East D St., Encinitas, 800/262-7837) located in downtown Encinitas. This station is not a stop for Amtrak. The closest Amtrak station is in Solana Beach.

The station is also a stop for several **bus lines,** including the north–south #101 from Oceanside to La Jolla's University Town Center, the #309 running north–south to Oceanside, and the #386 running east–west to the Wild Animal Park and Ramona.

Carlsbad

No, there are no caverns here (they're in New Mexico), but Carlsbad is still pretty darned cool. The town is home to a state beach, several ecological preserves, and a handful of museums and historical sights. It also plays host to world-class golf and tennis resorts, which are home to high-profile tournaments each year.

SIGHTS
Carlsbad Historical Sights

Carlsbad got its start as a jerkwater town along the route of the California Southern Railroad, which first chugged its way south in the 1880s. At that time it was just known as Frazier's Station, named for John Frazier, the man who dug the first well in town to keep

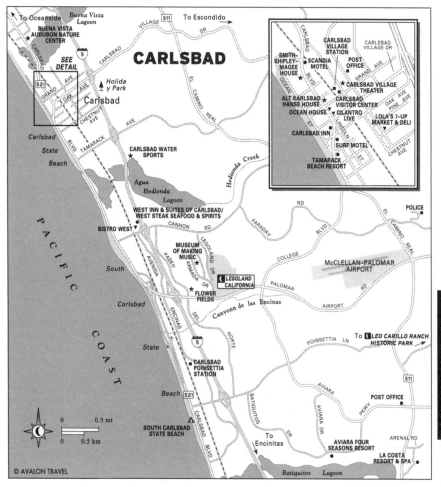

© AVALON TRAVEL

the steam engines well-supplied with water to keep the trains on schedule. The water supply still couldn't keep up with railway demands, so Frazier plumbed the earth again in 1883.

This time he stumbled upon something more valuable than the skunky engine water he dredged up from the first well. The new discovery was mineral water, with chemical composition so good that it matched the water at the best European health spa of the time, located in Karlsbad, Bohemia.

From the well sprang forth the town's name and newfound prosperity from the hotel and bottleworks that surrounded the water. Located in the heart of Carlsbad Village, Frazier's Mineral Well is on display today in front of **Alt Karlsbad Spa,** which still draws visitors to its healing waters more than a century after the well was dug.

The original train station that started it all was constructed by the **Old Santa Fe Depot** (400 Carlsbad Village Dr., 760/434-6093) in 1907, and acted as the community's hub for almost 60 years. At one time it operated as a

telegraph office, a post office, a Wells Fargo Express office, and a general store. The cross-gabled Stick Building is beautifully renovated and now acts as the Carlsbad Visitor Center.

North of the depot Magee Park is home to another well-maintained relic of Carlsbad's early years, the **Smith-Shipley-Magee House** (258 Beech Ave., 760/434-9189, www.carlsbadhistoricalsociety.com, noon–4 P.M. Fri., 10 A.M.–4 P.M. Sat.). This Craftsman-style house is known for its wraparound veranda accented by railings set with a herringbone balustrade. The house is decorated in period furnishing and is also the headquarters for the Carlsbad Historical Society, which runs tours from noon to 4 P.M. on Saturday.

🄲 Leo Carrillo Ranch Historic Park

One of Carlsbad's best historical properties is nowhere near the village. Recessed in a chaparral-covered canyon that is encroached by ever-multiplying tract homes, Leo Carrillo Ranch Historic Park (6200 Flying LC Ln., 760/476-

Leo Carrillo Ranch Historic Park preserves a piece of North County's rural past.

1042, www.carrilloranch.org, 9 A.M.–5 P.M. Tue.–Sat., 11 A.M.–5 P.M. Sun., closed Mon., free) is one of Carlsbad's last links to its wild ranching days. This property was owned by Leo Carrillo, the famous Hollywood actor who starred as Pancho on the TV version of *The Cisco Kid*. Carrillo was a descendent of two of the most famous Californio families in Southern California, the Bandinis and the Carrillos, and he was very proud of his heritage. In spite of his privileged lifestyle, Carrillo worked the ranch personally with the rest of his staff and helped to build the adobe home and pool that stands there today.

The property is but an echo of its former self, just a 10.5-acre sliver of what was once over 2,500 acres. But it is still a beautiful place to stroll and the house and surrounding ranch structures are in fantastic shape. The outdoor pathways and plazas are scattered with beautiful peacocks, succulents, citrus trees, and floral gardens.

Museum of Making Music

Drums, tambourines, player pianos, harps, and guitars—in untrained hands they make noise. In the deft fingers of an artist they are all mediums for the magical powers of music. The Museum of Making Music (5790 Armada Dr., 877/551-9976, www.museumofmakingmusic.org, 10 A.M.–5 P.M. Tues.–Sun., $7, $5 seniors, students, and military, free for kids 3 and under) puts these instruments and many others on display to give context to the craft of composing and the art of jamming. The exhibits here chronicle the history of American popular music and the instrument manufacturing business from 1890 to today. There are over 450 vintage instruments on display in total, but perhaps the coolest exhibit of all is the hands-on display that allows visitors to take a crack at the music-making process themselves.

The Flower Fields

Springtime visitors have the opportunity to walk through a real live Monet painting at The Flower Fields (5704 Paseo del Norte, 760/431-0352, www.theflowerfields.com, 9 A.M.–6 P.M.

daily Mar.–mid-May, $10 adults, $9 seniors, $5 children 3–10, wagon ride $5 adults, $3 children). Here, along the undulating Carlsbad hillsides, a sea of colorful ranunculus blossoms whisper in the breeze that blows from the ocean just a few miles away.

The fields originally started decades ago strictly as a commercial farm. But beach-bound visitors continued to stop off of the freeway to get a closer look at the blooming beauties, and the 50-acre farm became a tourist destination in and of itself.

◖ Legoland California

Legoland California (1 Legoland Dr., 760/918-5346, www.legoland.com, 10 A.M.–5 P.M. Thurs.–Mon. Nov.–mid-June, 10 A.M.–6 P.M. daily mid-June–July, 10 A.M.–8 P.M. daily July–Aug., 10 A.M.–6 P.M. daily Sept.–Oct., $67 ages 13–59, $57 children ages 3–12 and seniors, kids under 2 free) is an opus to those clickable bricks that have entertained generations of kids around the world. I was one of 'em, scheming up all the buildings and cars and

© LEGOLAND CALIFORNIA

Legoland California's cityscapes are impressive.

spaceships that I could possibly conjure from the mound of plastic Legos that littered my bedroom floor. If you were like me, the inner kid in you will squeal at the sight of what I consider the park's best section: Miniland. This amazing spectacle of ingenuity is a miniature-scale depiction of some of the nation's largest cities. Washington, D.C., New York, San Francisco, Las Vegas—they're all there and the details that the professional bricklayers built into these little dioramas are amazing.

Legoland is a park best visited by families with kids aged between about two and twelve. The park is scattered with rides and shows geared toward that age range. Though the promotional literature shows impressive roller coasters, the pictures are a bit misleading in my opinion. The coasters here are zippy little tracks, perfect for making the little ones squeal without losing their lunch, but not enough to excite the teens in the crowd.

Legoland Water Park

In 2010 Legoland Water Park opened its gates. The first-ever water park in the franchise, the park features four major water slides, including a family tube slide where four people can ride together down a single slope and an open body slide that careens riders down 240 feet into the splash-down area. There's a lazy river that lets kids build their own rafts before drifting along, using soft Lego "bricks" and a splash area designed for the toddlers. Admission to the water park is a $12 additional fee on top of the regular Legoland California admission.

Carlsbad State Beach

With flat and level sand, and lined with seawalls and smooth sidewalks, Carlsbad State Beach (Carlsbad Blvd. at Tamarack) is the picture of a classic beach scene. Joggers, inline skaters, and stroller mommies huff-and-puff their way along the sand-swept path. Multi-colored umbrellas flutter in the wind as happy nappers snooze underneath. Their uncovered neighbors soak in the rays, some breeze through trashy beach novels, others chatter with their friends about nothing in particular. Babies jam their

sandy hands into baggies full of cereal while their older siblings take a break to munch on smooshed-up peanut butter sandwiches. They all watch as the waves wash in waders, surfers, boogie boarders, and the occasional clump of seaweed onto the foamy shore.

This five-mile stretch of sand is most populated along the section known as Tamarack Beach, named for the nearby roadway that acts as the unofficial gateway to Carlsbad Village. Tamarack is easy walking distance for the visitors and locals who rest their heads nearby.

For a little more serenity, try **South Carlsbad State Beach** (7201 Carlsbad Blvd.), where Carlsbad meets Encinitas. This beach is overlooked by a state-run campsite and tends to see a lot fewer people kicking through the sand due to its more isolated location. It is also a better spot to cast for fish without fear of hooking a diaper with the baby still in it.

Lagoons

Carlsbad is dotted with estuaries and lagoons that are a source of natural serenity and aquatic fun.

Located between Encinitas and Carlsbad, **Batiquitos Lagoon** (accessible via the south end of Gabbiano Ln.) is one of the better-preserved coastal wetlands still remaining in Southern California. At one point in time this delicate ecosystem was doomed to be filled—like 90 percent of the waterways destroyed in the county—with several cockamamie development plans that included a glut of tract housing and even a theme park.

Luckily it was saved for prosperity and now the 610-acre lagoon and the surrounding wetland it rests in is open for gentle exploration. Hiking trails line the shores and a bird-watcher prepared with binoculars has a good chance of spotting the protected least tern that nests here. The lagoon is closed to watercraft, but shore-based anglers are welcome to take a crack at the fish that swim here. The foundation that champions the lagoon's health and future also runs a nature center for those curious about the wildlife and the history of Batiquitos.

Next there's **Agua Hedionda,** which is accessible via the **Agua Hedionda Lagoon Discovery Center** (1580 Cannon Rd., 760/804-1969), is a favorite recreational retreat for water sports fans. In Spanish, Agua Hedionda means "stinky water," a moniker earned by the brackish odor emitted by the marshy environs. If you can get over the slight smell you'll be well rewarded with opportunities to kayak, wakeboard, water-ski, and ride personal watercraft at this lagoon.

Finally, between Carlsbad and Oceanside is **Buena Vista Lagoon** (2202 South Coast Hwy.). This special marsh has long been a sanctuary for hundreds of species of birds. The area became California's first ecological preserve in 1939 when a young man, Maxton Brown, secured the agreement of local municipalities to ban shooting birds around the lagoon. He then headed off to war and eventually died in World War II, but his legacy lives on today. After development threatened the lagoon in the 1950s and 1960s, concerned citizens formed the Buena Vista Lagoon Foundation to acquire lagoon property and head off destruction. The foundation managed to save 223 acres of the wetland and 19 acres of watershed.

The wetland here is headquarters for the Buena Vista Audubon Nature Center, which has a collection of interpretive displays on plants and animals and holds classes and guided nature walks.

ENTERTAINMENT AND EVENTS
Carlsbad Village Theatre

This multipurpose venue (2822 State St., 760/720-2460, www.carlsbadvillagetheatre. com) is the cat's meow for all types of performing arts events: theater, cinema, stand-up comedy, music, dance, and even the occasional beauty pageant. This is no third-rate kiddie auditorium, either. Plush velvet seats and rich red curtains greet audience members as they file in before the lights go off and the curtains go up.

Festivals and Events

Carlsbad usually kicks off its event season with a little hustle at the **Carlsbad 5000** on the first Sunday in April. This 5K run is one of the most popular in the nation because of the ultra-flat course. Many professional runners are known to have attained their PR (personal record) here. Unlike many recreational runs, the Carlsbad 5000 holds its elite races at the end, that way all of the joggers can huff and puff their way to the finish, grab a brew from the beer garden, and cheer on the pros in style.

On the first Sunday in May, Carlsbad shuts down to welcome revelers for the **Carlsbad Village Faire.** This all-day event features arts and crafts vendors, music, and carnival treats. Can't make it in May? No worries. This event is so popular that the city holds it again on the first Sunday in November.

Come summer time, local parks are covered in blankets and picnic spreads on Friday evenings in preparation for the weekly **free jazz concerts.** The city has put these concerts on for more than 20 years, rotating the schedule between several parks each week between late June and the end of August. For schedule information, call 760/434-2904.

During the first week of August, the stars of women's tennis converge at La Costa for the **Mercury Insurance Open** (www.mercuryinsuranceopen.com) a competitive spectacle of serves, baseline rallies, and fast-paced net play.

On the second Sunday in August, the village is taken over by 200 arts and crafts vendors to showcase their sculptures, paintings, photos, ceramics, and handmade jewelry, furniture, and clothing.

And in September, art of another stripe hits the streets for **Art Splash.** This fun event features the best in mural and street arts, arming local and national artists with chalk and setting them loose on the streets near the Flower Fields to show that chalk art isn't just for kids.

One of the longest-running events in Carlsbad is held in October. The **Carlsbad Rotary Oktoberfest** celebrates beer, sausage, and, of course, oompah music at Holiday Park. Come in lederhosen or board shorts, it doesn't matter—just be prepared to wipe that sudsy mustache from your lips many times over.

SHOPPING

Fashionistas with dollar sense like to swerve off the Palomar Airport Road exit on I-5 to stop at **Carlsbad Premium Outlets** (5600 Paseo del Norte, 760/804-9000, 10 A.M.–8 P.M. daily) before hitting the beach. This chic outlet mall has all the brand-name stores that keep the fashion world ticking, including Kenneth Cole, Juicy Couture, Bebe, and Brooks Brothers.

The busy streets of Carlsbad Village have tons of unique shops to browse while letting your stomach settle between meal time and beach time. **Carlsbad Village Art and Antique Mall** (2752 State St., 760/730-9494, www.carlsbadartandantiques.com, 10:30 A.M.–5 P.M. daily) is a warren of antique dealers and art peddlers. Unique labels and vintage clothes can be found at shops like **Clothing Cottage** (620 Grand Ave., 760/720-5219, www.clothingcottage.com, 10 A.M.–6 P.M. Mon.–Sat., 11 A.M.–4 P.M. Sun.), **Janika Designs** (2969 State St., 760/729-1840, www.janikadesigns.com, 10 A.M.–5:30 P.M. Mon.–Sat., 11 A.M.–5 P.M. Sun.), and **OBJ's Collections** (630 Grand Ave., Ste. A, 760/730-9827, 11 A.M.–6 P.M. Mon.–Fri., 11 A.M.–5 P.M. Sat.–Sun.). If you actually like your mother-in-law, skip the grain of rice etched with her name and go straight for the good stuff. **The Bwarie Gift Basket Company** (100 Carlsbad Village Dr., Ste. 104, 760/730-1456, 11 A.M.–5 P.M. Mon.–Sat., closed Sun.) makes really cool custom baskets. For example, you can get her a "day at the beach" with a basket that includes a beach chair, flip-flops, goodies, and even a bottle of wine to sip during sunset. If you're really set on personalization, have her name etched in the wine bottle instead.

SPORTS AND RECREATION
Surfing

Carlsbad's natural beach landscape doesn't lend itself to consistent surf conditions. It is miles of flat sandy bottoms and not a reef in sight, a bitter pill for the wandering surfer.

But Carlsbad's natural beach landscape isn't completely natural.

In their concern for saving local lagoons from silt deposits and oxygen depletion, government agencies built two different sets of rocky jetties into the ocean to improve the flow between waterways. Those environmental enhancements yielded unintended benefits for surfers, because with that improved flow also came the buildup of sandbars surrounding the jetty outlets. And sandbars underfoot means better waves on the surface.

The better of the two spots is at a place called **Ponto** near the Batiquitos Lagoon outlet. The pair of jetties here creates two different breaks depending on the season. By summer the waves break left from the north jetty and by winter they peel right from the south.

Drive north up the 101 to reach the second spot, **Tamarack.** The break here isn't as consistent as Ponto, but it is known to send a stretch of left-handed curl off the north jetty pretty consistently with a moderate swell and tide.

In the summer the rest of the beach breaks along Carlsbad's strand are not the kind that the seasoned surfer writes home about. But they can be perfect for the beginner to learn the art of the pop-up. **Carlsbad Surf School** (4095 Harrison St., #3, 760/845-2272, www.carlsbadsurfschool.com) offers lessons locally that will run you $60 for two hours of semi-private instruction. This results-oriented school is so convinced that it can get you stoked about surfing that it offers a money-back guarantee. If you don't stand up in the first two hours it'll return your cash.

Those simply interested in rentals can try the gear at **Raw Skin Surf** (2796 Carlsbad Blvd., 760/434-1122, www.rawskinsurf.com, 10 A.M.–6 P.M. Tues.–Sat., 10 A.M.–5 P.M. Sun.–Mon.), where you can pick up a board rental for $25 per day or $100 per week.

Other Water Sports

Agua Hedionda, sometimes just known as Carlsbad Lagoon (www.carlsbadlagoon.com), is the best place to dip a paddle or rotor in the water. Due to restrictions on the lagoon, the only access available is through utilizing the outfitter **Carlsbad Water Sports** (2002 S.

U.S. 101, Oceanside, 760/434-8686), so don't plan on bringing your own equipment. This shoreline vendor offers both rentals and lessons. You'll be able to choose between wave runners, wakeboard and water-ski equipment, kayaks, pedal boats, and aqua cycles.

Spas

Inside the Bavarian-style Alt Karlsbad Hanse House, **Carlsbad Mineral Water Spa** (2802 Carlsbad Blvd., 760/434-1887, 9 A.M.–6 P.M. daily, 60 minute massage $85) taps into the same naturally carbonated mineral water that John Frazier drilled into in 1883. The house specialty is a dip in the healing waters infused with an herbal concoction, which will set you back $65 for 30 minutes of bath time. The spa also offers massages, mud baths, and facials.

In addition to the more traditional treatments offered elsewhere, the **Park Hyatt Aviara Spa** (7100 Four Seasons Pt., 760/603-6800, 5:30 A.M.–9 P.M., 50 minute massage $150) also offers Ayurvedic treatments, based on thousands of years of East Indian health traditions. These ritualistic treatments utilize natural oils and herbs in a method designed to improve the health of mind, body, and spirit.

The Spa at La Costa (2100 Costa del Mar Rd., 800/729-4772, www.lacosta.com/spa, 9:30 A.M.–7:30 P.M. Mon.–Fri., 7:30 A.M.–7:30 P.M. Sat.–Sun., 100-minute massage $265) has one of the most comprehensive facilities in the county; visitors are encouraged to stick around long after their treatments are over. The peaceful common area includes a pool, whirlpool, and a thundering roman bath, which showers a cascade of water from above to massage the neck and shoulders. Separate male and female facilities have the added benefit of steam rooms, saunas, additional whirlpools, and quiet lounge areas. The signature treatment here is the Spanish Herbal Treatment, a nearly two-hour affair that starts with a wrap in olive oil steeped in lavender and sage and concludes with a massage that will leave you feeling like a very contented limp noodle.

Golf

Carlsbad is home to the best golf in the county, period. The Arnold Palmer signature design at **Aviara Golf Course** (7447 Batiquitos Dr., 760/603-6900, www.golfaviara.com, 6 A.M.–sunset daily, $245) has garnered it many accolades, including being named as the top golf resort in Southern California by *Golf* magazine in 2006. Though not directly on the coast, this 18-hole course does overlook Batiquitos Lagoon and the water hazards are designed as visual extensions of the estuary environment.

Only a few miles from Aviara is **La Costa Golf Course** (2100 Costa del Mar Rd., 800/854.5000, 6 A.M.–sunset daily, $205), which has a storied past as the host of numerous PGA events. The course currently hosts the World Golf Championships Accenture Match Play Championship each year. As a club and resort, La Costa balances the use of its two 18-hole courses between members and guests. The resort alternates access to each course every other day.

Plane Rides

Imagine yourself as Snoopy, imagining himself as the Red Baron, on a biplane ride through **Barnstorm Adventures** (Montgomery Field Airport, 3750 John J. Montgomery Dr., Ste. D, 800/759-5667, www.barnstorming.com, by appointment only, $199–300 pp per ride). The rush is very real when you take to the open cockpit of its 1920s-era biplanes over the North County coastline. The company also offers flights on its restored World War II–era fighter craft and warbirds.

ACCOMMODATIONS
Under $150

Scandia Motel (2550 Carlsbad Blvd., 760/729-3585, $70 d) is located on the outskirts of Carlsbad and should inhabit a similar position on a potential hotel shortlist for anyone seeking anything more than a roof over their head and a bed to snooze on.

There's a reason that **Surf Motel** (3136 Carlsbad Blvd., 760/729-7961, www.surfmotelcarlsbad.com, $139 s, $149 d) doesn't show a picture of its rooms on its website—nobody wants to advertise a train wreck. However, and this is a big caveat, this motel is right in the middle of the village and across the street from the beach. It is one of the cheapest places in the village and can make a most excellent crash pad for a couple of surf pals interested in splitting the rate, which is still a bit high for what you get.

$150-250

The property at **Tamarack Beach Resort** (3200 Carlsbad Blvd., 760/729-3500, www.tamarackresort.com, $207 d pool view, $225 d ocean view) is not as large as Carlsbad Inn and it is across the street from the beach instead of sitting right on the sand. But the rooms here are cleaner and less cluttered than the ones up the street. Tamarack also offers activities and has a welcoming pool area in its center courtyard. It also features a games room with a pool table and table tennis.

$250-350

Set right along to the beach closest to Carlsbad State Park, **Carlsbad Inn** (3075 Carlsbad Blvd., 760/434-7020, www.carlsbadinn.com, $251 d) is a resort complex that consists of a hotel and beach condominiums sharing a pool area and beach cabana. The buildings are a funky mix of mock Tudor and Spanish Revival architecture, but these schizophrenic styles are no matter to the families that flock here for the location smack-dab in the middle of Carlsbad Village. The inn is right next door to several low-key restaurants that are geared towards family dining. Families looking to save a few bucks could also consider reserving a room with kitchenette, which costs $279 per night. Another big draw is the inn's daily schedule of activities, with everything from games to crafts to karaoke led by resort staff.

Halfway between Legoland and Carlsbad Village, **(West Inn & Suites of Carlsbad** (4970 Avenida Encinas, 760/448-4500, www.westinnandsuites.com, $229 d) has the easygoing and family-friendly atmosphere of a chain hotel with the amenities and rich decor of a high-class establishment. Rooms are equipped with plasma TVs, Egyptian-cotton linens, and pillow-top beds. This independently owned boutique invites furry family members as well as kids, hosting a number of pet-friendly services such as dog-walking and -sitting. The room rate includes a full buffet breakfast, free Wi-Fi access, and complimentary shuttle service through Carlsbad—a big plus on days when beach parking will be limited.

Over $350

Like a secret handshake, tales of a stay at **(La Costa Resort and Spa** (2100 Costa Del Mar Rd., 760/438-9111, www.lacosta.com, $400 d) are likely to elicit a knowing wink or a smile among the jet-setting crowd. This is one of San Diego's best-known destination resorts. The resort was built in the 1960s and has been a holiday getaway ever since. Its golf course has hosted several high-profile PGA events over the years. Tee times are still coveted at the storied golf course and the spa here invites guests to stay and relax under the thundering roman showers, the steam baths, and the pool well after their treatment is over. This is no stick-in-the-mud resort that looks down on kids, either. The main pool area features a kiddie wading pool and a water park–worthy slide. A daycare and activity center provide a full day of activity for the young'uns while Mom and Dad strut their stuff on the golf course or tennis courts. Similarly, teens are kept busy in a teen game room that includes a pool table, video games, and computer access.

Perhaps the only San Diego resort that can compete with such lavishness is just a couple of miles down the road. **Park Hyatt Aviara** (7100 Four Seasons Pt., 760/603-6800, http://parkaviara.hyatt.com, $455 d) also sports its own championship golf facilities—designed by Arnold Palmer—and an oceanfront view. Rooms are luscious, with fine linens, a deep soaking tub, and private patios and terraces. Kids are also made welcome here, with nightly milk and cookies delivered to the room and a family pool area. But couples who want to get away from the screeching are afforded that luxury as well with an adults-only pool area. The spa here is also one of the best in the county.

Camping

Set on a bluff above the beach, **South Carlsbad State Beach Campground** (7201 Carlsbad Blvd., 760/438-3143, www.parks.ca.gov) is a sprawling 222-campsite facility with nooks for tent and RV campers. Sites are pretty standard, equipped with a picnic table and metal fire ring, and nearby restrooms have flush toilets, spigots, drinking fountains, and pay showers with hot water. There's also a beach store and laundry facilities on-site. Dogs are allowed at the campground but not down on the beach. These $35-per-night sites are a hot item year-round, so don't expect to set your stakes down without a reservation.

FOOD

Set in one of the most distinctive Victorian mansions in Carlsbad, **Ocean House** (300 Carlsbad Village Dr., 760/729-4131, www. oceanhousecarlsbad.com, 11 A.M.–midnight Mon.–Wed., 11 A.M.–2 A.M. Thurs.–Sat., 9:30 A.M.–2 A.M. Sun., $14) is hard to miss as you drive U.S. 101 through Carlsbad Village. The vintage Queen Anne it occupies is a landmark in the area, built as the home of the president of the very first hotel and spa in town. Flanked by palm trees and processions of beachgoers hustling to the shore, this classic building has the charm of an old seaside resort. Inside, the restaurant serves up a mixture of burgers, pastas, and salads.

Joey's BBQ (6955 El Camino Real, Ste. 107, 760/929-1396, 11 A.M.–9 P.M. Sun.–Thurs., 11 A.M.–9:30 P.M. Fri.–Sat., $8) smokes its meat long and slow over hickory, divvying up ample portions of sweet and smoky ribs, chicken, and hot links. The meat is paired with all the usual suspects—beans, coleslaw, and cornbread—for a tangy and messy meal that'll have you reaching for the paper towels.

Get an authentic plate of tamales, chiles rellenos, or rolled *taquitos* to go from **Lola's 7-Up Market and Deli** (3292 Roosevelt St., 760/434-

2191, 7 A.M.–6 P.M. Mon.–Fri., 7 A.M.–5 P.M. Sat., closed major holidays, $6), in the heart of the Carlsbad Barrio. The Latino community here helped build the Carlsbad flower empire and in the center of it all, the Jauregui clan that owns Lola's has run a market here on this street for more than 70 years.

The hardest part about dining at ❰ **Bistro West** (4960 Avenida Encinas, 760/930-9008, www.bistrowest.com, 11 A.M.–10 P.M. Sun.–Fri., 11 A.M.–11 P.M. Sat., $16) is making up your mind. The menu is extensive; each section could make up a full menu at any other place. There's a selection of burgers that could satisfy J. Wellington Wimpy himself, homemade soups, and entrée-sized salads. If you've got a craving for pasta, take a crack at the puttanesca, a zippy little dish that features anchovies, olives, and capers. The braised meat is some of the best I've tasted, falling off the bone while maintaining all of its flavor.

For a more formal meal, right across the parking lot is the Bistro's intimate and posh sister restaurant, **West Steak Seafood & Spirits** (4980 Avenida Encinas, 760/930-9100, www. weststeakandseafood.com, 4:30 P.M.–10 P.M. Sun.–Thurs., 4:30 P.M.–11 P.M. Fri.–Sat., $50). This 20-table steakhouse serves prime cuts and doesn't nickel and dime you with the sides—they're included with your meat. Stick around for dessert here—the menu is replete with old favorites such as tiramisu, chocolate lava cake, and cherries jubilee.

INFORMATION AND SERVICES

The **Carlsbad Visitor Center** (400 Carlsbad Village Dr., 760/434-6093, www.carlsbadca. org, 9 A.M.–5 P.M. Mon.–Fri.) is located in Carlsbad Village at the Old Santa Fe Station. Mail can be sent from two **post offices** in town: in the village (2772 Roosevelt) or near Four Seasons Aviara (1700 Aviara Pkwy.).

Depending on where you are in Carlsbad, medical emergencies are best taken care of in Oceanside to the north or Encinitas to the south. In Encinitas visit **Scripps Memorial**

Hospital. In Oceanside, **Tri-City Medical Center.** The Carlsbad Police Station (2560 Orion Way) is located near the municipal airport just off El Camino Real.

Carlsbad City Library operates two branches: the **Georgina Cole Library** (1250 Carlsbad Village Dr., 760/434-2870, 9 A.M.–9 P.M. Mon.–Thurs., 9 A.M.–5 P.M. Fri.–Sat., 1 P.M.–5 P.M. Sun.) and the **Dove Library** (1775 Dove Ln., 760/602-2049, 9 A.M.–9 P.M. Mon.–Thurs., 9 A.M.–5 P.M. Fri.–Sat., 1 P.M.–5 P.M. Sun.). Both are appropriate stops for a respite from the sun and to borrow a computer for a few moments.

GETTING THERE AND AROUND

McClellan-Palomar Airport is the only airport besides San Diego International that offers daily flights from any of the major commercial airline services. United Express flies to and from LAX about seven times each day and US Airways operates a daily shuttle between Palomar and Phoenix.

Three car-rental agencies are based out of this small airport: **Avis** (760/931-1393), **Budget** (760/438-5527), and **Enterprise** (760/603-0240). Taxi service is available from **Coach Cab** (760/722-5100), **Coastal Cab** (760/722-7472), and **Yellow Cab** (760/722-4214). **Cloud Nine** (800/974-8885) offers a shuttle bus service as well.

The **Coaster** commuter train stops at two stations in Carlsbad, the **Carlsbad Poinsettia Station,** which primarily serves local bedroom communities, and the **Carlsbad Village Station** downtown. The closest Amtrak station is located north in Oceanside.

Bus route #310 will carry you down to University Town Center in La Jolla, where you can transfer to get downtown. It also travels north to Oceanside. **Route #322** circulates through Carlsbad and **Route #320** will take you east to Escondido.

Oceanside

The northernmost coastal town in San Diego County, Oceanside is invariably influenced by the massively sprawling Camp Pendleton Marine Corps base just north of city limits. Flattops are de rigueur in town, but recruits are well behaved. In fact, the number of military families that live close by probably helps to foster the family-friendly atmosphere in Oceanside. Also inland is Vista, a bedroom community that is a gateway to several regional parks as well as the foothills of the county's northern mountains.

SIGHTS
California Surf Museum
It has been called trivial, vulgar, and even a menace to youth, but at this point no one can deny that the surf culture in California has been a positive influence on the state's coastal way of life. Learn about the legends of wave riding at the California Surf Museum (223 N. U.S. 101, 760/721-6876, www.surfmuseum.org, 10 A.M.–4 P.M. daily, $3 adults, $1 students, seniors, and military, free kids under 12) in downtown Oceanside. This quirky museum exhibits boards, photos, and memorabilia that chronicle the sport's transition from 11-foot balsa-wood logs to the potato-chip shortboards of today.

Guajome Park
On the grounds of Guajome Park (3000 Guajome Lake Rd. 760/724-4489, www.co.san-diego.ca.us/parks, 9:30 A.M.–sunset daily) there stands one of the best examples of Californio architecture in the county. The **Rancho Guajome adobe home** (2210 N. Santa Fe Ave., 760/724-4082, www.history-andculture.com/guajome, free) was built in the 1850s by Cave Johnson Couts, a former U.S. Army lieutenant turned wealthy rancher, for his new wife Ysidora Bandini, a member

of Old Town San Diego's influential Bandini clan, who received the rancho's 2,200-acre plot as a wedding gift from her brother-in-law. Their 28-room home was a palatial estate in the mid-19th century and it became legendary for the parties and balls that the Couts family would host there. Today it stands as a State and National Historic Landmark and visitors can tour through the home on Saturday and Sunday at 11 A.M. and 2 P.M.

The adobe is only a part of Guajome Park's allure. Tramping on foot or clopping by on horseback, nature-loving explorers can look for more than 186 species of birds flitting across the miles of trails that crisscross the 557-acre park. Tread softly and there's a chance to come across long-tailed weasels, rabbits, and even bobcats. Also on the property is Guajome Lake, a pleasant spot to cast for fish or to dig into a picnic basket.

Antique Gas and Steam Engine Museum

Near Guajome, the little-known Antique Gas and Steam Engine Museum (2040 N. Santa Fe Ave., 800/587-2286, www.agsem.com, 10 A.M.–4 P.M. daily, $4 adults, $3 seniors, $2 children 6–12, free kids under 6) can make for a fascinating day trip for families and gear heads. This living-history museum is a 55-acre collection of old engines, a working farm, and antique farm equipment all bundled into one package. The best time to visit is on the museum's "show days" during the third and fourth weekends in June and October. Hordes of volunteers descend on the facility to fire up the tractors and the blacksmith forge and to work the farm for the benefit of visitors. Even on non–show days you are likely to see a volunteer running an odd piece of machinery here and there in the course of maintaining the property and the farm.

Oceanside Pier

Oceanside Pier (250 N. Pacific St., 760/966-1406, 24 hrs. daily) has been a landmark for generations of citizens and visitors, even though the pier itself has had multiple reincarnations. This, the sixth in the succession of water-bound structures, juts out to 1,954 feet,

© ERICKA CHICKOWSKI

Oceanside Pier

making it the longest wooden pier on the West Coast. The concrete approach is the oldest part of the pier, dating back to 1925; the wooden part was replaced in 1988.

It is a favorite among strolling couples, waddling toddlers, and the throngs of fishermen who flock here every day. The end of the pier is a good place to spot mischievous sea lions who enjoy stealing fish off anglers' lines. Or simply look out to sea and try to catch a glimpse of Catalina Island to the north and Los Coronados islands to the south. Visitors can also get a bite to eat at Ruby's Diner, located at the pier's terminus.

Below deck the pier is also frequented by surfers, who regard this as the best structurally improved break in the county.

◖ Mission San Luis Rey

Called the "King of Missions," Mission San Luis Rey (4050 Mission Ave., 760/757-3651, www.sanluisrey.org, 10 A.M.–4 P.M. daily, $6 adults, $4 ages 5–18, $5 military and seniors, free kids under 5) was one of the last of the 21 California missions to be founded by the Franciscans, but it ended up being the largest and wealthiest of all. At its height, this massive religious, farming, and ranching operation spanned over 1,000 square miles.

The church that was at the center of it all still rests within Oceanside city limits and is one of the few mission parishes still run by the Franciscans. The friars welcome visitors to meander through the sunken gardens, to look at the first pepper tree planted in California, and to hike through the trails that wander through the property's 56 acres.

The church itself is mostly a reconstruction, but the Catholic Church has taken care to painstakingly follow old design patterns found in books and textiles that have been maintained over the centuries.

There is also a museum on the property that contains exhibits on mission life, art work, and historical artifacts that document the rise, fall, and reconstruction of San Luis Rey.

San Onofre State Beach

Like the fertile crescent of Southern California beach culture, San Onofre State Beach (north

San Onofre State Beach

of Oceanside, exit off I-5, follow signs from Basilone Rd., 949/492-4872, www.parks.ca.gov, entrance fee $15 per car) has enticed beach revelers to its gentle shorelines since the days when surfers carved their own boards out of balsa wood.

This state beach is three and a half miles of untouched shoreline that represents everything the region has to offer. The bluffside campgrounds and beach connector trails are covered in coastal scrub and chaparral, with the occasional bunny hopping through the brush here and there. From the bluffs you can often see gray whales and dolphins swimming off shore. On the weekends the campground is packed with scouts, partying twenty-somethings, and with retirees in RVs with plates from all over the country. It's the friendly type of place where campers share their ice and their road-trip stories.

Meander down the trail and you'll find seclusion if you want it. Or you can join the crowds off the beach closest to the day-use parking. Guitars are a-strummin' here, barbecues sizzle, and people slip in and out of their wetsuits to hit the surf whenever they feel like it. Watches and schedules have no place here.

On the far northern end of the park is the San Mateo Creek Preserve, a marshland ripe for exploration via the nearby trails starting in San Mateo Canyon.

ENTERTAINMENT AND EVENTS
Nightlife

There's not a martini bar in sight in Oceanside. Nope, this town is pub and tavern territory through and through.

Young hotheads should be aware that if they're looking for a fight they might just find it in O'side, and probably a trip to the hospital to boot. The majority of the marines in town are respectable soldiers, but there are a few bad apples and they are drawn to the seedier bars like flies on a wheelbarrow full of manure. Keep your wits about you and your tone respectful to avoid a conflict.

With that said, there are a couple of mellow establishments that can provide a nice nightcap after a day on the water. The pirate-themed **Haunted Head Saloon** (207 N. Tremont St., 760/231-7600, 11 A.M.–2 A.M. daily) is festooned with Jolly Rogers and equipped with a pool table, foosball, and a giant TV. The place can get boisterous on the weekends but the vibe is still pretty chilled out.

The entertainment at **McCabe's Beach Club** (1145 South Tremont St., 760/439-6646, 10 A.M.–1:30 A.M. daily) is a grab bag of live country-and-western and cover bands, DJs spinning hip-hop, and American Idol wannabes warbling into the karaoke mic. The music schedule shifts with the sands—call ahead to find out what's on the agenda.

Festivals and Events

In July, Oceanside's military pride swells for **Independence Day.** The town celebrates for five days in a festival it likes to call Ofest. Highlights include a patriotic parade and a booming fireworks display off the pier.

Many of Oceanside's events are centered around the pier and the nearby **Oceanside Pier Amphitheater,** a classic band shell with bleacher seating built into the cliff that leads from street level to the beach.

There are numerous surfing competitions held near the pier and the jetties, but perhaps one of the longest running is the **Oceanside Surfing Club competition** that happens in mid-August each year.

Another adrenaline-pumped event that uses the pier as its centerpiece is the **Oceanside Pier Swim,** a freestyle competition that has run continuously every September for almost 80 years. Racers swim a one-mile course set around the landmark pier.

September is also the season for **Harbor Days,** the most popular street fair in town. In addition to live entertainment, food, and crafts vendors, this event also holds an annual fishing derby and a nail-and-sail competition that tasks participants to build a seaworthy craft and navigate it around a short course in the harbor.

SPORTS AND RECREATION
Surfing
The bros and wahines out in Oceanside primarily paddle out to the artificially made breaks created by Oceanside Pier and Oceanside's jetties.

Be careful not to get tangled up in anglers' lines as you carve the waves near the pier. People cast to the shallow water off of this fishing structure and surfing closer than 100 feet is prohibited. The rules might be a letdown when the peaks are pumping around the pier, but they are there for your safety. Tempers are short between the two groups and it isn't unheard-of for a grumpy angler to "enforce" the rules by casting for surfers.

Surf Oceanside Harbor and you'll have a choice between the reeling lefts off of the **North Jetty** and the breaking rights off the **South Jetty.** The beach off South Jetty is a nice place to hang between sessions. Build up a crackling fire in one of the rings provided by the city to cook up your meat caveman-style or rest beneath the rustling palapa umbrellas that are perched on nearby picnic tables.

For supplies and board rentals, **Real Surf Shop** (1101 S. U.S. 101, 760/754-0670, www. realsurfshop.com, 10 A.M.–6 P.M. daily) is a good option.

Officially the maps say that San Diego County ends at the northernmost boundaries of the expansive Camp Pendleton Marine base, but most San Diego residents will tell ya that **San Onofre State Park** ("San O" in local speak) is still on their turf. This massive coastal park butts right up against Camp Pendleton and is heaven for the longboard enthusiast. Seriously, don't even think about bringing one of those potato-chip boards out here. These waves are gentle and lazy, but consistent and perfect for hanging a few toes from the nose. From south to north the three major breaks here are the **Point, Old Man's,** and **Dogpatch.**

Just north of San O is one of the most storied breaks in all of Southern California, **Lower Trestles.** Named for the railroad track that surfers once had to scamper over to get to this out-of-the-way spot, Lower Trestles is now accessible from a one-mile trail that starts at the San Mateo Campground. This break's renowned left peak has been praised by legends from Kelly Slater to Rob Machado and frequently is the site of the kind of professional surf invitationals that draw international rippers to this shore. If it is too crowded here, your consolation prize is not so bad, with the breaks **Upper Trestles, Cottons,** and **Churches** all to the immediate north.

Cycling
Coast Highway (U.S. 101) merges with I-5 at Oceanside, so the only way to continue on and connect with U.S. 101 in Orange County is to make nice with the marines. If you bring government identification and promise to follow all of the road rules—including wearing a buckled helmet—the Marine Corps will let you ride through Camp Pendleton until its road reaches the main access road in **San Onofre State Park.** From there it is a straight route back to 101.

Access via Camp Pendleton is not always guaranteed, however, so it pays to give the Marine Corps Community Services Information line (760/725-3400) a call to ask about closures due to training exercises or changes in the base security posture.

Another cycling route option when the base is closed is to do an out-and-back along the **San Luis Rey River Bike Path,** which runs along the San Luis Rey River from Neptune Way to College Bridge.

Fishing
When you approach **Oceanside Pier** (250 N. Pacific St., 760/966-1406, 24 hrs. daily) from the beach in the right light it sometimes seems like a giant spider has woven a web of shimmering monofilament from the railings to the water. Under the moonlight, anglers try for squid. Once the sun rises they'll ply the deeper railings for pelagic varieties like bonito or mackerel. Halfway down the pier the biting's best with nibbles from multiple types of croaker, halibut, and sand sharks. And inshore

fishing yields corbina, croaker, guitarfish, and several kinds of rays.

Like all piers in Southern California, there's no license requirement to fish here. But be sure to bone up on local limits and regulations because state fishing deputies are known to wander these planks looking to bust poachers. Bait, lures, hooks, and lines are for sale at the **Pier Bait Shop** (760/722-3936, www.pierbait.com) halfway down the pier. The facility also sells snacks and drinks and rents rods and reels on an hourly basis. There are also basic restroom facilities on the pier, but I'd recommend bringing hand sanitizer, as there is no soap in sight.

ACCOMMODATIONS

Oceanside's lodging choices are extremely limited, with many "bargain" and chain motels that are dirty or threadbare still running above $110 per night in spite of the town's distance from metropolitan San Diego. Often the more decent options are ruined due to close proximity to the train lines that run through town. In a pinch it can make sense to stay in town, but unless you are camping I'd generally recommend driving south to Carlsbad, Encinitas, or Del Mar.

Under $150

If you are desperate and tired after driving through L.A. and Orange County, **Oceanside Inn and Suites** (1820 S. U.S. 101, 760/433-5751, $89 d) can shelter you for an evening. Make no mistake about it, this is a motel—of the by a busy thoroughfare, carpet held together by duct tape, and ceiling panels flaking variety—but you might consider making a pit stop here if you are in need of a bed for a night, have under a hundred bucks in your pocket, and can't find a place to stay near the beach during high season. The two redeeming qualities about this place are that it doesn't seem to attract the skeezy characters that are usually drawn to a motel of this caliber, and the beds are actually reasonably comfortable. Just don't even think about paying extra for the suite. It isn't worth it.

$150-250

Set on a private peninsula inside Oceanside Harbor, **Oceanside Marina Suites** (2008 Harbor Dr. N., 760/722-1561, www.omihotel.com, $169 d, $249 1-br suite) is one of the big exceptions in Oceanside accommodations. The facility is clean, quiet, safe, and nicely decorated. It is a family-oriented hotel that rents one- and two-bedroom suites that are all equipped with full kitchens and fireplaces. On the grounds you'll find barbecue equipment, a volleyball court, heated pool, and a gazebo with a view of the harbor.

$250-350

Like a comfortable pair of worn jeans, the **Southern California Beach Club** (121 South Pacific St., 877/477-7368, www.southerncalifbeachclub.com, $299 for 4 people) may be a bit faded in the looks department but it has the potential to fit with ease and could be the perfect option for a relaxed vacation. Sitting directly on the beach, this condo resort could use a bit of an update, but the rooms are clean nevertheless and families seeking some sandcastle building time can't beat the location. Units come decked out with full kitchens and are spacious enough for the little ones to sprawl out. The property is located close to the Oceanside Pier, just a few steps away from the sand. If the ocean's too cold for you, consider hoofing it up to the roof, which has a bubbly hot tub for guest use.

Camping

Some of North County's best campgrounds are in Oceanside or very close by. To the north, San Onofre State Beach has two of the best. The **San Onofre Bluffs Campground** (follow signs from Basilone Rd. exit off of I-5, 949/492-4872, May–Oct. only, $35 tent, $60 full hookup) sits above the beach. There are 176 tent and RV sites sitting on this long, rectangular campground. Sites are crammed together on gravel plots with no border shrubs or trees between most of them. But the crowd that comes here is generally respectful of your space if you want privacy and welcoming if you feel sociable. Dogs are allowed at the campground but not on the beach; there are restrooms with pedal-flush toilets and outdoor cold showers at regular intervals along the campground road. However, there are no hookups for RVs at this campground.

On the northern border of the park **San Mateo Campground** (follow signs from Basilone Rd. exit off of I-5, 949/492-4872, $35 tent sites, $60 full hookup sites) sits slightly inland and is a good backup when the bluffs are booked or closed. A mile-long nature trail leads from the campsite to the famous Trestles surf break. The grounds have 67 sites with electrical and water hookups. The rest of the 90 sites are for tent campers. The outer-loop sites offer a little more privacy, but this is another somewhat cramped facility. Bathrooms have flush toilets and hot-water pay showers and there is an RV water and dump station on-site.

Also in Oceanside is the small and sometimes overlooked campground at **Guajome County Park** (3000 Guajome Lakes Rd., 760/724-4489, sites $20, dog fee $1). This beautiful park has a historic adobe home and numerous trails and is very close to Mission San Luis Rey. The grounds have full restroom facilities with sinks, hot showers, flush toilets, and water spigots outside to wash your dishes. It also has an RV dump station and partial hookups at each site.

FOOD

There's no fancy nouveau cuisine in O'side, but the town really does shine when it comes to roadside diners and cafés. The most historic of the bunch is the 🄲 **101 Café** (631 S. U.S. 101, 760/722-5220, www.101cafe.net, 6:30 A.M.–midnight daily, $8), a classic counter-and-booth diner along U.S. 101 that has been scooping out hand-dipped milkshakes since before I-5 was a gleam in some engineer's eye.

In downtown Oceanside **Mary's Family Restaurant** (307 N. U.S. 101, #B, 760/722-3052, 7 A.M.–8 P.M. Mon.–Sat., 10 A.M.–3 P.M. Sun., $8) whips up hearty breakfasts like biscuits and gravy, huge burgers and sandwiches

for lunch, and comforting dinner entrées like meatloaf and country fried chicken. The friendly wait staff and the colorful murals depicting the pier, the city, and Camp Pendleton contribute to the homey atmosphere here.

If greasy food isn't your thing, skip on over to **Hill Street Café and Gallery** (524 S. U.S. 101, 760/966-0985, www.hillst.org, 7 A.M.–9 P.M. daily, $7) and choose between the organic and vegan options here. Tofu wraps, portobello steak with brown rice, and free-range chicken breasts are some of the culinary prospects at this arty café.

Finally, if all those fishing lines hanging off the pier have put ideas into your head, **Harbor Fish and Chips** (276A Harbor Dr. S., 760/722-4977, www.harborfishandchips.net, 11 A.M.–7 P.M. daily, $8) has got you covered. This salty seafood shack fries up fish hauled in fresh from a local fish market. Founded in 1969, the restaurant has accumulated a nostalgic collection of stuffed fish and photos of fishing trips long past.

INFORMATION AND SERVICES

The closest **post office** to the beach is at 517 Seagaze Drive. Only a few blocks away is the **Oceanside Library** (330 N. Coast Hwy., 760/435-5600, 9 A.M.–8 P.M. Mon.–Tues., 9 A.M.–5:30 P.M. Wed.–Sat., closed Sun.), which resides along the Coast Highway corridor.

Oceanside **police headquarters** (3855 Mission Ave., 760/435-4900, www.oceansidepolice.com) are located east of I-5 closer to the town's residential district. This is also where you'll find emergency medical service from **Tri-City Medical Center** (4002 Vista Way, 760/724-8411).

GETTING THERE AND AROUND

The **Oceanside Transit Center** (195 S. Tremont S.) is the first Amtrak station stop in San Diego County. Amtrak's **Surfliner** train provides service to and from Oceanside all the way up to San Luis Obispo.

The center is also Oceanside's major hub for local transportation. This is the northernmost station on the Coaster commuter line that runs to downtown San Diego. It is also be the easternmost station for the **Sprinter** commuter line that runs 22 miles to Escondido. Some of the **major bus routes** that run through the center include #395 north to Camp Pendleton and San Clemente, #310 express south to University Town Center in La Jolla, and #320 express that goes east to Escondido.

Escondido and San Pasqual

Located in the heart of the county, with its miles of mountain bike trails, Escondido is a key San Diego destination for fat-tire enthusiasts. Most trails are multi-use, so there are lots of opportunities to explore by foot as well. It is also home to the San Diego Zoo Safari Park, San Diego Zoo's 1,800-acre wildlife preserve.

SIGHTS

North County visitors often overlook Escondido, which is a shame because this small inland town has a lot to offer families in search of a change of pace from normal seaside activities. The best places to see are centered around Escondido City Hall and the surrounding Escondido Art District, which is a hub of museums and galleries.

California Center for the Arts

The centerpiece of the Escondido Art District is the California Center for the Arts (340 N. Escondido Blvd., 760/839-4138, www.artcenter.org, 10 A.M.–4 P.M. Tues.–Sat., noon–4 P.M. Sun., $5 adults, $4 seniors and military, $3 students, kids 12 and under free), a 12-acre campus for the arts that includes a 1,500-seat concert hall, a 400-seat theater, and a visual arts museum. The museum primarily celebrates the region by bringing in original art and traveling exhibits with work from American and Mexican artists who live and work in Southern California.

Escondido Children's Museum

Reward the little ones for suffering through the art gallery at California Center for the Arts by marching them right next door to the Escondido Children's Museum (380 N. Escondido Blvd., www.escondidochildrensmuseum.org, 10 A.M.–2 P.M. Tues., Thurs., Fri., noon–4 P.M. Wed., 11 A.M.–3 P.M. Sat., $5 adults and kids, babies under age 1 free). This hands-on museum teaches kids about art and science while making sure they always have fun. There's the "Wildlife Treehouse" exhibit, which features a climbing structure and learning exhibit about animals and plans; a toddler exhibit with games, toys, and obstacles designed to improve fine motor skills; and numerous other rotating exhibits. Outside there's a children's garden, play houses, and climbable sculptures by Niki de Saint Phalle.

Grape Day Park

Escondido's most celebrated gathering place, Grape Day Park (321 N. Broadway, 760/839-4691, sunrise–sunset daily, free) is the city's oldest park and since 1908 people from all over Southern California have come here to participate in the town's Grape Day Festival. After petering out in the 1950s, the festival was revived in 1996 and is held each year to celebrate the Escondido valley's agricultural heritage.

The three-acre park is centered around the grassy public green that is dotted by trees. There is a rose garden, a playground for kids, horseshoe pits, and picnic tables are scattered around the grounds.

What really makes Grape Day Park so special, though, is its collection of historic buildings. This lineup of vintage structures from all over Escondido was created as part of a bicentennial project in 1976. The buildings are owned by the city but they are maintained

NORTH COUNTY

by the **Escondido History Center** (321 N. Broadway, 760/743-8207, museum 1–4 P.M. Tues.–Sat.) which is based out of the park and has furnished each of the buildings to act as a museum. For $3 you can walk through an old Victorian house, a blacksmith shop, watch the breeze blow on two antique windmills, and clamber over the boarding platform of an old Santa Fe Train Depot, which has an authentic train car parked right outside.

◖ San Diego Zoo Safari Park

People who visit San Diego Zoo for the first time are often surprised to learn that the Zoological Society of San Diego runs not one, but two, mini-ecosystems for exotic and endangered wildlife.

The "other" zoo, San Diego Zoo Safari Park (15500 San Pasqual Valley Rd., 760/747-8702, www.sandiegozoo.org, 9 A.M.–9 P.M. June–Sept., 9 A.M. to 5 P.M. Oct.–May, $37 adults, $27 children), is actually far more expansive than its venerated counterpart. Set on 1,800 acres of rocky land in Escondido's San Pasqual Valley, this wildlife sanctuary tries to better approximate the natural landscapes that its largest beasts are used to roaming. The park's pride and joy is the "Journey to Africa" exhibit, a sprawling open-enclosure range that is grazed by rhinoceros, giraffes, onyx, and other roving animals used to coexisting peacefully in the wild. The park's decades-old monorail system was retired in 2007; now the way to check out open enclosures is through a special tram that winds through the Serengeti-like plain filled with roaming animals. The park's admission price includes a ride on the tram.

The full cost of admission will also gain you access to the other walkable exhibits, including Condor Ridge's American desert habitat, Elephant Overlook, Lorikeet Landing's hands-on aviary, and my favorite, Lion Camp. Part of this lion enclosure is built to look like an abandoned research camp and these massive felines are deceptively cute when they decide to snooze in the stripped-out Land Rover that's been set up as a kitty house for them. "Meow," indeed.

© ERICKA CHICKOWSKI

The exhibits at the San Diego Zoo Safari Park feature replicas of animals' natural habitats.

San Pasqual Battlefield

History buffs headed to the Wild Animal Park on a weekend afternoon may want to make time to take a brief detour to San Pasqual Battlefield State Historic Park (15808 San Pasqual Valley Rd., 760/737-2201, 10 A.M.–5 P.M. Sat.–Sun., free), which is just east of the animal sanctuary.

This was the site of one of the most controversial battles in the Mexican–American War, an 1846 clash between U.S. and Californio troops that lasted no more than 15 minutes but has had military historians arguing over its outcome for 150 years. The park's visitors center features exhibits that provide context to the battle, the history of the valley prior to the war, and the events leading up to it.

Wine Country

The history of Escondido has been intertwined with grape vines since the Franciscan padres first laid eyes on the wild grapes that grew naturally in the area's local soils. The neophytes of

Mission San Luis Rey first cultivated the area with wine-producing varietals and the region's reputation has fermented ever since.

As San Diego development has crept up to Escondido, though, many of the former vineyards have retreated north to the Temecula Valley in Riverside County. But there still remain a number of vineyards and wineries on San Diego turf that oenophiles swear by.

One of the best is **Orfila Vineyards and Winery** (13455 San Pasqual Rd., 760/738-6500, www.orfila.com) in the San Pasqual Valley. This 70-acre estate lies on the road that connects downtown Escondido with the Wild Animal Park. Travelers are invited to stop by at 2 P.M. each day for a 25-minute tour through the grounds and the cellar. The tasting room is open from 10 A.M. to 6 P.M. daily, and when the weather's fine (and it usually is this far inland) wines can be savored underneath the adjacent grape arbor just outside the tasting room. You'll be able to pick 5 wines for $6 and they let you keep the glass as a souvenir.

About six miles away from downtown, **Belle Marie Winery** (26312 Mesa Rock Rd., 760/796-7557, www.bellemarie.com) primarily uses grapes from Baja Mexico's Guadalupe Valley, but it does have a lovely demonstration vineyard on the property for those who insist on seeing grapes grow as they taste their wines. Tastings are held daily between 11 A.M. and 5 P.M. You'll get five sips for $5, along with a free wine glass.

Continue on about four miles farther north, near the Welk Resort, and you'll find **Deer Park Winery** (29013 Champagne Blvd., 760/749-1666, www.deerparkwinery. com, call for hours). Deer Park offers tastings, and the flights here are $5 for five tastes and a wine glass. If you stop here, be sure to check out the expansive auto museum on the premises. Housed within rustic barns on the property are dozens of old fantails and speedsters dating from 1886 all the way to the mid-1970s. The winery also operates a deli that serves sandwiches and accoutrements to go with the wine.

ENTERTAINMENT AND EVENTS
Casinos

More than 1,600 slot machines jingle, jangle, and whir loudly on the floor of **Harrah's Rincon** (777 Harrah's Rincon Way, Valley Center, 760/751-3100, www.harrahs.com, 24 hrs. daily). Located northeast of Escondido along Highway S-6, this gaming establishment also features seven different kinds of table games and an active poker room that spreads a Texas Hold–Em tourney every day of the week.

Kept sparkling clean by the attentive staff, **Pala Casino offers** (11154 Hwy. 76, Pala, 760/510-5100, www.palacasino.com) another gambling option in Escondido. The gaming floor is less smoky than the county's average tribal casino and its hotel and amenities have all other casino–hotel combo properties beat hands down. So take those winnings, book a hotel room, watch a concert at the arena and get a massage in the spa to cap it all off.

Festivals and Events

Escondido's **Grape Day Festival** has deep roots. Started in 1915, the yearly event held the day after Labor Day each year began as a celebration of the abundant grape harvest that at one point was the main economic driver for the region. As grape production declined in the middle of the century, the event did as well. By 1950 the event became but a memory. That is, until civic leaders decided to revive it in 1996 to pay homage to Escondido's long-running love affair with the Muscat grape. The all-day festival now features a parade, live music, grape stomping, and wine tasting.

SHOPPING

The Escondido Art District is a vibrant mesh of art studios and galleries clustered around the California Center for the Arts in downtown Escondido. There are dozens of storefronts to wander that showcase fine art paintings, folk crafts, handmade beads, ancient sculpture, and other work that spans the spectrum of perceived beauty.

NORTH COUNTY

One of the most eclectic collections is held at **Distinction** (317 E. Grand Ave., 760/781-5779, www.distinctionart.com, noon–5 P.M. Wed.–Fri., 10 A.M.–5 P.M. Sat.), a gallery that rents out 14 working studios to local artists. The contemporary work here is largely from emerging artists and exhibits change frequently, about once every two months. This is also the hub of activity on the second Saturday of each month when the gallery hosts the reception for **Escondido's Artwalk** between 5 and 8 P.M.

The art at **Bill Kasper Studio and Gallery** (415 W. Grand Ave., 760/310-7379, www.billkasperstudio.com, 11 A.M.–7 P.M. Mon.–Fri., 11 A.M.–5 P.M. Sat.) is hot. Really. It all reaches 2,300 degrees before Kasper blows it into flowing bulbous and vibrant glass displays that include bowls, vases, sculptures, and lighting fixtures. Visit the studio on Saturdays to watch the magic happen during the live glass-blowing demonstrations held on-site.

SPORTS AND RECREATION
Trapeze High

Ever want to run away and join the circus? Trapeze High (2470 Melru Ln., 760/740-2454, www.trapezehigh.com) can train you to make your escapist fantasies a reality without all the needless hassle. Ladies don't have to grow a beard, fellas needn't stick their head in a lion's maw.

The safe and supportive facility at Trapeze High is a fun way to learn the art of swinging from the rafters. Classes are held Tuesday and Thursday at 4 P.M. and on the weekend at 10 A.M., noon, 2 P.M., and 4 P.M. They last 90 minutes and cost $60 per person.

Mountain Biking

Escondido is the gateway to the North County backcountry. In fact, if you start at City Hall and drive in just about any direction you're likely to stumble upon one or more classic San Diego trailheads. The beauty of this area for the fat-tire enthusiast is that the great majority of these trails are still open to mountain bikers,

a rare phenomenon in the increasingly restrictive SoCal riding zone.

Best of all, these aren't just wide and planed fire roads or flat rails-to-trails gravel. There are a lot of windy, technical trails that have enough elevation change to satisfy the most sadistic bombers in your pack. And there is a lot of pretty single-track that leads through natural chaparral and coastal scrub that has been untouched except by the occasional forest fire.

Before heading out, consider stopping by **Hidden Valley Bicycle Shop** (1040 E. Valley Pkwy., Ste. B, 760/746-1509, www.hiddenvalleybicycle.com, 9 A.M.–6 P.M. Mon.–Fri., 9 A.M.–5 P.M. Sat., closed Sun.) in town to pick up spare tubes, water-bottle cages, and other essentials for the trail.

Some of the best riding in the county is right in town at **Daley Ranch** (3024 La Honda Dr., 760/839-4680, dawn–dusk daily, free), a 3,058-acre plot of land purchased by the city to open to the public and protect from the encroachment of tract homes. The ranch has 25 miles of interconnected single-track opened to hikers and bikers. The routes ramble past swaying meadows, seasonal ponds lined with cattails, irregularly shaped boulders, and shady stands of Engelmann oak.

For some real lung-burners, try the 7.6-mile round-trip up and down the hills of **Elfin Forest Recreational Reserve** or battle your way up the 3.6-mile trail to the top of Bernardo Mountain. Both have an elevation gain of about 1,000 feet and both offer unique views of nearby Lake Hodges. The reserve's trailhead parking lot is located between mile markers 6 and 6.5 on Harmony Grove Road in Escondido. Rangers can be contacted at 760/632-4212.

If you'd like to get a closer look at Lake Hodges, there are also numerous trails along the shoreline. These are ideal for family bike rides, especially the **Piedras Pintadas** (Painted Rocks) interpretive trail. The ancient Kumeyaay pictographs that lend this trail its name are restricted, but along the trail there are many signs that offer tidbits about the plants and animals native to the area and the culture of the natives that expressed themselves so long ago. To get there take the West Bernardo Road exit off of I-15 and head west along West Bernardo Road for about half a mile until you see the trailhead.

Hiking

All of the trails suitable for mountain biking are also great on foot. Hikers also have the added advantage of being granted access to even more trails in the immediate vicinity that don't allow mountain bikes.

If you're saddled with the wee ones, a fun and gentle spot is at **Kit Carson Park** in the southern part of Escondido. The park has a five-acre arboretum, a beautiful sculpture garden, and a network of nature trails that ramble past three little ponds.

Or hike down to the splishity-splash of the hidden **Hell Creek** at Hellhole Canyon Park, a deceptively named place that is actually quite pleasant to wander. Though a lot of the trails here traverse hot and dusty scrubland, the creek sluices through craggy boulders underneath the shade of oak and sycamore.

Between Escondido and Ramona you can also venture out to **Boden Canyon Ecological Reserve,** another oaky enclave that offers up to 5.5 miles of exploration through the canopy. The scrub and wild grapevines here provide cover for woodland creatures such as the endangered Arroyo toad, deer, mountain lion, and dozens of species of birds. To get to Hellhole Canyon Park, take the Valley Parkway exit off of I-15 and go east to Lake Wohlford Road. Turn right there, go up the hill and continue past the lake for three miles until you reach Paradise Mountain road. Take a right on Paradise Mountain Road and then another right on Los Hermanos Ranch Road. Then take a left on Kiavo Road and continue to the end. Boden Canyon Ecological Reserve is in Ramona off of Highway 78, five miles east of the Highway 78 and Highway 67 intersection.

Golf

There are a number of very satisfying links in Escondido's environs. One of the best is **The Vineyard at Escondido** (925 San Pasqual Rd., 760/735-9545, www.vineyardatescondido.com, $55 weekdays, $75 weekends), a municipal golf course that embraces the local grape-grower heritage by weaving through area vineyards.

Built around the trickling brook of the same name, **Castle Creek Country Club** (8797 Circle R Dr., 760/749-2422, www.castlecreekcc.com, $50 weekdays, $52 Fridays, $66 weekends) has a 50-year legacy. The course here is now public and provides a good straightforward challenge to intermediate golfers.

Welk Resort (8860 Lawrence Welk Dr., 760/749-3225, www.welksandiego.com, $42) offers two different courses to accommodate varying skill levels. For the beginner, the Oaks Course ($18) is a welcoming par-3 rambler. This walking-only course is a good one to hoof it without worrying about crazy cart drivers. And the Fountains is a well-regarded executive course that hosts the Junior Golf Championships every July.

ACCOMMODATIONS
Under $150

Located right off of I-15, **Palms Inn** (2650 S. Escondido Blvd., 760/743-9733, $89 d) is a pretty standard motel that is convenient to the downtown arts district and only a short jaunt away from the Wild Animal Park. Considering the 45-minute drive back into San Diego, this can make an excellent place to crash for the night after over-indulging in the wines of the Temecula and San Pasqual Valleys. The property has a pool and spa and the room rate includes continental breakfast.

$150-250

For an intimate experience, **Castle Creek Inn Resort and Spa** (29850 Circle R Way, 760/751-8800, www.castlecreekinn.com, $189 d) is a small inn set along the fairways of Castle Creek Golf Course. Six queen suites and a three-bedroom villa open their French doors onto patios overlooking the course. The facility also has tennis courts, a modest swimming pool, hot soaking pools, and a garden path that winds through a whole palette of floral colors.

$250-350

The one- and two-bedroom villas of **Welk Resort** (8860 Lawrence Welk Dr., 760/749-3225, www.welksandiego.com, 1-br suite $259, 2-br suite $359) are set on a 600-acre complex that has two golf courses, tennis courts, a pool with a water park–type slide, a dinner theater, and even a little museum dedicated to the onetime virtuoso of the variety show, Lawrence Welk. This is no counterpart to the luxury of La Costa or Aviara in Carlsbad, but it is a nice, comfortable one-stop vacation for middle-class families and retirees without an extravagant annuity. All the villas come with separate bedrooms, kitchenettes, and private patios.

Camping

Set adjacent to Daley Ranch, **Dixon Lake** (1700 North La Honda Dr., 760/839-4680, $25 tent, $35 full hook up) has 45 sites lining the shoreside campground loop. All sites at this city-run campground have a fire ring, table, and a locker to secure your food. Some sites also have hookups for RVs. The cost is $20 for basic sites and $25 for RV sites. The grounds here make a great place to settle before boating Dixon Lake with fishing poles in tow or exploring the surrounding 500-acre recreational area. Exploration of the ranch also awaits campers. This is also a quiet spot for those with accessibility challenges to get close to nature—the campground operates a wheelchair-accessible cabin that rents for $30 per night.

Northeast of Dixon Lake is another lakeside retreat on the water of Lake Wohlford. On the north end of the lake, **Lake Wohlford Resort** (25484 Lake Wohlford Rd., 760/749-2755, http://lakewohlfordresort.com, $22) is a private campground that offers sites with full RV hookups.

FOOD

Art lovers who have come to walk the galleries of Escondido can sup on a classy meal at nearby **Bistro 221** (221 E. Grand Ave., 760/737-7398, wwww.bistro221.8m.com, 11:30 A.M.–2 P.M. Tues.–Fri. and 5 P.M.–9 P.M. Tues.–Sat., closed Sun.–Mon., $15), which serves lunch and dinner indoors or on its foliage-ringed sidewalk patio. Lunchtime brings light salads, sandwiches, and pasta, while dinner leans on Continental favorites such as steak *au poivre* and chicken saltimbocca.

Who says you can't get good seafood farther inland? **Sandcrab Café** (2229 Micro Pl., 760/480-2722, www.sandcrabcafe.com, 11 A.M.–9 P.M. Mon.–Thurs., 11 A.M.–10 P.M. Fri., noon–10 P.M. Sat., noon–9 P.M. Sun., $22) proves all the naysayers wrong with its New England–style seafood feasts. Clams, crab, shrimp, and fish are boiled up with corn and potatoes and dumped on butcher-papered tables in front of eager diners waiting with mallets in hand. The only trick is finding the place—it is a bit out of the way on the east side of I-15 in a business park. The drive is only a couple of minutes from downtown, but be sure to consult a map before you heat out for those sweet, sweet crustaceans.

Lake Wohlford Café (25484 Lake Wohlford Rd., 760/749-6585, www.lakewohlfordcafe. com, 5:30 A.M.–9 P.M. daily, $9) also serves fish, but its specialties come from freshwater, not salt. The café is known for its all-you-can-eat catfish dinner on Friday night. This can be a tasty consolation prize if you've been skunked while out fishing Wohlford, or if you've just worked up a powerful hunger from scrambling the Escondido backcountry. If you can't make it on a Friday, the café still serves a full breakfast, lunch, and dinner menu with hearty omelets, patty melts, and fried chicken rounding out the bunch.

Best known for its highly popular Arrogant Bastard Ale, **Stone Brewing Company** (1999 Citracado Pkwy., 760/471-4999, www.stone-worldbistro.com, 11 A.M.–11 P.M. Sun.–Thurs., 11 A.M.–2 A.M. Fri.–Sat., $18) is a venerated institution among brewpub aficionados. The brewery runs a stylish restaurant to showcase Arrogant Bastard and its dozens of other sudsy concoctions. Sup and sip here amidst towering ceilings and a chic warehouse vibe that is accented by decor featuring lots of glass, metal, and—appropriately enough—stone.

INFORMATION AND SERVICES

Information about Escondido and North County can be gathered at **San Diego North Visitor Center** (360 North Escondido Blvd., 760/745-4741, 8:30 A.M.–5 P.M. Mon.–Fri.), which is located inside the California Center for Performing Arts. The post office is right across the street from the arts center. Also in the neighborhood is the **Escondido Public Library** (239 South Kalmia St., 760/839-4684, 10 A.M.–9 P.M. Mon., Tues., Thurs., 10 A.M.–6 P.M. Wed., Fri.–Sat., closed Sun.), just two streets away. The library has Internet access and computers available for public use.

The Escondido **police station** is also located downtown, just off of the Valley Parkway exit from I-15. It is a straight shot from there along Grand Avenue to **Palomar Medical Center,** about nine blocks away. This full-service hospital has a 24-hour emergency room. Grand Avenue is also your best bet for banks and gas stations. Several of each are scattered along this stretch between the police station and the hospital.

GETTING THERE AND AROUND

Escondido is serviced by the **North County Transit System's Breeze bus lines.** Routes through the city include #302 to Oceanside, the #308 to Solana Beach, #386 to the Wild Animal Park. The #351 and #352 circular routes provide service within the city.

The **Metropolitan Transit System of San Diego** also provides service from downtown San Diego to Escondido on the #810 route, an hour-long express ride that leaves Escondido every 15 minutes on weekday mornings and returns every 15 minutes from downtown each afternoon.

Additionally, NCTS also runs commuter train service to Oceanside aboard its light-rail **Sprinter** train.

JULIAN AND ANZA-BORREGO

Drive east from any point along the coast—doesn't matter which way, due east, northeast, southeast, on any old highway route—and within an hour you'll hit the yin to the ocean's yang. Here in the middle of the county are San Diego's mountains, a craggy and boulder-strewn collection of ten ragtag ranges that stretch all the way from the international border up into Riverside County.

The mountains are wrinkled with trails and scenic highways. Hidden in the valleys and meadows are quaint mountain communities that reveal the pioneer spirit that made San Diego what it is today. Visitors can relive the bygone era, taking a locomotive ride along a historic border railway in Campo or roaming through an abandoned mine built during the Julian gold rush. Outdoors enthusiasts will find peace in the shade of oak and pine forests on foot, by bike, or on horseback. And casual wanderers can rest their heels at the comforting bed-and-breakfasts scattered about the hillsides.

East of the green and granite-flecked peaks of the Lagunas, the Cuyamacas, and the Palomar Mountains lies the untamed beauty of the desert. About a quarter of the entire county is covered by one of the largest state parks in the United States, Anza-Borrego Desert State Park.

The amazing landscape here is made up of badlands, high and low desert, dry lakes, oases, and hidden waterfalls. Visitors can scramble up cactus-covered peaks, roam through groves of mesquite humming with bees, or jostle their way along dusty jeep roads. The park features smooth sandstone slot canyons and ancient

© ERICKA CHICKOWSKI

HIGHLIGHTS

◖ Cuyamaca Rancho State Park: Stands of statuesque oak, hills of golden grasses, and happily-splashing creeks shaded in green riparian vegetation can all be found at this serene recreational park (page 227).

◖ Historic Julian: This pioneer town crawled with gold prospectors in the 1870s. Now it is the premier mountain getaway in San Diego (page 235).

◖ Palomar Observatory: Built atop one of the region's highest peaks, this distinctive white observatory shelters the amazing 200-inch Hale Telescope (page 241).

◖ Anza-Borrego State Park Visitors Center: This award-winning interpretive center is an important stop for desert wanderers seeking historic and ecological perspectives about the surroundings (page 245).

◖ Font's Point: Easily accessible from Borrego Springs, this awe-inspiring outlook affords views of the forbidding Borrego Badlands (page 245).

◖ Vallecito Regional Park: Deep in the southern desert landscape is the Vallecito Stage Station, a reconstruction of one of the most-welcomed stops for wagon-bound travelers along the Butterfield Overland Stage (page 245).

LOOK FOR ◖ TO FIND RECOMMENDED SIGHTS, ACTIVITIES, DINING, AND LODGING.

pictographs. In the spring, the desert floor is awash in colors as the wildflowers give their annual show.

Those who want to witness the beauty needn't rough it, either: The resort town of Borrego Springs is centrally located.

PLANNING YOUR TIME

The wild country of San Diego will take some time to explore, if only just to allow time to get there. Northern outposts such as Palomar Mountain State Park and Warner Springs can take about an hour and a half to reach and the trip to some of the farthest points in Anza-Borrego Desert State Park can take longer than two hours.

If you plan on hitting any of the backcountry, you'll need to schedule it as a day trip at least. Some of the more accessible areas around Pine Valley, the Laguna Mountains, the Cuyamaca Mountains, and Julian are easily visited in one day if you only have a few specific spots you'd like to check out.

The desert is best explored as an overnight

JULIAN AND ANZA-BORREGO

RIVERSIDE COUNTY
SAN DIEGO COUNTY

Vail Lake

Aguanga

PALOMAR OBSERVATORY
Palomar Mtn State Park
DOANE VALLEY

Rincon
HARRAH'S RINCON CASINO & RESORT

To Escondido

Cleveland National Forest

GUY B. WOODWARD MUSEUM
Ramona

OASIS CAMEL DAIRY

Santa Ysabel
SANTA YSABEL ASISTENCIA
Santa Ysabel Open Space Preserve

Sutherland Reservoir

Lake Henshaw
SKYSAILING INC

Julian
HISTORIC JULIAN
William Heise Regional Park
CALIFORNIA WOLF CENTER

Volcan Mountains

WARNER SPRINGS RANCH
Warner Springs

Hot Springs Mountain

Pacific Crest Trail

Ranchita

Anza-Borrego Desert State Park

ANZA-BORREGO STATE PARK VISITORS CENTER
BORREGO PALM
Borrego Springs
BORREGO SPRINGS AIRPORT

Clark Lake

Santa Rosa Mountains

SALTON SEAWAY
BORREGO SPRINGS RD

FONT'S POINT
Borrego Badlands

OCOTILLO WELLS STATE VEHICULAR RECREATION AREA
Ocotillo Wells

Split Mountain

YAQUI PASS RD
Yaqui Pass
TAMARISK GROVE
GRAPEVINE TRAIL
Grapevine Cyn
Grapevine Mountain

Vallecito Mountains

PICTOGRAPHS
Blair Valley

trip or longer. It is definitely doable to trek out there in a single day, but it will be a long day with a lot of driving. Spending the night in Borrego Springs, at a designated campground, or just simply camped out anywhere in the park is part of the experience, anyway.

Anywhere you roam in the forests, meadows, cactus fields, and mountains, the more time you have to devote the better. There are countless trails to tromp, vistas to enjoy, and solitude to find. It is something you simply can't rush.

Campo to Julian

Home of the Laguna and Cuyamaca Mountains, this area is a fine place to stretch out the legs and explore a little. Recreation and scenic drives are the name of the game here, with dozens of trails just waiting to be discovered by bike or foot, and lakes that are meant to fished.

For those who don't want to try their luck against nature but still want to roll the dice, there are more than a few Native American casinos in the area also.

SIGHTS

Sequestered in the sleepy border town of Campo, there is a trio of museums that offers an interesting perspective on this region's position in San Diego's history. Located about 60 miles from the big city and only a mile from Mexico, Campo Valley is the crossroads of San Diego development. It lay on the alternate stage route to Yuma, Arizona, during the mid-1800s and when the San Diego and Arizona Railway laid its track to finish the last link of the transcontinental railway to San Diego, the trains chugged through Campo.

San Diego Railroad Museum

San Diego Railroad Museum (Hwy. 94 and Forest Gate Rd., Campo, 619/478-9937, www. sdrm.org, 9 A.M.–5 P.M. weekends and major selected holidays, museum entry and train ride $5 adults, $2.50 children 6–12 takes visitors on a trip through history over some of those same rails. For $10 visitors hop aboard the Golden State and rumble across the rugged landscape for a nostalgic ride. When the train returns to the Campo Depot, all are invited to wander

through the museum's warehouse of engines and cars, some restored and some romantically rusting away outside.

Motor Transport Museum

Trains weren't the only transportation link to San Diego that ran through Campo. In 1914, Old Highway 80 (it was new then) curved its way around the mountains and toward the sea. Here, trucks of all shapes and sizes kept the region rolling with goods from the eastern states. The Motor Transport Museum (31949 Hwy. 94, 619/478-2492, 9 A.M.–5 P.M. Sat.,

San Diego Railroad Museum in Campo

THE SAGA OF THE GASKILL STORE

In 1868, Silas and Luman Gaskill left Texas to start a brand-new life as shopkeepers in the wild backcountry of California. After some peaceful years of commerce, they soon got a taste of how wild it really could be. Their journey landed them in the dusty frontier town of Campo, just across the border from Tecate. It was there that the Gaskills built a wooden building complete with a trap door so they could draw water from Campo Creek and lower goods down for cold storage.

They lived a quiet backcountry existence until 1875, when they experienced the type of showdown that gave the West its crazy reputation. Sometime in the winter of that year the brothers were tipped off that a gang of Mexican banditos intended to rob the store. They hid firearms throughout the property in preparation for the fight, but were still surprised by the attack that started on the morning of December 4th, when Cruz Lopez and his band of cutthroats came calling.

The robbers announced their arrival by shooting Lumen Gaskill in the chest, leaving him critically wounded. Hearing the noise from the neighboring blacksmith's shop, Silas grabbed a hidden shotgun and unloaded on the thieves still in the store, helped out by the guns of a French ranchhand and another gentleman who just happened to be passing by and joined in the fracas. When the powder cleared, the Frenchman and one thief were dead and several others wounded.

In true Western vigilante style, two members of the slow and wounded gang were picked up by a posse the next day. That night, while being held for trial, both were hanged from a nearby tree by anonymous hands.

It's no surprise that the Gaskill store that you can visit today, which now houses the **Mountain Empire Historical Society,** is not the wooden one the brothers started with. They rebuilt their building to resemble a fort, with thick concrete and red-brick walls. It was used actively as a store until 1920 and also served as a post office, a bank, and a sort of town hall before the area became a one-acre county park.

free) pays tribute to those wheeled ferries of progress with its extensive collection of antique trucks, tractors, and trailers. Volunteers work on one or two restorations at a time; there are hundreds of vehicles in various states of disrepair scattered across the yard outside of the museum's cavernous workshop. It is enough to make a gearhead's eyes widen to the size of dish platters. Although admission is free, but donations are always welcome—those restorations aren't cheap!

Mountain Empire Historical Society

It hasn't always been easy traveling in the borderlands, though. Campo has been on the front lines of frontier border disputes since the United States gained possession of this land after the Mexican–American War. One of the most famous incidents was the Campo Gunfight in 1875, when a group of Mexican bandits attacked the **Gaskill Brothers Stone Store and Hotel.** This historic building now houses the Mountain Empire Historical Society (31130 Hwy. 94, 619/478-5707, http://mehs.net) museum, which recounts this incident and how it precipitated the establishment of the U.S. Customs Service station in Campo. The museum also covers the history of Camp Locket, which was built in Campo in 1941, remaining the last operational horse cavalry post in the country until its closure in 1946. Though the army was fully mechanized at that point, it believed that soldiers on horseback would be the most expedient way to guard the rough terrain at the border. This base was also a notable prisoner-of-war camp during World War II, interring Italians and Germans captured during the North African campaign against Rommel.

Laguna Mountain Recreation Area

San Diego is known for fun, sun, surf, and… snow? Yes, that's right. The mountains in the heart of the county are known to get a dusting of snow each year, and none receive more of the white stuff than Mount Laguna. The mountain is a part of the Cleveland National Forest's Laguna Mountain Recreation Area. Situated along the Sunrise Highway, this outdoor playground has lots of hills to sled down and terrain to traverse by cross-country ski when there's enough powder. Be sure to pack your hiking boots, too, because snow only hits a few days of the year and isn't very predictable.

You won't be disappointed either way. This mixed pine and oak forest area is home to hiking and mountain-biking trails galore, plus plenty of campgrounds and picnic areas. There's a serene mountain meadow here, and some amazing views of the desert floor to the east.

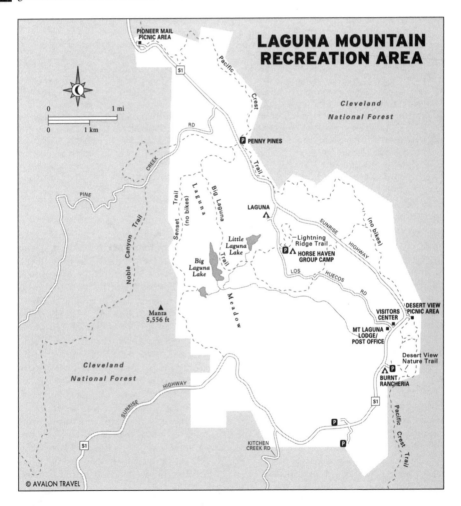

To learn about the flora and fauna, be sure to stop off at the **Laguna Mountain Visitor Information Center** (10 mi north of I-8 on Hwy. S-1, 619/473-8547, 9 A.M.–5 P.M. Sat., 9 A.M.–3 P.M. Sun., 1–5 P.M. Fri.). Usually staffed by a kindly volunteer, the center has interpretive displays and a collection of books and maps to get you started on your adventure. If you stop there, be sure to keep a lookout for the Desert View Picnic Area, just a quarter mile north. This offers one of the best lookouts to Anza-Borrego State Park along the entire length of Sunrise Highway.

Cuyamaca Rancho State Park

The country south of Julian, filled with rising and falling peaks and meadows dotted with fluttering oak trees, was called "Ah-ha-Kwe-ah-mac" by the indigenous people here, translated roughly as "the place of rain." The name has stuck, albeit modified by the Europeans, and the area is now known as the Cuyamaca Mountains. Much of this beautiful area has been saved for posterity, set aside by the state within the 25,000-acre Cuyamaca Rancho State Park (12551 Hwy. 79, Descanso, 760/765-0755, www.parks.ca.gov, www.cuyamaca.us, dawn–dusk daily).

Indeed, it does rain here more than in the surrounding regions and the resulting woodland forest offers some of the greenest natural landscapes in the county. The Cuyamacas are no stranger to drought, however, and the land here is subject to the natural cycle of growth, wildfire, then regrowth that is so common in Southern California. In 2003 these mountains were ravaged by one of the most devastating wildfires in decades, the Cedar Fire. Driving along Highway 79 through the heart of the state park, visitors will see the effects of this conflagration as the forest heals itself from the flames. The area is a powerful testament to Mother Nature's power of destruction and rebirth. In the areas where the flames swooshed through, great stands of "ghost forest" remain like legions of burnt and spindly matchsticks. But it is far from a desolate sight. Saplings, lowland scrubs, and wildflowers cover the

© ERICKA CHICKOWSKI

The trails in Cuyamaca Rancho State Park lead through mixed oak and pine forests.

woodland floor and this greenery continues to grow taller and thicker each year.

With over a hundred miles of trails that roam through grasslands and boulder-specked mountains, this state park offers a lifetime's worth of exploration.

ENTERTAINMENT AND EVENTS
Casinos

Stow some cash in those hiking boots and make a wager at any one of the numerous Native American casinos based in the area. Most convenient to the city is **Sycuan Casino** (5459 Sycuan Rd., El Cajon, 800/279-2826, 24 hrs. daily) and **Viejas Casino** (5000 Willows Rd., Alpine, 800/847-6537, 24 hrs. daily), which are both located just off of I-8. Both are Vegas-style ventures with loads of slot machines, plus table games (except craps, which is not legal in the state of California) and dedicated poker rooms. Sycuan also has a full resort and golf

© AVALON TRAVEL

course on its property, while Viejas features a concert venue and an outlet shopping center.

Halfway between I-8 and Ramona, **Barona Valley Ranch** (1932 Wildcat Canyon Rd., Lakeside, 888/722-7662, www.barona.com, 24 hrs. daily) is a slightly smaller casino that is lighter on the slot machines but has one of the largest collections of table and poker games of any of the casinos in the county.

Concerts

Also adjacent to the casino, Viejas hosts **Concerts in the Park** at its 1,500-seat outdoor concert arena. Shows here are all over the map, with frequent sets from country megastars, rock-band reunion tours, stand-up comedians, and emerging artists.

SHOPPING

Located adjacent to Viejas Casino, **Viejas Outlet Center** (5005 Willows Rd., #229, Alpine, 10 A.M.–9 P.M. Mon.–Sat., 10 A.M.–7 P.M. Sun.) is a popular spot to pick up brand-name items on the cheap. It has over 60 different outlet stores from shops like Borders, Eddie Bauer, Tommy Hilfiger, and Ralph Lauren.

SPORTS AND RECREATION
Hiking

Some of the most accessible San Diego backcountry trails lie between Alpine and Pine Valley, on the south side of I-8. Here Pine Valley Creek runs through Cleveland National Forest, which offers a number of easy-to-reach trails, such as the scramble to the top of **Lawson Peak** off of Lyons Valley Road. Take the Japatul Valley Road exit and head south on that road until you can take a left on Lyons Valley Road. Continue south on Lyons until you reach mile marker 13 and the unpaved Carveacre road. This road twists and winds its way to the granite-topped Lawson, where it is an easy enough scramble to the top. Or you can take on **Espinosa Trail** in Horsethief Canyon or **Secret Canyon Trail,** which both offer long exploration of chaparral-draped mountain sides. For both, take the Japatul

MOUNTAIN DRIVE

You don't need to huff and puff your way up the side of a cliff to enjoy San Diego's alpine scenery. Some of the best views unwind before you from the ribbon of pavement that winds through the county's mountains. My favorite drive takes you through the oak and pine forests of both the Laguna Mountains and the Cuyamacas.

From downtown San Diego, take I-8 past Pine Valley and exit onto Sunrise Highway. Take this windy road up through the chaparral, into the pine of the Lagunas. If you get a chance, be sure to stop off at the Desert View platform to get a look at the desert floor to the east. Then continue northeast until the junction with Highway 79.

Take a left to complete the loop. You'll curve south past Lake Cuyamaca and into Cuyamaca Rancho State Park. Here you'll be greeted by majestic oak and swaying grasslands. Keep following the road back down the mountainsides until you reach I-8 for the return trip back into town.

Valley Road exit off I-8 and head in the same direction as Lawson Peak, but only go as far as the Japatul Fire Station. The trailhead is right at the fire station.

For an easier jaunt, Roberts Ranch is a short stroll through a meadow sprinkled with dignified oaks. Feel free to bring along your furry pal on any of these dog-friendly trails. This is also off of Japatul Valley Road, less than a mile from the freeway. Park at the Caltrans maintenance station to explore here.

The town of Campo maintains a special place in the heart of the endurance hikers who have tromped over hill and dale to make the 2,650-mile hike from the Mexican border to the Canadian border. Campo marks the start of the **Pacific Crest Trail** (PCT) one of the most famous long-distance trails in the Americas. You don't have to hike the whole thing, though.

© ERICKA CHICKOWSKI

Big Laguna Meadow's mixed-use trail is a fun spot to hike with your furry friends.

There are numerous trailheads between Campo and Julian that are good places to set out on a day hike along the PCT. The trail runs right by **Lake Morena County Park** (2550 Lake Morena Dr.). Or you can start at the Boulder Oaks Campground just south of where the PCT crosses under I-8 and hike 2.25 miles north of the freeway to **Kitchen Creek Falls.** Here a spray of rivulets cascade 150 feet down alternately smooth and blocky chunks of granite mountainside. To get to the trailhead, take the Buckman Springs Road exit of I-8 and take Old Highway 80 south for two miles.

Farther north, the PCT wanders along a pine-covered ridge that looks east to majestic desert vistas. Park at Burnt Rancheria Campground (9.4 mi north of I-8 on Sunrise Hwy.) and travel this stretch of the PCT that is alternately known as **Desert View Trail** at this point. The opportunities to make up your own route along this trail are nearly limitless, but be sure to leave your pup at home, since dogs are restricted on this route.

Cuyamaca Rancho State Park and the

surrounding Cleveland National Forest land in the Cuyamacas is another prime region to trod in hiking boots. Just in the park alone there are over 100 miles of trails. Peak baggers will enjoy the ascent up **Stonewall Peak Trail,** reachable from Paso Picacho Campground (12551 Hwy. 79), or along **Monument Trail** to the top of Japacha Peak. Along the latter route, at about 4,700 feet elevation, there is an old biplane engine block mounted on a concrete monument in honor of a pioneering airman who crashed here in 1922. The trailhead is located on Highway 79 approximately 7.5 miles north of I-8.

Another notable trail on flatter terrain is the **California Riding and Hiking Trail** along the south shore of Lake Cuyamaca, which passes the site of an old gold mine, the Stonewall Mine. Park at the trailhead 10.7 miles north of I-8 along Highway 79 to hike here.

For an easy nature walk of less than a mile, try the **West Side Trail,** which is known for the Native American grinding holes that pock the granite here. These *mortreros* are some of the last signs of the Kumeyaay people who would spend the summers here collecting acorns to grind into meal. This trail is also reachable from Paso Picacho Campground.

Mountain Biking

Within an easy 30-minute drive from downtown San Diego, **Wright's Field** in Alpine makes for a quick taste of the country or a good warm-up before hitting the more remote trails in the county. This 230-acre nature preserve has a two-mile loop that rolls up and over meadowland that is speckled with boulders. The occasional oak dapples the route with shade. To get here, take the Tavern Road exit off I-8 and follow Tavern Road a little over a mile until you reach MacQueen Middle School. Park near the school; Wrights Field is adjacent to it.

Cuyamaca Rancho State Park doesn't allow any mountain biking on its trails, so the best single-track in this region is located south in the Laguna Mountains. The quintessential San Diego backcountry fat-tire route runs here through the tranquility of the **Big Laguna Meadow.** Here you can roll through the grassland of Big Laguna Trail, around Laguna Lake, and through the herds of cattle that graze here. The flat trail is perfect for recreational riders and families who are interested in a leisurely ride, and it is easily accessible from the Laguna Campground (12.6 mi north of I-8 on Sunrise Hwy., $17 per site). Those looking to get their fill of the picturesque and still get their heart rate pumping can use the Big Laguna route as a link to the **Noble Canyon Trail,** which humps it way up and down the mountainsides for ten miles until it reaches Pine Valley. This trail is also accessible on its own from Penny Pines Trailhead, which is about 14 miles north of I-8 along Sunrise Highway.

Though there is no riding along trails within Cuyamaca Rancho, the fire roads here are open to exploration by wheel. The coup de grace of them all is the 2.8-mile road up to San Diego County's second-tallest mountaintop, **Cuyamaca Peak,** from Paso Picacho Campground. This is a real lung-buster, with 1,700 feet of elevation gain bunched together in a number of very steep ascents. The reward at the top is your view of the Pacific, the desert, and the mountain ranges that stretch between them.

Cycling

The back roads of the southern mountain ranges are very popular with endurance and touring cyclists. Some favorite routes include the out-and-back along **Old Highway 80** and the loop from Pine Valley through the Lagunas on **Sunrise Highway** (Hwy. S-2) and down through the Cuyamacas and back to Pine Valley on **Highway 79.**

World Cycles (9621 Campo Rd., Ste. A, Spring Valley, 619/337-2817, www.worldcycles.com, 11 A.M.–7 P.M. Mon.–Sat., closed Sun.) in Spring Valley and **Big Ring Cyclery** (8691 La Mesa Blvd., La Mesa, 619/463-2453, 10 A.M.–7 P.M. Mon.–Sat., 11 A.M.–4 P.M. Sun.) are good sources for bike rentals.

Fishing

The mountainous corridor from the border up to Julian offers some of the most fruitful freshwater fishing in all of San Diego County, perhaps in all of Southern California. Close to the city along the I-8 corridor, **El Capitan Reservoir** is a 1,562-acre lake stocked with Florida-strain largemouth bass, crappie, bluegill, channel catfish, blue catfish, green sunfish, and carp. Though there are about four miles of accessible shoreline for fishing, the best access is by boat or float tube. There is a boat launch here, but no concession, so come prepared with a fishing license and all the bait you'll need. Also bring cash to pay the $5 lake-use fee.

Only 10 miles from El Cap, **Lake Jennings** (10108 Bass Rd., Lakeside) is the centerpiece of a popular county park. In addition to a boat ramp there are picnic areas, campsites, and a concession stand here. You'll find largemouth bass and bluegill all year, blue and channel catfish in the summer, and rainbow trout in winter.

Lake Morena (2550 Lake Morena Dr., Campo, 858/694-3049, 8 A.M.–5 P.M. Mon.–Fri.) is another popular county holding. Located just outside of Campo, this lake stocks similar strains to Lake Jennings, with the addition of crappie in the summer and German brown trout in winter. There is a boat ramp and the county operates a boat rental facility here, letting out motorboats for $35 per day and rowboats for $15 per day. This includes a lake-use fee, which is $6 per day for private boats.

Just north of Cuyamaca Rancho State Park, **Lake Cuyamaca** is the only lake in the county that stocks trout all year long. Also in the lake are catfish, smallmouth and largemouth bass, bluegill, crappie, and sturgeon. This 110-acre lake is open to float tubes during the week and boats daily. There is a full tackle shop and a boat concession that rents motorboats for $40 per day, rowboats for $15 per day, and kayaks for $10 per hour. Also on the lake is a full-service restaurant and a campground open to RVs and tent campers.

Golf

Some of San Diego's best golf courses are owned and maintained by the same tribal entertainment outfits that run the local casino complexes. The well-regarded **Singing Hills Resort at Sycuan** (3007 Dehesa Rd., El Cajon, 619/442-3425, www.sycuanresort. com, weekdays $57, Fri. $62, Sat.–Sun. $79, cart $13) is considered by many locals to be home to the finest set of links in the county. Set back into the foothills that sprout up around the Sweetwater River, Singing Hills boasts two full-sized courses and one executive par-3 course ($19–26) for those eager to head to the casino tables after their round. Water features, traps, doglegs, and trees abound at the challenging par-72 Willow Glen and Oak Glen courses, so don't forget the extra balls and your game face.

Meanwhile, **Barona Creek Golf Club** (1000 Wildcat Canyon Rd., Lakeside, 619/387-7018, www.barona.com, weekends $160, weekdays $120) offers more sweeping vistas and a more forgiving course with wide-open, undulating fairways and sprawling greens. Be sure to bring a nice, big driver. This course extends well over 7,000 yards.

ACCOMMODATIONS

Most of the best overnight options in this part of the county involve a stay under the starry skies. But there are a couple of places to take advantage of a soft bed and a warm shower.

Under $150

The rooms at **Ayres Inn** (1251 Tavern Rd., Alpine, 619/445-5800, www.ayreshotels.com/alpine, $112 s, $122 d) in Alpine are surprisingly plush for what looks like a gussied-up motel on the outside. The rooms have leather-upholstered chairs and dark mahogany furniture, with top-of-the-line linens. A stay here comes with an expanded continental breakfast and a free shuttle to the local casinos.

You can choose between modest motel rooms or rustic cabins at **Laguna Mountain Lodge** (10678 Sunrise Hwy., Mt. Laguna, 619/445-2342, www.lagunamountain.com, motel rooms $55–73 d, 1-br cabin $75–88 d, six-person 2-br cabin $108–183), which is within walking distance to the Laguna Mountain Visitor Information Center and the Pacific Crest Trail. The property is shaded by the pine and oak typical of the Laguna Mountains; each cabin comes with its own picnic table and barbecue. There are also pet-friendly cabins available here.

$150-250

Located on the border between the outskirts of town and the middle of nowhere, **Sycuan Resort & Casino** (3007 Dehesa Rd., El Cajon, 619/442-3425 or 800/457-5568, www.sycuanresort.com, $240 d) offers the complete casino resort experience. The golf course here is perennially rated as one of the best in the county and there is also a spa, tennis courts, and 72-hole golf course on the property.

$250-350

Pine Valley Inn (28940 Old Highway 80, Pine Valley, 619/473-8560, www.pinevalleyinn.com, $70 d, weekly $350 d) is an ideal place to stay when you are planning on hitting the road at the first light of day and would rather not pay city prices if you aren't going to be around to enjoy the region. It is a simple motel with a re-frigerator and microwave in each room, along with Internet access.

Camping

Camping in this region is plentiful, with a full range of camping experiences available, from primitive forest-service sites to full-hookup RV campgrounds.

Near the border, **Lake Morena County Park** (2550 Lake Morena Dr., Campo, 858/694-3049, tent $19, partial hookup $24, cabin $50) has spots for tenters and RV sites with partial hookups. The sites here are situated in an oak grove near the lake, with views of the granite-studded hillsides that surround the park. There are numerous hiking trails nearby, including the Pacific Crest Trail.

The most popular campground in the Laguna Mountains is the aptly named ◖ **Laguna Campground** (12.6 mi north of I-8 on Sunrise Hwy., $19). Located along the very scenic Big Laguna Meadow, this facility has primitive bathrooms and cold-water faucets. These woodland sites are mostly designed for tent campers, equipped with picnic tables and fire rings. There are no RV hookups, but there are a few sites with paved spurs.

Also nearby in the Laguna Mountain Recreation Area is the large **Burnt Rancheria** campground, which has direct access to the Pacific Crest Trail, and the primitive hike-in site **Aqua Dulce**. Prices are $19 per site per night for Burnt Rancheria; Aqua Dulce is free. Inquire at the Laguna Mountain Visitor Information Center for directions (10 mi north of I-8 on Hwy. S-1, 9 A.M.–5 P.M. Sat., 9 A.M.–3 P.M. Sun., 1–5 P.M. Fri.).

The two largest sites in Cuyamaca Rancho State Park are **Green Valley Campground** and **Paso Picacho**. Green Valley has a pretty little creek running right through the campground, a real treat for the kids in the summer. And Paso Picacho is only two miles south of Lake Cuyamaca. Both sites accept RVs, but there are no hookups. All campsites come with picnic ta-bles and fire rings, and both sites have flush toi-lets and pay showers and cost $30 per night.

Just north of the state park, **Lake Cuyamaca** (15027 Hwy. 79, Julian, 760/765-0515 or 877/581-9904, www.lakecuyamaca.org, $25) is one of the best places for RV travelers in the area. Here they have 23 RV sites with power and water hookups. The grounds are scenic, ringing the lake to provide good views of an-glers plying the waters.

FOOD

It is catch as catch can in this region when it comes to food. Unless you've packed your own lunch, you'll be relying on a few roadside diners and markets sprinkled between the vast tracts of open land dominating the landscape. Fortunately, many of them are quite good.

As you head east along the I-8 corridor, Alpine is the last bastion of civilization eas-ily accessible from the off-ramp until you hit the county line. If you'd like to fill your belly before heading to the hinterlands, this little hamlet is a reliable stop with a good selection of fast-food joints and a few cafés that will do the trick. Same goes for when you are speed-ing back into town on an empty stomach, just looking for the first place you can find.

If you don't feel like eating the same old fast food, **Fred's Old Fashioned Burgers** (2754 Alpine Blvd., Alpine, 619/445-1264, 10:30 A.M.–8 P.M. daily, $5) is a homey ham-burger stand that cooks up fresh patties and crispy fries. Another quick and delicious al-ternative is the affordable Mexican fare at **Mi Ranchito** (1903a Alpine Blvd., 619/445-8907, 8 A.M.–9 P.M. Sun.–Thurs., 8 A.M.–10 P.M. Fri.–Sat., $7). Both restaurants are accessible from the Tavern Road exit in Alpine.

Hands down, my favorite roadside diner in all of San Diego County is ◖ **La Posta Diner** (32337 Old Highway 80, Pine Valley, 619/478-5600, 7 A.M.–8 P.M. daily, $10). It's got big, two-handed burgers that taste so fresh I wouldn't be surprised to hear mooing coming from the kitchen. The chicken-fried steak is tender and crisp, and served with real mashed potatoes and fresh veggies. Finish with one of their tempting slices of pie and you'll be unbuttoning your pants for the rest of the drive. La Posta is also open for breakfast and lunch.

Near the border, **Campo Diner** (1367 Dewey Pl., 619/478-2888, www.campodiner. com, 8 A.M.–8 P.M. daily, $11) can really hit the spot after taking a ride on the San Diego Railroad Museum's Golden State. It might sound weird considering how far from the ocean this '50s-style diner is situated, but it has some of the best fish-and-chips in the whole county. Portions are huge, so don't be afraid to split a plate. Also on the menu are lumberjack-sized breakfasts and lots of sandwiches.

Drivers headed up Highway 79 to Julian have two diner choices along the way. **Descanso Junction Restaurant** (8306 Hwy. 79, Descanso, 619/659-2199, www.descansojunction. com, 7 A.M.–8 P.M. daily, $11) is in the blink-or-you'll-miss-it town of Descanso. Adorned with old-timey Coke ads and other frilly bits you'd see in grandma's house, this eatery has a selection of steaks, barbecue, burgers, and sandwiches, plus breakfast in the morning. Like grandma's house, the staff here is usually happy to whip up something off-menu if they have the ingredients for it.

Lake Cuyamaca Market and Restaurant (15027 Hwy. 79, Julian, 6 A.M.–8 P.M. daily, $9) is a nice little café with a view of the lake. Sandwiches, salads, and burgers are all on the menu, as are a host of breakfast standards. The market has a decent selection of goodies and cold drinks for the rest of the ride.

INFORMATION AND SERVICES

The closest major medical center in this area is **Sharp Grossmont Hospital** (5555 Grossmont Center Dr., 619/740-6000) just west of Alpine in La Mesa.

The **San Diego County Sheriff** runs substations in Alpine (1347 Tavern Rd., #2, 619/659-2600), Campo (378 Sheridan Rd., 619/478-5378), and in Pine Valley (28848 Old Highway 80, 619/473-8774). This particular section of the San Diego backcountry has pretty decent cell phone coverage, especially near the I-8 corridor, so you may just be able to call 911 in the case of an emergency. Always play it safe by telling someone when you plan on exploring the wilderness, giving them details about where you'll be and for how long.

GETTING THERE AND AROUND

This far out of the city there aren't many good public transit options available. Your best bet is to travel by car. Most routes this way will head east along I-8; you'll then veer off north or south depending on your destination. To the south the major roadways are Old Highway 80, Buckman Springs Road, and Highway 94. Going south to Campo from San Diego it might make sense to take Highway 94 the whole way and completely bypass I-8. To the north, the major thoroughfares are Sunrise Highway, also known as S-1, and Highway 78.

If you plan on parking at any of the trailheads within Cleveland National Forest, you'll be required to display an Adventure Pass parking permit. These passes are available at a number of outdoor supply stores in the city, including Sport Chalet and REI. You can also pick one up at the **Laguna Mountain Visitor Information Center** (10 mi north of I-8 on Hwy. S-1). Daily passes cost $5 and annual passes are $30.

Julian

Once upon a time this was San Diego's home to gold prospectors; now it plays host to dozens of bed-and-breakfasts, museums, and shops. Located more than 4,000 feet above sea level, the town is also a center for winter activity when the snow falls. San Diegans are awfully proud of this fact, as the area is one of the few in the United States where you can conceivably take a dip in the ocean and frolic in the snow within an hour. West of town is the "big city" of Ramona. This is the gateway to San Diego County's mountain and desert retreats, and a great place to stop for affordable lodging and convenient grub.

SIGHTS
◖ Historic Julian
The gold-mining operations that were once the lifeblood of Julian are long since shut down, but you can relive the fervor for that shiny stuff at **Eagle & High Peak Mine Tours** (2320 C

The guided tours provided by Eagle & High Peak Mine Tours are one of the highlights of sightseeing in Julian.

St., 760/765-0036, 10 A.M.–3 P.M., last tour 2:30 P.M. daily year-round, $8 adults, $4 children 5–15, free children 4 and under) right in the center of Julian. At one time these were two separate mine shafts, but they're connected now and open for a look-see. The affable and knowledgeable guides here will lead you through the timbered passageways, shedding light on how these dark caverns were worked. Once you reemerge and give your eyes some time to readjust, you'll have a chance to see the giant stamp press on property and try your hand at panning for gold.

A perfect complement to the mine tour is a visit to the **Julian Pioneer Museum** (2811 Washington St., 760/765-0227, 10 A.M.–4 P.M. Fri.–Sun. Apr.–Nov., 10 A.M.–4 P.M. Sat.–Sun. Dec.–Mar., $3) only a couple of blocks away. The museum has an interesting collection of mining equipment and rock samples on top of the other exhibits highlighting the establishment of this historic town. There's a restored stagecoach, household equipment, photos of the town's earliest residents, and a remarkable lace collection. Also on display are numerous artifacts from the Native Americans who predated the gold-seeking settlers.

Once you've learned about all those hardy town founders, you can pay your respects to many of them at the **Julian Pioneer Cemetery** (Farmer Rd. and A St.). This small-town burial ground has graves marked back to 1870.

At the town's primary intersection at Main and Washington Streets, you can wave down a horse-drawn carriage from **Country Carriages** (corner of Washington and Main, 760/765-1471, call to schedule a ride, $30 for two people) to get some more perspective on the town's history. You'll clip-clop around the town and some of the surrounding scenic roads while the driver regales you with Julian lore.

Woodward Museum
Julian doesn't have the lock on historic sights in in San Diego's backcountry. Settled in an 1886

pioneer home, the Guy B. Woodward Museum (645 Main St., Ramona, 760/789-7644, www. woodwardmuseum.org, 1–4 P.M. Thurs.–Sun., free) tells the unique stories of the Native Americans, farmers, cowboys, vaqueros, miners, and stagecoach drivers who once populated San Diego's mountains and deserts.

Santa Ysabel Asistencia

Situated between Julian and Ramona, Santa Ysabel Asistencia (Hwy. 79, Santa Ysabel, 760/765-0810, 8 A.M.–4 P.M. daily winter, 8 A.M.–5:30 P.M. daily Memorial Day–Labor Day) was built as a "sub-mission" of Mission San Diego de Alcalá in 1818. The original church fell to ruins after the secularization of the missions, but the adobe chapel erected in its place in 1924 still stands. There is a small museum on the property, as well as a cemetery.

Oasis Camel Dairy

Driving the back roads of Ramona goes a little something like this: horse, horse, cow, horse, cow, barn, camel…screech. What? Yep, right in the middle of the typical American rural landscape of Highway 78 is the first and only camel dairy in the United States, Oasis Camel Dairy (26757 Hwy. 78, 760/787 0983, www. cameldairy.com). The curious humpbacked creatures are milked here to create a line of smooth camel-milk soap. Tours are available, though infrequent. Check the website or give a call to see when the next scheduled tour occurs. Tours cost $10 for adults, $7 for children, and $8 for seniors.

California Wolf Center

Dedicated to the preservation of the North American Gray Wolf, the California Wolf Center (449 KQ Ranch Rd., 760/765-0030, www.californiawolfcenter.org) shelters recovering wolf packs so that they can breed and be released into the wild. Every Saturday staff and volunteers here sponsor an hour-and-a-half program meant to educate the public about the beauty of these mysterious canines. Watch a slide show, ask the program leaders questions, and encounter the wolf ambassadors

© ERICKA CHICKOWSKI

Take a ride in a horse-drawn carriage for a historical tour through Julian.

THERE'S GOLD IN THEM THAR HILLS

Julian may have never been much more than a few shacks in the mountains if it weren't for a freed slave named A. E. "Fred" Coleman. In 1869 Coleman was watering his horse while herding cattle near Volcan Mountain when he saw a shimmery glint in the small creek they stood near. This was more than two decades after gold rush fever hit California at large with the discovery of the shiny stuff at Sutter's Mill, so Coleman knew right away what to start doing. He unpacked his skillet and started panning.

Though the gold near Julian was hardly the second coming of the Mother Lode, it was enough to draw prospectors and pioneers to build a town. The height of Julian's gold production only lasted a couple of decades and the gold mined here only totaled about $5 million. But San Diegans are still awfully proud of their one and only mining town out in the county's hillsides.

at this animal sanctuary. Open for program tours only on Saturdays at 2 P.M. sharp for $10. Reservations are required.

ENTERTAINMENT AND EVENTS
Performing Arts

If you are in Julian on a Sunday afternoon, be sure to mosey over to Main Street to check out a performance by the **Julian Doves & Desperados.** These 1880s-era historic reenactors perform skits starring characters who very well could have roamed these same streets when the mines were flush with gold. Shows are north of Washington Street and are held at 1 P.M., 2 P.M., and 3 P.M.

Festivals and Events

July brings bunting and fanfare for the annual **Independence Parade** down Main

Street, a homey event known by San Diego locals as a means to get away from the crazy crowds at the beach. Don't expect serenity here either, though. The crowds throng town on the Fourth.

The best-known event all year is the **Apple Days Festival** in October, a fall classic celebrating the crisp fruit that has kept Julian on the map since the gold ran out.

In November, the R&B Bicycle Club holds its annual **Tour de Julian,** featuring a mountainous 55-mile or 28-mile road course.

SHOPPING

Both Julian and Ramona are well known as repositories of vintage relics, western heirlooms, and general miscellany from bygone times. Ramona is preferred by serious antique hunters, while Julian's shops tend to wrap a big ribbon round their collections, surrounding their stock with candles, soaps, postcards, and newer knick-knacks to appeal to the typical tourist.

For creaky treasures in Ramona, try **The Original Old Town Ramona Antique Fair** (734 Main St., 760/789-0574, 10 A.M.–5 P.M. Mon.–Fri., 10 A.M.–5:30 P.M. Sat., 11 A.M.–5:30 P.M. Sun.) and **Country Town Antiques** (746 Main St., 760/788-0076, 10 A.M.–5 P.M. Mon.–Sat.), which are two of the biggest and located close together.

Some favorites include **Antique Boutique**'s (2626 Main St., 760/765-0541, 10 A.M.–5 P.M. daily) cottage packed full of old stuff from dozens of grannies' attics, the old jewelry at **Julian Yesteryears** (2116 Main St., Ste. D, 760/765-1020), and the old and not-so-old books at **The Julian Bookhouse** (2230 Main St., 760/765-1989).

There are many straight-up gift shops as well. One of my favorites is the **Old Julian Garage** (2126 Main St., 760/765-1836, 9:30 A.M.–5:30 P.M. daily), a one-time mechanic building and now a shop full of candles, jams, toys, and souvenirs. Another is **The Birdwatcher** (2775 B St., 760/765-1817, www.thebirdwatcher.net, 9 A.M.–5 P.M. daily), which holds bird feeders, books, wind chimes,

CDs with bird calls, and anything else having to do with our winged friends.

SPORTS AND RECREATION
Hiking

A short drive northeast of Julian along Farmer Road leads you to **Volcan Mountain Wilderness Preserve** (www.volcanmt.org). Hike the three-mile round-trip trail that leads up, up, up to find a ridge with a whopper of a view of the town and the surrounding Pine Hills. On Saturdays and Sundays a five-mile loop up to the summit of the mountain is also open.

The lightly forested humps southeast of Julian are known as Pine Hills. Head here via Pine Hills Road off of Highway 79 to find trailheads to two of the county's best waterfall hikes. At the terminus of Eagle Peak Road's dirt section is the trailhead to the cataract of **Cedar Creek Falls,** a 4.5-mile round-trip. Or continue southwest where Cedar Creek Road intersects with Eagle Peak Road until you reach the trailhead to **Three Sisters Waterfalls,** an impressive three-tiered cascade.

Also in the Pine Hills vicinity is **William Heise County Park** (4945 Heise Park Rd., 760/765-0650), which has several miles of trails throughout the park. One of the most popular routes is along Kelly Ditch Trail, which syncs up with the trails in Cuyamaca Rancho State Park south of town.

Mountain Biking

Santa Ysabel Open Space Preserve (northwest of Santa Ysabel on Hwy. 79) offers over eleven scenic miles of riding through grassy meadows, a splashing creek shaded by sycamore trees, and hillsides covered in pine trees. Don't be surprised to find yourself cruising past a rafter of wild turkeys at dusk or dawn. These birds roam freely around the hills of Julian.

Another scenic ride follows the **Old Banner Toll Road,** a mile east of Julian off Highway 78. Once a wagon road that linked Julian to the desert, this 1.5-mile trail rides through mine country. You'll see boarded up shafts along the route and at about the mile mark you can explore the ruins at the old Warlock Mine, one of the longest-running in Julian.

For mountain bike rentals and tours, **Julian Stables** (760/765-2200, www.julianactive.com) is the only gig in town. Open by reservation only. Call for directions.

Horseback Riding

There are several outfitters in the Julian area that can help you enjoy the scenery on top of an equine buddy. The oldest in town is **Julian Stables** (760/765-1598, www.julianactive.com, reservation only, $55), which guides one- and two-hour tours on its private ranch trails near Volcan Mountain. Another option is **Kenner Ranch** (17550 Harrison Park Rd., 760/473-5681, www.julianhorsebackriding.com, $50). In addition to the standard one- or two-hour guided jaunts around its property, Kenner also offers advanced riders the option to take longer four-hour rides on local trails.

© ERICKA CHICKOWSKI

William Heise County Park

ACCOMMODATIONS

The bed-and-breakfast reigns supreme in Julian, which boasts over 20 bed-and-breakfasts of all stripes in the immediate vicinity. The following are just a few tried-and-true picks. For a survey of some of the other choices, talk to the folks at the **Julian Bed and Breakfast Association** (760/765-1555, www.julianbnb. com) to see if they can hook you up with suitable digs.

Under $150

If fancy bed-and-breakfasts aren't your thing, the **Julian Lodge** (2720 C St., 760/765-1420) offers straightforward and sensible motel rooms with refrigerators for about $120 per night. It is only a block away from Main Street and the standard room rate includes continental breakfast each morning.

Another affordable option are the motel accommodations at **Ramona Valley Inn** (416 Main St., Ramona, www.ramonavalleyinn. com, $74 d). Located on the northeast part of downtown Ramona, the property has the added benefit of a pool.

$150-250

◖ **Julian Gold Rush Hotel** (2032 Main St., 760/765-0201, www.julianhotel.com, $165 d) is the longest continually operating hotel in Southern California. Built in 1897 by a freed slave, Albert Robinson, and his wife, Margaret, this well-kept two-story charmer is furnished with authentic Victorian antiques. Afternoon tea and a full-service breakfast, both of which are included in the room rate, are served in the library sitting room downstairs. As for Mr. Robinson, he's said to be close even now: Guests have reported ghostly activity in the upstairs bedrooms.

Perched just above the desert on a 4.5-acre lot just outside of Julian, the **Observer's Inn** (3535 Hwy. 79, 760/765-0088, www.observersinn.com, $160 d) is a favorite retreat of astronomy buffs, who flock to the Inn for its nightly Sky Tours ($10 per guest, $20 per non-guest) that allow visitors to spot celestial objects through research-strength telescopes.

© ERICKA CHICKOWSKI

The Julian Gold Rush Hotel is Southern California's second-oldest hotel.

Each of the two guest rooms, Andromeda and Orion, are located in a special guest house in the oak-draped property. Rooms come with full baths and are decked out in astronomy-themed decor.

Over $250

The Craftsman-style lodge and cottages at **Orchard Hill Country Inn** (2502 Washington St., 800/716-7242, www.orchardhill.com, $250–425) sit on a picturesque plot of land that rises gently above Julian. There's a gurgling crick that splashes down into a lily pond complete with fat koi. Antique farm equipment rusts gently into gardens full of native flowers. And trails on the property lead to views of town and to a nearby gold mine. Rooms are elegant but unpretentious. The room rates vary depending on if you stay in a lodge or cottage. The room rates include an evening cocktail hour and a full-service breakfast. The gourmet kitchen here also offers four-course meals on Tuesday, Thursday, Saturday, and Sunday.

Camping

The campground at **William Heise County Park** (4945 Heise Park Rd.) is lightly wooded with oak and pine. About half of the 80 sites here are for tent camping only, the other half allows RVs but doesn't have hookups. All sites are $19 per night. There are flush toilets, hot showers, and outside spigots with potable water. Also available are rustic wilderness cabins for $50 per night.

FOOD

For a small village of only a couple of blocks, Julian offers a pretty decent dining selection. Most places are diners or cafés featuring their own spin on country cooking, such as the **Julian Café and Bakery** (2112 Main St., 760/765-2712, 8 A.M.–7:30 P.M. Mon.–Thurs., 8 A.M.–8:30 P.M. Fri., 7 A.M.–9 P.M.

Sat., 7 A.M.–8:30 P.M. Fri., $11). The lodge-like interior is decked out in Americana and the chicken pie is rich and scrumptious.

The long and skinny dining room at **Miner's Diner** (2143 Main St., 760/765-3753, 10:30 A.M.–5 P.M. Mon.–Thurs., 10:30 A.M.–6 P.M. Fri., 8 A.M.–6 P.M. Sat., 8 A.M.–5 P.M. Sun., $6) showcases the old-fashioned soda counter. Burgers and sandwiches abound, meant to be washed down with a root beer float served up by the soda jerk. Kids will want to wander to the pharmacy and gift store next door, which has a few stairs leading down to the candy store **Mine Shaft** (10:30 A.M.–6 P.M. Fri., 8 A.M.–6 P.M. Sat., 8 A.M.–5 P.M. Sun.).

The smoky aroma coming from **Bailey's Woodpit Barbecue** (2307 Main St., 760/765-3757, www.baileybbq.com, hours vary, $13) is

APPLE COUNTRY

After the mines dried up, Julian's gold was replaced by Golden Delicious. The soil and the weather near this mountain town make it well suited for growing apples, so the town has made a name for itself through the production of area orchards.

Ask any San Diegan from sea to desert what Julian is best known for and they won't skip a beat: It's the apple pie, of course! Just about every restaurant in this tiny town has its own variation of the flaky treat. Here's a primer on the best pies in town:

- **Best No-Sugar-Added Apple Pie:** Julian Pie Company (2225 Main St., 760/765-2449)

- **Best Old-Fashioned Pie:** Mom's Bakery (2119 Main St., 760/765-2472)

- **Best Dutch Apple Pie:** Julian Café (2112 Main St., 760/765-2712)

- **Best Apple-Berry Pie:** Apple Alley Bakery (2122 Main St., 760/765-2532)

Pie isn't the only gig in town, of course. There are also lots of great cider and jams to be had

as well. The best of the best in either department can be found at **Julian Cider Mill** (2103 Main St., 760/765-1430), right smack in the middle of town.

If you'd prefer to get your own bushel full to try your hand at your very own pies (or to just snap into a bite of fresh apple), seek out a couple of spots just outside of town. About halfway to Banner on Highway 78, **Meyer Orchards** (3962 Hwy. 78, 760/765-0233) operates a fruit stand with many varieties of apples when they're in season, along with veggies and other fresh fruits.

If you prefer the thrill of the pick, visit **Calico Ranch U-Pick Orchard** (4200 Hwy. 78, at Calico Ranch Rd., 760/765-3620), which lets visitors roam its trees in search of plump and juicy apples during harvest season, which is late September and October.

Harvest season is great for those who'd like to taste the fruit during its peak of flavor. But be warned – there are lots of like-minded folks in town after the same thing. The bakeries have lines out the door in autumn and those who wait to pick up pies until the end of the day risk going home empty-handed.

intoxicating, albeit frustrating because of this place's sporadic hours. If you can catch it while it is open you are in for very large, pioneer-sized portions of barbecue with coleslaw, cornbread, and other fixin's.

An intimate bungalow decorated in old photos and frilly fabrics, **Julian Grille** (2224 Main St., 760/765-0173, 11 A.M.–2 P.M. and 4:30 P.M.–8 P.M. Tues.–Sun., 4:30 P.M.–8 P.M. Mon., $21) prepares steak and seafood dinners for a sophisticated palate. Lunch is simpler fare like sandwiches and homemade soup, but equally delicious.

Romano's Dodge House (2718 B St., 760/765-1003, www.romanosjulian.com, 11:30 A.M.–8:30 P.M. Wed.–Mon., closed Tues., $15) offers an alternative to homestyle cooking with its menu of Italian dishes such as halibut in Florentine sauce and chicken cacciatore, as well as its crispy pizzas.

Most places in Julian shutter the doors early. **Rongbranch Restaurant** (2722 Washington St., 760/765-2265, www.rongbranchrestaurant.com, 11 A.M.–9 P.M. Sun.–Thurs., 11 A.M.–10 P.M. Fri.–Sat., $10) is the only place in town open during later evening hours. If you want some grub, you can either eat there or drive 22 miles to Ramona for a late dinner. If you eat at Rongbranch, do yourself a favor and order a burger. The restaurant likes to tout its barbecue, but I found the meat a little tough.

INFORMATION AND SERVICES

The **Julian police** (760/765-4718) have an office at 2907 Washington Street. Speaking from experience, obey the traffic laws in this area—they will pull you over if you break them. Just off of main street, the Julian **public library** (2133 Fourth St., 760/765-0370, noon–8 P.M. Tues., 10 A.M.–6 P.M. Wed.–Thurs., 10 A.M.–5 P.M. Fri.–Sat.) is a quiet retreat that offers free wireless Internet.

The **town's doctor** (760/765-1223, 8 A.M.–5 P.M. Mon.–Fri.) is also nearby at 2721 Washington Street. For critical care you'll need to trek back to La Mesa or Encinitas.

Palomar Mountain and Vicinity

Palomar Mountain is home to the famous observatory and to a scenic state park. The area's undeveloped nature is what makes it such a good place for stargazing, so other than the nearby Warner Springs Ranch, refined accommodations are limited. But camping abounds in this thickly forested zone of the county.

SIGHTS
C Palomar Observatory

Palomar Observatory (35899 Canfield Rd., 760/742-2119, www.astro.caltech.edu/palomar, free) is a distinctive white bullet of a building that is home to one of the world's most powerful telescopes, the 200-inch Hale Telescope. First established in 1936, this famed astronomical outlook is still a major research installation for Caltech's storied astronomy department.

You can get a look at the Hale Telescope and the three other major telescopes when you come for a tour at the observatory's visitors center. Be sure to check out the collection of dark-sky photos here. Because the observatory is still a place of serious scientific research, it is primarily open only during the daylight hours, 9 A.M.–3 P.M. daily November–March and 9 A.M.–4 P.M. daily March–November. Tours of the Hale Telescope ($8) are offered at 11:30 A.M. and 2:30 P.M. on Saturdays from April through October.

Those who want to get the full experience can try snagging a spot on one of the monthly nighttime tours offered through the Reuben H. Fleet Science Center during the summer. These $65-per-person tours depart from San Diego and return at midnight. Tours sell out quickly, so book in the spring to assure yourself a seat.

HALE TELESCOPE FACTS

- It took ten years of polishing the mirror to perfect it before being installed
- Over 10,000 pounds of glass was shaved away during the process
- Was dedicated in 1948
- Mirror diameter is 200 inches
- Was world's largest telescope for nearly three decades
- Still acts as the cornerstone of the famed Caltech astronomy department

Palomar Mountain State Park

San Diegans like to consider Palomar Mountain State Park (east of Hwy. 76 along Nate Harrison Rd.) their little slice of the Sierras. The high country here is densely wooded with the most diverse collection of evergreens in the region. There's ponderosa pine, Jeffrey pine, Coulter pine, white fir, big-cone Douglas fir, and incense cedar. The three-acre Doane Pond is a tranquil spot for bird-watching, fishing, picnicking, and camping.

Surrounding the park boundaries is the northern sector of **Cleveland National Park,** which has miles of trails and additional campgrounds and picnic areas to choose between.

SPORTS AND RECREATION
Hiking

In Palomar Mountain State Park, **Doane Valley Nature Trail** (east of Hwy. 76 along Nate Harrison Rd.) offers an easy one-mile loop through the aromatic cedar and pine woodlands of the mountain. The loop is intersected with other longer treks along notable routes such as **Thunder Spring Trail, Chimney Flats Trail,** and **Weir Trail.**

Outside of the park's boundary, and therefore open to hikers with dogs, **Observatory Trail** winds a little over two miles up the

mountain from Observatory Campground to the Palomar Observatory. There is a meadow view, a bubbling creek in the winter and spring, and a thick canopy of needles for much of the route.

The country north of Warner Springs is a good place to pick up the Pacific Crest Trail. The trail follows **Agua Caliente Creek** for about four miles, sometimes over the shady creek's shore, sometimes scrambling over baked hillsides covered in chaparral and cactus.

Golf

The subtly undulating golf course at **Warner Springs Ranch** (31652 Hwy. 79, Warner Springs, 760/782-4200, 6 A.M.–sunset) is open to public play Monday through Thursday. The course is fairly straightforward but scenic. On the horizon you can see Hot Springs Mountain, San Diego County's highest peak, plus views of Palomar Observatory and Lake Henshaw. The greens fee with a cart is $30 on weekdays, $55 on Saturdays, and $45 on Sundays and holidays.

Sky Sailing

The truly adventurous can soar the skies above Palomar and Hot Springs Mountains, and the meadows and foothills between them. **SkySailing Inc.** (31930 Hwy. 79, Warner Springs, 760/782-0404, www.skysailing.com, 9 A.M.–5 P.M. daily except Thanksgiving and Christmas) offers sailplane rides on their gliding and graceful motorless aircraft. You'll rumble along the tarmac connected by rope to a tow plane that pulls you up above 7,000 feet. Release the rope in midair and from there the sailplane harnesses the power of the strong geothermic thrust above this region to stay aloft. You'll then have the opportunity to take over the controls of the plane from your professional copilot to test your hands at gliding. Rides available from 9 A.M. to sunset, starting at $125 for 20 minutes in the air.

Fishing

It's shoreline-fishing-only at the postcard-perfect **Doane Pond** (Palomar Mountain State

© ERICKA CHICKOWSKI

preparing for takeoff; sky sailing above Warner Springs

Park, east of Hwy. 76 along Nate Harrison Rd.). Hunt trout by reel or fly all year long. Other than Lake Cuyamaca this is the only San Diego lake to stock trout in the summer.

Lake Henshaw (26439 Highway 76, Santa Ysabel, 760/782-3501, www.lakehenshawresort.com) is a large reservoir that's well-stocked with a variety of warm-water species, including largemouth bass, crappie, bluegill, and catfish. Day-use fees are $7.50, plus $5 to use the boat ramp. Boats are available for rent as well. The cost is $35/day for motorboats and $10/day for rowboats.

ACCOMMODATIONS

Accommodations are few and far between in this remote region of the county. However, there are a couple of real gems that are perfect for weekend getaways.

Under $150

On top of the list for outdoorsy types and horse lovers is **Warner Springs Ranch** (31652 Hwy. 79, Warner Springs, 760/782-

4200, www.warnersprings.com, $115 d). This 2,500-acre resort drapes over the foothills and meadows east of Palomar Mountain. Lodging is rustic, with no phones or TVs in the rooms, but you'll want to spend most of the time roaming the grounds anyway. There's hiking, biking, horseback riding, tennis, and golf here. But the real centerpiece of the ranch experience is the hot springs pool, fed from the historic springs that lend the resort its name. The property is member-owned, and advanced reservations are restricted because members have priority to make reservations. However, if you can make back-up plans and deal with only a month of lead time, you will be well rewarded for the hassle.

$150-250

Right on Palomar Mountain, **Bailey's Palomar Resort** (33691 Bailey Meadow, Palomar Mountain, 760/742-1859, www.baileyspalomarresort.com, $150 per night for two people) rests on a picturesque property with shady walnut and apple trees and a private pond. Guests at this pet-friendly establishment are invited to stay in a circa-1888 pioneer home or to opt for private cabins.

Practically bordering the county line, **Pala Casino and Resort** (11154 Hwy. 76, 760/510-5100, www.palacasino.com, $199 d) is a respite from the rugged country up here. This classy retreat towers over ranch lands and scenic byways and the rooms play up the scenery with picture windows that lend great views of the surrounding landscape. The pool area is huge, with an inviting adults-only whirlpool tub to retreat from the kiddies when they're roughhousing in the pool. Also on-site is a relaxing spa and, of course, the excitement of the casino floor.

Camping

At Palomar Mountain State Park, **Doane Valley Campground** (east of Hwy. 76 along Nate Harrison Rd.) is in a shady glen near Doane Pond. Each of the 31 sites ($30) here comes with a picnic table and either a pedestal barbecue or a campfire circle with a grate. Bathrooms on-site have flush toilets and pay showers and there are water spigots dotted between the sites. There are no hookups, but small RVs can park here.

Slightly down the mountain from the actual observatory, **Observatory Campground** is a National Forest Service facility. Campsites ($30) are equipped similarly to the Doane Valley sites, but bathrooms only come with vault toilets. Most weekends during the summer, rangers lead a Star Party, offering celestial tours for campers interested in being regaled about the constellations on view from this breathtaking perch. Call the Palomar Observatory or visit its website for more details about these tours.

FOOD AND SERVICES

Come stocked with food, because there are precious few restaurants and no grocery stores around here. On top of the mountain your only choice is **Mother's Kitchen and Bakery** (junction of Hwys. S-6 and S-7, Palomar Mountain, 760/742-4233, www.motherskitchenpalomar.com, 11 A.M.–4 P.M. Thurs.–Fri., 8:30 A.M.–5 P.M. Sat.–Sun., closed Mon.–Wed., $9), which is only open four days a week. If you can catch Mother's while it is open you'll be able warm up with a bowl of the homemade chili, get your greens fix at the salad bar, and then overindulge on a slice of pie or fresh cookies. On weekend mornings breakfast is also an option here.

Farther east at Pala Casino and Resort (11154 Hwy. 76, 760/510-5100) you can fill up at one of eight different restaurants and cafés, including **Mama's Cucina Italiana** (760/510-5100, 5–10 P.M. Mon.–Thurs. and Sun., 5–11 P.M. Fri.–Sat., $18) You'll find huge portions of pastas, including spaghetti with softball-sized meatballs.

Gas is available at the Pala Station and the Warner Springs Station.

Anza-Borrego Desert State Park

As the highways twist and wend their way down the eastern slopes of San Diego's mountains, pine and chaparral transitions to teddy-bear cactus and ocotillo. The descent leads to Borrego Desert, a massive chunk of the Sonoran Desert that covers much of eastern San Diego. Wander here and you'll find badlands and dry lakes, lush palm oases and hot springs. Summer bakes the desert floor and at its end brings torrential rains that carve washes and rivulets into the land and activate the aroma of ancient creosote bushes. Winter and spring are best for exploring. If the rain comes down hard enough in the fall, the desert is washed in blooming wildflowers the following spring.

The largest state park in the 48 contiguous states, Anza-Borrego Desert State Park spans more than 900,000 acres across eastern San Diego County and covers almost all of the Borrego Desert. The compound name is a combination tribute. The first part comes from Spanish explorer Juan Bautista Anza, the first European to establish an overland route from Mexico through the Sonoran Desert and to the Pacific Coast. The second is the Spanish word for bighorn sheep, a hardy species that roams the park's territory.

BORREGO SPRINGS

An island of private land in the state park, the little town of Borrego Springs offers convenience and accessibility to the untamed wilds of the desert. A handful of quaint shops and restaurants are collected here, as well as an assortment of resorts and golf courses. But the town is not overrun by glitz and fake greenery the way Palm Springs is. It is a desert community first and foremost, a place where it is still OK to go to dinner in hiking boots or with helmet hair.

© ERICKA CHICKOWSKI

Indian Head Mountain in Borrego Springs

◖ Anza-Borrego State Park Visitors Center

Conveniently located in Borrego Springs, the state park's visitors center (200 Palm Canyon Dr., 760/767-4205, 9 A.M.–5 P.M. Thurs.–Mon. Oct. 1–Apr. 30, 9 A.M.–5 P.M. weekends and holidays May 1–Sept. 30) is an award-winning information center and museum featuring exhibits on desert ecology and native peoples and a robust schedule of educational activities and events. The center is well staffed with friendly volunteers and stocked to the gills with maps and books to help you plan your adventure. It's even got a Wi-Fi hotspot for travelers hoping to look up last-minute hiking information. The center located is inside an attractive brick building settled into a hillside. Just outside the doors there is a gorgeous interpretive garden of native fauna to get you started on identifying plant life. Be sure to check out the pond featuring the rare desert pup-fish. Bet you never guessed there were fish in the desert!

◖ Font's Point

Only a few miles away from Borrego Springs, Font's Point (26 miles north of I-8 along Hwy. S2) affords one of the best (and most accessible) views of the **Borrego Badlands.** Come around during a winter sunset and you're likely to share the show with fellow travelers who often bring wine and hors d'oeuvres to help savor the moment. There is a short drive along a sandy road, but it is usually passable even in a passenger vehicle.

Agua Caliente Regional Park

This county park lies on land leased from the state park. It is known for its "warm waters." There are two popular hot spring–fed pools in the center of the park, a warmer indoor pool and a cooler pool set al fresco. Also nearby are a collection of nature trails. The day-use fee is $5.

◖ Vallecito Regional Park

Just four miles north of Agua Caliente, this is another sub-park run by the county. This historic valley has offered a patch of green refuge to people traveling this desert for over 150 years. The land was used as an army supply depot in the early 1850s. By 1857 it had evolved briefly as a stop for the "Jackass

© ERICKA CHICKOWSKI

view of the Borrego Badlands from Font's Point

Mail," a mounted mail service that traversed the county and rode to Arizona. Only a year later this service was made irrelevant by the establishment of the Butterfield Overland Stage, which at 2,800 miles long was the longest stage ride in the world. It closed the gap between Missouri and San Francisco and used Vallecito as a key resting point in the harsh desert clime. At the park, the **Vallecito Stage Station** is a rebuilt rendition of this circa-1859 stop along the Butterfield Stage. If you look out along the east side of Highway S-2 in this vicinity you can still see the wagon ruts between the cactus.

ENTERTAINMENT AND EVENTS

Without a doubt, the best entertainment in the desert is presented by Mother Nature. Provided there was enough rain in the fall, the **wildflower bloom** in the spring is the highlight of the year. The spindly whips of ocotillo flare up in green and orange, the sand verbena washes the floor with fluorescent purple, and even the teddy-bear cholla and barrel cactus sprout petals. To find out whether the desert is blooming, call the state park's wildflower hotline (760/767-4684).

Try to plan your wildflower visit around the **Circle of Art.** Held in Borrego Springs each March, this family-friendly art fair attracts painters, sculptors, and musicians from all over the country.

In April the storytellers come out of the woodwork to spin yarns at the **Peg Leg Liar's Contest** in Borrego Springs. The contest of wits and prevarication is named for the greatest fabricating scalawag the town has ever known. In the 1850s the mountain man Peg Leg Smith would saunter into Borrego Springs and spout tales of gold he'd found out in the desert hinterlands. Problem was, he couldn't quite remember where his strike was and never really could find his lost gold again. Travel about eight miles east of town on Highway S-22 and you'll see a plaque raised in his honor.

Summer is scorching and every moving thing either shutters its doors or scurries

DESERT TEMPERATURE EXTREMES

The Borrego Desert is formidable for its extreme temperatures. In the winter, evening temperatures frequently dip down below freezing. And in summer, daytime temperatures bump the mercury well over 100°F. The record high was set in June of 1997 at an incredible 121°F.

The following chart shows monthly averages for the last 60 years:

Annual Average Temp (F)	Jan.	Feb.	Mar.	Apr.	May	June	July	Aug.	Sep.	Oct.	Nov.	Dec.
Annual Average High	69.2	72.5	77.8	84.4	93.2	102.8	107.3	105.9	100.7	89.8	77.8	69.0

Annual average maximum temperature: 87.5

| Annual Average Low | 44.0 | 46.7 | 50.1 | 53.8 | 60.7 | 68.4 | 75.6 | 75.3 | 70.0 | 60.5 | 50.4 | 43.4 |

Annual average minimum temperature: 58.2

underground for respite. The desert comes alive again in October and Borrego Springs celebrates with the **Borrego Days Desert Festival.** There's a parade, live music, a carnival, and the annual Miss Borrego Pageant.

SHOPPING

Borrego Springs shopping is divided between two creatively named shopping centers, The Mall and The Center. At **The Center** (590 Palm Canyon Dr., 760/767-5164) you can check out the art at **Leisel Paris Art Studio** (www.lieselsart.com, 10 A.M.–4 P.M. Wed.–Sun.) or **Matson Gallery** (www.bretamatsonfusedglass.com, by appointment only) or pick up a souvenir at **The Desert Robin** (10 A.M.–4 P.M. Wed.–Sat. mid-Sept.–Memorial Day).

The Mall (590 Palm Canyon Dr., 760/767-5164), **Tumbleweed Trading Company** (www.tumble-weed.com, 10 A.M.–4 P.M. daily Oct.–May, 10 A.M.–4 P.M. Fri.–Mon. Jun.–Sept.) offers a hodgepodge of expensive furniture and decor. And **Gourmet Outfitters** (www.borregogourmet.com, 10 A.M.–5 P.M. Mon.–Fri.,

9 A.M.–4 P.M. Sat., 10 A.M.–4 P.M. Sun.) has a selection of culinary doodads and picnic-basket fillers.

If you are looking for more desert reference materials and maps, there are two great places to check out in Borrego Springs. The Anza-Borrego Foundation and Institute runs a store within the **park visitors center** (200 Palm Canyon Dr., 760/767-4205, 8 A.M.–4:30 P.M. Mon.–Fri.) with a selected collection of books, maps, and mementos commemorating the park. And in the middle of town, the Anza-Borrego Desert Natural History Association's **Borrego Desert Nature Center** (652 Palm Canyon Dr., 760/767-3098, www.abdnha.org) has an interesting collection of books, maps, jewelry, and desert fine art.

SPORTS AND RECREATION
4x4 Driving Tours

One of the best ways to really explore the deep backcountry in Anza-Borrego is to turn off the pavement and four-wheel your way along the hundreds of miles of dirt roads that criss-cross their way through this rugged terrain. Some roads are smooth enough to allow even a normal passenger car to traverse a short way, the majority require four-wheel-drive, and then there are a few rocky and treacherous routes that are only passable to the most sturdy of SUVs.

To find the perfect route, a visit to the park visitors center is highly recommended. In addition to a whole passel of books and detailed maps, the center is staffed by volunteers who are well versed in desert travel. They'll be able to point you to the best routes depending on what kind of terrain you'd like to see, how much time you have, and your means of travel.

Similarly, the Anza-Borrego Foundation and Institute is an excellent planning resource. It operates a bookstore and gift shop in Borrego Springs (587 Palm Canyon Dr., Ste. 220 & 224, 760/767-4063, 10 A.M.–4 P.M. daily Oct.–May, 10 A.M.–4 P.M. Fri.–Sat. June–Sept.) that is well equipped with maps and books to set you on the right path.

Some of the most popular routes that you can ask about include the boulder-strewn mountain area traversed by Old Culp Valley Road, the rugged high country in Sheep Canyon, the mostly smooth but scenic Blair Valley loop, and the route along Canyon Sin Nombre that leads to the Old Carrizo Stage Station in the southwest sector of the park.

Road conditions are determined year to year by what Mother Nature has been doing. During the rainy season violent downpours will sculpt the landscape, shifting dirt and debris so that one route that was easy to navigate one year may be rocky and rutted the next. Even between periods of rain, strong desert winds can shift lose dirt and sand in a way that will alter the roads' passability.

Before you head out, it is a good idea to visit or call the park visitors center and inquire about the state of the route you hope to take.

Or you can just abandon your own vehicle altogether and rely on someone else to do the heavy-lifting for you. Headquartered in Borrego Springs, **California Overland** (1233 Palm Canyon Dr., 760/767-1232, www.californiaoverland.com) offers a mix of group rides aboard its fleet of retrofitted military

Take a ride aboard a rugged troop carrier with California Overland.

© ERICKA CHICKOWSKI

THE SOUTH FAMILY:
AN EXPERIMENT IN DESERT LIVING

It takes at least a little bit of eccentricity to live through the heat and the cold, the lack of water or resources, and the loneliness of the desert. Still, for a small and unique set of people, the quiet solitude and the beauty tend to make up for the isolation.

This was the conviction of Marshal South, whose supreme belief in the spiritual nature of desert living led him to convince his wife Tanya to give up the trappings of normal life to raise their family in the high desert.

The Souths spent several years building an adobe home on the top of Ghost Mountain. Completed in 1932, they named it Yaquitepec. They built an elaborate rain-catching cistern and hauled any additional water or necessities up the mountain. This included the schoolbooks Tanya used to educate their three children.

Marshal wrote about their ascetic life from 1930 to 1946 in a monthly column for *Desert Magazine* with help from Tanya, who occasionally also wrote stories and poems for the publication. Their experience as nudists who raised their children amongst the simple joys of primitive living captivated the magazine's readership.

It was a grand experiment in natural living that couldn't last, however. By the mid-1940s, Tanya was worried that the children might never have the chance to assimilate into normal society if they weren't introduced to it soon enough. She and Marshal fought bitterly about the subject, along with other endless squabbles that came as a product of isolation. Finally she and the kids hiked down the mountain one day in 1946, never to return to Yaquitepec again. Marshal soon followed. Some speculate the dissolution of his marriage took a toll on him physically. He died only two years later as the result of a heart condition.

The winds of Ghost Mountain have greatly eroded their home there, but remnants still remain. If you have the time, it is worth the steep hike up to the mountain just for the view alone.

---

troop carriers and Jeeps. Spend some true quality time with its informative and humorous guides on a 10-hour trip with lunch for $160 per person.

All of the park's roads are meant to be enjoyed by any street-legal vehicle whose driver isn't scared of a little dirt. However, you must remember that off-road travel is strictly prohibited. Anza-Borrego Desert State Park is an environmental treasure and taking your car or truck off of designated roads threatens its beauty.

Besides, if you really want to cut loose in a four-wheeler or motorcycle, there's a much better place to do it just east of the park. The Ocotillo Wells State Vehicular Recreation Area allows all forms of off-road travel. The whine of dune buggies and dirt bikes can be heard across the more than 40,000 acres of open desert here. **Sand and Sea Toyz** (4875 Highway 78, Ocotillo Wells, 760/714/920-8273, www.sandandseatoyz.com, 8 A.M.–5 P.M. daily) in the tiny settlement of Ocotillo Wells offers quad ORV rentals starting at $79 per day.

Hiking

There are hundreds of miles of hiking in the 1,000 square miles of Anza-Borrego. Many isolated trails test the wits and physical endurance of some of the best-conditioned navigators. My intention here is not to give you any semblance of a complete hiking guide. Instead, I offer a few classics with the easiest access from the paved roads.

Should you need supplies before heading out, **Borrego Outfitters** (579-E Palm Canyon Dr., 760/767-3502, www.borregooutfitters.com, 10 A.M.–5 P.M. Mon.–Fri., 9 A.M.–5 P.M. Sat., 10 A.M.–4 P.M. Sun.) has an assortment of apparel, bags, and gear at its Borrego Springs location.

The quintessential hike in Anza-Borrego is an easy 1.5-mile scoot through a rocky gulch called **Borrego Palm Canyon.** The trailhead is one of the most accessible in the entire park, located only a half mile from the visitors center. The terminus of the trail was once home to the largest grove of naturally occurring palms in North America, but a violent flash flood in 2004 uprooted a good chunk of the palms and carried them down the canyon. Their trunks remain a striking reminder of the power of desert gully-washers. What remains of First Palm Grove is still an impressive stand of greenery and the splashing waterfall and pool at the grove is perhaps even more enjoyable now that some of the thick vegetation has been cleared away.

If falls are your thing, then you might want to carve out some time for a hoof up to **Maidenhair Falls.** The trailhead is only three miles west of the visitors center off Highway S-22. You'll tromp 2.4 miles into Lower Hellhole Canyon until you reach the thundering roar of the falls. Sycamores, palms, and cottonwoods all clamor for moisture near the pool and mosses and ferns cling to the rocks surrounding the spray. After a thorough cooldown here it is hard to remember you're still in the desert.

© ERICKA CHICKOWSKI
hikers at Anza-Borrego Desert State Park

Formed by millennia of flood and wind erosion, the undulating slot canyons here are ripe for hiking and scrambling. One of the most popular slot canyon explorations in the park is the squeeze through **Palm Wash** and its tributaries. Located about 19 miles east of Borrego Springs along Highway S-22, the route here runs through smooth, sculpted sandstone walls with interesting strata and occasional rocky accretions. Even with little knowledge of geology, it is easy to admire the natural artwork of these canyons. Be aware that there are tight quarters here and it is not a hike for the claustrophobe. Also use common sense—don't come here if there's even a hint of rain. Desert storms can cause the slots to flood in the blink of an eye.

One of my favorite areas in the park is **Blair Valley,** south of Borrego Springs along the quiet ribbon of Highway S-2. Here between Granite Mountain and Whale Peak it is easy

to fall in love with the calm serenity of the desert. The wind whooshes through the valley like a thousand whispers over the barren beds of two dry lakes. Jackrabbits scamper through the creosote and agave. The valley is crossed by two flat dirt roads, usually easy to drive in a passenger vehicle, which take to you the trailheads of several hikes that have real payoffs at the end. In the southeast corner of the valley there is a flat hike through a cut in the mountains called Smuggler Canyon. Less than a mile from the trailhead you'll find ancient rock paintings left by the Kumeyaay people, which lends this route its name, **Pictograph Trail.**

Just southwest from that trailhead there is another starting point, this one up the side of Ghost Mountain. The short one-mile trek up the mountain leads you to the desolate and haunting site of **Yaquitepec.** In the 1930s and '40s this was home of the desert ascetic Marshal South, his wife, Tanya, and their three children. South gained renown for his dispatches to *Desert* magazine describing the primitive life his family eked out here, an experiment in simplicity. The Souths built an adobe hut and an intricate rain-catching system up here, hauling water up the mountain as necessary. The ruins of their crude buildings still remain, slowly being reclaimed by the desert.

Mountain Biking and Cycling

All 500 miles of the primitive jeep roads and paved stretches in the park are open to exploration on bike. Most trails are closed, unless otherwise designated as bike trails. Some of the most popular mountain bike areas include **Grapevine Canyon** and **Split Mountain.** At Grapevine Canyon, take Old Culp Valley Road down to Jasper Trail, where you'll head south amid the creosote and cactus as many as 16 miles to Yaqui Well. Be sure to remember that the exhilarating downhill ride out means a punishing slope back up to the tent, so only go as far as your body will let you. And don't forget to pack more than enough water for your journey—a gallon at the very least.

Road cyclists often get their kicks by touring the blacktop along **Borrego Springs Road, Palm Canyon Drive,** and **Highway S-22** east of Borrego Springs. The really motivated will make the 60-mile out-and-back along S-22 from Borrego Springs all the way into Imperial County to the Salton Sea.

Unfortunately there are no bike shops in Borrego Springs, so repairs and rentals will need to be taken care of before you make the drive. **Ranchita Bike and Hike** (760/782-3900) does offer one option to those who don't have the means to haul their own bikes out to the desert: This tour operation supplies you with bikes and drives you up the steep and curving Montezuma's Grade on S-22 for an exhilarating plunge down the mountain and back into Borrego Springs. Call for pick-up and location information.

Golf

This is a good time to repeat the fact that this is not Palm Springs. There are no courses here designed by golf legends. But, the courses in town do provide enough entertainment to visiting duffers to keep them busy weeks at a time. Of the four public courses here, probably the nicest of the bunch are the three nine-hole courses at **Borrego Springs Resort** (1112 Tilting T Dr., 760/767-5700, 6 A.M.–sunset, $65). These rolling courses offer a decent challenge with a robust bunker system and five lakes shared between the 27 holes.

For beginners or those looking for a quick nine holes, **The Springs at Borrego RV Resort and Golf Course** (2255 Di Giorgio Rd., 760/767-5457, 7 A.M.–sunset, $30) has a well-kept course that has a fun island green, waterfalls, and abundant palm trees. Right next door, the **Road Runner Golf and Country Club** (1010 Palm Canyon Dr., 760/767-5373, 7 A.M.–sunset Mon., Wed., and Fri.–Sun., noon–sunset Tues. and Thurs., $25) is an executive three-par course open to those beginners or practicing golfers who'd like a slightly longer course.

Another no-fuss option is at **Club Circle Golf Course** (Club Circle W., 760/767-5944, 7 A.M.–sunset, $20) a three-par, nine-hole course that lets golfers play as much as they'd like for $20 a day.

ACCOMMODATIONS

There's no need to go without the conveniences of modern living while kicking up dust in the desert. Borrego Springs has a healthy mix of affordable lodging and swanky digs to suit most price ranges.

Under $150

Oasis Inn (366 Palm Canyon Dr., 760/767-5409, www.oasisinnborrego.com, $98 d) is a simple cinderblock motel with a pool, spa, and barbecue.

Palm Canyon Resort (221 Palm Canyon Dr., 760/767-5341, www.palmcanyonresort.com, $115 d) offers a step up from that with its Western-themed hotel. The clapboard building is lined with verandas on the outside and river-rock accents inside the lobby. Also on the property is a popular RV park, as well as a pool and two restaurants.

$150-300

The rooms at **Borrego Springs Resort** (1112 Tilting T Dr., 760/767-5700, www.borregospringsresort.com, $150 d) are comfortable, clean, and spacious, but don't come expecting a five-star resort experience. Fortunately, the rates are adjusted accordingly, so you can head out for a golf vacation for under $150 per night.

Located near the park visitors center, **The Palms at Indian Head** (2220 Hoberg Rd., 760/767-7788, www.thepalmsatindianhead.com, $159 d, suites $229 d) is a quirky little inn housed in a 1950s-era hotel building that was once a part of a resort getaway for Hollywood hipsters. This restored midcentury beauty presides over a giant Olympic-sized pool that is viewable from every room.

For a quiet desert retreat, consider the **Borrego Valley Inn** (405 Palm Canyon Dr., 800/333-5810 or 760/767-0311, www.borregovalleyinn.com, $215–280 d) a secluded but centrally-located property featuring pretty adobe buildings that blend into the well-manicured desert landscapes. If you're adventurous, consider skinny dipping in the clothing-optional pool—there's also a more conservative pool for those who prefer bathing suits to birthday suits. Or cool off in the air-conditioned, casual guest lounge. Guests are served an expanded continental breakfast each morning and the innkeepers are available to offer plenty of advice to help you plan your desert adventure.

Camping

Outdoor adventurers not yet head-over-heels for Anza-Borrego are usually tipped over the scale when they learn that there is an open camping policy in the entire park. You can pull over and pound in stakes wherever you please, with no fee or pass required. Campfires are allowed as long as they are built in a contained metal receptacle of some sort.

The downside to this nomadic lifestyle is that there are no bathroom facilities and no water in sight when you're out in the backcountry. If squatting in the bushes and hauling in

your own water doesn't do it for you, then you're still in luck. There are a handful of public and private developed campsites scattered throughout the park.

The immediate vicinity around Borrego Springs affords the most options. The go-to site for most casual desert visitors is at the spacious **Borrego Palm Canyon Campground** (200 Palm Canyon Drive, 760/767-5311, www.reserveamerica.com, $30 tent, $65 full RV hookup) on the east side of town. This is the larger of the two state campgrounds in the park, with 120 sites total. Be sure to book in advance during the cooler months, because it still fills up fast. There are numerous tent sites, as well as about 52 full hookup RV sites. There are restrooms with flush toilets, water spigots, wheelchair-accessible nature trails, and a host of ranger-led activities in the winter.

Also in town is **The Springs at Borrego** (2255 DiGiorgio Rd., 760/767-0004, www.springsatborrego.com, $68 per site), an RV resort that hardly even qualifies as a campground. Guests are invited to pull their rigs into the full hookup sites that also include wireless Internet and cable TV connections. The lush grounds are lined with palms and include a nine-hole golf course, tennis courts, swimming pools, hot mineral baths, and a catch-and-release fishing hole.

For something a little simpler but still in town, **Oasis Inn** (366 Palm Canyon Dr., 760/767-5409, www.oasisinnborrego.com, $95 d) has an RV park with water and power connections, picnic tables, and fire grates. Guests here are welcome to use the motel's small pool and whirlpool tub.

South of Yaqui Pass from Borrego Springs on Highway S-3, **Tamarisk Grove Campground** (junction of Rte. 78 and Hwy. S-3, 760/767-5311, www.reserveamerica.com, $30 tent) is another state park–run site with running water and bathrooms featuring flush toilets. All the sites here have the added benefit of ample shade from the tamarisk trees that cover the campground.

If you prefer to explore the southern reaches of the Anza-Borrego via Highway S-2, there are three convenient sites to seek shelter. Within four miles of one another, **Agua Caliente Regional Park** (39555 Hwy. S-2, 760/765-1188, $15 tent, $25 full RV hookup) and **Vallecito Regional Park** (37349 Hwy. S-2, 760/765-1188, $15 per site) are county-run parks that both feature developed campgrounds. There are no hookup sites available, but RVs are allowed there. Agua Caliente has the added benefit of two mineral pools on the grounds, but most of the campsites are exposed to the elements and the pools tend to attract more crowds. Vallecito is quieter, home of the Vallecito Stage Station. Many of the sites here are situated under mesquite and smoke trees.

Just a little north of these sites, **Butterfield Ranch** (14925 Hwy. S-2, 760/765-1463, $20 camping, $25 full RV hook up, $95 cabins) is a private facility that offers RV and tent camping, primitive camping huts, and more comfortable cedar cabins. This very family-oriented property takes the rough out of roughing it. There are two swimming pools on-site, a clubhouse with games and books, and a small general store. Also on site is a comfortable lounge with a big-screen TV, fireplace, and wireless Internet access.

FOOD

Borrego Springs is pretty much the only place to find restaurants out in the desert. Most places here are informal, but foodies will find refuge at **The French Corner** (721 Avenida Sureste, 760/767-5713, www.thefrenchcorner.biz, 5–9 P.M. Wed.–Sun., $15) an oasis of European cuisine such as crêpes, quiche, homemade pâté, and escargot. The atmosphere is casual, but the limited dining options in town still make it advisable to set reservations for dinner if you don't want to be turned away.

On the opposite end of the spectrum, **Jilberto's Mexican Restaurant** (655 Palm Canyon Dr., #F, 760/767-1008, 7 A.M.–10 P.M. daily, $4) is the kind of place where you order at the counter and pick up your food when your number is called. This a favorite place for ravenous hikers and cyclists who come here to fill up on the absolutely huge portions for very cheap.

Across the street, **Carlee's** (660 W Palm Canyon Dr., 760/767-3262, 11 A.M.–9 P.M. daily, $10) is a sit-down bar and grill with a friendly vibe. The locals and snowbirds pack the place on winter weekends and most nights in the spring to select from pizza, steaks, burgers, and the like before crooning away on the karaoke machine. Call ahead to see if it's possible to make a reservation.

On the east end of town at the Palms at Indian Head, **Krazy Koyote** (2220 Hoberg Rd., 800/434-6835, 5:30 P.M.–8 P.M. Wed.–Thurs., 5:30 P.M.–9 P.M. Fri.–Sun., $25) is a good place to sip on a martini and enjoy an appetizer like baked brie or pâté with crackers. Entrées include beef Wellington, prime cuts of steak, and pork chops. They are tasty, but a bit overpriced for what you get. If you simply want to snack or indulge your sweet tooth, just go for appetizers and dessert. The menu of prepared sweets here is one of the best in town. The spot is shared by the **Red Ocotillo** ($12), the hotel's daytime eatery that offers huge breakfasts and lunches and even serves some to-go. The only downside to both is the service—it is notoriously slow, so if you're on your way out for a hike, be sure to pad your schedule or even consider buying supplies at the grocery store and bagging it instead.

Finally, if the mood strikes you for some ice cream, **The Fudge Factory** (590 Palm Canyon Dr., 760/767-5407, 8 A.M.–4 P.M. Tues.–Sun., $5) serves it up along with its tempting selection of fudge, locally cultivated honey, and other confectionaries.

If you are wandering around the southern section of the desert, there is a **general store** (39545 Great Southern Overland Stg Rte., 760/765-0676) at Agua Caliente that serves cold beverages and has a limited supply of snacks and groceries.

INFORMATION AND SERVICES

Emergency services are available in Borrego Springs. The local county **sheriff's office** is at 565 Palm Canyon Drive, and rangers can be reached at the **Anza-Borrego State Park Headquarters** (200 Palm Canyon Dr., 760/767-5311) on the same drive leading to the visitors center. The **Borrego Medical Center** (4343 Yaqui Pass Rd., Borrego Springs, 760/767-5051) offers a small emergency room and can facilitate airlifts in the event of major injuries.

GETTING THERE AND AROUND

Most people drive into the desert via car. There are three major routes from the west end of the county. You can take Montezuma's Grade along Highway S-22 from the Warner Springs area to Borrego Springs and beyond. Or you can head down Banner Grade along Highway 78 from Julian. Note: Montezuma's Grade is not accessible to RVs. If you drive an RV, you have to take Highway 78 from Julian to Yaqui Pass. This route will give you three choices along the way. You can either cut north

through Yaqui Pass and to Borrego Springs via Highway S-3. This is the favored route for San Diegans to reach the town. Or you can continue along Highway 78 into the tiny hamlet of Ocotillo Wells and the Ocotillo Wells State Vehicular Recreation Area. Or you can head southwest on Highway S-2, which will send you to the southern sector of the park. Another option for the southern reaches is to head east on I-8 until you cross the county line and then take Highway S-2 back northeast through the small town of Ocotillo and into the state park. This is the easiest route to Agua Caliente and Vallecitos from San Diego.

Gas is not readily available in most of the park, so plan ahead. Borrego Springs has three fill-up stations, Ocotillo Wells has one, and so does Ocotillo, just off I-8.

If your car is acting funny and you can limp it into Borrego Springs, **Tito's Auto Repair** (1233-A Palm Canyon Dr., 760/767-3029, 8 A.M.–5:30 P.M. daily) can help get you up and running again.

BACKGROUND

The Land

GEOGRAPHY

San Diego County is the most southwesterly county in the United States. Sitting against the Pacific Ocean, this 4,255-square-mile trapezoid of land is cushioned between Orange County and Riverside County to the north, Imperial County to the east, and Baja California in Mexico to the south.

The region is made up of a mix of terrain whose diversity is unmatched in just about any other part of the country. Along the coast there are sandstone cliffs, brackish marshes, and sandy beaches. Venture inland and encounter verdant mountainsides, grassy valleys, and rivers hidden in secret canyons. Trek even farther east and those mountains slope down to the desert floor and even more hillsides, these ones baked and covered in agave, cactus, and other succulents.

GEOLOGY

Experts break the county up roughly into thirds when explaining the geological makeup of the region. First comes the Coastal Plain, which is largely defined by the layers of sedimentary rock that tell the story of over 140 million years of aquatic life here. Visitors can view the "layer cake" themselves by visiting the cliff areas of La Jolla Cove or Sunset Cliffs Natural Park

SAN DIEGO QUICK FACTS

- Nickname: America's Finest City
- Incorporated: 1850
- Population: 1,311,162
- Land area: 342.5 square miles
- Time zone: Pacific Standard Time
- Second largest city in California
- Eighth most populous city in the United States
- County: San Diego
- Ethnicity: 46 percent white, 27 percent Latino, 15 percent Asian, 7 percent black
- Sunshine: 300 days per year
- High/low temperature averages: 66°F/54°F in winter, 74°F/62°F in summer
- Average rainfall: 9.32 inches annually
- Major employers: Federal government, state and municipal government, Qualcomm, Sharp Medical Center
- Area colleges and universities: University of California–San Diego, San Diego State University, University of San Diego, Point Loma Nazarene University, Thomas Jefferson School of Law, Mesa College, California Western School of Law, San Diego City College, San Diego Community College
- Median income in 2008: $62,820
- Sales tax: 7.75 percent
- Hotel tax: 10.5 percent

under, the North American Plate. During the process, the sediment surrounding the plates and the magma were also heated and metamorphosed, or changed, into amazing minerals and gems such as marble, quartzites, schists, and tourmaline.

A lot of this metamorphic sedimentation can also be found in the third geological zone, the Salton Trough. Here in the Anza-Borrego Desert, the sedimentation formed in the Peninsular and surrounding mountains, along with sediment carried by the ancient Colorado River, have filled a giant cavity in the earth's crust up to five miles deep. The cleft in the base rock is a tectonic extension of the Sea of Cortes, which separates Baja California from mainland Mexico.

The sediment filling the Salton Trough has left behind a treasure trove of rare gemstones and minerals, ancient marine deposits, and fossils.

Visiting rock hounds who are interested in more information should consider contacting the San Diego Mineral & Gem Society (www.sdmg.org), which runs classes and field trips to local areas in search of various rare gems and minerals. Within Anza-Borrego State Park there is a strict "look, but don't touch" policy regarding fossils and geological specimens. If you are interested in learning more about rock formations in the desert, your best source of information will be the Anza-Borrego Visitors Center. The center has an 18-mile self-guided tour along the "Erosion Road" that can provide a good introduction to the Santa Rosa Mountains, the Borrego Badlands, and the Salton Sea without ever leaving the pavement.

CLIMATE

San Diego's legendary Mediterranean climate is about as perfectly sunny and fair as it gets. But meteorologists here don't have it as easy as you'd think. The region is actually broken up into four distinct "microclimates" that can swing the weather significantly in as few as two or three miles.

in Ocean Beach. Next are the Peninsular Ranges, mountains forged through the combination of volcanic activity and tectonic plate shifts. At their base, these mountains are made up of granitic rocks formed from cooling magma produced from the force of an ocean plate being subducted, or pushed

Coastal

This is the pleasantly sunny microclimate that defines San Diego. Summer highs typically only poke the temperature up into the high 70s and winter lows rarely dip below the mid 40s.

The only break in the sunshiny days is when the marine layer, a high-level fog, rolls in from the ocean some evenings. It usually burns off by mid-morning, except for some days in June where the sun's rays can't quite push through. San Diegans call this phenomenon June Gloom.

Inland Valleys

Just a couple miles inland from the coast, temperature highs and lows are more extreme. These areas also tend to catch the brunt of rain and thunder showers that pass over the coast. In the summer the temperatures are regularly ten to fifteen degrees hotter than along the shoreline and in the winter they can drop below the coastal norms.

Mountains

Once in the mountains, you can encounter quickly fluctuating weather patterns. The

REGIONAL WILDFIRES

San Diego is a land of water and fire. Just as the ocean is an environmental constant in the region, so too are wildfires. The chaparral landscape that is so persistent in San Diego and Southern California in general is one that thrives on the natural cycle of fire and re-growth that occurs in the region. In fact, many plants in this ecosystem will only germinate after being exposed to the extreme temperatures found in a wildfire.

Typically, wildfire season is in October when the warm Santa Ana winds sweep in from the north and from eastern deserts. Vegetation is already dry from so little precipitation during the spring and summer months, so all it takes is one spark from human or natural sources to get a blaze started. Once the flames begin, the winds can potentially whip them up to monumental proportions.

One of the worst San Diego fire seasons on record occurred in 2007, when more than 325,000 acres burned across the county, with multiple simultaneous fires blazing at once. Fires licked the pine trees of Palomar Mountain, barreled through Rancho Bernardo and Poway, swept through Campo, and came dangerously close to Chula Vista.

Although many residents claim to have seen an increase in wildfire frequency and intensity in the region over the past few decades, most scientists beg to differ. According to the Center for Biological Diversity, cycles of wildfires in the San Diego area have been occurring for eons. Experts point to historical evidence of a massive 1889 fire in what is now Orange and San Diego Counties; it burned more than 100 miles in length and 10 miles in width and seems to be proof that there have always been big fires in San Diego.

The only difference now is that the region's ever-expanding population is now pushing into fire-prone terrain that was once desolate. Nowadays tract homes and McMansions lie directly within the fire path – in 2007 more than 500,000 people were evacuated in the wake of the fire.

Fortunately, San Diego's firefighting force continues to improve its techniques to keep residents and visitors safe from impending fires. They are prepared with high-tech equipment, trained to find and predict the path of fires, and they communicate freely with the media to keep people from danger.

If you are ever in town during fire season and you smell smoke, be sure to check the radio or television to find out if there are any blazes in your vicinity. And if you go camping in the back country, be conscientious and adhere to burn bans when the forest rangers enforce them. You don't want to be responsible for a potentially catastrophic fire if you can help it.

mountains here are the cause of a natural effect called a "rain shadow." Storm clouds blow over the county, and the mountains trap them from passing and generally get soaked as a result. Winter brings more rain here than at the coast, along with an occasional dusting of snow. Summer brings intermittent thundershowers. Weather can get hot in the summer, but once the sun goes down even tank-top days can turn to sweater evenings. Winter months are chilly, so be sure to pack a fleece.

Desert
There are two parts to every rain shadow. The desert microclimate is the mountains' foil. All of those storms trapped off of the mountains make for little cloud cover or rainfall in this microclimate. Average summer temperatures in the desert are up to 30° hotter than in the mountains. Borrego Valley's average high in July is 110° and sometimes the mercury hovers up at 120°. Winter nights are cold, sometimes plummeting into the low teens.

ENVIRONMENTAL ISSUES
San Diego's perfect climate and beautiful environment is, unfortunately, causing its own undoing. So many people come to live here and visit that urban development has created serious problems that threaten the region's whole appeal.

The coast is home to some of the biggest conflicts between environmental protection and the types of development that accommodate tourist traffic and new residents. Countless people want to live and stay around the beach, but more development cuts off access to the coastline and also threatens delicate beach and estuary habitats that can never be replaced once a development mars the landscape.

And the water itself is also a hot-button issue. Runoff from the streets and sewers frequently pollutes local waters, particularly after a bad storm. Area residents and environmental groups are working hard with municipal leaders to mitigate these problems, as this pollution causes long-term damage to fish populations, water vegetation, and reefs.

Flora and Fauna

It follows that an area with such a wide range of geological and climatic variations would also have a pretty broad scope in habitat. The breadth of plant and wildlife that flourishes here has a direct relationship with the wildly divergent geographic zones.

OCEAN
Sometimes the barren and choppy surface of the water can belie the teeming depths below. But look closely from shore or by boat and you will notice some of what beckons from beneath San Diego seas. Strands of kelp wash in with the tides, dolphins frolic in the waves, and fish skitter on the surface, distancing themselves from bigger predators below.

In terms of undersea flora, San Diego is best known for the Point Loma giant kelp beds just offshore. This is one of the largest kelp forests in the state. Other underwater plants include stands of eelgrass and other sea weeds, as well as a variety of algae.

Sea Mammals
San Diego is particularly blessed with a remarkable collection of sea mammals. Dolphins and porpoises are frequent sights in the water here. Sometimes they'll breach and spyhop just beyond the breakers, other times they'll snake a wave from resident surfers. You'll sometimes even see them in the shallow waters of Mission Bay.

As in many parts of the state, the charismatic California sea lion is a common sight near the marinas, piers, and rocky shores of San Diego. Their characteristic barks and honks are a portent of frustration for fishermen. These thieving mammals are well known

© PAM BURLEY/123RF.COM

seals at the Children's Pool in La Jolla

for poaching lunkers from right off the hook. They also like to bask on docks and rocks to soak up the sunshine.

Seals are also known to scoot up some of the sandy shores here. Children's Pool in La Jolla is a well-known hangout for these hefty pinnipeds.

Grab a pair of binoculars and look out in the distance during the winter months and you're eventually going to glimpse a spout or two from migrating gray whales. These gigantic mammals shuttle down south every year to give birth to calves in the warm shallows of the Sea of Cortez.

Other Sea Life

In the dark of the San Diego deep there are many pelagic species such as tuna, bonito, and mackerel. All swish away from several shark varieties: blue, mako, and thresher. In the kelp beds, barracuda and angel shark hunt while sheephead, calico bass, and whitefish hide.

Closer into the tidal zones you'll see corbina, croaker, and guitarfish splashing against the breakers. Sand sharks, halibut, and stingray all take cover in sandy bottoms and lobster and abalone sequester themselves in the rocky crags. In calmer coves the most colorful and notable Garibaldi floats about in orange resplendence. This territorial sunfish is like a giant goldfish, a protected species that California has chosen as its state saltwater fish.

BEACHES AND MARSHES

Where the ocean meets the land is a very special habitat, one that has been greatly altered by the encroachment of developers hell-bent on building homes and businesses as close to the water as possible. What remains of San Diego's lagoons and marshes is only 10 percent of what was there before we made our mark upon the environment.

Fortunately, there are still some remaining to appreciate. In and near the wetlands you'll encounter plants like goldenbush, saltgrass, cordgrass, and Southwestern spiny rush.

The water greatly varies in salinity in the lagoons, attracting an array of fresh and saltwater fish. In some saltier areas there are species like topsmelt and killifish, in other brackish and freshwater zones those like goby and striped mullet swish about.

Either way, the abundance of fish and invertebrates such as crab and clams attract hundreds of species. Bird-watchers can spot Great Blue Heron, egrets, terns, gulls, and pelicans circling and pecking at the water's buffet.

RIPARIAN

Closely associated with the marshy wetlands of the county are the region's river, or riparian, habitats. Many of these areas have been wiped out by development and damming of local rivers, but what remain are distinct ecological sectors consisting of plants that rely on a close and constant source of water. Some of the best-known riparian habitats include areas around the San Dieguito, San Luis Rey, and Santa Margarita Rivers. Cottonwood, willow, sycamore, and alder trees are all common in these areas. Water-loving animals that thrive here include California newt, Pacific tree frog, and belted kingfisher. You'll also see red-shouldered hawks floating in to feast on the frogs and fish in the river.

CHAPARRAL AND COASTAL SCRUB

The two most common habitats in the region are chaparral and coastal scrub, which share similarities but are actually distinct biospheres. Both are brushfields dominated by drought-resistant shrubs adapted to the Mediterranean climate. Animals common to both include gopher snakes, squirrels, brush rabbits, and coyotes.

Coastal scrub is sometimes nicknamed "soft chaparral" because the leaves and twigs of the plants in these zones are more supple than the traditional chaparral vegetation. The sight and smell of sage dominates coastal scrub, with several variations such as California sagebrush and black sage popping up. Other plant varieties

San Diego's mountains are primarily covered in chaparral.

© ERICKA CHICKOWSKI

include lemonadeberry, bush monkeyflower, buckwheat, and laurel sumac. The rare Torrey pine is a tree that only grows in the coastal scrub of San Diego County. If you are lucky you might spot Audubon cottontail hopping along, soaring red-tailed hawks, or the occasional rosy boa or horned lizard rustling the bushes in these areas.

Coastal scrub typically thrives from sea level up to 1,500 feet. As the altitude rises and as you go farther inland, chaparral takes over. The plants here grow taller and thicker than the coastal shrub, with bushes and trees so tightly set together that they sometimes seem all part of one giant plant spreading over a mountainside. The most common vegetation here is the chamise, a scratchy and needly bush that is well adapted to withstand many months of dry weather. Other low-lying plants include ceanothus, also known as wild lilac, and deerweed. Larger shrubs and trees include toyon, Mexican elderberry, California scrub oak, and at higher elevations, manzanita. Here you might encounter grey fox, bobcat, scrub jays, or California thrashers.

Chaparral is especially susceptible to wildfire—in fact, this habitat depends on the natural cycles brought on by these blazes. The moisture-saving oils covering many chaparral leaves act as a fire accelerant in many cases. Wildfire here sweeps away a dense canopy of mature shrubs and trees and makes way for a new layer of young foliage. Roots and seeds belowground survive the wildfires to spring anew. Some chaparral seeds don't germinate until after a fire. The heat cracks their thick shells and chemicals released by smoke and flames spur on the new growth.

WOODLANDS AND GRASSES

The statuesque coastal live oak and Engelmann oak are at the foundation of the oak woodland scattered over the inland foothills in San Diego. These open forests are often spread between patchy grassland made up of native grasses such as purple needlegrass and nonnative varieties such as cheatgrass, wild oats, mustard, and clover. Sometimes chaparral blends with these woodlands. Other times the understory and open spots will be filled with elderberry, coffee berry, and manzanita. Poison oak is also common here, especially in canyons and near streambeds.

Ground squirrels and acorn woodpeckers root for the oak's fruit in and around the trees. Other common sightings here include mule deer, California king snake, and woodrat.

Climb above 4,500 feet and oak woodland starts to be overtaken by coniferous forest. Oak might continue to grow here, but the landscape is more dominated by coulter pine, Jeffrey pine, incense cedar, and white fir. The occasional mountain lion stalks here, along with the great horned owl, and the high-flying golden eagle.

The canopy of these mountainous firs, cedars, and pines is occasionally interrupted by mountain meadows. One of the most well-known in San Diego is Big Laguna Meadow. These moisture-rich habitats are highlighted with lupines, evening primrose, and goldenrod among other grassy varieties. Here you might spot blackbirds, mallards, meadowlark, and meadow mouse.

DESERT

Over the Peninsular Mountains, the habitat changes drastically. At first blush the desert might seem a desiccated expanse of nothingness, but it is really animated with the hardiest stock of flora and fauna found in the entire region. Rocky slopes and desert floor are covered in cholla cacti of several varieties, barrel cactus, agave, and creosote. Desert willow and smoke tree billow in the wind and mesquite buzzes with bees collecting nectar for their hives. In the spring wildflowers like primrose and verbena burst into bloom and spindly ocotillo puts on its bright green jammies and orange nightcaps.

Keep still and quiet to catch sight of bighorn sheep, coyote, kit fox, and blacktailed jackrabbit. Roadrunner, kangaroo rat, chuckwalla, and spiny lizard skitter along the ground.

rocky and cactus-strewn desert landscape

© ERICKA CHICKOWSKI

History

ANCIENT CIVILIZATION

San Diego's beaches have been popular for quite a while. It's estimated that the first inhabitants of the county arrived some 20,000 years ago, following herds of migrating animals across the Bering Strait. These original residents became the San Dieguito people, but it wasn't long before the Yuman and Shoshonian peoples made the foray west, occupying much of San Diego County, as well as an estimated one third of California. Not yet aware of fish tacos, many of these groups lived off of a mush made by meticulously grinding acorns and mixing the flour with water. From these groups emerged the Cupeño, Cahuilla, Kumeyaay (also known as Ipai or Diegueño), and the Luiseños, the descendants of whom still live in Southern California today.

SPANISH COLONIALISM
Early Exploration

The thunder before the storm for these indigenous peoples came on September 28th, 1542, when Portuguese-born explorer Juan Rodriguez Cabrillo, flying under the flag of Spain, landed in San Diego Bay and claimed the area for the Spanish king. Even though Cabrillo left no permanent settlement, failed to find any cities of gold, died on his voyage, and even the name he gave the area (San Miguel) didn't stick, the expedition was still successful in proving that Alta California was not an island and cementing it into Spanish consciousness.

First European Settlements

Although Sebastian Vizcaíno was to visit briefly on behalf of Spain in 1602, the Spanish crown did much to lay the foundation for the leisureliness now common in San Diego by completely ignoring the area for over a hundred years. Not until Russia began establishing fur colonies in Northern California did Spain decide to assert its property claim in a more permanent way. Thus, in 1769, an expedition made up of Franciscan friars and Spanish soldiers set off for SoCal, some by ship and some

ancient Native American grinding holes, called *morteros*, in San Diego's hillside

© ERICKA CHICKOWSKI

Presidio Hill is the site of San Diego's first European settlement.

© PAUL CHICKOWSKI

by foot. Fraught with illness, bad weather, and maybe not the best of planning, the two groups of foot travelers finally met up with their ship-borne companions and built a fortified camp at the top of today's Presidio Hill overlooking what is now Old Town. The original Catholic Mission was hastily built on the site by legendary priest Father Junípero Serra, only to be moved five years later to be closer to reliable water supplies and the Native Americans they hoped to convert to Christianity. The mission system in California had begun its march northward, colonists arrived from Spain and Mexico, and the first of many transformations that would rock the area had commenced.

The Missions

The Spanish would go on to establish 21 missions in California, bringing the native people Catholicism, backbreaking labor, and European diseases. The ultimate goal of the missions in Southern California was to convert the Native Americans, teach them the basics of living in "civilized" society, and then to divest the mission land to the converted Native Americans (or neophytes) so they could live without the supervision of the clergy. Certainly, the system was heavily flawed, and to this day, controversy rages as to the degree to which the missions benefited those they hoped to help. The padres ranged from highly compassionate to nearly despotic, but shared a disdain for the native people's pagan ways. That their help was not always appreciated was evidenced by an uprising on the site of the present-day mission in 1775, during which angry Diegueños surrounded the grounds and killed two Spaniards and one Father Louis Jaime, making him California's first official Christian martyr.

MEXICAN RULE

In 1821, Mexico won its independence from Spain and just one year later, California swore allegiance to Mexico. Despite the first homes having been built at the foot of Presidio Hill, San Diego was still essentially a Mexican backwater, and it made little difference to the local citizenry which flag flew atop the Presidio. The activities of the Mexican government would soon have a major impact on the area, however. In 1833, the Secularization Act was passed, effectively closing the missions and handing control over to the Native Americans they had been built to serve. Over the objections of mission leadership, each head of a household of neophytes was given a homestead, some cattle, and grazing land in common. Although provisions were put in place to prohibit this land and cattle from being sold, it was not long before the neophytes were bullied, cajoled, and downright swindled into parting with their property, and forced back into the wilderness from which they came. Many disreputable locals became wealthy landowners very quickly at the expense of the church and the long-suffering native population.

During the years following Secularization, San Diego was on the decline. Populations fell and soldiers abandoned the venerable Presidio, allowing it to fall into ruin. The mission buildings themselves were plundered for their tiling and other building materials. The once-promising city became little more than a handful of ranchos and farms, and again, slipped into obscurity. Residents of the province re-branded themselves as "Californios," drawing a distinction between themselves and newer settlers as well as residents of the rest of Mexico. If not for a gradual yet steady stream of Americans trickling across the deserts to the east, and the sudden hostility of the Mexican–American War in 1846, the story of America's finest city may well have become a footnote in the history of Tijuana.

MEXICAN-AMERICAN WAR

On July 29, 1846, U.S. Marines from the warship USS *Cyane* seized the virtually undefended city of San Diego without firing a shot, consummating their victory by raising the American flag in the plaza in Old Town. A few months later, the legendary Admiral Robert F. Stockton arrived by ship and set up his base in the ruins of the old Presidio, creatively renaming the fortress Fort Stockton. From here, he organized the defense of the city, which became violent on only a few occasions. One of these was the Battle of San Pasqual, near present-day Escondido, where the Californios handed heavy casualties to the Americans led by General Stephen Kearney. Despite the embarrassing loss, the United States was eventually victorious, with the Treaty of Guadalupe Hidalgo ceding to the United States all of California, Utah, and Nevada, and big chunks of Colorado, Arizona, New Mexico, and Wyoming to boot. American rule commenced in earnest, and big changes were on the horizon yet again.

AMERICAN RULE

In the early days of American rule, life progressed much as it did in any growing western town, complete with its share of ranching, gambling, and minor controversy, albeit with more of a Latin flair than many other western locales. In 1855, the first lighthouse in San Diego was built at the tip of Point Loma, a miserable affair that was obscured by fog and clouds far too often to be useful. The famous Butterfield Stage cut a path through the eastern portion of San Diego County, breathing life into the dust surrounding present-day Borrego Springs. And in 1857, the colorfully and descriptively named Jackass Mail Line, originating in San Antonio, delivered the first overland mail to the area.

Echoes of the American Civil War

The outbreak of the American Civil War had little immediate impact on San Diego, but left a significant legacy. After the end of hostilities in 1865, a virtual flood of broken men seeking to escape the scenes of savagery struck out for the West and all the myths and hope associated with it. In 1870, A. E. "Fred" Coleman, a former slave turned rancher, discovered gold in the Cuyamaca Mountains. For the next six years, gold fever swept through like a firestorm, leaving the towns of Julian, Ramona, and Banner in their wake. Former slaves worked hand in hand with former Confederate soldiers, not only digging ore but also building profitable inns, stores, and restaurants in these out-of-the-way places.

New Town San Diego

Back in the western part of the county, controversy was brewing. In 1850, businessman William Heath Davis valiantly tried and failed to relocate the center of San Diego from the traditional Old Town location to a more sensible place closer to the harbor, to the profound satisfaction of Old Town supporters such as Thomas Whaley. Things were to change, however, when merchant Alonzo Horton turned his considerable fortune and business acumen toward making this move permanent. Horton himself was financially crushed when land prices took a nosedive in the late 1880s, but the lasting success of the Horton Addition has assured his legacy as the "Second Father" of San Diego.

For the next 40 years, San Diego shared in the growth, maturation, and technological advances that transformed the country as a whole. The county of roughly 30,000 souls got telephones, a public library, an opera house, and access to the transcontinental railroad. In 1885, San Diego's heroine horticulturist Kate Sessions moved to town and began beautifying everything she touched; her work is still evident in Balboa Park and many other city areas today. The city's infrastructure also took a huge leap forward during this period, with the arrival of electric street lights, cable cars, and numerous water flumes, dams, reservoirs, and aqueducts. In 1888, the fabulous and iconic Hotel del Coronado opened its doors, later to play host to 15 American presidents and luminaries such as Thomas Edison and Charlie Chaplin. And curiously enough, the city founded by Franciscan missionaries became home to Katherine Tingley and Madame Blavatsky's Theosophical Society as well as the site for the Villa Montezuma, showplace home of famed spiritualist and musical medium Jesse Shepherd, still standing today in all of its eclectic Victorian splendor.

Panama-California Exposes a Park

In 1915, San Diego got a tremendous boost with the opening of the Panama-California Exposition in today's Balboa Park. Built to celebrate the start of traffic on the new Panama Canal, the ornate Spanish colonial revival–style buildings and international exhibits served to promote San Diego as a stopping point for ships headed west through the canal. Not only did the exposition give San Diego some needed exposure, it also began the transformation of Balboa Park from largely open space into the cultural centerpiece it has become. Many of the stunningly ornate original buildings have been heavily restored and now house museums. The exposition is also said to have planted the seeds for the world-famous San Diego Zoo when several animals that had been on display were quarantined by federal officials and not allowed to leave the site.

NAVY TOWN

It's no secret that San Diego owes much of its success to the United States Navy. The careful and concerted efforts of city boosters brought the mighty USN to San Diego in a gradual

a sculpture of Kate Sessions, one of the civic leaders responsible for Balboa Park's ascendency during the Panama-California Exposition, by Ruth Hayward

© ERICKA CHICKOWSKI

way. After making the world's first successful seaplane flight in the waters just off Coronado, Glenn Curtiss invited army and navy officers to the city for complimentary pilot training. This led to the 1911 establishment of North Island Aviation Camp, an area still used for naval aviation. Just eight years later, San Diego was selected as the headquarters for the entire Pacific Fleet. Since that point, the military has played a huge role in the development of San Diego. From the submarine base at Ballast Point all the way to the Marine Corps's Camp Pendleton, the people and materials of the armed forces have been a vital component of the city's growth and well-being.

SAN DIEGO OF TODAY

A varied economy, based on tourism, defense, agriculture, and, lately, biotechnology, has seen the city through many of the ups and downs that have thrown other cities into serious decline. Despite budget mismanagement and pockets of corruption in city government, San Diego continues to chug right along. The Gaslamp Quarter, long ago a comfortable home for prostitutes and drug dealers, has been completely transformed into a chic destination for nightclubbers and fans of haute cuisine. Through careful management, San Diego's beach areas have (so far, at least) been spared the plague of being walled off by condos, as has been the fate of many other beach communities nationwide.

Government and Economy

As the home to the U.S. Navy's Pacific Fleet Headquarters and numerous military installations, San Diego's political and economic landscapes are deeply affected by the whims and wishes of Uncle Sam and those who work for him.

Military and defense is one of the top four economic industries in the region, along with tourism, manufacturing, and agriculture. It is only behind manufacturing in terms of financial impact to the area, bringing more than $13 billion into the local economy. In addition to the four biggest industries, the city also has a strong concentration of biotechnology companies, likely pulled in due to the heavy concentration of research colleges, clinics, and institutions in the area, including Scripps Institution of Oceanography, the Salk Institute, and the University of California–San Diego Medical Center.

Telecommunications is also an important niche in the city. In fact, the largest non-governmental employer in the city is Qualcomm, which has more than 10,000 employees.

In addition to the economic importance of the military to San Diego, it also has a political impact on the area. With so many military families living in town, the city skews conservative, especially compared to other major California cities such as Los Angeles and San Francisco. However, the city is far from the Republican stronghold it once was in past decades. Currently registered Democratic voters edge out Republicans by about seven to six within the county.

Because the federal government has such a large stake of land in the region, it often has a bigger say in municipal politics than it does in most other regions. For example, the region is currently in the process of planning a new international airport but it is currently embroiled in debate with military leaders over the preferred location, because its flight patterns could potentially conflict with the operations of Marine Air Station Miramar.

The city of San Diego is governed by a city council with a council president, but it has a strong mayoral system, so the mayor holds more power than in cities with a council executive. Currently the city is embroiled in an economic scandal that dates back to the early 2000s when city leaders voted to enact an overly ambitious—and some argue, illegal—pension system for the more than 11,000 workers employed by the city. The problem was exacerbated by political maneuvering that resulted in a delay of audits done by Wall Street financiers that ended up resulting in municipal bonds being downgraded to junk bond status. This particular problem has caused financial issues for the city that will likely linger for many years.

People and Culture

The people of San Diego are a living contradiction. Founded by priests and funded by the military, the region is full of independent and anti-establishment thinkers. At the same time these folks who rail against "the man" are hardworking family types, many of whom attend mass each Sunday or design advanced systems for the navy during the work week. The latest generation of San Diegans has a growing sense of stewardship over the oceans and beaches, mountains, and deserts that give them so much pleasure. They take advantage of the weather out on their surfboards or bikes, or out for runs and hikes, and they're reminded daily why they pay such a high cost of living and put up with expensive housing. They'd rather be throwing away rent money to live on the beach than be comfortably cooped up in a house on the prairie somewhere.

COMPAÑEROS DE MEXICO

San Diego's population and culture is inexorably intertwined with Mexican and Latino heritage. You see it in the sights, the street names, the language, and the family-loving atmosphere.

When the Americans won Alta California from Mexico in the Mexican–American War, many of the "Mexicans" that settled here so long ago stuck around. They called themselves "Californios." Many were tied to this beautiful region for generations, and they weren't about to let a new government push them away. In fact, some of these Californios embraced American rule, rejecting Mexico City's distant and disorderly oversight. These people aren't taking over San Diego. They've always been a part of the region.

MILITARY INFLUENCE

As the navy's Pacific Fleet headquarters, San Diego is home base for the largest naval fleet in the world. At Naval Station San Diego alone, more than 35,000 sailors and civilians staff the grounds. Thousands more are stationed at the county's nine other navy and marine installations, including the massive Camp Pendleton.

Beyond the economic impact of such a strong military showing, the presence is also felt within San Diego culture. The city leans to the right politically. Single soldiers and sailors kick loose in certain pockets of the city, and they've probably done a lot over the decades to keep beach-area bars and tattoo parlors in business. But they're largely reigned in and outnumbered by their family-oriented compatriots.

Probably the biggest cultural effect of this large military population is its diversity. Enlisted people come from all over the country to serve here and many stay or come back once their time is up. They bring with them new ideas, philosophies, and ways of life that are constantly freshening the San Diego scene.

SURFING CULTURE

Introduced to the region by Hawaiian legend Duke Kahanamoku in 1916, surfing is the sport that defines San Diego. It's soulful and it's aggressive. It's ragingly anti-establishment and relaxed to the point of indifference. Some surfers here spend their whole life in search of that perfect wave, happily renouncing steady employment and physical possessions in favor of their obsession. Others sneak into the ocean to steal a few mushy breaks, if only to have a moment of peace from their kids and jobs. It is blissful escapism in whatever dose they're willing to take.

Out of the water these athletes have been known as iconoclasts and as bums, nihilists and druggies, ever since the sport really started taking off here in the late 1930s. Surfing emerged as a frivolous pastime in a serious world, one that prompted young risk-takers to throw everything away to hang out at the beach. Or so said the elders. As time passed into the '50s and '60s, the nonconformists who practiced the art of waveriding embraced their bad reputation. They grew out their hair. They took drugs and partied. They invented skateboards so they could

SURF LINGO

Surf culture is full of colorful slang and lingo meant to describe riders, equipment, conditions, and emotions. The lexicon could probably fill a whole book of its own.

The following are some of the most common terms you might hear around town.

- **Aggro:** An adjective used interchangeably to describe aggressive surfing and angry behavior.

- **Bro:** A good friend or buddy. Also heard as "brah."

- **Dawn patrol:** As a noun, this is the crew that shows up to ride the waves in the early-morning hours while the waves are still glassy and free of wind interference. As a verb it is the act of waking up early to enjoy the good conditions.

- **Drop-in:** Also referred to as "snaking a wave," dropping-in is the act of catching a wave that is already occupied by a rider. This is surfing's number one no-no.

- **Duck dive:** A method of pushing your body and your surfboard under a wave so that it washes over you rather than sending you back to shore. This is the preferred technique to get past the breakers.

- **Getting tubed:** A perfect moment in surfing when the lip of a steep wave curls over the surfer as he or she rides to create a cylindrical tunnel of water around the rider. Sometimes called "getting shacked."

- **Goofy foot:** Surfing with your right foot forward.

- **Grommet:** A young surfer. Often abbreviated to just "grom."

- **Hang ten:** Longboarding trick where the rider stands with all ten toes dangling off the nose of the board. Takes a great deal of practice and agility. Also known as "toes on the nose."

- **Hodad:** A non-surfer who hangs out at the beach. Often used as a negative term for surfing wannabes.

- **Impact zone:** The point where most of the waves are crashing down.

- **Inside:** Anywhere between the breaking waves and the shore. To be "caught inside" is to be unable to make it past the crashing waves to the lineup. The best bet is to wait for a calm time between sets to paddle out.

- **Kook:** A derisive term for beginner surfers.

- **Leash:** A piece of tubing fixed to the back of a board that attaches the board to the surfer's ankle or knee. Keeps the board from hurtling toward shore upon wiping out. Some surfers pride themselves in their ability to surf without a leash, but it is generally considered bad manners to others around them.

- **Lineup:** The group of surfers bobbing just outside the breakers waiting to catch a wave.

- **Quiver:** A surfer's collection of boards.

- **Regular foot:** Surfing with your left foot forward.

- **Set:** A group of waves.

- **Soul surfer:** A surfer who sees the art of wave riding as a spiritual unity with the elements and who loves to share the joy of surfing with any bro or wahine willing to listen.

- **Stick:** Another word for a surf board.

- **Turtle roll:** An alternative to the duck dive, surfers do this by flipping upside down with the board so that the wave washes over the underside. This method is used by those with longboards who can't push these buoyant sticks under for a duck dive.

- **Wahine:** A female surfer, generally a term of affection.

- **Whitewash:** The foamy leftovers from a wave that has already broken. This is where many beginners first learn to ride waves.

keep riding all hours of the day. And even as society's curmudgeons were wagging their fingers, these surfing bums were building a movement that would spring forth whole communities of like-minded individuals who understood the serenity of paddling out, the cosmic connection with the ocean when dropping into a tube. Communities like Ocean Beach, Encinitas, and Oceanside were all built on a culture tied to the sea and the stoke of surfing.

Today these places are inhabited with a new generation of surfers. There's still a wild streak ingrained in the surfing psyche, but the population has grown more mainstream. There will always be those surfing rebels living out of their vans, hopping beach to beach. But they're joined in the lineup by doctors and lawyers, students and teachers. And, every once in a while, by one of the old guard who remembers what it means to be a real surf bum.

ESSENTIALS
Getting There

BY AIR
San Diego International Airport

San Diego International Airport (SAN, 619/400-2404, www.san.org) is the largest in the region, with over 20 airlines routing domestic and international flights over its tarmac. Major airline carriers include:

- AirTran Airways (800/247-8726, www.airtran.com)
- Alaska Airlines (800/252-7522, www.alaskaair.com)
- American Airlines (800/433-7300, www.aa.com)
- America West Airlines (800/235-9292, www.americawest.com)
- Continental Airlines (800/525-0280, www.continental.com)
- Delta (800/221-1212, www.delta.com)
- Frontier Airlines (800/432-1359, www.frontierairlines.com)
- Hawaiian Airlines (800/367-5320, www.hawaiianair.com)
- JetBlue Airways (800/538-2583, www.jetblue.com)
- Midwest Airlines (800/452-2022, www.midwestairlines.com)

© IOANA DAVIES/123RF.COM

- Northwest Airlines (800/225-2525, www.nwa.com)
- Southwest Airlines (800/435-9792, www.iflyswa.com)
- United Airlines (800/864-8331, www.ual.com)
- US Airways (800/428-4322, www.usairways.com)

Los Angeles International Airport

One of the nation's largest airports, Los Angeles International (LAX, 310/646-5252, www.lawa.org), is also within striking distance. Depending on the fare, it might make sense for some international travelers to book a trip directly into LAX and drive the rest of the way down the coast.

If you are simply a domestic traveler looking to save a couple of bucks by choosing an LAX arrival, be forewarned that you'll still pay. Oh, yes, you will pay. It'll either come in the form of a ridiculous shuttle fare, up to $300 in some cases, or through the depletion of your precious vacation time.

Though Amtrak runs from downtown San Diego to L.A., it does not go directly to LAX. You'll have to make a transfer on the Los Angeles World Airport FlyAway Bus from Union Station to the airport. And the 124-mile driving distance is beguiling. That "easy two-hour drive" can potentially double if you're ensnared in L.A. rush hour (which, in my estimation, is between the hours of 6 A.M. and 5:30 A.M. the following day). Plus, rental cars are more expensive at this airport than at San Diego International.

Other Regional Airports

McClellan-Palomar Airport (2192 Palomar Airport Rd., Carlsbad, 760/431-4646) is the only other airport in the county that offers daily flights from any of the major commercial airline services. United Express flies to and from LAX about seven times each day and US Airways operates a daily shuttle between McClellan-Palomar and Phoenix.

Other municipal airports include **Gillespie**

Field (1960 Joe Crosson Dr., El Cajon, 619/956-4800), **Brown Field** (1424 Continental St., San Diego, 619/424-0455), **Borrego Valley Airport** (1820 Palm Canyon Dr., Borrego Springs, 760/767-7415), and **Montgomery Field Airport** (3750 John J. Montgomery Dr., San Diego, 858/573-1440).

Only a half hour away from San Diego, **Tijuana International Airport** (Carretera Aeropuerto, Tijuana, tel. 664/607-82-01) is often an economical alternative for those flying between San Diego and Mexico. Major airlines include: Aeromexico (tel. 800/021-40-00, www.aeromexico.com), Aerolitoral (tel. 800/021-40-00, www.aeromexico.com), Mexicana (tel. 800/502-20-00, www.mexicana.com), and Aerocalifornia (tel. 800/685-55-00).

BY BUS

San Diego County is serviced by **Greyhound Bus Lines** at six stations in the region. Three of the most convenient stops are Oceanside (205 S. Tremont St., 760/722-1587), downtown San Diego (120 W. Broadway, 619/239-3266), and at the border in San Ysidro (799 E. San Ysidro Blvd., 619/428-1194).

You can reach Tijuana and Rosarito in the plush shuttle buses run by **Mexicoach** (619/428-9517, www.mexicoach.com). These red buses depart San Diego from Old Town and San Ysidro.

Once you cross the border, you can step aboard the private buses run by **ABC** (800/025-0222, www.abc.com.mx) to reach Ensenada to the south.

BY TRAIN

Amtrak's Surfliner (800/USA-RAIL or 800/872-7245, www.amtrak.com) runs through Southern California's coastal cities all the way down to the Santa Fe Depot in downtown San Diego. This train makes several other stops in the county, including Oceanside and Solana Beach.

For easy travel from Los Angeles and Orange County, **MetroLink** (800/371-LINK or 800/371-5465, www.metrolinktrains.com) might also be an option. This network of trains north of San Diego County makes forays down to Oceanside Station.

BY CAR
Into San Diego
There are three major routes into San Diego. From the north, I-5 and I-15 run roughly parallel to one another until they start to converge and come to a point in San Diego's city center.

I-5 is the easiest route along the coast from Los Angeles and Orange County. I-15 is best for those headed down from Riverside and the rest of the Inland Empire. This is also the preferred route from Las Vegas. From the east, I-8 is the major route. In the summer this is the annual escape hatch used by Arizonans to flee the blazing temperatures in Phoenix, Scottsdale, Tucson, and Yuma.

Getting Around

BY CAR
Like most of SoCal, San Diego has more than its fair share of concrete cloverleaves. In addition to I-5, I-15, and I-8, there are also a number of other convenient freeways and highways that connect the county's sites.

In the center of the city both I-805 and Highway 163 are good north–south alternatives to I-15 and I-5.

In North County, Highways 52 and 56 are major east–west connectors between I-5 and I-15. Running parallel to these along the county line, Highway 76 is a two-lane highway that runs through the most remote stretches of the county's northern reaches. Similarly, Highway 78 runs across the middle of the entire county, from I-5 through Ramona, Julian, and the desert. In the central mountains, Highway 79 is the main north–south route, running through Cuyamaca Rancho State Park, Julian, and up through Warner Springs. In Anza-Borrego Desert State Park, Highway S-22 runs through the northern part of the park and Highway S-2 curves through the southwest corner.

From downtown, Highway 94 runs southeast into the county's border mountain ranges. Also south of downtown is Highway 904, a spur off of I-5 that leads down to the Otay Mesa border crossing.

Car Rental
San Diego has plenty of rental car agencies. Contact the following to compare rates: **Alamo** (2942 Kettner Blvd., 619/297-0311),

Avis (3180 N. Harbor Dr., 619/231-7171), **Dollar** (2499 Pacific Hwy., 619/234-3389), **Enterprise** (1691 Hancock St., 619/225-8881), **Hertz** (3202 N. Harbor Dr., 619/220-5222), and **National** (3280 N. Harbor Dr., 619/497-6777).

BY BUS
In the city of San Diego, **Metropolitan Transit System** runs a fairly robust bus system that covers most of the main tourist areas including downtown, the beaches, Uptown, and more. Some areas are serviced more sporadically than others. The MTS website (www.sdcommute.com) offers a good interactive planning tool to map out your travels in advance.

In North County the **North County Transit District** runs a more limited line of buses throughout the area communities. There are buses that run between North County and downtown, but they are mostly designed for commuters in these bedroom communities, so many routes are set up for rush-hour travel.

BY RAIL
The **San Diego Trolley System** is one of the most efficient means of public transport to reach your destination—as long as the tracks go there. You'll find the trolley rumbling through downtown, by Old Town, into Mission Valley, and down to the border. This rail system is run by Metropolitan Transit System. Visit the website (www.sdcommute.com) for route and schedule information.

Those traveling between downtown and North County should consider taking the Coaster (www.gonctd.com/coaster). This commuter train runs from downtown all the way to Oceanside with six stops along the way.

BY FERRY

Skip driving the Coronado Bay Bridge and head across the bay by boat. The **Coronado Ferry** leaves downtown at the **Broadway Pier** (1050 N. Harbor Dr.) every hour on the hour starting at 9 A.M. and arrives at **Coronado's Ferry Landing Marketplace** (1st St. and B Ave.) about a half hour later. Similarly, the ferry departs from Coronado at the half hour every hour starting at 9:30 A.M. During the week, the last ferry departs from downtown at 9 P.M. and from Coronado at 9:30 P.M. Operation is extended by one hour on Fridays and Saturdays.

Tips for Travelers

TRAVELING WITH PETS

With its plethora of dog-friendly parks, restaurants, hotels, and ample animal critical-care facilities, it is no wonder that San Diego was voted the most dog-friendly town in the United States by DogFriendly.com in 2010, and in *Dog Fancy* magazine the city was ranked in the top ten of the magazine's DogTown USA 2010 competition.

San Diego is a great town for traveling with pets. With a bit of careful planning you should be able to spend a maximum amount of time with your furry best friend while on vacation here. Throughout the book I've tried to include pet-friendly establishments, parks, and trails. In addition to those I've detailed there are a number of other notable off-leash parks in town, including Nate's Point and Morley Field in Balboa Park, Capehart Park in Pacific Beach, and Dusty Rhodes Neighborhood Park in Ocean Beach.

Unfortunately, pets are restricted from all trails in state parks. You'll also be barred from many of the larger attractions unless yours is a

WHAT TO TAKE

This is a no-brainer, but your vacation preferences will dictate your packing choices. San Diego is generally a very casual town – we residents like to consider it "beach-ready." The usual uniform is a T-shirt, board shorts, and flip-flops for guys, and tank top, beach sarong, and flip-flops for gals. Basically, if guys tuck a polo shirt into a pair of belted shorts or girls put on a flouncy sun dress, they're considered dressed up.

There are exceptions to these standards, of course. If you plan on going club-hopping in the Gaslamp, be sure to bring a set of dress clothes. Same goes for the fancy restaurants downtown, in La Jolla, or in North County.

No matter what time of year, be sure to bring a light jacket. Add a sweater to that in the winter.

The chill kicking off the coast at night tends to surprise first-time visitors. Don't skip the sunscreen in the winter, either. Even under cloud cover the sun is known to burn the unprepared.

If you plan to go to Mexico, be sure to pack a passport. New regulations from Homeland Security now require international travelers to present this form of ID when crossing back into the States. A Spanish-English dictionary also might help, but isn't completely necessary. Most of the service workers in the border cities are bilingual.

Finally, don't forget to pack a pair of comfortable and worn-in sneakers. The majority of San Diego County's best sites require a ton of walking. A blister early in the trip can really chafe your plans.

service dog. Should you like to bring your dog with you on vacation but still have the freedom to visit these pet-free areas, kenneling and day-care services are readily available throughout the county. My favorite place in the city to take my little Sandy is **Camp Diego** (2926 Garnet Ave., 858/490-6440) in Pacific Beach. Cages are only used in the evening; this boarding and day-care facility lets its dogs loose all day in its indoor/outdoor play yard. When I'm able to make the drive out to Alpine, my absolute favorite place to put Sandy up is **Alpine Dog Ranch** (619/659-5034, www.alpinedogranch. com). Set on a four-acre property, the ranch also adheres to the play-all-day philosophy. The owner, Thomas, has a very special connection with the dogs he tends to.

Finally, if an after-hour health issue arises there are several emergency vets in town, including **A Animal ER of San Diego** (5610 Kearny Mesa Rd., 858/569-0600) and **VCA Emergency Hospital** (2317 Hotel Circle S., 619/299-9068).

TRAVELING WITH CHILDREN

San Diego falls over itself to cater to vacationing families, which makes it pretty easy on parents looking for a restaurant or hotel with staff that won't bat an eye when the kids are fussy.

One great trick for Moms and Dads hoping for some time alone together is to send the kids to a surf day camp. Many of the surf schools mentioned in this book run half-day or all-day camps, allowing parents just enough time to visit a museum or just get a little peace and quiet. Most kids love learning to surf and parents will be returned a happy and tired brood at the end of the session.

A big challenge many families face while visiting San Diego is the expense. Hotels and food add up quickly, and that's not even including the cost of tickets to attractions. It is possible to do your San Diego touring on the cheap and still have fun, though. There are many very nice camping facilities in and around the city. And there are tons of free sights to visit. Here is a quick list of five free family-friendly places.

MAKING FRIENDS IN SAN DIEGO

San Diego is a transient town. Waves of residents are washed in and out with the tide. That high quality of life draws 'em in and the reality of expenses spits 'em out. Because of this the population is used to making friends quickly, opening themselves up like blooming flowers in the ever-present sunshine.

One sunny day in August, I was walking home from the beach when an unknown neighbor hailed me over and offered me a free beer from his keg. He and his girlfriend and a couple of people were sitting around on kitchen stools and folding chairs on the front lawn, sipping out of red plastic cups. The keg was left over from a charity event the day before and they were inviting every single person that walked, jogged, or biked by to stop for a pour or three to help them empty it. By the time I left this "stranger party," there were at least fifteen people huddled around the keg laughing and talking as if they'd known each other for ages. There was the German ex-pat in town to do research with Scripps Hospital, the hotel marketing director just cruising by on her bike to the grocery store, tatted-up surfers and primped-out beach babes. This event was a true testament to the San Diego community and the perfect embodiment of our city's spirit and style.

Beaches

Most of the city's municipal beaches are free to use and provide days of family enjoyment. Stay frugal by bringing plastic cups to craft sand castles instead of buying beach toys. Don't waste your money on a boogie board you'll need to throw away at the end of the trip. Instead, try your hand at bodysurfing. Catch the wave like you would on a boogie board and extend one of your arms out straight forward to increase your planing surface.

Trails

There are tons of easily accessible hikes that are kid-friendly. Trot along the trails at Torrey Pines, scramble up Cowles Mountain, or take a scenic walk along the sandstone at Sunset Cliffs. Other fun—and flat!—alternatives are the lagoon trails up in North County around Batiquitos Lagoon and Buena Vista Lagoon.

Tide pools

Get your hands on a tide chart and cart the kids out to one of San Diego's many tide pools when the water is low. These natural wonderlands are teeming with sea life that'll likely have toddlers squealing with delight and will fascinate older kids. The top tide pools with free access include Tourmaline Surfing Park and Shell Beach at the foot of Ellen Browning Scripps Park. If you're willing to pay a small entry fee, some of the very best pools are at Cabrillo National Monument and Cardiff State Beach.

Balboa Park

Sure the museums cost money, but your kids don't want to go inside anyway. You can easily spend a whole day exploring the gardens and looking at the pretty buildings at the park. On Sunday the family can rest a bit, listening to the free 2 P.M. concerts at the Spreckels Organ Pavilion.

Pepper Grove Playground

This is a very comfortable area where youngsters can easily spend a whole afternoon scampering around. There's a ton of playground equipment, swings, a tot lot, picnic tables, barbecues, and restrooms all at hand here.

MAKING THE MOST OF LEAVE: MILITARY VISITS

San Diego is one of the best places in the country for military personnel to catch a little R&R. The weather is perfect and this navy town is inviting and supportive of the troops and their families. The high percentage of sailors and marines in the county works to your advantage, as almost every sight in town and many of the hotels and restaurants offer discounts to active-duty military members.

The city is also home to two USO Centers. At Lindbergh Field's Terminal Two, **Airport USO Center** (San Diego Lindbergh Field Terminal 2, 619/296-3192, 8 A.M.–11 P.M. daily) is the largest airport center in the entire world. There's free coffee, pastries, and Internet access, as well as plenty of couches for sitting back and watching a little bit of television.

The **Downtown USO Center** (303 A Street Suite 100, 619/235-6503, 11 A.M.–9 P.M. daily) also offers free Internet access, plus two big-screen televisions, pool tables, and a very robust list of activities and holiday events. Every Tuesday night this center cooks up a complimentary dinner for active-duty military and their families.

Both active-duty and retired military members can also take advantage of the local area Navy Lodges and Marine Inns to save on accommodations. These military-run hotels offer up to a 40 percent savings over San Diego's expensive hotels. Some of the most popular include **Navy Lodge San Diego** (619/234-6142) at Navy Base San Diego, **Navy Lodge North Island** (619/435-0191) at North Island Naval Air Station, and the **Marine Inn Ward Lodge** (760/725-5304 or 760/725-5194) at Camp Pendleton.

Similarly, active and retired military members can take advantage of some of the very well-respected navy golf courses in town. Two of the best are **Admiral Baker Golf Course** (Admiral Baker Way, Mission Gorge, 619/556-5520, 6 A.M.–dusk daily) and **Sea 'n' Air Golf Course** (Naval Air Station North Island Building 800, Coronado, 619/545-9659, 6 A.M.–dusk daily).

Navy Federal Bank has numerous ATMs in the San Diego area, as well as a large Mission Valley branch (8660 Rio San Diego Dr., 866/454-3135, 8:30 A.M.–6 P.M. Mon.–Fri., 8 A.M.–2 P.M. Sat.) in the Rio Vista Shopping Center.

TRAVELERS WITH DISABILITIES

San Diego is an extremely accessible town and most of the major tourist attractions, hotels, and restaurants provide means for those with disabilities to enjoy their vacation as much as the next person.

Before making a trip to San Diego, consider getting in contact with **Accessible San Diego** (858/279-0704, www.accessandiego. org). This is one of San Diego's oldest travel service organizations and an excellent planning resource. The group has published an annual Accessible Travel Guide to the city for over fourteen years.

San Diego is a beach town and the city has made every effort to ensure that those with disabilities aren't left out of the fun. The following beaches offer accessibility via roll-out mats: **Silver Strand State Beach** (619/435-0126), **Ocean Beach** (619/522-7346), **Mission Beach** (619/221-8899), and **La Jolla Shores** (619/235-1169). The latter three beaches also provide free motorized sand chairs. Call the lifeguard numbers provided to ask about reservations.

If you're the active type, get wet at Mission Bay. The **Mission Bay Aquatic Center** (1001 Santa Clara Point, 858/488-1036) rents adapted equipment for those with disabilities to enjoy activities such as water-skiing, sailing, canoeing, and riding personal watercraft.

All of San Diego's public transit systems are designed for maximum accessibility. In addition, **USA Cab** (619/231-1144) offers taxi rides in accessible vehicles. If you prefer the freedom of your own ride, **Wheelchair Getaways** (877/388-4883) rents vehicles with wheelchair ramps or lifts, hand controls, power doors, and outside entry controls.

Those travelers with disabilities who wish to visit Baja should be aware that Mexico is decades behind the United States and European nations when it comes to accessibility regulations. This can make it difficult to travel south of the border, but definitely not impossible. Many of the expensive resorts do make an effort to accommodate those with disabilities, so don't be afraid to call ahead and ask what kind of accessibility options are offered. A good resource for information about sights, hotels, and tours while in Mexico is the **Society for Accessible Travel & Hospitality** (212/447-7284, www.sath.org).

GAY AND LESBIAN TRAVELERS

San Diego might be one of the most politically conservative cities in all of California, but don't let this fool you. The people here are an accepting lot.

Maybe it's the happy weather or the devil-may-care Southern California attitude, but most folks don't give a hoot about sexual orientation in this town. In a July 2007 story about the many gay and lesbian political officials in the city, Eric Wolff of *San Diego CityBeat* put it most succinctly: "Forget 'Don't ask, don't tell.' In millennial San Diego, the motto these days is, 'Who knows, who cares?'"

As a result, there's no real "lavender line" here. However, there is a thriving gay and lesbian community focused around the neighborhood of Hillcrest, a sanctuary of tolerance since the 1960s, when San Diego's residents weren't nearly so open-minded. Hillcrest is a nerve center for the community at large, with many gay-friendly bars, hotels, and businesses. It is also the main gathering place during Pride Week festivities in July.

At Hillcrest's core is The Center, a gay, lesbian, bisexual, and transgender community center that is extremely active and hosts events throughout the year. This is a good resource to get the scoop on current happenings within the community.

And what of the military influence? Does it spur on any homophobia around here? Not really. In fact, you're likely to see plenty of fresh flattops interspersed in the crowds at Hillcrest's craziest watering holes. Guess even Uncle Sam doesn't know or care around here.

When traveling to Mexico, gay and lesbian travelers should remember that Mexico is a very conservative Catholic country whose residents will not be nearly as welcoming to gays and lesbians as San Diegans are. Nevertheless, Baja is known to be one of the most open-minded parts of the country and Tijuana is especially known for its acceptance of gays and lesbians. In fact, the Zona Norte is well known to have a number of gay bars that cater to both Americans and locals.

ON THE ROAD

San Diegans are one of the friendliest groups of people I've ever met. But there is a dark side to all the graciousness. Put those same affable people behind the wheel of a car and they become, well, a wee bit obnoxious. Granted, not all of it is intentional. Some of them are absentminded. Some are just bad drivers, period. But the net effect is all about the same. Accidents are frequent and near-misses happen every day. Don't believe me? Ask an insurance adjuster. When I moved here from Seattle my insurance doubled!

So be forewarned. Drive defensively and keep an eye out for loony-toon drivers. If it looks like they're about to do something crazy, they probably will. Give 'em a wide berth.

Freeway Driving

The driving style here is fast and sudden. Be prepared to be cut off. You'll frequently encounter a lot of zippy seamsters and seamstresses—they like to weave in and out of lanes to get that extra millisecond lead in congested traffic. And you'll often need to make way for people moving over quickly to make an exit. Part of the reason this happens is because folks around here just don't like to let people into their lanes. It is also likely a result of tourists who don't know their exit has come up until the last minute. Avoid contributing to the problem by planning your route in advance and knowing approximate mileage to your exit.

Intersections

I grew up in a town where people were courteous to a fault at intersections. They'd fall over themselves to let you go first if you even appeared to hit the intersection before them. Here, not so much. Be ready to go when it's your turn or wait until everyone else has gone, because if you blink for a second people will take that as their cue to cut ahead of you.

In the same vein, be wary of inattentive drivers flying through stop signs. This is particularly a problem in the wild-and-woolly beach areas, so watch out.

Pedestrians

Another problem that is particularly bad in the beach party zones is careless pedestrians. Jaywalking in San Diego is an Olympic sport. Many people like to train by walking out in front of speeding cars from every point in the road. Even though these people don't really have the right of way, that won't matter one bit to your conscience if you accidentally hit one of them.

Driving Under the Influence

Contrary to what you may have read or heard about Hollywood starlets' drunk driving "punishments," the DUI laws in California are some of the strictest in the country. So think of that before you selfishly or absentmindedly put other people at risk by driving intoxicated.

Do everybody a favor and call a cab, ride the trolley, or use a designated driver. Another option is to call the **Designated Drivers Association of San Diego** at 866/373-SAFE (866/373-7233). This organization offers a free, safe ride home for you and your car, no questions asked.

Health and Safety

CRIME

If you don't count every time SeaWorld charges $5 for a drink, San Diego's crime statistics are quite low. According to the FBI, the city ranks below the national average in almost every violent and property crime category that is tracked. The only exception is car theft, which is 1.65 times the national average. So, be sure to use common sense when parking your car. Keep the doors locked and bring valuables with you or stow them in the trunk in order to take away any temptations. Also, be sure to keep tabs on your keys at the beach. Surfers especially have been known to suffer at the hands of plotting thieves who watch them exit their cars and place the keys in a "safe spot." Once the car owner is out in the water the thief strikes. Find a way to fasten a key around yourself or consider wearing a wetsuit with a place to put a car key.

Beyond that, exercise the same caution you would in any midsize to large city. Keep an eye on your kids, don't leave your valuables unmonitored, and don't go walking alone in dark alleys at night.

WATER SAFETY
Water Pollution

Rain is a welcome phenomenon to this region in all respects but one: water pollution. Because rain is so infrequent here, all of the nasty street runoff in the cities concentrates on the asphalt and in storm drains until the heavens open up. A good rain will send this pollution right into ocean drainages. On top of this, San Diego County's sewage system is notoriously rickety. A heavy rain is sometimes all it needs to push the system into overflow mode, sometimes sending thousands of gallons of raw sewage into Mother Ocean. It is a disgusting trend and environmental groups like **Surfrider Foundation** (www.surfrider.com) have been working to improve the way that we care for our oceans and beaches. But for now the reality remains, and for this reason the rule

of thumb around here is to avoid any ocean contact for 72 hours after a rain.

Rip Currents

According to the United States Lifesaving Association, 80 percent of the rescues that ocean lifeguards make involve saving swimmers caught in rip currents. These seaward-moving currents are responsible for about 100 deaths a year in the United States. Sometimes misunderstood as "undertow" or "rip tide," a rip current is actually neither.

It only moves horizontally, never pulling someone under water. People drown not from any kind of sucking motion in the water, but instead from tiring after trying to beat the rip by swimming directly into the current towards shore.

As for the tide, it isn't directly linked with tidal phenomenon. Instead a rip current is usually formed when strong waves break around areas where there is a depression in the ocean floor, perhaps where there is a break in a sand bar. As the water gets pulled back to sea it tends to follow the path of least resistance, where the waves coming in are the least strong. Since the onshore depressions can diminish wave size, this is the route the water takes. Other natural and artificial features that can weaken wave size and facilitate the formation of a rip are rock jetties, piers, natural reefs, and even large groups of people. Either way, the result is effectively a river of ocean water heading out to sea. The phenomenon is sometimes so pronounced that you can spot a rip current from shore by looking for a strip of discolored or churning water where the break is less pronounced.

Depending on the size of the waves and the beach conditions, rip currents vary in speed. Some of the fastest move at a rate that even world-class swimmers can't overcome. Fortunately, they are isolated channels of water, usually only a couple of yards across. For this reason lifeguards advise swimmers caught in a rip to swim parallel to shore until they are out of the current. At that point they can try

San Diego's lifeguards have got your back, but common sense is important.

swimming toward shore. Above all else, don't panic while you're in a rip current. Conserve your energy as best as possible—exhaustion is the only real killer in the situation.

Jellyfish

When the ocean water warms up in the summertime, San Diegans aren't the only ones that come for a swim at the local beaches. The higher temperatures tend to attract purple-striped jellyfish. These gelatinous sea creatures are more of an irritant than a danger, but they do sting when you come into contact with them.

No matter how badly your buddy wants to pee on you, don't let him. That popular saw about urine being the best relief for a jellyfish sting is a bunch of bunk. In fact, it may activate some of the remaining nematocysts on your skin, making the sting worse.

Here's what to do if you're stung. First, rinse the affected area with salt water, or vinegar if it is handy. Salt water is key, because fresh water changes the pH on your skin and releases more venom from the nematocysts. The only exception is an eye sting, for which you should irrigate the eye with about a gallon of fresh water. Mouth stings can be treated with a quarter-strength solution of vinegar.

For particularly bad stings, you'll next need to remove any remaining tentacles. Then you should apply either shaving cream or a baking soda paste to the sting area and either shave it or scrape it with a credit card. The shaving cream counteracts the toxin and the scraping gets rid of the last invisible jelly bits from the skin.

If for some odd reason, you don't go to the beach armed with vinegar, shaving cream, and razors (a beach list that sounds like the set-up for a dirty joke), ice will keep the venom from spreading until you can get the necessary supplies. San Diego lifeguards are also very handy in these kinds of situations, so feel free to ask for help if you are near a lifeguard shack.

Stingrays

Ever done the "stingray shuffle"? No, it isn't

that dance you did with your Gram-gram at the retirement home. It's a way of scuffing the sand as you enter the surf to avoid the painful barbs of lurking stingrays.

These oddly shaped fishes enjoy shallow and warm water, sandy bottoms, and the tasty little invertebrates that live there. Their number one dislike? Being stamped on the head by tourists. They don't usually voice their displeasure with a complaint letter, instead opting for an unceremonious jabbing to the feet with a venomous barb. It usually gets the point across pretty quickly.

The best way to treat a sting is to avoid it altogether, hence the shuffle. Kicking up sand in front of you will let the stingrays know you're a-comin' and will usually make them skedaddle before they have to resort to blows. It's usually how you tell the locals from the tourists. One slowly slogs into the water, the other happily high-steps and splashes in.

Sometimes a barb is unavoidable, though. I once came down off of my surfboard straight onto a poor ol' ray.

In this instance, pee is still not the answer. For some reason, old wives just really like to tell tales of urinating on each other at the beach, because this is their erroneous remedy for stingray stings as well. But it doesn't work.

First of all, if you are allergic to bee stings you need to get immediate medical attention. Stingray venom has the same chemical makeup as bee venom and a sting can send an allergic person into anaphylactic shock.

Most stingray stings can be relieved by putting your foot into a bucket of fresh water that is as hot as you can possibly tolerate for about a half hour. This will relieve the pain and flush the wound. Once that is out of the way, give it a good washing with soap and water and apply topical antibiotic as needed.

Sometimes, though, the stingers or even the whole barb will remain in your foot. You'll need to remove this with tweezers. Particularly large rays can also gash the skin, causing bleeding. As much as it hurts, be sure to get in there once the stingers are removed and really clean the wound well. The larger the wound, the more

important an antibiotic is. In fact, if it looks pretty bad don't be afraid to go to a clinic and ask for an oral antibiotic. This is the best way to prevent a stinger-induced infection. If you do that, don't forget the sunscreen. Antibiotics tend to make your skin more sensitive to sun.

BACKCOUNTRY TIPS
Rattlesnakes

Outdoor enthusiasts will need to keep their eyes and ears alert on the trail for signs of rattlesnakes. Four species of this venomous reptile live in the county, but if you encounter one at all, it's most likely to be a western rattlesnake. They live throughout the county, from coastal scrublands into the mountains and parts of the desert.

Experts advise that most rattlers can strike about half their body length. Give these suckers a wide berth when you see or hear them and you'll likely be fine. Most of the rattlesnake bites that county hospitals treat are struck in defense when the "victim" goes all Jeff Corwin on the snake. They might be dangerous, but rattlesnakes are an important part of the ecosystem and they don't need to be killed when you come across them. So don't try, OK?

Most rattlers like rocky outcroppings. Be sure to look under that nice-looking boulder before you sit on it and never stick your hands or feet into areas you can't see. Also avoid tall grass without heavy boots and try to stick to the trail.

If you are bitten, seek medical attention as soon as possible. Rattlesnake bites are rarely fatal but are still serious enough to warrant professional care. Area clinics and hospitals usually have antivenin at the ready. In the interim don't apply ice or tourniquets, and don't make incisions on the wound. All of these methods can cause further injury. The best first aid is to wash the bite with soap, immobilize the wound, and keep it above the heart. Suction cups that come with snake-bite kits can also be used to help draw the venom from the wound. Again, don't make an incision. Finally, if you think it will be longer than 30 minutes before you can get to a hospital you can wrap a

Please respect the rules of hiking trails.

pressure bandage above the bite wound to slow the venom as long as it doesn't completely restrict blood flow.

Rattlesnake bites are deadly to pets, so take care to keep your dog on a leash in the backcountry. The venom works very quickly, especially on smaller breeds, so act as swiftly as possible to get your buddy straight to a critical-care vet center. Again, incisions, ice, and tourniquets do more harm than good. Try to keep the dog quiet and immobilized to slow the venom's spread and hurry! Time is of the essence.

Cougars

Cougar sightings are fairly rare in San Diego County compared to northern regions of California. Nevertheless, these big cats do roam the mountainous areas, especially near Julian and the Cuyamacas. One of the best ways to protect yourself is to hike with a companion and be sure to keep your dog on a leash so that it won't attract a mountain lion toward you. If you encounter a cougar, don't run. This can trigger its predator instinct and might elicit an avoidable attack. Don't play dead, either. The best way to scare one off is

to make yourself look big—spread out your coat, wave your arms, and make a lot of noise. Maintain eye contact and even throw rocks or sticks at the animal. If it does attack, keep fighting back. You want to convince it that you are not dinner.

Plants to Avoid

Other than a trip to the naughty parts of Tijuana, the most likely places to find yourself the recipient of an unbearable itch are in the backcountry canyons east of the desert. These areas are so full of poison oak that I wonder if San Diego's dermatologists are planting the stuff.

Probably not, though. Poison oak just really thrives in the partial shade of oak trees and the moist soil near streambeds. Remember: "Leaves of three, let them be!" The best way to avoid a rash is to wear long-sleeved shirts and pants. If your clothes do come into contact with poison oak, be sure to take them off and give them a good washing. The irritating oil in this plant can remain on clothing and still cause a rash if you come into contact with it later.

In the desert, you're more likely to curse the existence of teddy-bear cholla, also known as "jumping cholla" because its spines manage to jump right off the plant and onto passersby. Desert rats like to carry around combs to help pull the cactus clusters from their skin and clothes. Tweezers and pliers also come in handy. Especially be sure to have them around if you're hiking with kids or dogs, both of whom have a knack for attracting owies out in the desert where almost everything has thorns or spines. Other desert plants to avoid include cat claw, a thorny shrub that you'll often see along washes, and agave, which has a rosette of broadsword-shaped leaves that have a thorn at the tip laced with a natural irritant.

Desert Survival

Exploring remote desert areas is an exhilarating experience that can quickly turn deadly without taking the proper precautions. Dehydration, heat stroke, losing one's way, and even drowning are all dangers that you might face without appropriate safety measures.

First and foremost, be sure to pack in plenty of water. The rule of thumb is about a gallon a day, more as the thermometer gauge or your activity level rises.

Most desert experts tell you that the best way to store water in the desert is inside your body, not in a water bottle. Keep drinking, even if the situation seems dire. Instead of conserving water in the bottle, try to conserve your sweat. Travel during the cooler hours of the day, seek shelter during the hot hours if you can. If not, rest off the ground—it is usually much cooler that way. Wear a broad-brimmed hat for shade and light-colored long-sleeved and loose clothes to keep your sweat from evaporating. In that same vein, keep your mouth closed as much as possible. Water evaporates quickly from the mucous membranes in your mouth. Some people suggest sucking on a pebble or a button to keep saliva from drying out inside the mouth.

Finally, don't eat if you are running low on water. The digestive process uses up your system's water stores and you can survive much longer without food than you can without water.

If you do lose your way, remember this little tip. In all Anza-Borrego regions except for the Carrizo Badlands, all of the desert washes flow east toward some highway or settlement. Follow the washes east and you'll have a better chance of flagging down help. In Carrizo, follow the washes west.

Loose-fitting clothes and hats will keep you cool on the desert trails.

© ERICKA CHICKOWSKI

Speaking of washes, be aware that it isn't always dry in the desert. When the rain comes, it comes hard. Flash floods are a common occurrence during these downpours. If it looks like it might rain, don't camp or hang around the slot canyons or gullies.

One last concern to think about is the temperature extremes you'll encounter in the desert. Even on some of the hottest days in Anza-Borrego, the temperature can dip quite low in the evening. In the winter months the nightly averages are in the low 40s. Come prepared with a warmer layer to snuggle up in once the sun drops below the horizon.

Road Kit

If you plan on exploring the backcountry by car, you should prepare yourself for a breakdown. Finding yourself stranded on a remote byway is a major inconvenience at best, dangerous at worst.

Packing some necessities in the trunk will help you get yourself back on your way or at least keep you safe until help arrives. The following road kit is a loose guide to get you started:

- An inflated spare tire, preferably full-size
- A jack
- Basic tools, especially wrenches and screwdrivers
- Duct tape or electrical tape
- Extra car fluids, including water, washer fluid, antifreeze, and oil
- Signal flares
- A charged cell phone
- Extra food and water
- A warm change of clothes

This is by no means a comprehensive list if you plan on traveling very rugged roads, especially in the desert. In that case I'd recommend finding a specialized book about desert off-roading for a better list. And, most importantly, be sure to have your car inspected before leaving the pavement.

Information and Services

MAPS AND TOURIST INFORMATION

While planning your trip, the **San Diego Convention and Visitors Bureau** (619/232-3101, www.sandiego.org) is an excellent resource for information about the region at large. Contact the organization to ask for a free mailing that includes a booklet about activities and events in town, a comprehensive list of lodging and food, and informative maps.

If you'd prefer, you can also get information once you are in town at the bureau's **International Visitor Information Center** (1040 ⅓ W. Broadway, at Harbor Dr., 619/236-1212 or 619/230-7084, 9 A.M.–5 P.M. daily June–Sept., 9 A.M.–4 P.M. daily Oct.–May) on the Embarcadero or at the **La Jolla Visitor Center** (7966 Herschel Ave., 619/236-1212) in La Jolla Village.

If you require maps of anywhere in the region, including Baja, the best source in the entire city is **Map Center** (7576 Clairemont Mesa Blvd., 858/278-7887 or 888/849-6277, www.mapworld.com) in Clairemont. In addition to local, regional, and international maps, it also has a full spate of nautical maps and GPS units.

MONEY

San Diego's currency is the U.S. dollar. Sales tax throughout the region is 7.75 percent and hotel tax within the city is 10.5 percent. Tipping practices are similar to those throughout the states, with the customary gratuity coming out to between 15 and 20 percent of the total bill. The exception to this is when the tip has already been added to the bill.

In Baja, the currency is the Mexican peso but most places in Tijuana, Rosarito, and Ensenada typically accept U.S. dollars.

San Diego has ample opportunities for backroad traveling, but be sure to pack the necessities in case of a breakdown.

COMMUNICATIONS AND MEDIA
Telephone

There are three major area codes in San Diego. Within the city center, downtown, and south, the code is 619. Some city beach neighborhoods and northern parts of the city use 858. Everywhere else in the county, the area code is 760. Cell-phone reception is good throughout the city and North County coastal areas, but can be spotty in the mountains and desert.

In Baja there are two major area codes, 646 and 661, but to call Baja telephone numbers from the U.S. you will need to start by dialing (011-52) and then the ten-digit number.

Throughout the book I have written all seven-digit numbers as they'll usually appear in Mexico, with two hyphens, in order to distinguish them from domestic calls.

Internet Access

San Diego is a very connected city and there are numerous hot spots throughout. However, if you are having a difficult time finding free access quickly, don't worry about wandering around looking for an Internet café. Instead, make a beeline to one of the many branches of the San Diego library (www.sandiego.gov/public-library), all of which offer free access. Almost every branch has computers available to use.

If you need Wi-Fi access upon your arrival or departure, the San Diego International Airport also offers free access within its terminals.

WEIGHTS AND MEASURES

San Diego uses the Imperial system of measurements, but Baja is on the metric system. While in Mexico, you'll notice that gas is sold by the liter and distance is measured in kilometers.

The entire San Diego region is in the Pacific Time Zone and also practices Daylight Savings Time. Between the second Sunday in March and the first Sunday in November, clocks are pushed one hour ahead.

RESOURCES

Suggested Reading

Davis, Mike, Kelly Mayhew, and Jim Miller. *Under the Perfect Sun: The San Diego Tourists Never See.* New York, NY: New Press, 2003. Gets inside the scandals and the gritty reality behind San Diego politics.

Innis, Jack S. *San Diego Legends: Events, People, and Places That Made History.* El Cajon, CA: Sunbelt, 2004. A collection of stories, both historical and mythical, that make up the region's lore.

Jackson, Helen H. *Ramona.* Charleston, SC: BiblioBazaar, 2007. Often compared to *Uncle Tom's Cabin,* this social commentary wrapped within a fictional novel turned the nation on to the troubles facing Native Americans when it was published in 1884.

Kohner, Frederick. *Gidget.* Berkeley, CA: Berkeley Trade, 2001. This reprint of the 1957 myopic on the adventures of a teenaged girl growing up in the early days of SoCal's surfer scene offers a glimpse into the birth of the beach-shack subculture that still defines San Diego today.

Lindsay, Diana. *Anza-Borrego A to Z: People, Places, and Things.* Osceola, WI: Voyageur Press, 2000. The comprehensive guide to the nature and history of San Diego's expansive desert.

MacPhail, Elizabeth C. *Kate Sessions: Pioneer Horticulturist.* San Diego, CA: San Diego Historical Society, 1976. This is the definitive biography of Kate Sessions, the city's first gardener and the "Mother of Balboa Park."

McLaughlin, David J. *Soldiers, Scoundrels, Poets & Priests: Stories of the Men and Women Behind the Missions of California.* Scottsdale, AZ: Pentacle Press, 2006. The founding of the California mission system played an integral part in the establishment of San Diego. This book details the religion, politics, and scandals that drove the development of the missions.

Saldivar, Jose D. *Border Matters: Remapping American Cultural Studies.* Berkeley, CA: University of California Press, 1997. A textured and well-rounded look at the collision of cultures that occurs within the nation's border towns.

Schad, Jerry. *Afoot and Afield in San Diego.* 3rd edition. Berkeley, CA: Wilderness Press, 1998. Known as the adventure bible for most outdoors enthusiasts in San Diego, this tome offers the most comprehensive collection of regional trail descriptions.

Schaelchlin, Patricia. *The Newspaper Barons: A Biography of the Scripps Family.* Carlsbad, CA: Kales Press, 2001. After the family made a fortune in the news business, the Scripps clan made a difference in San Diego with a legacy of philanthropy that still extends into the city's art, science, and nature preservation today.

Smythe, William. *History of San Diego 1542–1908*. San Diego, CA: The History Company, 1908. This is one of the classic books on early history in San Diego. The original is long out of print, but readers can find the entire book online at the San Diego History Society's website, www.sandiegohistory.org.

Wolfe, Tom. *The Pump House Gang*. New York, NY: Farrar, Straus and Giroux, 1965. The namesake story in this collection is based on the surfers and rebels who hung out at the pump house set near Windansea Beach in La Jolla during the mid-1960s.

Internet Resources

Balboa Park
www.balboapark.org
Comprehensive site about America's second-largest municipal park. It contains background information, hours, and detailed information about the numerous attractions and gardens at Balboa Park.

Cleveland National Forest
www.fs.fed.us/r5/cleveland
Learn about the open space that dominates San Diego County's backcountry at this official site for Cleveland National Forest.

Discover Baja California
www.discoverbajacalifornia.com
Information and tips about Baja travel are offered here by the State Tourism Secretariat of Baja California.

Gaslamp.org
www.gaslamp.org
The official site of the Gaslamp Quarter Association, with historical background and information about this historic district.

San Diego Association of Governments
www.sandag.org
Demographic and geographical information about the entire county can be found at this site, the official website of the San Diego Association of Governments.

San Diego Convention and Visitors Bureau
www.sandiego.org
The official site of the San Diego Convention and Visitors Bureau. Includes comprehensive information about sightseeing, dining, lodging, and events.

San Diego Golf
www.sandiegogolf.com
One of the most comprehensive regional golf sites, this one offers local course descriptions, information on green fees, and online tee time reservations.

San Diego History
www.sandiegohistory.org
Run by the San Diego Historical Society, this site has hundreds of articles and photos that chronicle the city's extensive history.

San Diego Reader
www.sdreader.com
Run by the *San Diego Reader,* this site is a good resource to find out about local shows and events through its online entertainment calendar.

Sign On San Diego
www.signonsandiego.com
The online portal for San Diego's major daily newspaper, the *San Diego Union Tribune.*

Index

List of Maps

www.moon.com

DESTINATIONS | ACTIVITIES | BLOGS | MAPS | BOOKS

MOON.COM is ready to help plan your next trip! Filled with fresh trip ideas and strategies, author interviews, informative travel blogs, a detailed map library, and descriptions of all the Moon guidebooks, Moon.com is all you need to get out and explore the world—or even places in your own backyard. While at Moon.com, sign up for our monthly e-newsletter for updates on new releases, travel tips, and expert advice from our on-the-go Moon authors. As always, when you travel with Moon, expect an experience that is uncommon and truly unique.